CAMBRIDGE TEXTBOOKS IN LINGUISTICS

General Editors: W. SIDNEY ALLEN, B. COMRIE, C. J. FILLMORE
E. J. A. HENDERSON, F. W. HOUSEHOLDER, R. LASS, J. LYONS, R. B. LE PAGE
P. H. MATTHEWS, F. R. PALMER, R. POSNER, J. L. M. TRIM

TRANSFORMATIONAL SYNTAX

A student's guide to Chomsky's Extended Standard Theory

947

B6 L

gen ϕ, γ

TRANSFORMATIONAL SYNTAX

A STUDENT'S GUIDE TO
CHOMSKY'S EXTENDED STANDARD THEORY

ANDREW RADFORD

PROFESSOR OF LINGUISTICS
UNIVERSITY COLLEGE OF NORTH WALES

CAMBRIDGE UNIVERSITY PRESS

CAMBRIDGE
LONDON   NEW YORK   NEW ROCHELLE
MELBOURNE   SYDNEY

Published by the Press Syndicate of the University of Cambridge
The Pitt Building, Trumpington Street, Cambridge CB2 1RP
32 East 57th Street, New York, NY 10022, USA
296 Beaconsfield Parade, Middle Park, Melbourne 3206, Australia

First published 1981

Printed in Great Britain at the Pitman Press, Bath

Library of Congress catalogue card number: 81–10025

British Library Cataloguing in Publication Data
Radford, Andrew
Transformational syntax. – (Cambridge
textbooks in linguistics)
1. English language – Grammar, Generative
I. Title
425   P1097

ISBN 0 521 24274 6 hard covers
ISBN 0 521 28574 7 paperback

CONTENTS

Contents

PREFACE

The aim of this book is to provide a clear, simple introduction to recent work in Syntax by Chomsky and his followers, for all those who find Chomsky unintelligible. In an obvious sense, it is an introduction to works like his *Essays on Form and Interpretation* (1977), 'Filters and Control' (1977, with H. Lasnik), 'On Wh-Movement' (1977), *Rules and Representations* (1980), 'On Binding' (1980), 'Markedness and Core Grammar' (1980), *Pisa Lectures* (1980) and 'On the representation of form and function' (1980). Setting yourself such a goal raises a number of questions. Let me try and answer them.

'Why concentrate on Chomsky's work,' you might ask, 'rather than including detailed discussion of alternative models such as those developed by Brame, Bresnan, Gazdar and others?' There are several answers to this question. One is that Chomsky is the name that everyone associates with TG, Chomsky is the only linguist you are ever likely to see on television, Chomsky is the one linguist whose work is widely known in neighbouring disciplines like Psychology and Philosophy, and Chomsky is the primary linguist that students want to know about. A second reason is that much of the work described here is of an extraordinary technical complexity: presenting this in a form in which it will be intelligible to beginners is in itself a major undertaking, and leaves no room for discussion of equally complex research by others.

'But why concentrate on Chomsky's recent work, instead of tracing the historical development of his work over the past three decades?' First, to concentrate on the past twenty-five years rather than the past five years would have meant curtailing discussion of more recent work to such an extent that either I would have had to omit any discussion of certain ideas, or I would have had to make the presentation much more dense, and therefore less readily intelligible. Secondly, the past five years has seen a major theoretical reorientation in aims, methods, terminology, argumentation and so forth – to such an extent that it is no longer clear that reading yesterday's Linguistics helps you understand today's Linguistics (on the contrary, many students find the historicist approach tiresome, and bewildering). In any case, there are already endless introductions to early work in TG on the market, including Bach, *Syntactic Theory* (1974), Akmajian and Heny, *Principles* (1975), Huddleston, *Introduction* (1976), Culicover, *Syntax* (1977), Baker, *Introduction* (1978), Jacobsen, *TG Grammar* (1978), and Perlmutter and Soames, *Argumentation* (1979) – why waste good ink writing another textbook that's years out of date before it's printed?

'But why not give a *critical evaluation* of Chomsky's recent work, at least?' Well, a critical evaluation of a theory presupposes that the reader understands the theory in the first place. But to suppose that anyone other than the very brightest PhD student could read 'On Binding' or the *Pisa Lectures* by himself and digest the ideas is naive in the extreme. What is needed first is a clear, simple *exposition* of the theory: the first stage in being able to criticise a theory is to be able to understand it! And what this book seeks to do is to develop in the reader a basic *understanding* of the views and ideas of Chomsky and his followers; the reader should then be able to go on and read for himself some of the works cited. Only after that does it make sense to talk about attempting to make a critical evaluation of the theory. And that would be the subject for another, very different kind of book.

I have designed the book to be used with a variety of different students for courses at a variety of different levels. For the beginning student, chapters 1–5 provide a basic introduction to TG syntax; for an intermediate course, chapters 3–9 would be useful; and for an advanced course on recent work, chapters 3 and 6–11 provide invaluable preparatory reading and practice material which should enable the student to go on to read the primary literature (i.e. the original source material). The text is sequenced in such a way that the student can 'stop' at any point beyond chapter 5, and still have covered a reasonably coherent set of ideas.

I should also say something about the Exercises at the end of each chapter. These are an integral part of the text (i.e. it would be foolish to 'skip' them), and are of three types: (i) *reinforcement* exercises (which give the reader practice at applying the ideas discussed in the text); (ii) *advancement* exercises (which serve to introduce new concepts and terminology which will be presupposed in the rest of the text: these are marked by a prefixed single asterisk *); and (iii) *problem* exercises (which attempt to get the reader to look rather more critically at some of the assumptions, arguments and analyses given in the text; these are marked with a prefixed double asterisk **).

I'd like to thank a number of friends and colleagues for their encouragement, helpful discussion, critical comments and so on – especially Michael Anthony, Bob Borsley, Memo Cinque, Jacques Durand, Frank Heny, Giulio Lepschy, Peter Matthews, Frank Palmer, Deirdre Wilson and Nigel Vincent. Lack of time and energy has meant that I have been unable to take account of the more radical revisions that they proposed. Special thanks are due to the Press for agreeing to take the manuscript in its original mimeographed form, and for making an effort to publish it sooner than possible!

Finally, let me add that this book is dedicated to the person who did more than anyone to awaken my interest in language, and to persuade me that just maybe linguistic theory wasn't quite as pointless as it seemed at the time – Joe Cremona.

Andrew Radford
October 1980

I

Goals

Why study language? For Chomsky, the answer is that language is a mirror of the mind – i.e. by detailed study of language, we might hope to reach a better understanding of how the human mind produces and processes language. As Chomsky himself remarks:

> There are a number of questions that might lead one to undertake a study of language. Personally, I am primarily intrigued by the possibility of learning something, from the study of language, that will bring to light inherent properties of the human mind.
>
> (Chomsky, *Language and Mind* (1972), p. 103)

Chomsky seeks to attain two parallel, interrelated goals in the study of language – namely to develop (i) a Theory of Language, and (ii) a Theory of Language Acquisition. The Theory of Language will concern itself with what are the defining characteristics of natural (i.e. human) languages, and the Theory of Language Acquisition with the question of how children acquire their native language(s). Of the two, the task (i) of developing a Theory of Language is – in Chomsky's view – logically prior to the task (ii) of developing a Theory of Language Acquisition, since only if we first know what language is can we develop theories about how it is acquired; moreover, we shall see shortly that a Theory of Language is an important subpart of the Theory of Language Acquisition that Chomsky seeks to develop.

So, the primary aim of Linguistics, for Chomsky, is to develop a Theory of Language. But what is it that such a theory seeks to characterise? The answer is that any adequate Theory of Language must provide answers to questions such as the following:

> What is language?
> What is it that you know when you know a language?

What are the essential defining characteristics of natural
languages which differentiate them from e.g. artificial languages like those used in Mathematics or Computing, or
other forms of communication?
Do languages differ from each other in unpredictable ways, or
do they all share certain common, universal properties?

But how do we attempt to develop a Theory of Language which will
answer such questions? The first step is to formulate detailed
descriptions (known technically as *grammars*) of particular languages (e.g. English): this is the study of *Particular Grammar*.
The second step is to abstract from particular grammars common,
universal properties that they all share: this is the study of
Universal Grammar – i.e. the search for linguistic universals.

Consider first the study of Particular Grammar. What is a
grammar of a particular language? Chomsky gives an essentially
mentalist answer to this question: for him, a grammar is a *model* (=
systematic description) of those linguistic abilities of the native
speaker of a language which enable him to speak and understand his
language fluently. These linguistic abilities, Chomsky terms the
competence of the native speaker. Thus, *a grammar of a language is
a model of the linguistic competence of the fluent native speaker of
the language. Competence* (the fluent native speaker's knowledge of
his language) is contrasted by Chomsky with *Performance* (what
people actually say or understand by what someone else says on a
given occasion): competence is 'the speaker–hearer's knowledge of
his language', while performance is 'the actual use of language in
concrete situations' (Chomsky, *Aspects* (1965), p. 4). Very often,
performance is an imperfect reflection of competence: e.g. the fact
that people make occasional 'slips of the tongue' in everyday
conversation does not mean that they don't know their language, or
don't have fluency (i.e. competence) in it. 'Slips of the tongue' and
like phenomena are – for Chomsky – *performance errors*, attributable to a variety of performance factors like tiredness, boredom,
drunkenness, drugs, external distractions, and so forth. Linguistics
is – for Chomsky – primarily concerned with competence, since a
Theory of Competence will be a subpart of an eventual Theory of
Performance: that is, you have to understand what a native speaker
knows about his language before you can study the effects of
tiredness, drunkenness, etc. on this knowledge.

Chomsky distinguishes two types of competence: (i) *pragmatic competence*, and (ii) *grammatical competence* (see e.g. Chomsky, *Essays* (1977), p. 40). Pragmatics is concerned with the rule played by nonlinguistic information such as background knowledge and personal beliefs in our use and interpretation of sentences. To take one of Chomsky's own examples (from *Essays* (1977), p. 40), suppose I have a friend who says to me 'Today was a disaster.' If I know (by way of background information) that he was giving a special lecture today, then on the basis of this background knowledge I infer that he probably means that his lecture went down very badly. It is the native speaker's *pragmatic competence* which enables him to bring into play nonlinguistic information in the interpretation of such sentences. By contrast, in the case of a sentence such as:

(1)   He thinks that John is wrong

it is the native speaker's *grammatical competence* (his knowledge of the grammar of his language) which tells him that *he* cannot be interpreted as referring to the same person as *John* in (1). Chomsky's own work is almost exclusively concerned with the attempt to characterise *grammatical competence*: by contrast, his work in Pragmatics hitherto has been little more than anecdotal in nature.

Grammatical competence in turn subsumes three primary types of linguistic ability – *syntactic, semantic* and *phonological*. The principal syntactic ability which forms part of the native speaker's grammatical competence is the ability to combine words together to form grammatical sentences in his native language, and to know which sequences of words form grammatical or ungrammatical sentences in his language. For example, any native speaker of English would intuitively recognise (leaving aside for the moment differences of style or dialect) that all of the examples in (2) below are grammatical (i.e. syntactically well-formed) sentences in English:

(2) (a)   I gave back the car to him
    (b)   I gave the car back to him
    (c)   I gave him back the car
    (d)   I gave him the car back

but that the following are ungrammatical as sentences of English:

(2) (e)   *I gave the car to him back
    (f)   *I gave back him the car

(an asterisk in front of a sentence means that it is ungrammatical –
i.e. syntactically ill-formed in some way; by convention, any
sentence which does not have an asterisk in front of it is assumed to
be grammatical).

However, there is – for Chomsky – a second aspect of the native
speaker's syntactic competence which a grammar should
characterise – namely the native speaker's intuitions about the
syntactic structure of sentences in his language. For example, in a
sentence like:

(3)   John likes very fast cars

any native speaker would agree that *very* modifies *fast* (and not
likes), and that *very fast* modifies *cars* and not *John* – and so
forth. Thus, the native speaker has two types of syntactic intuition:
intuitions about well-formedness, and intuitions about structure.
We should perhaps add that the word *intuition* here is used in a
technical sense which has become standardised in Linguistics: by
saying that a speaker has *intuitions* about sentence well-formedness,
all we mean is that he has the ability to make *judgements* about
whether or not a given sequence of words is grammatical in his
native language.

Among the *semantic* abilities which form part of the native
speaker's grammatical competence are his intuitions about the
semantic well-formedness or ill-formedness of sentences: thus, any
native speaker of English would agree that (4) (a) below is
semantically well-formed, but that (4) (b) is semantically ill-formed
(i.e. 'odd' in some way by virtue of its meaning):

(4) (a)   I thought Mary was ill, but it turned out that she wasn't
   (b)   ! I knew Mary was ill, but it turned out that she wasn't

(! in front of a sentence means that it is semantically ill-formed). A
second type of semantic intuition which native speakers have about
their language concerns semantic structure, and semantic relations:
for example, any native speaker of English will tell you that *the fool*
can be interpreted as *coreferential to* (i.e. referring to the same
individual as) *Harry* in (5) (a) below, but not in (5) (b):

(5) (a)   I don't like Harry, because the fool hates Linguistics
    (b)   Harry says that the fool hates Linguistics

Hence, intuitions about coreference relations in sentences are part of the set of intuitions we have about semantic relations in and between sentences.

Among the *phonological* abilities subsumed under grammatical competence are the native speaker's intuitions about the phonological well-formedness or ill-formedness of sentences in his language. All speakers of English would agree, for example, that (6) (a) below is phonologically well-formed, but that (6) (b) is phonologically ill-formed (the syllables receiving primary stress are italicised):

(6) (a)   *This* is a gram*ma*tical *sen*tence
    (b)   *This* is a *gra*mmatical sen*tence*

A second type of phonological intuition which native speakers have in their language is intuitions about phonological structure: any English speaker intuitively feels, for example, that the sequence *black bird* can either be a single phonological word (*black*bird, with primary stress on *black* = a species of bird, like thrush, robin, etc.), or two independent phonological words, each with its own primary stress (*black bird* = bird which is black, as opposed to *white bird*).

Overall, then, we see that grammatical competence subsumes two types of intuition: (i) intuitions about syntactic/semantic/phonological well- or ill-formedness; and (ii) intuitions about syntactic/semantic/phonological structure. Before we go any further, however, it is useful to clear up a number of problems which arise with the notion of *ill-formedness*. One of these is that it is important not to confuse the descriptive notion of *well-formedness* with the corresponding prescriptive notion of *correctness*. For example, there are many dialects of English in which sentences like:

(7)   Mine is bigger than what yours is

are perfectly grammatical, and for speakers of these dialects such sentences are perfectly well-formed. But at the same time, sentences like (7) are of a type stigmatised as 'incorrect', or 'bad grammar' by a certain self-styled socio-cultural elite (e.g. schoolmasters). This poses an apparent dilemma for the linguist: should he *describe* what people actually say, or should he attempt to *prescribe* what he or others think they ought to say? In other words, should Linguistics be *descriptive*, or *prescriptive*? In actual fact, it is hard to see how anyone could defend the *prescriptive* approach: in any other field of enquiry, it would be seen as patently absurd. What would we say of the sociologist who, instead of describing the way a given society is, sets about prescribing how he thinks it ought to be? And what would we think of the scientist who, regretting the unfortunate tendency for objects to fall downwards by gravity, instead proposes an alternative model in which everything is attracted upwards towards the sky, simply because he thinks things *ought* to be that way? No one these days would take any such enterprise seriously; and the same is true of Linguistics. Modern Linguistics is purely descriptive, not prescriptive.

A more serious problem that arises with Chomsky's conception of a Grammar as a model of the linguistic intuitions of the average native speaker of a given language concerns what to do about disagreements among native speakers about the well-formedness or structure of particular sentences. One of the abstractions that Chomsky makes in studying language is to assume that speech communities are homogeneous: i.e. to assume that all native speakers of a given language will have essentially the same well-formedness intuitions: as Chomsky himself says (*Aspects* (1965), p. 3): 'Linguistic theory is concerned primarily with an ideal speaker–listener, in a completely homogeneous speech community. . .' But this is plainly not the case: all native speakers have to some extent their own individual way of speaking (or *idiolect*) which may not be exactly the same as that of any other member of the same speech community. There are, of course, larger linguistic groupings within society: speakers with a common geographical background may share a common *dialect*, while speakers from a common social background may share a common *sociolect*. We can illustrate the linguistic differences within a given speech community in terms of the examples in (8) below: each of these sentences would probably be accepted as well-formed by only a certain percentage of English speakers (hence the use of the % prefix):

(8) (a) %Your car wants mending
   (b) %That's to do tomorrow
   (c) %I gave it her

(d)   %There's a man delivers vegetables in the village
(e)   %It was me what told her

The obvious question to ask is what the linguist is to do in such cases. The broad answer is that in general the problem of linguistic variation within a speech community is one which is more appropriately dealt with in a partially separate discipline (*Sociolinguistics*), and since it is not a problem which is essentially *syntactic* in nature, it is not the kind of problem which ought to be the primary focus of attention in the attempt to develop an adequate theory of *Syntax*. For practical purposes, most linguists describing a language of which they are native speakers rely on their own intuitions, and thus the grammar they devise is essentially a grammar of their own idiolect, which they assume is representative of the language as a whole.

An even more tricky problem which arises with the notion of *ill-formedness* concerns the attempt to identify in what way a given sentence which 'sounds odd' is ill-formed. Let's first draw a distinction between sentences which are 'pragmatically odd' in some way, and those which are 'linguistically ill-formed'. While the distinction may be clear enough in principle, it is often very hard in practice to decide which side of the dividing line a given sentence falls. For example, what is the status of sentences such as the following (taken from George Lakoff, 'Presupposition and relative well-formedness' (1971), p. 332):

(9) (a)   My uncle realises that I'm a lousy cook
    (b)   My cat realises that I'm a lousy cook
    (c)   My goldfish realises that I'm a lousy cook
    (d)   My pet amoeba realises that I'm a lousy cook
    (e)   My frying pan realises that I'm a lousy cook
    (f)   My sincerity realises that I'm a lousy cook
    (g)   My birth realises that I'm a lousy cook

Intuitively, most people would regard (9) (a) as perfectly well-formed, (9) (b) as slightly less natural, (9) (c) as a little eccentric, (9) (d) as implausible, (9) (e) as just plain daft, and (9) (f) and (g) as absolutely inconceivable. But what precisely is the nature of the oddity in the more unusual sentences? The answer is that the oddity seems to be largely *pragmatic* (i.e. nonlinguistic) in nature. Thus, whether or not you find expressions like *My goldfish thinks that* . . . well-formed depends on whether or not you believe that

7

goldfish do (or might) possess powers of thought; a sentence like
(9) (c) presupposes that goldfish are capable of thought, and a
person who rejects sentences like (9) (c) is in effect rejecting the
proposition that goldfish are capable of thought. Why should he
reject such a proposition? Presumably because it conflicts with his
personal beliefs about the world. Thus, sentences like (9) (c) are not
linguistically ill-formed in any way, but rather simply pragmatically
odd, in the sense that they express ideas which do not conform to
our view of the way the world is organised.

But surely, (9) (f) and (g) are a very different case: surely
nobody in any culture could accept such a sentence as well-formed?
In this regard, Lakoff (ibid.) remarks:

> (9) (f) and (9) (g) are another matter. That properties and
> events have mental powers might seem to be an impossible
> belief, not just a strange one. If this were true, it would follow
> that (9) (f) and (9) (g) were universally impossible. However,
> Kenneth Hale informs me that, among the Papagos, events are
> assumed to have minds (whatever that might mean), and that
> sentences like (9) (g) would be perfectly normal.

In other words, our judgements about the ill-formedness of sentences like (9) depend entirely on our cultural, religious, or
personal beliefs – not on any *linguistic* knowledge that we have
about our language. Sentences like (9) are thus linguistically
well-formed: they are neither ungrammatical (e.g. they don't
involve a plural verb with a singular subject), nor semantically
ill-formed (e.g. it is not the case that we find such sentences as
completely incomprehensible or meaningless as a sentence from a
language we do not speak).

The distinction between sentences which are pragmatically or
linguistically 'odd' in some way has been the cause of a great deal of
confusion in the linguistic literature. For example, Katz and Postal
(*An Integrated Theory of Linguistic Descriptions* (1964), p. 16)
observe that a phrase like *honest geranium* is literally 'meaningless'
(sic): this presupposes that the oddity of such a phrase is purely
linguistic (and more particularly semantic) in nature. But this
seems a remarkably obtuse statement, since most of us would have
no difficulty in assigning a meaning to the phrase *honest geranium*:
we might paraphrase it (in typical lexicographical jargon) as 'a
flower of the genus pelargonium which is upright in word and

deed'. Of course, those narrow-minded bigots (or linguists) who can't imagine geraniums having essentially human properties like 'not telling fibs' would doubtless feign to be mystified by such a phrase. They *ought* to stare in blank incomprehension at the following extract from a fictitious episode of *The Magic Round-about*:

> Dougal was looking for his dog-biscuits. 'Have you been nibbling my Kanine Krunchy-Munchies again?' he asked Gerald the geranium. 'I'm awfully sorry, old chap,' replied Gerald, 'But I was so hungry . . .' 'Oh well, never mind!' retorted Dougal, 'At least you're an honest geranium.'

In such a context (i.e. a 'fairy story' context in which one's beliefs about the real world are suspended), such a phrase is clearly acceptable to anyone with a little imagination. But that is precisely the point: whether or not you find a phrase like *honest geranium* well-formed depends on your powers of imagination, not on any linguistic fact.

Let's take another problematic case. What is the status of a sentence like:

(10)   Gary Gay never loses her temper with anyone

Are we to say that such sentences are linguistically ill-formed – i.e. *ungrammatical* by virtue of the fact that the feminine pronoun *her* does not agree in gender with the masculine subject *Gary Gay*? Or are we to say that such sentences are semantically ill-formed – i.e. uninterpretable, and hence incomprehensible? Again, surely not. (10) is perfectly meaningful: it carries the implication that Gary Gay is effeminate. Of course, a person who finds any such insinuation distasteful may well object to such a sentence – but for nonlinguistic reasons.

Similar problems arise with phrases like:

(11) (a)   the tree who we saw
     (b)   the man which we saw

An obvious initial reaction to such phrases would be to regard them as syntactically ill-formed: but this is surely a very myopic view. (11) (a) is neither syntactically nor semantically ill-formed: the use of *who* referring back to *tree* carries with it the implication that the tree concerned is thought of as having e.g. humanlike qualities (i.e.

in traditional terminology, it is personified). As such, (11) (a) would be fully acceptable in a 'fairy story' context (where beliefs about the real world are suspended) – as in the following fictitious extract from *The Magic Forest*:

> The naughty tree who we passed waved his cheery branches at Mary and said 'You can tickle my leaves any time, darling.'

Support for this way of looking at phrases like (11) (a) (i.e. as pragmatically, rather than linguistically 'odd'), comes from the title of Pamela McCorduck's (1979) book *Machines who Think* (W.H. Freeman and Co., San Francisco). Likewise, (11) (b) is again both grammatical and meaningful: but the phrase carries the clear implication that the man referred to is somehow thought of as being an inferior being of some sort. Hence, (11) (b) might be appropriate if uttered by an arrogant Martian or Dalek, or even if uttered by a human in relation to a plastic model of a man, or a robot-man, etc.

Thus, it is easy to be deceived into thinking that a sentence is linguistically ill-formed in some way, when in fact very often the sentence is merely 'pragmatically odd' – i.e. it expresses an idea which (to people with certain beliefs, culture, education, etc.) may seem unacceptable. But if we now turn instead to sentences which do appear to involve some kind of *linguistic* ill-formedness, we again find many uncertainties: in particular, we find that it is sometimes very difficult to distinguish between sentences which are *semantically ill-formed* (or *unsemantic*, to use more recent terminology introduced by Chomsky), and those which are *syntactically ill-formed* (or *unsyntactic*). There are, of course, relatively clear cases of semantic ill-formedness, like:

(12) (a)   !I killed John, but he didn't die
    (b)   !All my friends are linguists, but I have no friends

and relatively clear cases of syntactic ill-formedness, like:

(13) (a)   *John very Mary much loves
    (b)   *All are linguists friends my

But there are also awkward intermediate cases, where it is clear that a sentence is linguistically ill-formed, but less clear whether it is syntactically or semantically ill-formed: consider, for example, the sentence:

(14)   We respect himself

A traditional way of looking at such sentences is to say that they are ungrammatical (i.e. *syntactically* ill-formed), by virtue of the fact that *himself* is a third person masculine singular reflexive pronoun, and does not agree in number or person with the first person plural nonreflexive pronoun subject *we*. But there is another, less traditional but equally plausible way of looking at such sentences: we might argue that they are syntactically perfectly well-formed: after all, a reflexive pronoun like *himself* can occur as the direct object of a verb like *respect* in a sentence like:

(15)   John respects himself

and hence there is clearly no overall syntactic restriction in English against using *himself* as the object of a transitive verb, and hence no reason to suppose that (14) is any more ungrammatical than (15). Instead, we might argue that (14) is in fact semantically ill-formed – i.e. simply uninterpretable. What's wrong with (14) – we might say – is that reflexive pronouns like *himself* have no independent reference, but rather must take their reference from some *antecedent* in the same sentence which is compatible in number, gender, and person with the reflexive. But in (14) – unlike (15) – there is no compatible antecedent for *himself*; hence, *himself* cannot be assigned any reference, and the resulting sentence as a whole is uninterpretable (or *unsemantic*, to use Chomsky's term) – i.e. 'meaningless'.

Faced with two equally plausible ways of looking at the ill-formedness of a sentence like (14), the obvious question to ask is how we decide whether to analyse (14) as syntactically, or semantically ill-formed. It might seem that the natural answer to this question is to rely on the intuitions of the native speaker. 'Do native speakers feel that such sentences are syntactically, or semantically ill-formed?' we might ask. However, as Chomsky has repeatedly emphasised, this is an unrealistic and unreasonable question to ask of an *informant* (= a native speaker who you are questioning about his language): for the simple fact is that very often all an informant can tell you is that one sentence 'sounds OK', and another 'sounds odd' – without being able to say how or why it sounds odd. As Chomsky himself remarks:

> We may make an intuitive judgement that some linguistic expression is odd or deviant. But we cannot in general know, pretheoretically, whether this deviance is a matter of syntax, semantics, pragmatics, belief, memory limitations, style, etc., or even whether these are appropriate categories for the interpretation of the judgement in question. It is an obvious and uncontroversial fact that informant judgements and other data do not fall neatly into clear categories: syntactic, semantic, etc.
>
> (Chomsky, *Essays* (1977), p. 4)

Indeed, it is not surprising that informants should not be able to tell you whether a sentence is syntactically or semantically ill-formed; for the very notions 'syntactically ill-formed' and 'semantically ill-formed' are terms borrowed from linguistic theory: and like all theoretical terms, they are meaningless to those not familiar with the theory. An informant simply gives judgements about ill-formedness: it is up to the linguist to decide, on the basis of the internal organisation of his own theory, what category a particular type of ill-formedness represents within his theory.

So now let's ask a rather different question about sentences like (14): 'Within Chomsky's theory, would (14) be analysed as syntactically, or semantically ill-formed?' Before we can answer this question, however, we should first say something about Chomsky's view of the overall organisation of a grammar. Chomsky takes an essentially *modular* approach to Linguistics: as we have already seen, he believes that Pragmatics should be separated from (and studied independently of) *Grammar*; within the domain of Grammar, Chomsky also believes that Syntax, Semantics, and Phonology should all three be treated as autonomous of each other, and studied independently. What is of more direct concern to us here is his insistence that Syntax should be studied independently of Semantics: this is known as the *Autonomous Syntax* thesis, and is defended at length in his *Essays* (1977), pp. 36–59 (not for beginners). Chomsky repeatedly emphasises that his claim that a distinction can and must be drawn between syntactic and semantic phenomena is an *empirical* one – i.e. a working hypothesis to be judged solely on the basis of whether it leads to interesting generalisations about Syntax on the one hand, and Semantics on the other. As he himself remarks:

The thesis . . . constitutes an empirical hypothesis about the organisation of language, leaving ample scope for systematic form-meaning connections while excluding many imaginable possibilities.

(Chomsky, *Essays* (1977), p. 42)

In principle, the dividing line between Syntax and Semantics seems clear enough: *Syntax* studies how words can be combined together to form sentences, what positions in the sentence a given word or phrase can occupy, and so forth; *Semantics* studies the meaning of words, phrases and sentences. *Syntax* answers the question 'Is such-and-such a sentence grammatical, and, if so, what is its syntactic structure?'; whereas Semantics answers the independent question 'Is such-and-such a sentence meaningful, and, if so, what does it mean?' But in practice, the issues may not be as clearcut: returning to our earlier problem, are we to treat (14) as syntactically or semantically ill-formed? In pre-1970 work in TG, sentences like (14) would undoubtedly have been considered ungrammatical; but in post-1970 work, they would be considered grammatical, but uninterpretable (i.e. *unsemantic*). The difference in attitude to such sentences reflects a difference in the overall organisation of grammars between Chomsky's earlier, and later work. Many phenomena dealt with as syntactic in earlier work have been reanalysed as semantic in more recent work. Subsequent discussion will give a fairly clear idea of where the dividing line between Syntax and Semantics is currently drawn, so we shall not dwell on the issue here.

Hitherto, we have been concerned with a variety of problems which arise with the notion of sentence ill-formedness (ill-formed relative to whose idiolect, and in what way(s)?). But there is one further distinction which we should draw – namely between sentences which are *ill-formed* (e.g. unsemantic, unsyntactic (= ungrammatical), etc.), and those which are *unacceptable*. This distinction which Chomsky draws is related to the distinctions which he draws between Competence and Performance on the one hand, and Pragmatics and Grammar on the other. Native speakers give judgements about the *acceptability* of sentences (i.e. they indicate whether they find them *acceptable* or *unacceptable*); acceptability is a *Performance* notion. If a native speaker says that a sentence is unacceptable in his language, this may be for a variety of reasons: one possibility (discussed earlier in relation to (9)) is that the sentence is simply *pragmatically* odd in some way (i.e. it expresses an idea which the speaker finds distasteful, or otherwise unacceptable); as we have already seen, sentences which are pragmatically odd are not necessarily linguistically ill-formed. However, it may be that a speaker will find unacceptable a sentence which is not pragmatically odd in any way: does this mean that the sentence concerned is ill-formed? Not necessarily. It may be that the informant is confused, or tired, or bored with all those questions about his language, and hence makes a hasty, and perhaps erroneous judgement: in such a case, Performance is a poor reflection of Competence. Or it may be that the informant is influenced by prescriptive notions inculcated at school: thus, some English speakers asked about a sentence like:

(16)   Who did you meet at the party?

would reply that such a sentence is *unacceptable* because it is 'bad grammar', and should be 'corrected' to:

(17)   Whom did you meet at the party?

But of course this is nonsense: a sentence like (16) is perfectly well-formed, and is characteristic of everyday conversation. In this case, a performance factor (prescriptive education) is interfering with the natural competence of the native speaker, with the result that the *acceptability* judgements which he gives are not an accurate reflection of the well-formedness or otherwise of sentences in his language.

To summarise: native speakers of a language have the ability to make performance judgements about sentence acceptability, on the basis of which the linguist seeks to capture the intuitions about sentence well-formedness which form the basis of their competence. But the remarkable fact about these abilities – Chomsky argues – is that they hold not only for familiar sentences that we have heard before, but equally for sentences that we have never heard before – or, as Chomsky calls them in his earlier work, *novel utterances*: herein lies what Chomsky refers to as the essential creativity of language: cf.

> The most striking aspect of linguistic competence is what we may call the 'creativity of language', that is, the speaker's ability to produce new sentences, sentences that are im-

mediately understood by other speakers although they bear no
physical resemblance to sentences which are familiar.

(Chomsky, *Topics* (1966), p. 11)

To cite one of Chomsky's own examples (from *Logical Structure*
(1975), p. 132), you have probably never encountered any of the
following sentences before:

(18) (a) Look at the cross-eyed elephant
    (b) Look at the cross-eyed kindness
    (c) Look at the cross-eyed from

And yet – if you are a speaker of English – you intuitively know
that (18) (a) is acceptable in English, whereas (18) (b) is odd, and
(18) (c) almost inconceivable. Any native speaker is capable of
producing, and understanding 'new sentences' like (18) (a), or
making judgements about their well-formedness. What is the
significance of the fact that all native speakers have the ability to
form, interpret and pronounce sentences that they have not come
across before? Chomsky argues that this essential creativity of
language shows that language can't simply be learned by imitation:
i.e. learning a language doesn't simply involve learning a list of
sentences produced by others, and repeating them parrot-fashion.
On the contrary, argues Chomsky, very few of the sentences we
produce or hear are repetitions of previous utterances:

> The normal use of language is innovative in the sense that
> much of what we say in the course of normal language use is
> entirely new, not a repetition of anything that we have heard
> before, and not even similar in pattern – in any useful sense of
> the terms 'similar' and 'pattern' – to sentences or discourse that
> we have heard in the past.
>
> (Chomsky, *Language and Mind* (1972), p. 12)

The novelty of most utterances we produce or hear provides a
strong argument against the claim made by behavioural psycholog-
ists that language-learning simply involves the acquisition of a set of
'linguistic habits'. As Chomsky remarks:

> This creative use of language is quite incompatible with the
> idea that language is a habit-structure. Whatever a habit-
> structure is, it's clear that you can't innovate by habit, and the
> characteristic use of language, both by a speaker and a hearer,
> is innovative. You're constantly producing new sentences in
> your lifetime – that's the normal use of language.
>
> (Chomsky, interview reprinted in *The Listener* (1968), p. 687)

So, if language isn't learned by imitation, how is it acquired? Chomsky argues that in order to account for the native speaker's ability to produce and understand new sentences, we must postulate that the child learning a language and faced with a certain set of data (i.e. the speech of people around him) abstracts from the data a set of general principles about how sentences are formed, interpreted and pronounced. These principles (or *rules*) must be of a sufficiently general nature to allow the child to form, interpret and pronounce new sentences that he hasn't come across before. In other words, acquisition of a language involves acquisition of (at least) the following:

(i)   a set of rules of sentence-formation (which specify how to combine words together to form grammatical sentences)

(ii)   a set of rules of sentence-interpretation (which specify how to interpret what sentences mean)

(iii)   a set of rules of sentence-pronunciation

This is what Chomsky means by saying that Language is *rule-governed*. The task of the linguist seeking to account for this creative aspect of grammatical competence is to formulate a set of rules of sentence-formation (= *syntactic rules*), rules of sentence-interpretation (= *semantic rules*), and rules of sentence-pronunciation (= *phonological rules*). A grammar of a language will thus comprise three interrelated components: a syntactic component, a semantic component, and a phonological component.

In Chomsky's view, then, learning a language involves learning a set of syntactic, semantic and phonological rules. But is there any evidence that learning a language actually does involve learning a set of rules? Some evidence in support of this assumption comes from studies of child language acquisition. Jean Berko in her (1958) paper 'The child's learning of English morphology' describes a simple experiment designed to prove the point: she drew a picture of an imaginary animal on a piece of paper, and told a child that it was called a *wug*; then she drew a picture of two of the same animals on another piece of paper, and asked the child what they were. The child replied: 'Wugs.' The significance of this was that the child had produced the plural form, even though it could never have heard the plural form *wugs* before, since this was an invented word. What does this tell us? The only way to account for the elicitation of the form *wugs* is by assuming that on the basis of hearing pairs such as *dog–dogs*, *bug–bugs*, *log–logs*, *rod–rods*, *flood–floods*, etc., the child formulates a rule which in effect says 'You form the plural of nouns by adding an -*s* on the end.'

Another source of evidence supporting the conclusion that children learn language by formulating a set of rules comes from *errors* that they produce: a case in point are past tense forms like *comed*, *goed*, *seed*, *buyed*, *bringed*, etc., frequently used by young children. Such forms cannot have been learned by imitation of adult speech, since they do not occur in adult speech (instead we find *came*, *went*, *saw*, *bought*, *brought*). So how is it that children produce such forms? The obvious answer is that, on the basis of pairs such as *love–loved*, *close–closed*, *use–used*, etc., the child formulates for himself a rule to the effect that 'You form the past tense by adding -*(e)d* to the stem of the verb'; the rule is then overgeneralised to 'irregular' verbs like *come*, *go*, *see*, *buy*, *bring*, etc.

The observations above suggest that children learn morphology (i.e. to construct past tenses, plural forms, etc.) by constructing for themselves (albeit subconsciously) a set of morphological rules. There is parallel evidence that the same is also true of Syntax. For example, Akmajian and Heny (*Principles* (1975), p. 17) report one group of American children observed producing direct yes–no questions like:

(19) (a)   Is I can do that?
     (b)   Is you should eat the apple?
     (c)   Is Ben did go?
     (d)   Is you be here?
     (e)   Is the apple juice won't spill?

Clearly, no adult English speaker would produce sentences like (19). So how does the child come to produce them? The obvious answer is that on the basis of sentences such as:

(20) (a)   Is daddy staying out again tonight?
     (b)   Is mummy getting dinner ready?
     (c)   Is Uncle Harry spending the night here again?

the child formulates for himself a rule to the effect that 'You form a question by putting *is* as the first word in the sentence.' Of course, the rule is 'wrong' to the extent that it doesn't correspond to the adult rule – and will be corrected at a later stage of acquisition by

17

the child. But these 'novel utterances' produced by the child provide strong evidence that learning a language does indeed involve learning a set of linguistic rules – and hence that language is indeed *rule-governed*.

A further illustration of children formulating rules of their own comes from the speech of my own daughter: between the ages of 48 and 54 months, she consistently produced sentences such as:

(21) (a)   I can't undone it
     (b)   I want daddy to undone it for me
     (c)   Will you undone it for me?

Equally interesting is the following conversation between her and me at the age of 49 months:

> Suzy: Don't make me lost it
> Daddy: No, don't make me *lose* it
> Suzy: No, not *lose* . . . *losed*!

It is quite clear that she is systematically replacing adult infinitives by past participles; she seems to have formulated for herself a rule to the effect that all nonfinite clauses in English contain participles. Once again, it is clear that sentences like (21) cannot have been produced by imitation of any adult pattern, since they do not occur in adult speech. Rather, the child is formulating rules of her own – 'guessing' at the rules of sentence-formation for English, and occasionally making the 'wrong guess', and hence producing sentences which are ungrammatical in adult speech. Another of Suzy's 'creations' from the same period is the following sentence-type (which lasted for about three months):

(22)   What was that noise was?

To summarise: there is a certain amount of evidence from studies of child language acquisition that learning a language involves learning a set of syntactic, semantic, morphological, phonological, etc. rules. The *grammatical competence* of the fluent native speaker of a language is therefore characterisable in terms of just such a system of rules of sentence-formation, sentence-interpretation and so forth: in the words of Chomsky:

> The person who has acquired knowledge of a language has internalised a system of rules that relate sound and meaning in a particular way. The linguist constructing a grammar of a

language is in effect proposing a hypothesis concerning this internalised system.

(Chomsky, *Language and Mind* (1972), p. 26)

We can introduce some technical terminology here. A grammar incorporating an explicitly formulated set of syntactic, semantic, and phonological rules which specify how to form, interpret and pronounce a given set of sentences is said to *generate* that set of sentences. Such a grammar is called a *generative grammar*. For a grammar to be adequate, it must *generate (i.e. specify how to form, interpret and pronounce) all and only well-formed sentences of the language* (i.e. the grammar must generate all the well-formed sentences, and no ill-formed sentences).

But this raises the question of how many well-formed sentences there are in any given language. Chomsky argues that the set of well-formed sentences in any language is *infinite*. This follows from the fact that there is no theoretical upper limit on the length of sentences in any language (though there are of course *performance* limitations – e.g. you might die before you finished a sentence of more than a million words!). For example, we can have indefinitely many attributive adjectives qualifying a noun in English:

(23) (a)   John is a handsome man
    (b)   John is a dark, handsome man
    (c)   John is a tall, dark, handsome man
    (d)   John is a sensitive, tall, dark, handsome man
    (e)   John is an intelligent, sensitive, tall, dark, handsome man
    (f)   Etc.

And there is in principle no upper limit to the number of quantifying expressions we can use to modify an adjective:

(24) (a)   Debbie Harry is very attractive
    (b)   Debbie Harry is very, very attractive
    (c)   Debbie Harry is very, very, very attractive
    (d)   Debbie Harry is very, very, very, very attractive
    (e)   Debbie Harry is very, very, very, very, very attractive
    (f)   Etc.

Nor is there any limit on the number of times that we can use one clause as the complement of another:

(25) (a)   John said that Mary was ill
    (b)   Fred said that John said that Mary was ill

(c)   Harry said that Fred said that John said that Mary was ill
(d)   Etc.

And there is no limit on the number of phrases that we can conjoin together by *and* (or *or*):

(26) (a)   I met Debbie and Harry
     (b)   I met Debbie, Noam and Harry
     (c)   I met Debbie, Noam, the dustman and Harry
     (d)   I met Debbie, Noam, the dustman, the President and Harry
     (e)   Etc.

Likewise, there's no upper limit on the number of relative clauses a sentence can contain:

(27) (a)   I chased the dog
     (b)   I chased the dog that chased the cat
     (c)   I chased the dog that chased the cat that chased the rat
     (d)   I chased the dog that chased the cat that chased the rat that chased the mouse
     (e)   Etc.

In other words, given any sentence of English, we can always form a longer one by adding another adjective, adverb, relative clause, etc. In consequence, it is literally true that there are an infinite set of well-formed sentences in English (or any other language, for that matter). And the native speaker is capable of making acceptability judgements about any of these; hence, his competence ranges over an infinite set of sentences. And yet, this infinite competence is acquired on the basis of a finite experience (i.e. a child learns a language in a finite period of time, on the basis of having been exposed to a finite sample of speech): as Chomsky himself observes:

> A speaker of a language has observed a certain limited set of utterances in his language. On the basis of this finite linguistic experience, he can produce an indefinite number of new utterances which are immediately acceptable to other members of his speech community.
>
> (Chomsky, *Logical Structure* (1975), p. 61)

Thus, the task of the linguist devising a grammar which models the linguistic competence of the native speaker is to devise a *finite* set of rules which are capable of specifying how to form, interpret and pronounce an *infinite* set of well-formed sentences.

To summarise: a Grammar is a model of the grammatical

competence of the native speaker of a language. It comprises a finite system of rules which generate (i.e. specify how to form, interpret and pronounce) the infinite set of well-formed sentences in the language. Accordingly, the task of the linguist describing a particular language is to devise a finite system of rules of sentence-formation, interpretation and pronunciation that will generate the infinite set of well-formed sentences in the language.

But how do we establish what the rules are? It might seem that the obvious approach is to ask a native speaker what the rules are which he has internalised, and which enable him to speak and understand his language fluently. But this is not of course possible, because the speaker has only *tacit* (i.e. subconscious) knowledge of the rules, and cannot bring them to consciousness: as Chomsky remarks:

> A person who knows a language has mastered a system of rules that assigns sound and meaning in a definite way for an infinite class of sentences . . . Of course, the person who knows the language has no consciousness of having mastered these rules or of putting them to use, nor is there any reason to suppose that this knowledge of the rules can be brought to consciousness.
>
> (Chomsky, *Language and Mind* (1972), pp. 103–4)

So, if we cannot get direct evidence about the nature of linguistic rules by asking native speakers what the rules are, how can we establish what they are? The linguist who asks this question is in essentially the same position as the scientist who want to study the laws (i.e. rules) which determine the motion of the planets. Of course, the laws of planetary motion are not themselves directly observable: only the effects produced by the operation of the laws can be observed. So, the scientist who wants to determine what these laws are has to proceed indirectly: i.e. first collect a set of data about the observed motion of the planets, then hypothesise principles which might explain this motion. The linguist is in an exactly parallel position, and has therefore to proceed in the same way: viz.

(i)   collect a set of data relevant to the phenomenon being studied
(ii)   hypothesise a set of principles (i.e. rules) which account for the data
(iii)   test the hypothesised rule(s) against further data

Natural questions to ask are: 'What count as *data*? How do you collect *data*?' There are two different types of data which linguists typically work with in formulating grammars: the first are recorded samples of speech or text (such samples are known technically as a *corpus of utterances*); we assume (perhaps simplistically) that in general people speak and write well-formed sentences. The second type of data that linguists work with are *informant intuitions*: for example, we might ask a Swahili speaker questions like 'Can you say "—" in Swahili? If so, what does it mean? What's the corresponding negative form? What effect does it have if I alter the stress pattern?', and so forth. There are lengthy, but rather sterile debates in the linguistic literature about which is the 'best' method of collecting data. For practical purposes, most linguists accept that it is sensible to use both types of data, and to check one against the other.

Suppose that we have now collected our data, and want to process it: how do we determine what are the explanatory principles which account for the data? Unfortunately, there are no known set of inductive procedures which the linguist (or anyone else) can apply to a given set of data to find generalisations. The simple answer is that you have to make an intelligent, informed 'guess' about what principle or rule might be needed to account for a particular phenomenon (linguists like to intellectualise their work by talking about *formulating hypotheses* rather than 'making guesses', however!).

To avoid the discussion becoming excessively abstract, let's take a concrete example. Suppose we are interested in the use of reflexive (i.e. *-self*) pronouns in modern English, and more particularly in the syntax and semantics of reflexives. Given Chomsky's view of Syntax as autonomous from Semantics, we might assume that the division of labour between Syntax and Semantics in the case of reflexives would be:

Syntax: specifies the positions in a sentence in which reflexive pronouns can occur

Semantics: specifies which expression(s) in a sentence a given reflexive pronoun can be interpreted as referring to (i.e. specifies the range of possible *antecedents* for a reflexive pronoun)

To confine our discussion within manageable bounds, let's just concentrate on the single problem of formulating a semantic interpretation rule which will tell us what the possible range of antecedents for reflexives is. In this regard, consider:

(28)   She never talks to us about herself

What can and cannot be the antecedent of *herself* here – i.e. the expression that *herself* refers to? Clearly, the antecedent can be *she*, but not *us*; but why? The traditional answer is that *she* is a third person feminine singular pronoun, as is the reflexive pronoun *herself*, while *us* is a first person plural pronoun; and it is generally assumed that reflexives can only have as their antecedent an expression which has the same number, gender, and person as the reflexive. In other words, we might provisionally propose a Reflexive Interpretation rule along the lines of:

(29)   A reflexive can be construed with (i.e. understood as core-ferential to) any expression in the same number, gender and person as the reflexive

Our rule (29) provides a simple account of why *herself* can be construed with *she*, but not with *us* in (28).

But now consider the following mini-discourse:

(30)   SPEAKER A: What do your friends think about Fred?
          SPEAKER B: John doesn't like himself very much, but I'm
          not sure about Mary

In (30), *himself* is third person masculine singular, as are both *Fred* and *John*; so, rule (29) predicts that either *Fred* or *John* can be interpreted as the antecedent of *himself*. But this is false; in fact, *himself* can only be construed as *anaphoric* (i.e. referring) to *John*, not to *Fred*. Thus, our initial rule (29) breaks down in the face of new data like (30); or, to use the appropriate technical terminology, (30) is a *counterexample* to (29). Accordingly, we need to modify (29) in some way so as to make it compatible not only with data like (28), but also with new data like (30). Why is it that *himself* can be anaphoric to *John*, but not to *Fred* in (30)? A likely answer is that *John* is contained in the same sentence as *himself*, but *Fred* is not. Accordingly, we might revise our earlier Reflexive Interpretation rule (29) along the lines of:

(31)   A reflexive can be construed with any expression in the same
          sentence which has the same number, gender and person

However, our revised rule (31) can be *counterexemplified* by further data, such as:

(32)   John thinks that Fred hates himself

Here, *himself* is third person masculine singular, as are both *Fred* and *John*: moreover, *Fred*, *John* and *himself* are all contained in the same sentence. Hence, our new rule (31) predicts that *himself* can be construed with either *Fred* or *John*. But this is simply wrong: *himself* can only be interpreted as coreferential to *Fred* here, not to *John*. Why? One relevant factor might be that *Fred* and *himself* are both part of the *hates*-clause, whereas *John* belongs to a different clause, the *thinks*-clause. In view of this, we might propose to reformulate (31) as:

(33)   A reflexive can be construed with any expression in the same clause which has the same number, gender and person

Rule (33) makes correct predictions about the sentence (32): *himself* is the object of the *hates*-clause, and can therefore be construed with *Fred*, which is the subject of the *hates*-clause, but not with *John* since *John* is the subject of the *thinks*-clause. But our revised rule (33) is in turn counterexemplified by:

(34)   John never talks to himself about Fred

because (33) wrongly predicts that *himself* can be construed with either *John* or *Fred* (since *John*, *Fred* and *himself* are all part of the *talks*-clause). But this is not the case, since *himself* can only be coreferential to *John*, not to *Fred*. Why? An obvious answer would be because *John* precedes the reflexive, and *Fred* follows it, and reflexives in general seem to require a *preceding* expression to refer to. To get round the problem posed by (34), we might modify (33) along the lines of:

(35)   A reflexive is construed with any expression which precedes it in the same clause which has the same number, person and gender

If we say that two expressions which have the same number, gender and person are *compatible*, and that two expressions which occur in the same clause are *clausemates*, we might reformulate (35) more succinctly as:

(36)   A reflexive is construed with any preceding compatible clause-mate expression.

In actual fact, we could demonstrate that our revised rule (36) is also inadequate in a number of respects; but that is not the point of our discussion. The point that we have been making is a methodological one: what the linguist does is collect a set of data relevant to a particular problem, formulate a hypothesis, test the hypothesis against further data, modify the hypothesis as necessary, test it against yet more data . . . and so on and so forth. By repeating this process time and again for a range of different phenomena, the linguist gradually builds up a set of rules of sentence-formation, interpretation and pronunciation which form the basis of his eventual *grammar* of the language.

But how do you know whether the grammar you propose for a particular language is adequate or not? Chomsky has proposed a number of *criteria of adequacy* for grammars (and for the linguistic theories associated with them). The weakest requirement for any grammar of a language is that it attain *observational adequacy*: this we might define as follows:

> A grammar of a language is *observationally adequate* if it correctly predicts which sentences are (and are not) syntactically, semantically and phonologically well-formed in the language

A higher level of adequacy is *descriptive adequacy*, which we can define as:

> A grammar of a language is *descriptively adequate* if it correctly predicts which sentences are (and are not) syntactically, semantically and phonologically well-formed in the language, *and also* correctly describes the syntactic, semantic and phonological structure of the sentences in the language in such a way as to provide a principled account of the native speaker's intuitions about this structure

We can illustrate the differences between observational and descriptive adequacy in Syntax in terms of the following example:

(37)   These boys don't like those girls

Any grammar of English which specifies that the sequence of words in (37) forms a grammatical sentence of English would attain observational adequacy (at least, in respect of this one example). To attain descriptive adequacy, the grammar would have to specify in addition what the syntactic structure of the sentence (37) is – i.e. it would have to specify that *these* modifies *boys* and not *girls*, and that *those* modifies *girls* and not *don't* . . . and so on and so forth.

The highest level of adequacy set by Chomsky for grammars (and linguistic theories) is *explanatory adequacy*: this we might attempt to define as:

> A grammar attains *explanatory adequacy* just in case it correctly predicts which sentences are and are not well-formed in the language, correctly describes their structure, *and also* does so in terms of a highly restricted set of optimally simple, universal, maximally general principles which represent psychologically plausible natural principles of mental computation, and are 'learnable' by the child in a limited period of time, and given access to limited data

Thus, to attain explanatory adequacy, a grammar must in effect be 'psychologically real'; in addition, it must be maximally *constrained*. But what does it mean for a grammar (or indeed a linguistic theory) to be *constrained*? And why should a grammar be *constrained* in any case?

To understand this, let's look at the problems associated with the alternative – namely, a totally unconstrained theory. In such a theory, where no constraints are put on what could be a 'possible syntactic rule of some language', there would be no reason not to expect to find some language with a rule along the lines of:

(38)   Invert any word beginning with 'p' with any word meaning 'tree' or 'motor car' on Sundays after 6 p.m. in a leap year

And yet no linguist describing any language has ever proposed any syntactic rule even remotely resembling (38): and in fact all of us would agree, I am sure, that we would want to rule out (38) as an 'impossible rule' in any language. But this amounts to saying that we want to *constrain* our theory in such a way as to rule out rules like (38) as 'impossible' in any language. What's wrong with (38) – i.e. how can we *constrain* our theory so as to 'bar' such rules? One obvious thing that seems to be wrong with (38) is that here we have a syntactic rule whose application depends on *pragmatic* information (i.e. information about the date and time when a sentence is uttered); one way of ruling out (38) would be to build into our linguistic theory the following *constraint*:

(39)   No syntactic rule can make reference to pragmatic information

However, the condition (39) is not strong enough, since it would still not preclude 'absurd' rules like:

(40)   Invert any word beginning with 'p' with any word meaning 'tree' or 'motor car'

How can we rule out (40)? One possibility would be to suggest a constraint along the lines of:

(41)   No syntactic rule can make reference to phonological information (e.g. whether or not a given word begins with 'p')

But even (41) would fail to rule out intuitively implausible rules like:

(42)   Invert any word meaning 'tree' in a sentence with· any word meaning 'motor car'

How can we rule out (42) as an 'impossible' rule? One answer would be in terms of a constraint along the lines of:

(43)   No syntactic rule can make reference to semantic information

Conflating our three constraints (39), (41) and (43) gives us:

(44)   No syntactic rule can make reference to pragmatic, phonological or semantic information

– and this returns us by another route to Chomsky's affirmation of the mutual autonomy (i.e. independence) of Syntax, Semantics, Pragmatics and Phonology.

Even if the idea of constraining a grammar or theory is relatively easy to understand, we might still ask *why* it is important to do so. Chomsky's answer is that only a maximally constrained theory of language can lead to the development of an adequate theory of language acquisition. That is, only if we assume that grammars contain a highly restricted set of principles of a highly restricted set of types, and that the child is born with this knowledge (i.e. genetically preprogrammed with a 'blueprint' for language), can we explain the rapidity of language acquisition in children. In other words, Chomsky assumes that the child is innately endowed with the knowledge of what are 'possible' and 'impossible' linguistic rules, so that his task in learning a language is thereby vastly simplified: i.e. a child attempting to learn the rule for the use of reflexives in English (for example) can automatically discount certain possibilities as 'linguistically impossible' (e.g. some arbitrary 'never-on-a-Sunday' condition to the effect that reflexives are never used on Sundays). As Chomsky himself remarks:

> I think it is reasonable to postulate that the principles of
> general linguistics regarding the nature of rules, their organisa-
> tion, the principles by which they function, the kinds of
> representations to which they apply and which they form, all
> constitute part of the innate condition that 'puts a limit on
> admissible hypotheses.' If this suggestion is correct, then there
> is no more point in asking how these principles are learned
> than there is in asking how a child learns to breathe, or, for that
> matter, to have two arms.
>
> (Chomsky, *Language and Mind* (1972), p. 171)

To summarise: on the basis of a detailed study of particular
grammars, the linguist hypothesises a set of linguistic universals
which form the basis of his proposed theory of language. This
theory of language in turn constitutes an essential subpart of the
theory of language acquisition that Chomsky seeks to develop.
Universals provide the key to understanding language acquisition,
since – in Chomsky's view – only if we hypothesise that the child
has innate knowledge of these universals can we account for the
rapidity of language acquisition. Universals also provide the key to
explanation since (according to Chomsky) explanation can only
proceed from universal (and hence hypothesised-to-be-innate)
principles.

One word of caution should be added, however. That is, it is not
necessary to accept Chomsky's views on innateness in order to go
along with his views on the goals of linguistic theory, the nature of
linguistic structure and rules and so forth. In fact, it is perfectly
possible to accept part or the whole of Chomsky's Linguistics,
without accepting his Philosophy of Mind (i.e. the Innateness
Hypothesis). In spite of Chomsky's own pronouncements to the
contrary, the two *are* separable, and raise distinct issues. It is one
thing to accept that Chomsky's way of analysing language is
interesting, and often insightful and revealing, but quite another to
accept his view that we cannot explain language acquisition unless
we posit some innate language faculty genetically preprogrammed
with a highly specific set of linguistic universals.

Returning now to the question of *universals*, Chomsky distinguishes two distinct types of universal: (i) *absolute* universals, and
(ii) *relative* universals. An absolute universal is a property which all
languages share without any exception; a *relative* universal represents a general tendency in languages, but one which has some

exceptions (which might in turn be attributable to other universal principles). Related to the notion of relative universals (i.e. general tendencies) is the *Theory of Markedness*; within markedness theory, we distinguish between *marked* and *unmarked* phenomena. An *unmarked* phenomenon is one which accords with general tendencies in language; a *marked* phenomenon is one which goes against these general tendencies, and is hence 'exceptional' in some way. For example, suppose we establish as a relative universal that most syntactic rules in most languages have property P, but that there are a mere handful of syntactic rules in a few languages which don't appear to have property P; in such a case, any rule in any language which has the property P will be an *unmarked rule*; and any rule which does not have property P will be a *marked* rule.

Related to the Theory of Markedness in turn is the *Theory of Core Grammar* which Chomsky seeks to develop. This represents the attempt to establish a common, universal 'core' of linguistic principles which characterise the full range of unmarked grammatical phenomena found in natural language (i.e. the set of 'general tendencies' observed in language). Thus, any rule which conforms to these general principles is a 'rule of Core Grammar' (or core rule), whereas any (marked – i.e. exceptional) rule which does not obey the principles concerned is not (i.e. is a noncore rule). Since the mid-1970s, Chomsky has increasingly focussed his attention on the attempt to develop, firstly, a particular 'core grammar' for English and, secondly, a more general universal Theory of Core Grammar; this inevitably means concentrating on the search for greater generalisations, often at the expense of any attempt to account for apparent 'exceptions'. Chomsky justifies this approach in the following terms:

> Linguistics would perhaps profit by taking to heart a familiar lesson of the natural sciences. Apparent counterexamples and unexplained phenomena should be carefully noted, but it is often rational to put them aside pending further study when principles of a certain degree of explanatory adequacy are at stake.
>
> (Chomsky, 'On Binding' (1980), p. 2)

Chomsky also seeks to integrate his proposed Theory of Markedness and Core Grammar into his associated Theory of Language Acquisition: he suggests as one possibility that children may be innately endowed with just such a Theory of Markedness and Core Grammar which defines for them the set of 'unmarked' rules which could be found in natural language; children would then have 'genetic help' in learning unmarked (or core) rules, and hence would master these relatively quickly. But they would have no such assistance in learning marked (or noncore) rules, and hence these would be expected to take much longer to learn. Needless to say, this work is so new that it has not yet filtered through to Developmental Psycholinguistics (i.e. studies of child language acquisition), and so at the moment is no more than an as yet unsubstantiated hypothesis, albeit an interesting one.

While a theory of relative or absolute universals (when suitably developed) will take care of the *similarities* between languages, an obvious question to ask is how we deal with the apparent *differences* between languages. As Chomsky himself observes, 'Plainly, rules can vary from language to language. . .' ('On Wh-Movement' (1977), p. 75); however, this variation is by no means random – e.g. there is no language with any rule like (38). On the contrary, languages vary, but 'within fixed limits' (Chomsky, ibid.). Accordingly, one of the essential tasks for linguistic theory is to define the set of possible *parameters of variation* across languages. That is, linguistic theory (and hence Universal Grammar) is concerned with 'the attempt to discover . . . what are the limits within which languages can vary, what are the [universal!] terms by means of which this variation can be described' (Bach and Harms, *Universals* (1968), p. vi).

Summary

The aim of Linguistics is (i) to develop a *Theory of Language*, and (ii) to develop a *Theory of Language Acquisition*. We attempt to develop a Theory of Language by formulating grammars of particular languages, and abstracting from these *absolute universals* on the one hand, and *relative universals* (i.e. general tendencies in language which form the basis for the development of a *Theory of Markedness and Core Grammar*) on the other. A grammar of a language is a *model* of the *competence* of the average native speaker of the language. Competence subsumes both *intuitions about sentence well-formedness* (derived from the *acceptabil-*

ity judgements given by informants) and *intuitions about sentence structure*. The task of the linguist in formulating a grammar of a language is to devise a *finite* set of syntactic, semantic and phonological rules which will *generate* the *infinite* set of well-formed sentences in the language. Grammars (and the linguistic theories they are based on) must meet three criteria of adequacy: *observational, descriptive* and *explanatory* adequacy. Linguistic theories (and grammars) can only attain explanatory adequacy if they are based on a maximally constrained, psychologically plausible, universal set of general principles.

EXERCISES

Exercise I

Discuss the question of whether any or all of the following sentences are ill-formed and, if so, what the nature of the ill-formedness is (pragmatic, syntactic, semantic, etc.)

(1)   John's a living dead man
(2)   My wife is not my wife
(3)   This is a five-sided hexagon
(4)   This oats is of rather poor quality
(5)   You can see the taste in a Fox's glacier mint
(6)   Two and two is five
(7)   I order you to know the answer/be tall/have black hair
(8)   My toothbrush is pregnant again
(9)   Colourless green ideas sleep furiously
(10)   I eat much cereal for breakfast

Exercise II

Two traditional prescriptive rules are the following:

A.   *Who* is used as the subject of a verb, and *whom* as the object of a verb or preposition
B.   Never separate a preposition from its object

Decide for yourself which of the sentences below are grammatical in your idiolect. On the basis of the judgements you make, decide whether rules A and B are an adequate reflection of your intuitions about English. If they are not, try and formulate a more adequate set of rules which would describe the way *you* speak more adequately.

(1)   Who came to the party?
(2)   Whom came to the party?
(3)   Who did you meet at the party?
(4)   Whom did you meet at the party?

(5)	Who did you buy those flowers for?
(6)	Whom did you buy those flowers for?
(7)	For who did you buy those flowers?
(8)	For whom did you buy those flowers?

Exercise III

Earlier, we proposed a rule to the effect that reflexives require a clausemate antecedent (see (36)). Which of the examples below are ill-formed in your idiolect; and which are consistent with/are counterexamples to this rule?

(1)	I know someone who hates myself
(2)	John is anxious for himself to get the prize, not Mary
(3)	John thinks that himself is sick
(4)	The book which I gave John impressed himself

*Exercise IV

In the following examples, show how the predictions that our clausemate reflexive rule (36) makes about whether they are well-formed or not depends on whether we assume that the italicised reflexive is the object of the verb preceding it, or the subject of the verb following it:

(1)	John considers *himself* to be tall, dark, handsome and intelligent
(2)	Every senator wants *himself* to get elected, not his rivals
(3)	I'd very much prefer *myself* to win, rather than you

**Exercise V

On the basis of your judgements about the following sentences, discuss the problems involved in determining whether a reflexive is *compatible* with its antecedent on the basis of person, number and gender agreement:

(1)	Gary Gay cut herself while shaving this morning
(2)	Every Soviet woman engineer is capable of asserting himself on the factory floor
(3)	The trouble with Gary Gay is that he never shaves herself
(4)	That nasty little brat next door hurt itself this morning
(5)	The tree tried to steady himself/itself/herself against the rock
(6)	Does a Dalek ever wash themselves?

**Exercise VI

A number of linguists have argued that when reflexives are used as complements of nouns (as in expressions like 'a picture of *herself*' where *herself* is a complement of the noun *picture*: hence reflexives used in this type of construction are known as 'picture noun reflexives'), they are not subject to the same restrictions as 'ordinary' reflexives. Bearing in mind our suggestion in (36) that 'ordinary' reflexives generally require a preceding clausemate antecedent, discuss the differences between 'ordinary' and 'picture-noun' reflexives in sentences such as the following (assuming the judgements given):

(1) (a) I would never show a photo of himself to John
    (b) *I would never show himself to John
(2) (a) Rumours about himself annoy John
    (b) *Himself annoys John
(3) (a) John thinks that stories about himself are interesting
    (b) *John thinks that himself is interesting
(4) (a) John says that there was a picture of himself in the paper
    (b) *John says that there was himself in the paper

FURTHER READING

Bach (1974) *Syntactic Theory*, pp. 1–28
Grinder and Elgin (1973) *Guide*, pp. 1–29
Huddleston (1976) *Introduction*, pp. 1–34
Jacobsen (1978) *TG Grammar*, pp. 1–63
Smith and Wilson (1979) *Modern Linguistics*, pp. 1–74

2

Structure

Thus far, we have conceived of a grammar as comprising at least three components (or sets of rules), namely:

(1) (i) *syntactic* rules of sentence-formation, which specify how to form sentences
  (ii) *semantic* rules of sentence-interpretation, which specify how to interpret the meaning of sentences
  (iii) *phonological* rules of sentence-pronunciation, which specify how to pronounce sentences

Henceforth, we shall be concerned almost entirely with the *syntactic* rules. Thus far, we have required that the sentence-formation rules of the syntactic component of a generative grammar perform two tasks:

(2) (i) generate all and only the grammatical sentences of the language (i.e. specify how words can be combined to form sentences)
  (ii) assign an appropriate syntactic structure to the sentences concerned which accounts for the native speaker's intuitions about the structural relations between the words in a sentence

Before we look at how we might go about tackling (2) (i), let's look more closely at (2) (ii) – the question of what we mean by saying that sentences have an internal syntactic structure, and how we can represent that structure.

Chomsky argues that the native speaker intuitively knows more about the syntax of his language than just which sequences of sounds can be combined in what order to form grammatical sentences. More specifically, the native speaker intuitively recognises that sound-sequences in sentences are structured into successively larger sets or groups which we call *constituents*. Even the spelling system of English recognises this (albeit sporadically), by grouping sound-sequences into *words* (bounded by a space),

34

phrases (bounded by a comma) and *sentences* (bounded by a capital letter and full stop). If sound sequences had only *linear* structure (whereby one sound precedes the next), then sentences would be written as a continuous sequence of sounds – e.g.

(3)   Thisboywillspeakveryslowlytothatgirl

But sentences aren't unstructured linear sequences of sounds: any native speaker of English can tell you that the sounds in (3) are grouped into *words*, and can tell you what the word-divisions are. We'd all agree, for example, that the word-divisions in (3) are those in (4) below:

(4)   This boy will speak very slowly to that girl

and not those in (5) below:

(5)   Th isb oywillsp eakv erys lowlytot hatg irl
           T his boyw ills peak ver ysl owly toth atgi rl

But although the English spelling system provides a systematic representation of the way sounds are structured into words, it generally provides only a very inadequate, inconsistent and sporadic representation of the way in which words are structured into phrases. For instance, we'd all agree that in (4) *very* 'goes with' or 'modifies' *slowly*, and not e.g. *speak* – and yet our spelling system provides no representation of this fact. One way in which we could represent this type of structural relation diagrammatically is by grouping the two words together into a single set, e.g. as follows:

(6)
        This boy will speak ver͞y slo͞wly to that girl

Likewise, we'd all agree that *that* in (4) 'goes with' *girl*, not with e.g. *to*. Once again, we could represent this intuition by grouping the two words together into a single set as follows:

(7)
        This boy will speak ver͞y slo͞wly to tha͞t girl

And in much the same way, we all share the intuition that *this* 'goes with' *boy* – a fact which we can represent as:

(8)
        Thi͞s boy will speak ver͞y slo͞wly to tha͞t girl

35

Furthermore, it seems intuitively obvious that *to* modifies the phrase *that girl* (not e.g. *very slowly*); this we can represent as:

(9)

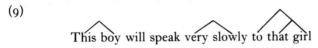

This boy will speak very slowly to that girl

Thus far, we'd probably all agree on the groupings that we have proposed. At this point, however, our intuitions tend to become rather more cloudy. Some people would argue that *speak very slowly to that girl* is also a structural unit, a *phrase*: if so, we might represent this as in (10):

(10)

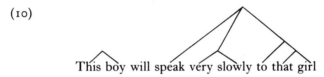

This boy will speak very slowly to that girl

Finally, the whole sequence *This boy will speak very slowly to that girl* is also a structural unit or constituent – one which we traditionally call a *clause* or a *sentence*: i.e. we intuitively know that the words in (4) form a single sentence, rather than two or three separate sentences. We can represent this by grouping all the phrases we have established so far into a single set, as follows:

(11)

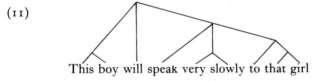

This boy will speak very slowly to that girl

The diagram (11) now provides a schematic representation of our intuitions about the internal syntactic relations between the various words and phrases in the sentence (4).

But even now we haven't exhausted our intuitive knowledge of the syntactic structure of sentences such as (4). For, we know not only which sequences of sounds form constituents (i.e. structural units), but also which constituents are *constituents of the same type*. So if someone asked us whether we feel intuitively that *boy* and *speak* are constituents of the same type, we'd probably say: 'No, *boy* is a *Noun*, and *speak* a *Verb*.' But we'd want to say that *boy* and *girl* are constituents of the same type – namely *Nouns*. By the same token, we'd intuitively recognise that *this* and *that* are constituents of the same type, which we might call *Determiners*. Similarly, we'd probably recognise that *will* is the same kind of constituent as *can*, *may*, *must*, *would*, *might*, etc. – i.e. is a constituent of the type traditionally called an *Auxiliary*. And we'd intuitively recognise that *to* is the same kind of constituent as *with*, *from*, *by*, *at*, *in*, *for*, etc. – namely a *Preposition*. Finally, we'd probably agree that in traditional terminology *slowly* is an *Adverb* (of manner) just like *carefully*, *quickly*, *patiently*, etc., and that *very* is a *Degree Adverb* like *quite*, *rather*, *somewhat*, and so forth. We can represent this information in an obvious way by labelling each of the words in (4) according to its type or *syntactic category* – e.g. as follows:

(12)

DET	N	AUX	V	DEG	ADV	P	DET	N
This	boy	will	speak	very	slowly	to	that	girl

DET = Determiner; N = Noun; AUX = Auxiliary; V = Verb; DEG = Degree Adverb; ADV = Adverb; P = Preposition

We can do this with the larger constituents as well: for instance, we'd want to say that *this boy* and *that girl* are constituents of the same type – phrases whose major constituent or *head* is a Noun in each case; hence we might label them *Noun Phrases* (NP):

(13)

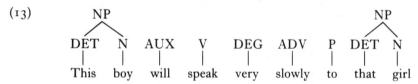

Likewise, the phrase *very slowly* is a constituent of the same type as phrases like *rather quickly*, *somewhat rudely* – i.e. a phrase whose *head* (*slowly*, *quickly*, *rudely*) is in each case an Adverb, so we might label such phrases *Adverbial Phrases* (ADVP):

(14)

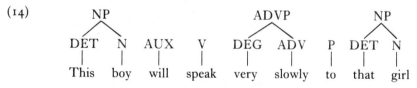

The phrase *to that girl* is a phrase of the same type as e.g. *from the headmaster*, *into the room*, *for Mary*, and in each case the head of the phrase is a Preposition (*to*, *from*, *into*, *for*), so we might call

such phrases *Prepositional Phrases* (PP); accordingly, we can label
to that girl as a Prepositional Phrase (PP):

(15)

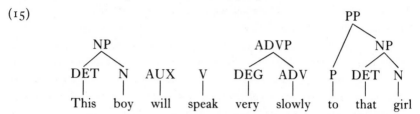

If it is also the case that *speak very slowly to that girl* is a
constituent, then it appears to be a constituent of the same type as
e.g. *give a present to Mary, run back home, close the door, die
tomorrow* – i.e. a constituent whose head is a Verb, and which
accordingly we might label Verb Phrase (VP):

(16)

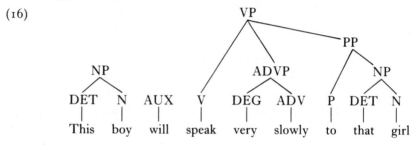

Finally, the whole sequence *This boy will speak very slowly to that
girl* is a constituent of the type we usually call a *Clause* or *Sentence*
(S): this we can represent as follows:

(17)

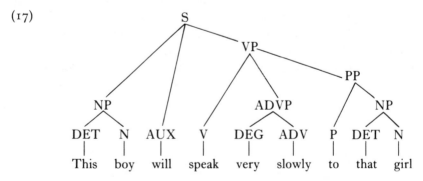

A diagram such as (17) provides a visual representation of the
hierarchical structuring of the words in (4) into *Constituents*
(structural units): i.e. (17) provides a visual representation of the

Constituent Structure (or *Phrase Structure*) of the sentence (4). Hence, the type of diagram used in (17) is referred to as a *Phrase-Marker* (P-marker), because it marks the hierarchical grouping of words into phrases, and phrases into sentences. The P-marker (17) thus provides a visual representation of the superficial syntactic structure – or *Surface Structure*, as Chomsky calls it – of the sentence (4).

The method of representing syntactic structure visually by the use of tree-diagrams (P-markers) such as that in (17) is in fact only one of many alternative systems which have been devised in order to provide a visual representation of structure. Another (logically equivalent) method of visual display frequently used in the linguistic literature is to make use of *labelled brackets* rather than tree-diagrams. Within this alternative system we could represent the constituent status of each of the words in (4) as:

(18)   [$_{DET}$ this] [$_N$ boy] [$_{AUX}$ will] [$_V$ speak] [$_{DEG}$ very] [$_{ADV}$ slowly] [$_P$ to] [$_{DET}$ that] [$_N$ girl]

Likewise, we could represent the fact that *this boy* and *that girl* are NPs (Noun Phrases), that *to that girl* is a PP (Prepositional Phrase), that *very slowly* is an ADVP (Adverbial Phrase), that *speak very slowly to that girl* is a VP (Verb Phrase), and that *This boy will speak very slowly to that girl* is an S (Clause) as follows:

(19)   [$_S$ [$_{NP}$ [$_{DET}$ this] [$_N$ boy]] [$_{AUX}$ will] [$_{VP}$ [$_V$ speak] [$_{ADVP}$ [$_{DEG}$ very] [$_{ADV}$ slowly]] [$_{PP}$ [$_P$ to] [$_{NP}$ [$_{DET}$ that] [$_N$ girl]]]]]

(By convention, only the left-hand member of any pair of brackets is usually labelled with the relevant category label.) The resultant diagram (19) is entirely equivalent to (17) – i.e. the two diagrams contain exactly the same information as each other. Generally speaking, tree-diagrams are easier to read, and this is the reason why they are frequently preferred by many linguists as a form of visual representation of syntactic structure.

Diagrams like (17) and (19) provide a virtually complete representation of the syntactic structure of a sentence like (4). Quite often, however, the linguist may prefer to give a less detailed account of the structure of a sentence, where he does not want to include absolutely every minute detail of the structure, but rather just wants to give a partial representation of the structure. For this reason, it is quite common to find in the relevant literature partial tree-diagrams, or partial labelled bracketings. For example, suppose that, for the purposes of some argument that I am developing, it is essential to assume that a sentence like (4) contains three major constituents, the Noun Phrase *this boy*, an Auxiliary *will* and a Verb Phrase *speak very slowly to that girl* – but that it is irrelevant to my argument what the internal structure of the Noun Phrase and Verb Phrase may be. In such a case, in place of the tree diagram (17), I might prefer the partial P-marker (20):

(20)

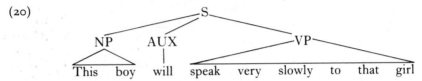

(In partial P-markers like (20), it is quite common to use a 'triangle' to represent constituents with a complex internal structure that you don't choose to represent.) Or, in place of the detailed labelled bracketing (19), we might prefer the partial bracketing (21) below:

(21)   [NP this boy] [AUX will] [VP speak very slowly to that girl]

(In what respect is (21) not quite *exactly* equivalent to (20)?) Generally speaking, linguists tend to use tree-diagrams (P-markers) for a full representation of the syntactic structure of a sentence (because at that level of detail, they are easier to read) and labelled bracketings for a partial representation of structure (because they occupy less space on the printed page). But recall that the two systems of representation are logically equivalent (whatever structure can be represented in the one system can be represented in the other, and vice-versa), so the question of whether you adopt one or the other is entirely a matter of typographical convenience, *not* a matter of any theoretical significance. Accordingly, we shall use both systems freely in our discussions here.

Earlier on, we said that the syntactic component of a grammar comprises a set of sentence-formation rules which have two tasks to fulfil: viz. (2) (i) and (ii) above; that is (i) specify which sequences of words form grammatical sentences in a language, and (ii) specify the internal syntactic structure of such sentences. We have now seen that the surface syntactic structure of a sentence can be represented in the form of a tree-diagram or P-marker like (17). Accordingly, we might reformulate the goal of the syntactic component of a grammar as being that of generating (= specifying how to form) all the grammatical sentence-structures (surface structures) in a language. That is, we want to devise a set of rules which specify how sentences are built up out of phrases, and how phrases are built up out of words. If we further assume that surface structures can be adequately represented by P-markers such as (17), then the problem in effect reduces to devising a set of rules which will generate P-markers such as (17).

But what kind of rules could we devise which would generate tree-structures like (17)? One suggestion made by Chomsky is that structures such as (17) could be generated by a set of rules which he calls *Phrase Structure Rules* (or PS rules) – so called because they specify how sentences are structured out of phrases, and phrases out of words. Consider, for example, the following set of Phrase Structure Rules:

(22) (a)   S → NP – AUX – VP
    (b)   VP → V – ADVP – PP
    (c)   ADVP → DEG – ADV
    (d)   PP → P – NP
    (e)   NP → DET – N
         (S = Clause/Sentence; NP = Noun Phrase; AUX = Auxiliary;
         VP = Verb Phrase; V = Verb; ADVP = Adverbial Phrase;
         PP = Prepositional Phrase; DEG = Degree Adverb;
         ADV = Adverb; P = Preposition; DET = Determiner;
         N = Noun
         → = 'can consist of/can be formed from'
         – = 'immediately preceding')

Given the gloss at the foot of (22), rule (22) (a) can be regarded as specifying 'You can form a Clause by taking a Noun Phrase immediately followed by an Auxiliary immediately followed by a Verb Phrase.' More formally, we can say that rule (22) (a) will *generate* the partial tree-structure (23) below:

(23)

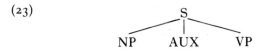

                NP   AUX   VP

Rule (22) (b) specifies that we can form a Verb Phrase by taking a Verb immediately followed by an Adverbial Phrase immediately followed by a Prepositional Phrase: i.e. from (23) by application of rule (22) (b) we can generate:

(24)

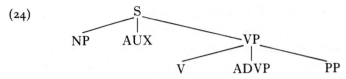

Rule (22) (c) specifies that we can form an Adverbial Phrase by taking a Degree Adverb followed by an Adverb; applying this rule to the structure (24), we expand (24) into:

(25)

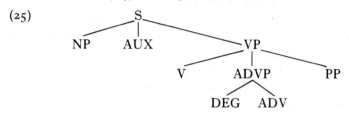

Rule (22) (d) specifies that we can form a Prepositional Phrase out of a Preposition immediately followed by a Noun Phrase; applying rule (22) (d) to the structure (25) will give us:

(26)

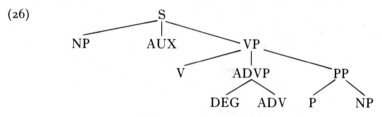

Rule (22) (e) says that we can form a Noun Phrase by taking a Determiner immediately followed by a Noun; if we apply this rule to expand both the Noun Phrases in (26), we *derive* the structure:

(27)

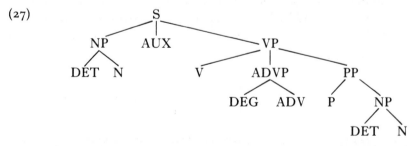

Let's now assume that in addition to the *Categorial Rules* (22) – i.e. rules expanding categories into other categories – the syntactic component of our grammar also contains a *Lexicon* (= dictionary), or list of all the words in the language. And let us further assume that the *Lexical Entry* (= dictionary entry) for each such *Lexical Item* (= word) contains (in addition to other information) a specification of the syntactic category that the word belongs to. For present purposes, we might imagine that our Lexicon contains (inter alia) the following entries:

(28)   *boy*, N, . . .
        girl, N, . . .
        slowly, ADV, . . .
        speak, V, . . .
        that, DET, . . .
        this, DET, . . .
        to, P, . . .
        very, DEG, . . .
        will, AUX, . . .

And finally, let us also postulate a *Lexical Insertion Rule* by which any lexical item (= word) belonging to a given lexical category (i.e. word-category like N, V, P, ADV, etc. as opposed to *Phrasal Categories* like NP, VP, PP, ADVP, etc.) can be inserted in a structure like (27) under the corresponding category – e.g. any N (= Noun) can be inserted under N, any V (= Verb) under V, any ADV (= Adverb) under ADV, and so forth. Given such a Lexical Insertion Rule, we can insert e.g. *this* under the first DET in (27), *boy* under the first N, *will* under AUX, *speak* under V, *very* under DEG, *slowly* under ADV, *to* under P, *that* under the second DET, and *girl* under the second N, thereby deriving from (27) the Surface Structure (29):

(29)

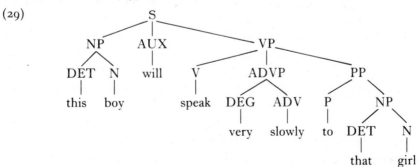

Thus, we see that a set of Categorial Rules like (22) (which specify how categories are formed out of other categories), together with a

Lexicon like (28) and an associated Lexical Insertion Rule expanding lexical categories into Lexical Items ('real words'), will prove adequate to generate a surface structure such as (29), which is the same as (17) or (19). We have thus now achieved our aim of formulating a set of syntactic rules which will generate sentence-structures like (17).

But notice that our existing system of rules will generate not only the sentence-structure (29): the very same set of rules (together with the same Lexicon) can also be used to generate the surface structures associated with any of the following set of sentences:

(30)   This boy will speak very slowly to this girl
             That boy will speak very slowly to that girl
             That boy will speak very slowly to this girl
             This boy will speak very slowly to this boy
             This boy will speak very slowly to that boy
             That boy will speak very slowly to this boy
             That boy will speak very slowly to that boy
             This girl will speak very slowly to this girl
             This girl will speak very slowly to that girl
             That girl will speak very slowly to that girl
             That girl will speak very slowly to this girl
             This girl will speak very slowly to this boy
             This girl will speak very slowly to that boy
             That girl will speak very slowly to that boy
             That girl will speak very slowly to this boy

In other words, the simple grammar we have devised will generate not only the surface structure (29), but also fifteen other similar surface structures corresponding to the fifteen sentences listed in (30). Thus, a grammar incorporating a set of Phrase Structure Rules like (22), a Lexicon like (28), and an appropriate Lexical Insertion Rule can provide a partial account of the *creativity* of natural language, insofar as the set of rules necessary to generate one surface structure like (29), will also generate 'novel' surface structures such as those associated with the sentences in (30).

Of course, structures like (29) and (30) constitute only a tiny subset of the infinite set of well-formed surface structures found in English. We can increase the *Generative Capacity* of our grammar (= the set of structures that it generates) either by expanding the Lexicon on the one hand, or by expanding the Categorial Rules on the other. For example, we might add to our Lexicon Auxiliaries such as *must, may, might, can*, etc., Nouns such as *man, woman, student, person, waiter*, etc., Determiners like *the* and *a*, Degree expressions like *rather, quite, too*, etc., Adverbs like *carefully, sincerely, thoughtfully*, etc., Verbs like *gesture, whisper, signal, talk*, etc. . . . and so on and so forth. In consequence, our grammar would then generate thousands of sentence-structures similar to (29), including those associated with sentences such as:

(31)   This girl will speak very carefully to the waiter
         A boy must speak very sincerely to a girl
         That student may signal rather carefully to the waiter
         Etc., etc.

Alternatively, we might modify or expand our existing categorial rules so that they generate more types of surface structure than before. Thus, for example, bearing in mind that the occurrence of the Adverbial Phrase in sentences like (30) is optional, so that alongside (30) we also find sentences such as:

(32)   This boy will speak to that girl

we might propose to make the Adverbial Phrase an *optional* constituent of the Verb Phrase: this we could do by replacing rule (22) (b) by rule (33):

(33)   VP → V – (ADVP) – PP

where a constituent in parenthesis is, by convention, taken to be optional. Rule (33) is equivalent to the two rules (34) below:

(34) (a)   VP → V – ADVP – PP
     (b)   VP → V – PP

Clearly, we need an enormous expansion of both our categorial rules and our Lexicon in order to achieve anything like an adequate grammar of English. But the main point that we are concerned with illustrating here is simply that it is possible to devise a system of sentence-formation rules that will indeed generate a wide range of surface structures for any given language.

Thus far, we have relied essentially on *intuition* to justify the postulation of an abstract hierarchical surface constituent structure associated with every sentence in a given language. But constituents and categories, in addition to having a basis in *intuition*, also have a rather different status – namely that of *theoretical constructs*: i.e. they are abstractions which we postulate in order to provide a principled account of a number of linguistic facts which would otherwise remain unexplained. In what follows, we shall examine some of these facts in detail.

Perhaps the most important linguistic argument in favour of postulating that sentences are structured into constituents belonging to various categories is a *distributional* one. Syntax is essentially concerned with the distribution of words and phrases – i.e. specifying which words or phrases can appear in which positions in which types of sentence. Now, it turns out that any attempt to formulate a set of sentence-formation rules dealing with the distribution of words and phrases without using a set of syntactic categories encounters considerable difficulties, as we shall see.

One such problem is that any noncategorial grammar (i.e. a grammar which does not make use of categories) will miss important generalisations about significant regularities in the distribution of words and phrases. Consider, for example, the problem of generating a simple set of sentences like the following in a noncategorial grammar:

(35) (a)   The noble king will introduce the rich count to the kind princess
  (b)   This wicked count may present that noble princess to a rich count
  (c)   The wicked princess can describe the rich king to the kind count
  (d)   That noble count must present a rich princess to the wicked king
  (e)   A wicked count may introduce a kind king to a rich princess

Now it might seem at first sight that we can directly generate sentences like those in (35) in a noncategorial grammar, simply by listing the set of words that can occur in first position, second position, third position, fourth position, and so forth, in the sentence: this we might do as follows:

(36)

1	2	3	4	5	6	7	8	9	10	11	12
the	noble	king	will	introduce	the	noble	king	to	the	noble	king
a	kind	count	may	present	a	wicked	count		a	wicked	count
this	rich	princ-	can	describe	this	kind	prin-		this	kind	princess
that	wicked	ess	must	. . .	that	rich	cess		that	rich	. . .
. . .	. . .	. . .	. . .		. . .	. . .	. . .		. . .	. . .	

We might then stipulate that we can form a grammatical sentence by taking any word from column 1, immediately followed by any word from column 2, immediately followed by any word from column 3 . . . and so on and so forth. Any grammar incorporating a list like (36) would be noncategorial in the sense that it does not make use of syntactic categories, but rather simply of words. Could we not formulate an adequate syntax of a language like English using word-lists like (36)?

The answer to this question is that any noncategorial grammar suffers from a number of serious defects. One such drawback is that word-based grammars lack generality in the sense that they fail to capture important linguistic generalisations about the distribution of words. Notice, for example, that the set of words which can occur in column 1 is exactly the same as the set of words which can occur in columns 6 and 10. A list-based grammar like (36) makes this seem entirely coincidental, since each column represents a distinct sentence-position, and hence we might expect that each column will contain a different set of words, with no significant overlap between columns. But in fact, there clearly is significant overlap between the columns in three respects; firstly, columns (1), (6) and (10) contain the same set of words; secondly, columns (2), (7) and (11) contain the same set of words; and thirdly, columns (3), (8) and (12) contain the same set of words. The degree of overlap here is so great that we cannot dismiss these correspondences as coincidental – on the contrary, they clearly represent a significant distributional fact, namely that the same set of elements may occur in a variety of different sentence-positions. The function of grouping words into category-sets is precisely to capture such distributional generalisations, by assigning words which have essentially the same distribution to the same lexical category (= word-class), and then formulating our sentence-formation rules in terms of sequences of categories, rather than sequences of words. In the present case, for example, we achieve much greater generality by replacing the list (36) by a category-based rule like:

(37) S $\rightarrow$ *DET* $-$ *A* $-$ *N* $-$ AUX $-$ V $-$ *DET* $-$ *A* $-$ *N* $-$ P $-$ *DET* $-$ *A* $-$ *N*

where DET is the category of Determiners (including *the*, *a*, *this*, *that*), A is the category of Adjectives (including *noble*, *wicked*, *kind*, *rich*) N is the category of Nouns (including *king*, *count*, *princess*), AUX is the category of Auxiliaries (including *will*, *may*, *can, must*), V is the category of Verbs (including *introduce, present, describe*), and P is the category of Prepositions (including *to*, etc.).

But even rule (37) still misses at least one important distributional generalisation – namely that the sequence $DET - A - N$ recurs in three separate sentence-positions (italicised in (37)) in the sentences (35) viz. immediately before AUX, immediately after V, and immediately after P. Clearly we are missing another obvious generalisation here, and rule (37) is unnecessarily cumbersome and repetitive in repeating the same sequence of categories ($DET - A - N$) three times. We can capture the relevant generalisation if we assume that the sequence $DET - A - N$ in each case forms a larger phrasal category, a Noun Phrase (= NP): in which case, we can replace rule (37) by the more general set of rules (38) below:

(38) (a)   S → NP – V – NP – P – NP
    (b)   NP → DET – A – N

Rule (38) can itself be made more general if we assume that the $P - NP$ sequence together forms a PP, and that the V and the categories which follow it together form a VP; we shall discuss the motivation for positing VP and PP constituents later, so we shall not dwell on the matter here.

The essential motivation for setting up categories, and formulating sentence-formation rules in terms of categories should now be clear; namely that categories enable us to achieve much more general statements about distribution (i.e. much more general sentence-formation rules) than could be achieved by arbitrary lists of words like (36). Accordingly, we might define a category distributionally in the following terms:

(39)   A *category* is a set of elements that have essentially the same distribution, and that recur as a structural unit in a variety of different sentence-positions and sentence-types

Thus far, we have argued that a category-based syntax achieves a greater level of generality than a word-based syntax. But, in fact, we can go further than this, and demonstrate that it is doubtful that word-based syntaxes can even achieve *observational adequacy* (at least in terms of a finite set of rules or lists). For natural languages typically have the property that they allow (potentially infinite) *recursion* or *iteration* of categories – a process which can easily be handled in a category-based grammar, but cannot be handled in any finite way in terms of a grammar using word-lists. To illustrate the problem, consider how we might generate a set of sentences such as the following:

(40) (a) John knows Joe
    (b) Fred knows John knows Joe
    (c) Jim knows Fred knows John knows Joe
    (d) Pete knows Jim knows Fred knows John knows Joe

Any attempt to write a word-based set of sentence-formation rules to generate sentences like (40) faces the problem that there is no upper limit to the (potential) length of such sentences: hence, any set of rules which attempts to simply list the set of possible word-combinations in such cases will have to be *infinite*. But this violates the most fundamental criterion of adequacy imposed on grammars – namely that they contain a *finite* system of rules capable of generating a potentially infinite set of sentences. By contrast, in a category-based grammar, we can generate an infinite set of sentences like (40) in terms of a very simple *recursive* set of rules including:

(41) (a) S → NP – VP
    (b) VP → V – $\begin{cases} NP \\ S \end{cases}$
    (c) NP → N

where (41) (a) specifies that we can form a Clause (= S) out of a Noun Phrase immediately followed by a Verb Phrase, (41) (b) specifies that we can form a Verb Phrase by taking a Verb immediately followed by a Noun Phrase or a Clause, and rule (41) (c) says that we can form a Noun Phrase out of a Noun on its own (i.e. a Noun like *John, Joe, Fred, Jim*, etc.). By applying rule (41) (a), we generate the structure:

(42)

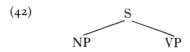

Rule (41) (b) tells us that we can expand the VP in (42) into a V followed by either an NP, or an S. If we choose the former option and expand VP into the sequence V – NP, we obtain:

(43)

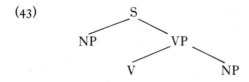

Subsequent application of rule (41) (c) to both NPs in (43) will then yield:

(44)

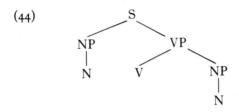

and (44) is precisely the surface structure of sentences like (40) (a), *John knows Joe*. Alternatively, if instead we take the second option in rule (41) (b) and expand the VP in (42) into the sequence $V - S$, we derive:

(45)

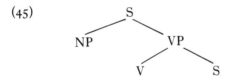

If we now reapply rule (41) (a) to expand the embedded (= lower) S in (45) into $NP - VP$, we derive:

(46)

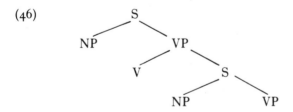

If we now expand the embedded (= lower) VP in (46) into $V - NP$ by rule (41) (b), we obtain:

(47)

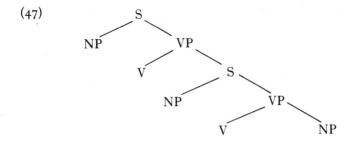

If we then further expand all the NPs in (47) into N by rule
(41) (c), we get:

(48)

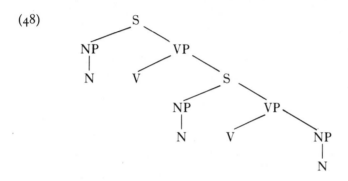

i.e. precisely the abstract structure associated with sentence like
(40) (b), *Fred knows John knows Joe*. But now suppose that instead
of expanding VP in (46) into *V – NP*, we expand it into *V – S* by
rule (41) (b) instead: this would give us:

(49)

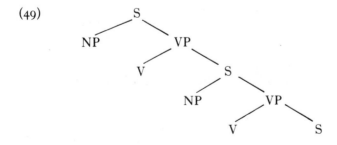

If we now expand the most deeply embedded (= lowest) S in (49)
into *NP – VP* by applying rule (41) (a) once again, we obtain:

(50)

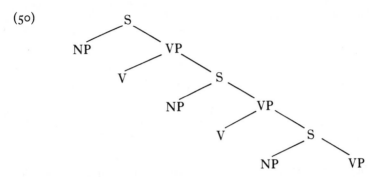

And if we then apply rule (41) (b) to expand the most deeply embedded VP in (50) into the sequence $V - NP$ by rule (41) (b), we derive:

(51)

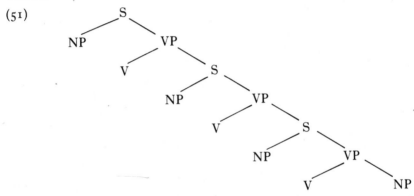

Finally, if we now apply rule (41) (c) to expand all occurrences of NP in (51) into N, we obtain the structure:

(52)

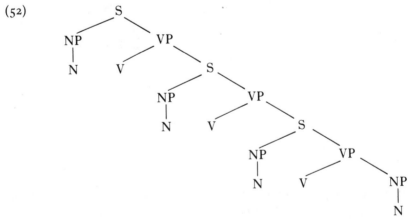

and (52) is the abstract superficial syntactic structure associated with sentences such as (40) (c), *Jim knows Fred knows John knows Joe.*

It should be clear enough from the above discussion that by reapplying the same set of rules (41) more and more times, we can generate more and more complex sentences. In fact, there is potentially no limit on the number of times we can keep reapplying the rules; and, in consequence, there is no limit on the length or number of such sentences that we can generate. In other words, the rules (41) will generate an infinite set of abstract sentence-structures. The interesting property that the rule-system (41) has which enables a finite set of rules to generate an infinite set of sentence-structures is that of *recursion*. That is, the rules are recursive in the sense that rule (41) (a) generates as part of its output a category (VP) which itself serves as input to rule (41) (b); and rule (41) (b) in turn generates as part of its output a category (S) which in turn can serve as input to rule (41) (a).

Thus far, we have seen two advantages of category-based grammars: firstly, they capture distributional regularities and, secondly, they can handle recursion. A third advantage is that category-based grammars are more *constrained* than word-based grammars. For, in a category-based syntax, it may be possible to impose two very strong constraints on the nature of all sentence-formation rules in natural language: viz.

(53) (i)   All syntactic rules in all natural languages are category-based (or, in Chomsky's terminology, *structure-dependent*)

    (ii)   The set of lexical and phrasal categories found in any language is drawn from a highly restricted finite universal set including S; N, NP; V, VP; P, PP; ADV, ADVP; A, AP; AUX; DET; etc.

The conditions in (53) impose very strong constraints on what constitutes a 'possible syntactic rule' in natural languages: e.g. (52) rules out any rule incorporating word-lists like (36) as an 'impossible syntactic rule'.

Any grammar incorporating the constraints (53) can also achieve greater *explanatory adequacy* than word-based grammars: i.e. it offers a more plausible model of language acquisition. If our linguistic theory imposes the condition that all grammars of all natural languages are subject to the constraints (53), then the task facing the child learning a language is a relatively simple one: i.e. the child has to identify which words and phrases belong to which categories in the language he is learning, and which categories can occur in which sentence-positions. For example, if a child learns that in English the words *a, the, this, that, my, your, his*, etc. all belong to the category DET (= Determiner), and if he hears a sentence like:

(54)   I want *a* toy

then, given the constraint that all syntactic rules are category-based, he can immediately infer that not only *a* but also all other members of the same category (DET) can occur in the italicised position – i.e., having heard (54), he will be able to infer that the sentences in (55) below are also grammatical in English:

(55) (a)   I want *the* toy
     (b)   I want *this* toy
     (c)   I want *that* toy
     (d)   I want *my* toy
     (e)   I want *your* toy
     (f)   I want *his* toy
             Etc.

Furthermore, given the same assumption that all syntactic rules are category-based (or *structure-dependent*), he can also infer that in place of *toy* in (54) he can substitute any other item belonging to the same category (N, = Noun), and thus generate e.g.:

(56) (a)   I want a *ball*
     (b)   I want a *television*
     (c)   I want a *blackboard*
     (d)   I want a *banana*
             Etc.

In short, the twin assumptions that syntactic rules are category-based, and that there are a highly restricted finite universal set of categories in natural language, together with the assumption that the child either *knows* (innately) or *learns* these constraints (53), provide a highly plausible model of language acquisition, in which languages become learnable in a relatively short, finite period of time (a few years).

Another, very different reason for assuming that sentences have a hierarchical constituent structure concerns the fact that such an assumption makes it possible to provide a principled account of certain types of *ambiguity* characteristic of natural languages. Here, it is important to distinguish between two very different kinds of ambiguity: (i) *lexical* ambiguity, and (ii) *structural* ambiguity. Lexical ambiguity is ambiguity attributable to the fact that some particular lexical item (= word) has more than one meaning. For example, the word *ball* is ambiguous as between one sense in which it means a 'round object', and a second sense in which it means a 'dance'; the ambiguity here is purely lexical. But there is a second type of ambiguity characteristic of natural languages, illustrated by the phrase:

(57)   very old men and women

Clearly, (57) is ambiguous, but the ambiguity does not lie in the words themselves: i.e. it isn't the case that *old*, or *men*, or *women* has more than one distinct sense. Rather, the ambiguity rests on whether *very old* is taken as qualifying only *men* (so that (57) has the sense of 'women and very old men') or as qualifying the phrase *men and women* (so that (57) means 'very old men and very old women'). Thus, it would appear that the ambiguity is not lexical in nature, but rather *structural*, insofar as it resides in the question of which part of the structure of (57) is modified by *very old*. Hence a natural way of representing the ambiguity would be to say that (57) has two distinct constituent structures: if *very old* is taken as qualifying only *men*, then (57) will have the structure (58) below; but if *very old* qualifies the phrase *men and women* then (57) will have the structure (59):

(58)

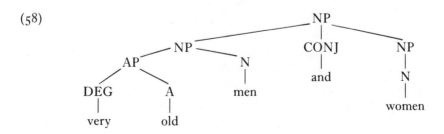

(59)

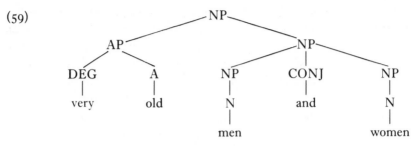

AP = Adjectival Phrase; A = Adjective; CONJ = Conjunction

Against this, it might be objected that in a model of language where Syntax is treated as autonomous of Semantics, it is not the task of a *syntactic* theory to answer questions like 'Is such-and-such a sentence structurally ambiguous, and if so how can its ambiguity be formally represented?' Ambiguity, we might object, is a *semantic* property, and hence falls within the scope of a *semantic* theory, not a syntactic one. Chomsky's reply to this type of objection would be the following:

(60)   The phenomena presented to us do not, of course, come provided with a system of appropriate categories or explanatory principles. It is only in the light of a particular theory that we can draw conclusions as to how some phenomenon is to be interpreted. . . It is an obvious and uncontroversial fact that informant judgements and other data do not fall neatly into clear categories: syntactic, semantic, etc.

                                      (Chomsky, *Essays* (1977), p. 4)

What Chomsky is saying here is that the question of whether we decide to treat a particular phenomenon as syntactic or semantic should not be decided on the basis of private prejudices, but rather in terms of the overall organisation of a linguistic theory. If – as in the present case – Syntax (by means of the constituent structure it assigns to sentences) provides a natural means of characterising structural ambiguities of the type found in (57), and in terms of a device (constituent structure) which is required for independent reasons in syntax, then there is no reason not to represent structural ambiguity in syntactic terms – provided we can do so (as in the present case) using existing constructs (constituents and categories), without the need to posit new kinds of syntactic constructs.

Now let's turn to look at a very different type of justification for positing that sentences are hierarchically structured into constituents assigned to various categories: this time we shall argue that categories have independent *morphological* motivation. In English, Verbs take a characteristic range of inflections including *-ing*, *-s*, *-ed*, giving us paradigms like:

(61)   like – liking – likes – liked
         kiss – kissing – kisses – kissed
         smack – smacking – smacks – smacked
         float – floating – floats – floated
         etc.

By contrast, Prepositions do not permit the same range of verbal inflections: cf.

(62)   at – *atting – *ats – *atted

In much the same way, only (a subset of) Adjectives have a comparative form in *-er*: cf.

(63)   tall – taller; fat – fatter; lovely – lovelier; etc.

and not e.g. Nouns: cf.

(64)   boy – *boyer; girl – *girler; cat – *catter; etc.

Conversely, only Nouns – not Adjectives – have a plural inflection (usually *-s*): hence the contrast in:

(65)   They are fools/*foolishes

In much the same way only Pronouns are inflected for *nominative* and *accusative case* (in traditional Latin terminology), giving rise to alternations like:

(66)   I – me; he – him; she – her; we – us; they – them; etc.

whereas Nouns, by contrast are not morphologically marked this way. Finally, only Noun Phrases can take a possessive-*'s* inflection, as in:

(67)   John's; the king's; that poor man's; the king of England's; etc.

and not e.g. Adverbial Phrases: cf.

(68)   *very slowly's; *rather too quickly's; *much too soon's; etc.

Thus, we need to posit *categories* (i.e. different types of constituents) not only to account for syntactic facts, but equally to account for morphological facts as well.

Just as constituents and categories prove essential constructs for any model of syntax and morphology in natural languages, so too they also prove essential prerequisites for any adequate description of the phonology of natural language sentences. Consider, for example, the problem of formulating a phonological rule for English which will provide a principled account of word-stress in cases such as the following (where stress is indicated by italics):

(69) (a) I really must pro*test* about it
     (b) Why make a *pro*test about it?

(70) (a) I don't want to con*test* your claim
     (b) I don't think it was a fair *con*test

(71) (a) I wouldn't re*ject* him outright
     (b) This one is a *re*ject

Notice that in each of the (a) sentences, the stress falls on the second syllable (italicised) of the relevant word; whereas in each of the (b) sentences, the stress falls on the first syllable. Why should this be? An obvious answer is that in each case the relevant word (*protest, contest, reject*) has the categorial status of a *Verb* in the (a) sentences, but the categorial status of a *Noun* in the (b) sentences. That is, the relevant generalisation is that words like *protest* carry stress on the second syllable when used as verbs, but on the first syllable when used as nouns. But any such generalisation presupposes that phonological rules have access to categorial information: i.e. that such rules have to know what the category of a constituent is before they can apply to it.

As a second example of how constituent structure determines pronunciation, consider the contrast between the following two examples, where italics are used to indicate (primary) stress:

(72) (a) *black*bird (a species of bird, like *thrush*, *robin*, etc.)
     (b) *black bird* (a bird which is black, as opposed to a *white bird*)

The different stress patterns here appear to correlate with a difference in constituent structure: in (72) (a) the sequence *blackbird* represents a single Noun, whereas in (72) (b) it represents an *A – N* (Adjective – Noun) sequence. Overall, then, there seems little doubt that constituent structure has phonological, as well as syntactic and morphological motivation.

Let's move on to look at a further (syntactic) phenomenon which lends support to the postulation of constituents and categories –

namely the phenomenon of *coordination*. English and other languages have a variety of *coordinating conjunctions* (CONJ) which can be used to *conjoin* (or *coordinate*) words or phrases: cf.

(73) (a)   He has *a cat* and *a dog*
    (b)   I met *John* and *Mary*
    (c)   Do you know *the man next door* and *his girlfriend*?
    (d)   It was raining *yesterday* and *the day before*

In each of the sentences in (73) *and* has been used to conjoin the italicised pairs of words or phrases. Clearly, any observationally adequate grammar of English will have to provide a principled answer to the question:

(74)   What kind of elements can and cannot be conjoined (or coordinated) in English?

Now, it turns out that we can't just coordinate any random pair of elements in English, as we see from the ungrammaticality of:

(75)   *John rang *up his mother* and *up his sister*

Why can the italicised items be conjoined in (73), but not in (75)? One possible answer could be that the italicised elements can be conjoined in (73) because they are constituents, whereas the coordinate sequences in (75) are not constituents. That is, we might suggest a constraint along the lines of:

(76)   Only constituents can be conjoined; nonconstituent sequences cannot be conjoined

But can a constituent of one type (or category) be coordinated with a constituent of another type? Consider the following paradigm:

(77) (a)   John wrote *to Mary* and *to Fred* (= PP and PP)
    (b)   John wrote *a letter* and *a postcard* (= NP and NP)
    (c)   ?John wrote *a letter* and *to Fred* (= NP and PP)
    (d)   ?John wrote *to Fred* and *a letter* (= PP and NP)

(? in front of a sentence means that it is 'marginal' – i.e. of doubtful well-formedness, hence unidiomatic and unnatural.) (77) shows us that we can conjoin two PPs or two NPs quite freely, but that any attempt to conjoin an NP with a PP, or a PP with an NP leads to an unnatural, unidiomatic and 'forced' sentence. This suggests that we might revise our constraint (76) as:

59

(78)   Only identical categories can be conjoined, idiomatically

We can now test the predictions made by the constraint (78) for a wider range of categories: it predicts that the following sentences will all be grammatical, because the conjoined (italicised) pairs of elements belong to the same category:

(79) (a)   Good *linguists* and *philosophers* are rare (N and N)
     (b)   John is a very *kind* and *considerate* person (A and A)
     (c)   There are arguments *for* and *against* this claim (P and P)
     (d)   J.R. *walks* and *talks* like a true Texan (V and V)
     (e)   You can bring *these* and *those* books (DET and DET)
     (f)   He opened the door quite *slowly* and *deliberately* (ADV and ADV)

In each case in (79) we have conjoined identical *lexical* categories; but the constraint (78) also predicts that we should be able to conjoin identical *phrasal* categories as well. And – as the sentences (80) below indicate – this prediction seems to be correct:

(80) (a)   *The man next door* and *his wife* are nice (NP and NP)
     (b)   He is a *very shy* and *rather inarticulate* person (AP and AP)
     (c)   He went *to London* and *to Paris* (PP and PP)
     (d)   He may *go to London* and *visit his mother* (VP and VP)
     (e)   John drives *very slowly* and *very carefully* (ADVP and ADVP)

It thus seems that the principle (78) has considerable empirical support. But note that the principle makes crucial reference to constituent structure and category membership: in other words, it is not clear how we could provide any principled account of coordination if we did not posit that sentences are structured into sets of *constituents*, each of which belongs to a particular *category*. This discussion serves to illustrate our earlier remark that constituents and categories have the status of *theoretical constructs* – i.e. elements without which it is not obvious how we could provide a principled explanation of linguistic phenomena such as coordination.

Let's now turn to look at another linguistic phenomenon whose systematic description also seems to require the postulation of an abstract constituent structure associated with sentences – and this is the phenomenon we shall call *intrusion*. Not infrequently, speakers may insert some parenthetical expression like 'if you ask me', 'I suspect', 'in all probability', 'almost certainly', 'quite obviously', etc. somewhere internally within a sentence. But such elements cannot be freely inserted anywhere in a sentence, as we see from (81):

(81) (a)   *The, almost certainly, cat will eat his dinner
     (b)   The cat, almost certainly, will eat his dinner
     (c)   The cat will, almost certainly, eat his dinner
     (d)   ?The cat will eat, almost certainly, his dinner
     (e)   *The cat will eat his, almost certainly, dinner

That is, an Adverbial Phrase like *almost certainly* can intrude between certain sequences of words, but not between others. How can we account for this fact?

Once again, if we assume that sentences are hierarchically structured into constituents assigned to a restricted set of categories, we can perhaps begin to gain some insight into what might be going on. Suppose we posit, for example, that a sentence like:

(82)   The cat will eat his dinner

has the constituent structure:

(83)

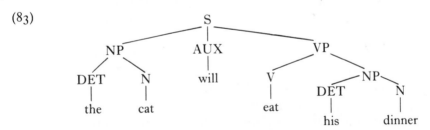

And suppose we further postulate the following condition on the distribution of parenthetical adverbial expressions like *almost certainly*:

(84)   Parenthetical adverbial expressions like *almost certainly* can be inserted only immediately under an S, not a VP, or NP, or PP, etc.

We can now provide a principled account of the contrast between e.g. (81) (a) and (81) (c); for (81) (a) would have the structure:

(85)

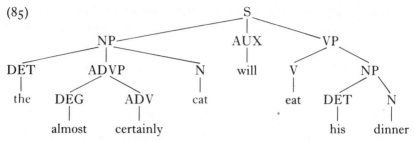

But (85) would of course violate the condition (84), since in (85) the Adverbial Phrase has been inserted immediately· under an NP – in spite of the fact that (84) only allows parenthetical adverbials to be inserted immediately under an S. By contrast, (81) (c) would have the structure:

(86)

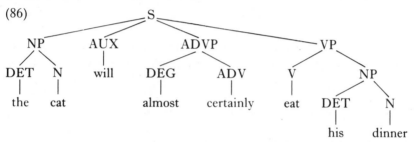

and (86) does indeed satisfy the condition (84), since in (86) the Adverbial Phrase *almost certainly* has indeed been inserted immediately under S.

The 'immediately under S' condition (84) will of course also be met if *almost certainly* is positioned between the subject NP *the cat* and the AUX *will*, as in (81) (b). In addition, the condition will also be satisfied if *almost certainly* is positioned either at the beginning or at the end of the whole S; and the resultant sentences are indeed well-formed:

(87) (a) Almost certainly, the cat will eat his dinner
     (b) The cat will eat his dinner, almost certainly

Thus, condition (84) seems to have a fair amount of empirical support.

So we find that yet a further phenomenon – that of the intrusion of certain types of phrase in various positions internally within a sentence – cannot be accounted for adequately unless we posit that sentences are hierarchically structured into constituents and categories. Now we shall go on and show that this is also true of a further phenomenon characteristic of natural languages – the phenomenon of *anaphora*.

It is a general property of natural languages that they possess *anaphoric devices* – i.e. devices for referring to entities mentioned elsewhere in the same sentence or discourse. Consider the following dialogue:

(88)   SPEAKER A: What do you think of Fred?
        SPEAKER B: I can't stand *the bastard*

In (88) the italicised phrase is an anaphoric expression whose *antecedent* is *Fred* (i.e. *the bastard* refers back to *Fred*). In addition to anaphoric expressions like *the bastard*, *the fool*, *the idiot*, etc., natural languages typically possess another type of *anaphor* termed *anaphoric pronouns* in traditional grammars. One such anaphoric pronoun in English is *him*; this we could have used instead of *the bastard* in (88):

(89)   SPEAKER A: What do you think of Fred?
        SPEAKER B: I can't stand *him*

However, the term *pronoun* is peculiarly inappropriate here, for two reasons. Firstly, it is by no means the case that the antecedent of a word like *him* is invariably a *Noun*: for example, in a discourse such as:

(90)   SPEAKER A: What do you think of *the man next door*?
        SPEAKER B: I can't stand him

the antecedent of *him* is *the man next door*, so that it would be more appropriate to describe *him* as a *pro-Noun-Phrase* (= pro-NP) rather than as a *pro-Noun* (pro-N). Secondly, if we look at the distribution of so-called *pronouns*, we find that they typically occur in the sentence-positions which Noun Phrases can occupy, not in the sentence-positions which Nouns can occupy. Thus, in a sentence like (91) (a), we can replace the whole Noun Phrase *the woman in the blue hat*, but not the Noun *woman*, by the corresponding pronoun *her*: cf.

(91) (a)   I like the woman in the blue hat
     (b)   I like her
     (c)   *I like the her in the blue hat

Thus, the term *pronoun* is doubly inappropriate, since it is not an accurate description either of the distribution of such items, or of the class of expressions which can serve as their antecedents. Words like *him*, *her*, etc. are more accurately described as *pro-NPs*, since they occur in NP-positions in a sentence, and generally have NPs as their antecedents. Not all *pro-constituents* are pro-NPs, however. One might argue, for example, that in a discourse like:

(92)   SPEAKER A: Have you ever been to Paris?
         SPEAKER B: No, I have never been *there*

the word *there* is a *pro-PP* (pro-Prepositional-Phrase), in that it has as its antecedent, and occurs in the same sentence-position as the Prepositional Phrase *to Paris*.

Any adequate description of pro-constituents (or *proforms*) will have to be concerned with both the syntax and semantics of them. Any adequate syntax of proforms will have to specify which sentence-positions particular proforms can occur in; while any adequate account of the semantics of proforms will have to specify what kind of expressions can be construed as the antecedent of a given proform. But it turns out that any adequate description of either the syntax or the semantics of proforms will have to make crucial reference to *constituents* and *categories*.

We can make this discussion more concrete in relation to the proform *it*. An adequate syntax for *it* will have to answer the question 'What range of sentence-positions can *it* occupy in English?' The answer is that *it* can occupy the same range of sentence-positions as a typical Noun Phrase like *the book on the table*, as we see from (93):

(93) (a) $\left\{ \begin{array}{c} \text{The book on the table} \\ \text{It} \end{array} \right\}$ is interesting

     (b)   Is $\left\{ \begin{array}{l} \text{the book on the table} \\ \text{it} \end{array} \right\}$ yours?

     (c)   I like $\left\{ \begin{array}{l} \text{the book on the table} \\ \text{it} \end{array} \right\}$

     (d)   I've read about $\left\{ \begin{array}{l} \text{the book on the table} \\ \text{it} \end{array} \right\}$

Syntactically, then, *it* has the same distribution as a typical Noun Phrase: i.e. syntactically, it functions like a pro-NP.

But what about the semantics of *it*? What kind of expression can be interpreted as the antecedent of *it*? All the italicised expressions in (94) can be interpreted as possible antecedents for *it*:

(94) (a)   *My car* is OK when it works
   (b)   *The back seat of my car* has got books on it
   (c)   The trouble with *the table* is that it's too small
   (d)   If I find *the lid of the kettle*, I'll give it to you
   (e)   I never use *that bone-handled knife*, because it's blunt

What have the italicised expressions in (94) got in common? The obvious answer is that they are all Noun Phrases, since they can all occur in the (bracketed) NP-positions in (93). Thus, an obvious generalisation about the semantics of *it* is that *it* can be interpreted as having an NP as its antecedent.

But is it only Noun Phrases which can serve as the antecedent of *it*? Data like (95) cast doubt on this:

(95) (a)   SPEAKER A: *Mary has finished her assignment*
          SPEAKER B: I don't believe it
   (b)   *Jean is pregnant again*, I just know it
   (c)   If *I don't turn up*, it won't be fair on you
   (d)   SPEAKER A: *Is there snow outside?*
          SPEAKER B: Does it matter?
   (e)   They say *he's planning to give up his job*, but it may not be true

Each of the italicised phrases in (95) can serve as the antecedent of *it*, and each appears to have the categorial status of an S (= Clause). So it would appear that not only an NP, but also an S can be interpreted as the antecedent of the proform *it*.

This shows up an important discrepancy between the syntax and semantics of certain types of proform: syntactically, *it* occurs only in typical NP-positions, not in typical S-positions. Thus, for example, a verb like *hope* can take a following S-complement, but not a following NP-complement:

(96) (a)   I hope *you will come* (= hope – S)
   (b)   *I hope *the pen on the table* (= hope – NP)

Significantly, *it* cannot be used as a direct complement of *hope*:

(96) (c)   *I hope it

This shows us that *it* cannot occur in a typical S-position in a sentence; on the contrary, syntactically *it* occurs only in NP-positions; but semantically, *it* can have as its antecedent either an NP, or an S.

Thus, any adequate description of proforms must include both a syntactic and a semantic characterisation of their function. It's not much use simply specifying that such-and-such a form is a pro-NP, pro-VP, or pro-S: is that meant to be a description of its syntactic distribution, or of the class of expressions which can serve as its antecedent, or both?

The conclusion to be drawn from the discussion of proforms here is that any adequate account of either the syntax or the semantics of pro-constituents will have to make crucial reference to structural properties of sentences. For it turns out that proforms have the same syntactic distribution as certain categories on the one hand, and that the class of expressions which can serve as their antecedents is most simply characterised in categorial terms on the other. Once again, then, we find a linguistic phenomenon which cannot adequately be described without appealing to notions of constituent structure.

Now let's turn to a further linguistic phenomenon which supports the same conclusion. Under certain discourse-conditions, it is possible in English (and other languages) to omit some sentence-fragment identical to one which occurs elsewhere in the same sentence or discourse: for example, in a discourse such as (97), it is possible to omit the slashed material, where it is identical to the italicised material:

(97)   SPEAKER A: John won't *wash the dishes*
         SPEAKER B: I bet he will w̶a̶s̶h̶ ̶t̶h̶e̶ ̶d̶i̶s̶h̶e̶s̶ if you're nice to him

and again in (98):

(98)   John won't *help me with the dishes*, but Paul will h̶e̶l̶p̶ ̶m̶e̶ ̶w̶i̶t̶h̶ ̶t̶h̶e̶ ̶d̶i̶s̶h̶e̶s̶

An obvious question which any observationally adequate grammar of English is going to have to answer is:

(99)   What kind of elements can be omitted in this way, and under what conditions?

In actual fact, we can't just omit *any* random set of words in a sentence when they are identical to another set, as we see from the fact that the following sentences are ungrammatical if the slashed material is omitted:

(100) (a)   *John won't put the car in the *garage*, but Paul will put the car in the g̶a̶r̶a̶g̶e̶
      (b)   *John won't put the car *in the garage*, but Paul will put the car i̶n̶ ̶t̶h̶e̶ ̶g̶a̶r̶a̶g̶e̶

(c)   *John won't put the *car in the garage*, but Paul will put the c̸a̸r̸ i̸n̸ t̸h̸e̸ g̸a̸r̸a̸g̸e̸

(d)   *John won't put *the car in the garage*, but Paul will put t̸h̸e̸ c̸a̸r̸ i̸n̸ t̸h̸e̸ g̸a̸r̸a̸g̸e̸

Although we can't omit any of the slashed sequences in (100) above, we can delete that in (101) below:

(101)   *John won't *put the car in the garage*, but Paul will p̸u̸t̸ t̸h̸e̸ c̸a̸r̸ i̸n̸ t̸h̸e̸ g̸a̸r̸a̸g̸e̸

Why is it that the slashed material can be omitted in (101), but not in (100)? It appears that we can only give a principled answer to this question in terms of constituent structure. Consider the structure of a sentence such as *Paul will put the car in the garage*: this is

(102)

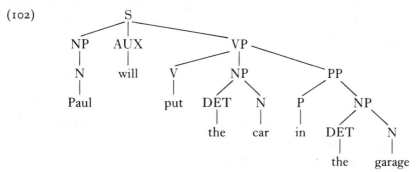

Given the assumption of a constituent structure such as (102) above, we can suggest as a tentative answer to the question we asked earlier that:

(103)   Only Verb Phrases (VPs) can be omitted, if they are identical to some other VP in the same discourse

Principle (103) would provide a ready account of why omission of the slashed material was possible in (101), but not in (100); for in (101) the slashed material was a VP, whereas in (101) (a) it was an N (= Noun), in (101) (b) it was a PP (= Prepositional Phrase), in (101) (c) it was an N – PP sequence, and in (101) (d) it was an NP – PP sequence. Confirmation of the validity of (103) comes from the fact that it correctly predicts that the slashed VPs in (104) below can be omitted if they are identical to the italicised VPs:

(104) (a)   He may *come home early*, but then again, he may not c̸o̸m̸e̸ h̸o̸m̸e̸ e̸a̸r̸l̸y̸

67

(b)   Mary wants to *close the shop*, but I don't want to ~~close the shop~~
(c)   *Fetch me an apple*, if you can ~~fetch me an apple~~
(d)   SPEAKER A: Could you *have a look at the car*?
      SPEAKER B: OK, I will ~~have a look at the car~~.

What's interesting about the above discussion is that it tells us that we cannot attain any adequate description of the phenomenon in question, unless we recognise that sentences are hierarchically structured into sets of constituents assigned to categories.

In the foregoing discussion, we have presented a number of arguments in support of postulating that sentences are hierarchically structured into constituents, each of which is assigned to a particular category. In general, these twin assumptions are uncontroversial – i.e. virtually any linguist working on Syntax from any theoretical perspective will accept the need to recognise the existence of an abstract syntactic structure associated with sentences. Where linguists disagree with each other is over the question of just how many categories there are in a particular language or universally – not over the question of *whether* there are categories.

What we have argued hitherto is that certain linguistic phenomena cannot adequately be described without assuming that every sentence in every natural language has a specific syntactic (constituent) structure. But an obvious question that arises is:

(105)   How do we determine what the constituent structure of a given sentence in a given language is?

Sometimes, we can rely on intuition: but while linguists tend to acquire fairly refined intuitions about this sort of thing over a period of years, nonlinguists very frequently have few if any strong intuitions about the structure of sentences in their language. So, when our intuitions fail us, how can we determine what the constituent structure of a given sentence is?

Perhaps we can best answer this question by asking another question: 'Why do we posit the existence of constituents and categories?' The answer we have given is: 'In order to provide a principled account of e.g. distribution, coordination, intrusion, anaphora, omissibility, etc.' An obvious answer to the question: 'How do we determine whether a given sequence of words is a constituent of a given type?' is thus: 'On the basis of whether it behaves like a constituent of that type with respect to distribution, coordination, intrusion, anaphora, omissibility, etc.' More precisely, we might propose the following *diagnostics* for determining whether a given set of words in a sentence is a constituent or not, and if so, of what type (= category):

(106)   A given string of elements is a *constituent* just in case it has one
         or more of the following properties:
    (i) It behaves distributionally as a single structural unit – i.e.
         it recurs as a single unit in a variety of other sentence-
         positions
   (ii) It can be coordinated with another similar string
  (iii) It does not readily permit intrusion of parenthetical
         elements internally (intrusion generally being permitted
         only at the boundaries of major – especially phrasal –
         constituents)
   (iv) It can be replaced by, or serve as the antecedent of, a
         proform
    (v) It can be omitted, under appropriate discourse conditions

Let's look at how we might apply these diagnostics to help us determine the constituent structure of a sentence such as:

(107)   I will wash the dishes

Intuitively, it seems plausible to assign to (107) a superficial syntactic structure along the lines of:

(108)

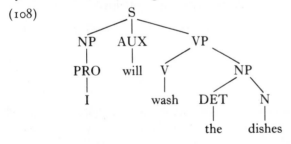

PRO = proform – in this case, = pro-NP

Let's see first of all whether there is any motivation for assuming that the string *wash the dishes* is a constituent – a Verb Phrase (VP) in fact. If *wash the dishes* is indeed a constituent, then the *distributional* criterion (106) (i) would tell us that we would expect it to recur as a single structural chunk in a variety of other sentence-positions. And sure enough this does indeed seem to be the case, as (109) illustrates:

(109) (a)   I said that I will wash the dishes, and *wash the dishes* I will
(b)   What shall I do – *wash the dishes*?
(c)   What I will do is *wash the dishes*
(d)   There's one thing I will not do: *wash the dishes*
(e)   *Wash the dishes*, will you?
(f)   SPEAKER A: What will you do?
      SPEAKER B: *Wash the dishes*

In addition, the coordination criterion (106) (ii) also suggests that *wash the dishes* is a constituent, since it can be conjoined with other similar strings: cf.

(110)   I will *wash the dishes* and *clean the floor* (= VP and VP)

And the *intrusion* criterion (106) (iii) supports a tripartite division of the sentence into NP – AUX – VP, since it is possible for Adverbs like *certainly* to intrude between NP and AUX, and between AUX and VP, but not elsewhere:

(111) (a)   I certainly will wash the dishes
(b)   I will certainly wash the dishes
(c)   ?I will wash certainly the dishes
(d)   *I will wash the certainly dishes

The *proform* criterion (106) (iv) also suggests that *wash the dishes* is a constituent, since it can serve as the antecedent of a variety of proforms, including those italicised in (112) below:

(112) (a)   I promised that I will wash the dishes, *which* I will
(b)   I said that I will wash the dishes, and *so* I will
(c)   I will wash the dishes, and *so* will Mary
(d)   SPEAKER A: I will wash the dishes
      SPEAKER B: You will *what*?

Finally, the *omissibility* criterion (106) (v) also suggests that *wash the dishes* is a constituent, since it can be omitted in an appropriate discourse setting: cf.

(113)   SPEAKER A: Who will *wash the dishes*?
           SPEAKER B: Mary will w̶a̶s̶h̶ ̶t̶h̶e̶ ̶d̶i̶s̶h̶e̶s̶

All in all, then, there appears to be considerable empirical support for postulating that *wash the dishes* is a major constituent in the syntactic structure of sentences like (107).

   There is also an equal amount of evidence for claiming that the string *the dishes* is also a constituent (an NP, or Noun Phrase) in

(107). For example, it recurs as a single distributional unit in other sentence-positions:

(114)   *The dishes*, I will wash – but not the floor

Likewise, *the dishes* can be coordinated with other NPs:

(115)   I will wash *the dishes* and *the floor* (NP and NP)

And *the dishes* can occur in the same sentence-positions as, and serve as the antecedent of, a pro-NP like *them*: cf.

(116)   SPEAKER A: Will you wash the dishes?
          SPEAKER B: Yes, I will wash them

and so on and so forth. Hence it seems clear that *the dishes* is a constituent, and furthermore a constituent belonging to the category NP.

It might seem at first sight that there is something paradoxical in saying that both *wash the dishes* and *the dishes* are constituents of the sentence (107) *I will wash the dishes*. But closer reflection reveals that there is no contradiction here at all, since *the dishes* is an NP (= Noun Phrase) which is itself a constituent of (= included in) the larger VP (= Verb Phrase) constituent *wash the dishes* – as represented diagrammatically in (108).

Notice that the same arguments which we use to justify the postulation of a VP constituent in a sentence like (107) can also be used to justify the postulation of a VP constituent in sentences which contain no overt auxiliary: that is, we can argue that in an auxiliary-less sentence such as:

(117)   John *washed the dishes*

the italicised string is also a VP constituent, so that (117) has the constituent structure:

(118)

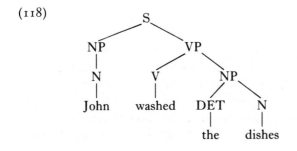

For example, *washed the dishes* can occur as an independent (elliptical) sentence in an appropriate context like:

(119)   SPEAKER A: What did John do?
         SPEAKER B: Washed the dishes

so that distributionally it might be argued to function as a constituent. Likewise, *washed the dishes* can be coordinated with another VP: cf.

(120)   John *washed the dishes* and *polished the floor*

And an Adverb like *certainly* can intrude between the NP *John* and the VP *washed the dishes*, though not elsewhere in the sentence: cf.

(121) (a)   John certainly washed the dishes
      (b)   ?John washed certainly the dishes
      (c)   *John washed the certainly dishes

Likewise, *washed the dishes* can be replaced by, and serve as the antecedent of an appropriate proform: cf.

(122)   SPEAKER A: John washed the dishes
         SPEAKER B: John *what*?

and so on.

Overall, then, we see that we do not have to rely purely on (often rather elusive) intuitions to support the postulation of a hierarchical syntactic structure associated with sentences: to some extent, it is also possible to make use of diagnostics like (106) to confirm – or indeed refute – our intuitions. The status of 'tests' like (106) is of course purely *empirical*: they are, in general, traditional tests, but tradition is no substitute for truth. Future research may show that some – or even all – of the assumptions underlying (106) are incorrect, and have to be replaced by an alternative set which yields different results.

Summary

Sentences are not just unstructured sequences of sounds; rather, they are hierarchically structured into successively larger sets of *constituents*, with each constituent belonging to a given *category*. There are two types of category: *lexical* (i.e. word-based) categories like A, N, P, V, etc., and the corresponding *phrasal* categories like AP, NP, PP, VP, etc. The claim that sentences have a hierarchical structure is based not simply on native speaker intuitions, but more importantly on empirical evidence relating to phonology, morphology, structural ambiguity, distribution, coordination, intrusion, anaphora, omissibility and so forth. Since sentences are hierarchically structured into words and phrases, we require of our syntactic sentence-formation rules that they specify how sentences are built up out of phrasal categories, how phrases are built up out of lexical categories, what range of words can be inserted in a given lexical category position, and so forth. To do this, we posit a set of *Phrase Structure Rules* generating abstract nonlexical (i.e. wordless) *Phrase-markers*, plus a *Lexicon* containing a list of all the words in the language and a specification of what category (or categories) they belong to, together with a *Lexical Insertion Rule* inserting words from the Lexicon under appropriate lexical categories in the P-marker.

EXERCISES

Exercise I

Draw six different Phrase-markers which can be generated by a set of Phrase Structure Rules like (1) below, together with a Lexicon containing the entries in (2):

(1) (a) $S \rightarrow NP - AUX - VP$
   (b) $VP \rightarrow V - NP$
   (c) $NP \rightarrow DET - (AP) - N$
   (d) $AP \rightarrow (DEG) - A$

(2) *a(n)*, DET; *apple*, N; *arrest*, V; *buy*, V; *can*, AUX; *fairly*, DEG; *girl*, N; *handsome*, A; *may*, AUX; *nice*, A; *policeman*, N; *pretty*, A; *rather*, DEG; *ripe*, A; *sparrow*, N; *tall*, A; *tasty*, A; *that*, DET; *the*, DET; *this*, DET; *very*, DEG; *will*, AUX.

Are any of the structures generated by (1) and (2) ill-formed and, if so, what is the nature of their ill-formedness?

In addition, take one of the Phrase-markers generated by the above rules, and represent its structure instead by an equivalent set of labelled brackets.

Exercise II

Many linguists would argue that one of the sentences in (1) below:

(1) (a) The boy brought in the chair
   (b) The boy sat in the chair

has the structure (2) (a) below, while the other has the structure (2) (b):

(2) (a)

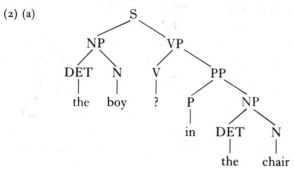

(2) (b)

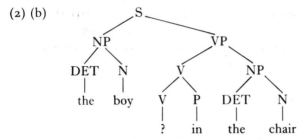

But which sentence has which structure? In order to determine this, decide for yourself which of the sentences below *you* regard as grammatical, and which as ungrammatical (indicate ungrammaticality by a prefixed*). Then, on the basis of (106), discuss how the resultant data can be used as diagnostics to determine the constituent structure of sentences (1) (a) and (1) (b).

(3) (a)   *In the chair* sat a tall, dark, handsome stranger
   (b)   *In the chair* brought a tall, dark, handsome stranger

(4) (a)   He sat *in the chair* and *in the hammock*
   (b)   He brought *in the chair* and *in the hammock*

(5) (a)   He sat *quietly* in the chair
   (b)   He brought *quietly* in the chair

(6) (a)   He sometimes sits *in the chair*, but I never sit *there*
   (b)   He sometimes brings *in the chair*, but I never bring *there*

Exercise III

The sentences below might be argued to be *structurally ambiguous*. How might we represent this ambiguity in terms of a difference of syntactic structure?

(1) (a)   I like Egyptian cotton shirts
   (b)   They found the boy in the library
   (c)   You could not go to the party
   (d)   John ran down my garden path

*Exercise IV

Consider the sentence:

(1)   He may have been writing a letter.

In (2)–(7) below are a number of suggested analyses of the superficial syntactic structure of this sentence (adapted in minor ways):

(2)   Chomsky, *Syntactic Structures* (1957)

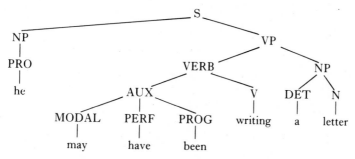

PERF = perfective auxiliary; PROG = progressive auxiliary

(3)   Chomsky, *Logical Structure* (1975) (written in 1955)

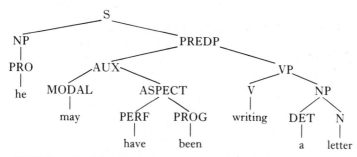

PREDP = Predicate Phrase

(4)   Chomsky, *Studies* (1972)

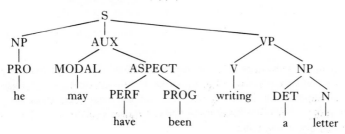

(5)   Jackendoff, *Semantic Interpretation* (1972)

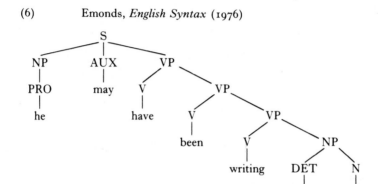

(6)   Emonds, *English Syntax* (1976)

(7)   Ross, 'Auxiliaries as main verbs' (1969)

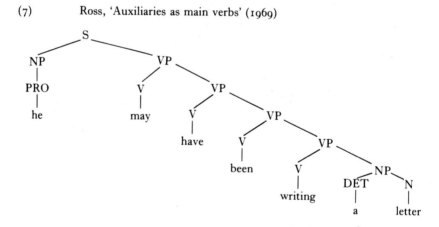

Below are a set of sentences. Decide for yourself which are grammatical and which are ungrammatical. Then determine for each of the six analyses given earlier whether it is, or is not, consistent with your data. Is it possible to make a definite choice as to the optimum analysis – or is there more than one such analysis?

(8)   SPEAKER A: What might he have been doing?
           SPEAKER B: Writing a letter
                       Been writing a letter
                       Have been writing a letter

(9) (a)   He may have been *writing a letter* or *watching TV*
   (b)   He may have *been writing a letter* or *been watching TV*
   (c)   He may *have been writing a letter* or *have been watching TV*

(10) (a)   He may – *for example* – have been writing a letter
   (b)   He may have – *for example* – been writing a letter
   (c)   He may have been – *for example* – writing a letter

(11) (a)   Mary thinks he may have been writing a letter, and *so* he may have
           been
   (b)   Mary thinks he may have been writing a letter, and *so* he may have
   (c)   Mary thinks he may have been writing a letter, and *so* he may

(12)   SPEAKER A: Do you think he may have been writing a letter?
           SPEAKER B: Yes, he may have been ~~writing a letter~~
                       Yes, he may have ~~been writing a letter~~
                       Yes, he may ~~have been writing a letter~~

Exercise V

Write a separate set of sentence-formation rules to generate each of the
sentence-structures in (2), (3), (4), (5), (6) and (7) in Exercise IV
(i.e. one set of rules for (2), another for (3), another for (4), and so on).

Exercise VI

What kind of arguments could be advanced to support the claim that in a
sentence like:

(1)   Mary likes flowers

both *Mary* and *flowers* are not only Nouns, but also Noun Phrases? That
is, what reasons might we give for saying that (1) has the structure (2) (a)
below, not (2) (b)?

(2) (a)   (2) (b)

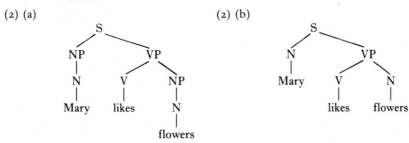

FURTHER READING

Akmajian and Heny (1975) *Principles*, pp. 1–75
Bach (1974) *Syntactic Theory*, pp. 37–57
Fromkin and Rodman (1978) *Introduction*, pp. 195–215
Huddleston (1976) *Introduction*, pp. 35–46
Keyser and Postal (1976) *Grammar*, pp. 1–66 (read with care: unconventional)
Palmer (1971) *Grammar*, pp. 1–134 (for historical background)

3
X-bar Syntax

Hitherto, we have argued that sentences are hierarchically structured into sets of category-labelled constituents, and that the constituent structure of a sentence can be displayed graphically in the form of a tree-diagram (or *Phrase-marker*). But what exactly is a Phrase-marker? It's useful to think about this problem for a while, and to have some convenient terminology for describing the internal structure of P-markers.

Essentially, a P-marker is a set of points (or *nodes*, to use the appropriate technical terminology), connected by lines or *branches*. The nodes at the (bottom) end of each complete tree-structure are called *terminal nodes*; other nodes are *nonterminal*. Each node carries a *label*. Nonterminal nodes carry category-labels (N, NP; V, VP; etc.); terminal nodes (unless they are *empty* – a possibility which we will discuss later) are labelled with an appropriate lexical item (= word). There are two types of relation between any given pair of nodes contained in the same P-marker; *precedence*, or *dominance*. To say that one node *precedes* another is to say simply that it occurs *to the left of* another in a given P-marker. Consider, for example, the P-marker in (1) below:

(1)

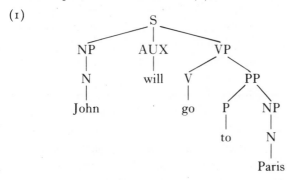

Here, for example, the AUX-node *precedes* the VP-node to its right; it also *precedes* the V-node; it also precedes the PP-node; it also precedes the word *Paris*, and so on and so forth. To say that one node *immediately precedes* another is to say that it occurs *immediately to the left of* the other node; so, for example, the AUX-node in (1) *immediately precedes* the VP-node; it also *immediately precedes* the V-node; and it also *immediately precedes* the word *go*; but it does not *immediately precede* (though it does *precede*) the PP-node, or the word *Paris*, etc. There is thus a clear distinction between the relation *precedes*, and the relation *immediately precedes*. It is therefore essential in any careful description to use these terms appropriately – and not e.g. say *precedes* when you mean *immediately precedes*.

Precedence relations are not explicitly indicated in P-markers like (1); rather, they are *tacitly* indicated (by convention) by the relative left-to-right ordering of nodes on a page. Of course, we could indicate precedence relations graphically, e.g. by dotted arrows in the manner indicated in (2) for the NP (= Noun Phrase) *the dishes*:

(2)

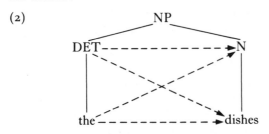

But such diagrams become extraordinarily complex to read once we attempt to represent the precedence relations which hold between sets of – say – more than ten nodes. So, we suppress any explicit visual representation of precedence (= left-to-right linear ordering) relations in favour of a convention that precedence relations are tacitly indicated by relative left-to-right ordering on the printed page.

The second type of relation between nodes in the same P-marker is *dominance*, represented by solid lines (= branches) connecting nodes in a tree. One node *dominates* another just in case it occurs higher up in the tree than the first node, and is connected to the first node by an unbroken set of solid lines (branches): e.g., the

S-node in (1) *dominates* all the other nodes in the tree; and the VP-node dominates the node labelled V, the node labelled *go*, the node labelled PP, the node labelled P, the node labelled *to*, and so on, but not the node labelled AUX, or the node labelled *will*, or the node labelled S, or the node labelled *John*, etc. One node is said to *immediately dominate* another if it is the next highest node up in the tree, and connected to the other node by a single branch (solid line). Thus, the S-node in (1) immediately dominates only the NP-node, AUX-node, and VP-node immediately beneath it. As before, for the sake of precision, it is essential to be careful in using the terms *dominates* on the one hand, and *immediately dominates* on the other: any confusion between the two will result in a nonsensical description.

Overall, then, a P-marker is a type of *graph* consisting of a set of points (called nodes) each carrying a label, with each pair of nodes in the graph being related *either* by a precedence relation, *or* by a dominance relation. The *either . . . or* condition here is quite significant: it rules out certain P-markers as 'impossible natural language sentence-structures'. To see this, consider two possible representations of the superficial structure of a sentence like:

(3)   John picked Mary up

A conventional representation of the structure of (3) might be:

(4)

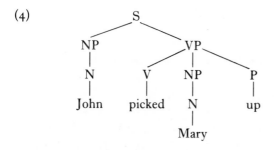

in which *picked* and *up* are represented as distinct, unrelated constituents. We might, however, object to (4) on the grounds that intuitively we feel that *pick . . . up* is some kind of *discontinuous constituent*, a sort of 'complex verb'. In such a case, we might propose an alternative analysis of (3) along the lines of:

(5)

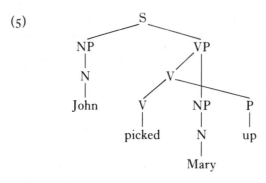

Notice that in (5) two of the branches 'cross', whereas in (4) there is
no 'crossing of branches' at all. A number of linguists have
proposed a *constraint* (= well-formedness condition) on P-markers
to the effect that no well-formed P-marker representing the structure of any sentence in any language may contain crossed branches.
The motivation behind this constraint is essentially as follows: on
general metatheoretical grounds, we want to restrict the class of
P-markers which qualify as 'possible natural language sentence-
structures' as narrowly as possible, and rule out as many 'impossible' structures as we can; we find that in general the structure of
most sentences in most languages can be described quite adequately
without the need to posit structures with crossing branches; hence,
in order to *constrain* the class of possible sentence-structures in
natural languages, we propose to 'ban' the use of P-markers with
crossing branches as a representation of sentence-structure in
natural languages. In what sense is our theory more *constrained* if
we impose the 'no crossing of branches' condition? The answer is
that the set of admissible P-markers without the 'no crossing of
branches' condition is vastly greater than the set of admissible
P-markers would be if we impose the 'no crossing of branches'
condition. To take a concrete illustration, if we say 'Branches can
either cross or not cross', then either (4) or (5) would be a possible
representation of the structure of sentence (3): but if we say
'Branches cannot cross', then (5) is not a possible structure for (3),
only (4) is. Incidentally, there is a further, nontrivial complication
posed by 'crossed branches' structures such as (5): namely that they
could not be generated by conventional Phrase Structure Rules (to
see this, try to devise a set of PS rules which would generate (4) on
the one hand, and (5) on the other).

So, let us suppose that, in the interests of attaining a more constrained theory of syntactic structure, we impose the 'no crossing of branches' restriction on all P-markers used to represent natural language sentence-structure. What this means in more formal terms is that we are in effect proposing the condition:

(6)   If a node x dominates two nodes y and z, and if y precedes z, then any node dominated by y must precede both z and any node dominated by z

Earlier, we noted another well-formedness condition on P-markers, which amounted to:

(7)   Given any pair of nodes x and y in a P-marker, then for that P-marker to be well-formed, then either x must precede *or* dominate y, or y must precede *or* dominate x.

It follows from (7) that one node cannot both precede and dominate another; and this in turn means that if a node dominates another node, it cannot precede or be preceded by that other node. This shows up an important inaccuracy in our earlier statement that precedence relations between nodes are indicated by relative left-to-right ordering on the printed page. To see this, consider again a structure like (2), repeated here as (8):

(8)
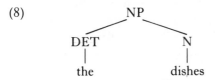

Notice here that the DET-node actually occurs to the left of the NP-node on the printed page; but this does *not* mean that the DET-node *precedes* the NP-node. On the contrary, the fact that the two are linked by a branch (solid line) indicates that the NP-node actually dominates (and in fact immediately dominates) the DET-node; and (7) tells us that where one node *dominates* another, then neither node can *precede* the other. Hence, a more careful formulation of the relevant convention might have been:

(9)   If one node occurs to the left of another, and neither node dominates the other, then the lefthand node precedes the other node

Now for some more human terminology. Nodes can have *mothers*, *daughters*, and *sisters* (though not, alas, *fathers*, *sons*, and *brothers*). These terms can be defined as follows:

(10) (i)   One node is the *mother* of another node if it immediately dominates the other node

   (ii)   One node is the *daughter* of another node if it is immediately dominated by that other node

   (iii)   A set of nodes are *sisters* if they are all immediately dominated by the same (mother) node.

To illustrate these relations, consider a sentence-structure like:

(11)

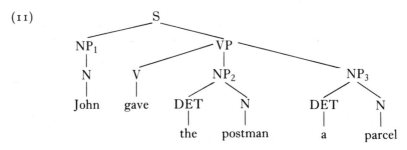

(the subscripts here have no theoretical significance – they are just added for ease of identification). Let's concentrate in particular on the constituents of the VP (= Verb Phrase). Here, we can say that the VP-node is the *mother* of three constituents – V, NP_2, and NP_3; these three constituents (V, NP_2 and NP_3) in turn are *daughters* of the VP-node; and furthermore, they are all *sisters* of each other.

Let's summarise what we have said so far. Sentences have a hierarchical constituent structure, which can be represented in terms of a *Phrase-marker*. A P-marker is a type of graph consisting of a set of points (called *nodes*) with each such point carrying a label, and with each pair of nodes being related either by a *precedence* or a *dominance* relation. These P-markers can be *generated* by a set of *Sentence-Formation Rules* comprising *Phrase Structure Rules*, an associated *Lexicon* and an appropriate *Lexical Insertion Rule* or convention. The P-markers so generated provide a visual representation of the way in which sentences are structured out of *constituents*, each such constituent being assigned to an appropriate *category*. Categories are drawn from a highly restricted

finite (and putatively universal) set including those in (12) (and a
few others we shall encounter subsequently):

(12)   S = Clause/Sentence   ADV = Adverb
         N = Noun   ADVP = Adverb Phrase
         NP = Noun Phrase   DET = Determiner
         V = Verb   DEG = Degree Expression
         VP = Verb Phrase   CONJ = Coordinating Conjunction
         AUX = Auxiliary   PRO = Pro-constituent
         A = Adjective
         AP = Adjectival Phrase

Categories are of two types: *lexical* and *phrasal*. Lexical categories
are word-categories (e.g. N, V, AUX, A, ADV, DET, DEG,
CONJ, PRO, etc.); phrasal categories are those categories in (12)
which carry the suffix -P (= Phrase), together with S (hence S;
NP, VP, AP, ADVP, etc.). However, the relationship between
lexical categories and their phrasal counterparts is by no means as
straightforward as one might imagine.

By way of illustration, consider a sentence such as:

(13)   Cars can be useful

There doesn't seem to be anything controversial in saying that *cars*
is an N (= Noun) in (13), *can* is an AUX (= Auxiliary), *be* is a V
(= Verb), and *useful* is an A (= Adjective); in addition, given
traditional syntactic diagnostics, we might argue that *be useful* is a
VP (= Verb Phrase), and the whole sequence *Cars can be useful* is
an S (= Clause/Sentence). Hence, it might seem reasonable to
suppose that (13) has the structure:

(14)

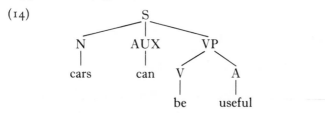

But in fact, this analysis would probably be rejected by most
linguists: instead, they would want to say that *cars*, in addition to
being an N (= Noun) is also an NP (= Noun Phrase); and that
useful, in addition to being an A (= Adjective), is also an AP (=
Adjectival Phrase): thus, in place of (14), they would prefer the
analysis (15) below:

(15)

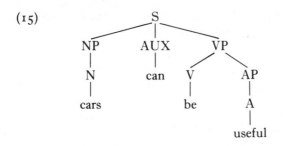

But, we might object, surely it is absurd to say that *cars* is a Noun Phrase and *useful* an Adjectival Phrase when each of these constituents contains only one word: after all, isn't it in the very nature of things that a *Phrase* is a sequence of two or more words? The answer to this is simply: 'No, not the way that we use the term *Phrase* here.' Any theory defines the technical terms it uses in terms of the way in which it uses them: and within the kind of model we are discussing, the term *Phrase* is used to mean simply 'a *set* of elements which form a constituent', with no restriction on the number of elements that the set may or must contain.

But of course it isn't enough merely to say that if we define the notion *phrase* liberally enough, then we *could* call expressions consisting of a single noun like *cars* Noun Phrases. The real question posed by such an analysis is: 'What is the empirical justification for doing so?' – i.e. what set of facts could we explain thereby which might otherwise go unexplained? One such set of facts concerns the distribution of expressions like *cars*. Notice that in place of *cars* in a sentence like (13) we could also have any of the italicised expressions in (16) below:

(16) (a) *Fast cars* can be useful
    (b) *Very fast cars* can be useful
    (c) *Those very fast cars* can be useful

There seems little doubt that the italicised expressions in (16) are all genuine Noun Phrases – and that they occupy exactly the same sentence-position as *cars* does in (13). If we recognise that *cars*, *fast cars*, *very fast cars*, and *those very fast cars* are all Noun Phrases, then we can have a simple Phrase Structure Rule expanding Clauses of the form:

(17)   S → NP – AUX – VP

But if, on the other hand, we say that *cars* is an N (though not an NP), but *fast cars*, *very fast cars*, and *those very fast cars* are all NPs, then we need a more complex rule of the form:

(18) $S \rightarrow \begin{Bmatrix} NP \\ N \end{Bmatrix} - AUX - VP$

And in fact the same will be true of all rules specifying sentence-positions in which NPs like *very fast cars* can occur, since wherever we can have *very fast cars*, we can also have simply *cars*: cf. e.g.

(19) (a)   I like *very fast cars/cars*
     (b)   I like riding in *very fast cars/cars*
     (c)   What I dream about are *very fast cars/cars*

Thus, there will be considerable unnecessary duplication in our grammar in its statements about the distribution of constituents. The same kind of redundancy will also occur in other areas of the grammar: for example, if we insist on saying that *cars* is an N (but not an NP) in sentences like (20) (a) below, but that *very fast cars* is an NP in (20) (b):

(20) (a)   I like *cars* because *they* turn me on
     (b)   I like *very fast cars* because *they* turn me on

then we shall have to say that a proform like *they* has two distinct syntactic functions: namely that in sentences like (20) (a) above it is a pro-N, whereas in sentences like (20) (b) it is a pro-NP. If, on the other hand, we adopt the more sensible solution of recognising that both *cars* in (20) (a) and *very fast cars* in (20) (b) are NPs, then we can achieve a unitary account of proforms like *they* simply by saying that *they* is a pro-NP.

The same kind of reasoning can be extended to arguing that an adjective like *useful* is actually also an Adjectival Phrase in sentences like *Cars can be useful*; for of course here *useful* is occurring in exactly the position in which we could find an Adjectival Phrase like *very useful* (cf. *Cars can be very useful*). The same kind of reasoning also extends to other constituents: for example, we could argue that in:

(21)   John speaks slowly

the word *slowly* as well as being an ADV (= Adverb), is also an ADVP (Adverbial Phrase), since *slowly* here occurs in exactly the kind of sentence-position in which we could find an ADVP like *very slowly*: thus, the structure of (21) would be:

(22)

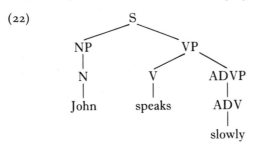

And what of a phrase like:

(23)   *many girls* (have long hair)

Here, *many* belongs to the category Q of *Quantifiers*; but notice that in place of *many* in (23) we might have had the QP (= Quantifier Phrase) *very many*: on this basis, we could argue that *many* in (23) is actually a Quantifier Phrase QP which just happens to contain only the Q *many*, though it could equally have had a more complex structure (cf. *rather too many*, etc.): this being so, then (23) will have the structure:

(24)

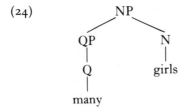

Again, the reasoning is the same: wherever we can find expressions like *rather too many*, we can also find simpler expressions like *many*; hence on the basis of similarity of distribution, we assign *many* to the same phrasal category as *rather too many*, *very many*, etc. And, finally, the same argument also extends to the analysis of simple verbs that lack following complements, e.g. *leave* in a sentence such as:

(25)   John may leave

Here we might be tempted to say that *leave* is simply a Verb; but note that in place of *leave* we could have a Verb Phrase like *leave home* – cf.

(26)   John may leave home

Wherever we can have *leave home* we can also have simply *leave*; hence we might assume that *leave* in (25) has the same categorial status as *leave home* in (26) – i.e. that of VP. Thus, the structure of (25) will be:

(27)

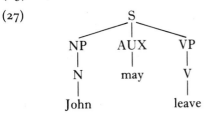

And just as *leave home* can serve as the antecedent of the pro-VP *so* in a sentence such as:

(28)   John may *leave home*, and *so* may Paul

so too *leave* can also serve as the antecedent of the pro-VP *so* in a sentence like:

(29)   John may *leave*, and *so* may Paul

To summarise, then: there are good reasons for assuming that an unaccompanied N or PRO is also an NP; an unaccompanied A is also an AP; an unaccompanied ADV is also an ADVP; an unaccompanied Q is also a QP; an unaccompanied V is also a VP . . . and so on and so forth.

   Now let's turn to a rather different issue: namely the question of what we mean by the term *generate*. A seemingly natural enough assumption to make is that a rule which *generates* a certain structure tells you how to form, create, or produce that structure. That is, we might interpret a Phrase Structure Rule of the form:

(30)   S → NP – VP

as an instruction of the form:

(31)   Plot three distinct points on a graph, and let them be called
           nodes. Let one node be labelled S, another NP, and the third
           VP. Let the S-node immediately dominate both the NP-node

and the VP-node, and let the NP-node immediately precede the VP-node

Given our earlier conventions about the way that we represent dominance and precedence relations, (30) – interpreted as (31) – could be regarded as specifying how to produce structures of the form:

(32)

The difficulty with interpreting rules like (30) in the manner outlined in (31) is that it is only too easy to fall into the obvious trap of unconsciously imputing to (31) some kind of psychological reality, by reinterpreting (31) as:

(33)   What a native speaker actually does in his mind when he produces a sentence is. . .

But any claim along the lines of (33) would be patently absurd; we simply have no idea what psychological processes are involved in the act of creating sentences – and it is absolutely pointless to speculate about them. Hence, the interpretation (33) is perverse, pointless and utterly misguided.

So what is the alternative to (31)? The answer is that we might instead choose to interpret rules like (30) as *Node Admissibility Conditions*, or equivalently *Node Well-Formedness Conditions*. Under this alternative conception, (30) would be interpreted as specifying:

(34)   Any node labelled S in a P-marker is well-formed as an S-node if it immediately dominates two other nodes, one labelled NP and the other labelled VP, and if the NP-node immediately precedes the VP-node

To interpret generative rules as well-formedness/admissibility conditions (i.e. conditions which admit a node as well-formed) is to disclaim any implications about the processes and mechanisms by which sentence-structures might be formed – i.e. to leave open the question of how structures like (32) might be produced, and simply to specify that structures like (32) are well-formed (at least in respect of the S-node), however they are produced.

Perhaps a simple analogy might help to clarify the point. Municipal regulations specify certain conditions that houses must meet: viz. they must be built out of certain materials, not others; they must contain so many windows of such-and-such a size, and so many doors; they must have a roof which conforms to certain standards . . . and so on and so forth. Such regulations are in effect well-formedness conditions on houses. What they do not do is tell you *how* to go about building a house; for that, you need a completely different set of instructions, such as might be found e.g. in *Teach Yourself Housebuilding.*

Thus far, we have looked at one system of representing the structure of sentences in natural languages – the system of *Phrase Structure Syntax*. Now we are going to look at a rather different system adopted by Chomsky in his more recent work, called *X-Bar Syntax* (though in some ways this second system dates back to earlier work by Zellig Harris in the 1950s).

Proponents of $\overline{\text{X}}$ (= X-bar) Syntax voice two types of objection to Phrase Structure Syntax:

(35) (i) It is too restricted in the number of types of categories it permits

(ii) It is too unconstrained in the sets of possible Phrase Structure rules it permits.

Let's concentrate initially on the claim (35) (i).

Within Phrase Structure Syntax, only two types of category are recognised: viz.

(36) (i) *Lexical* categories like N, V, P, A, ADV, Q, AUX, DET, etc.
(ii) *Phrasal* categories like NP, VP, PP, AP, ADVP, QP, S, etc.

In particular, there are no intermediate categories larger than the word but smaller than the phrase: e.g. there is no intermediate category larger than the Noun but smaller than the Noun Phrase: within the system of Phrase Structure Syntax, any nominal constituent must either be an N, or an NP. But there seems to be a considerable amount of empirical evidence that such 'intermediate' categories actually do exist, and that accordingly our theory of syntactic categories should make provision for them.

We can illustrate the nature of the problem by considering the internal structure of a Noun Phrase like:

(37)   this very tall girl

Within the traditional system of Phrase Structure Syntax, (37) would probably be assigned the structure (38):

(38)

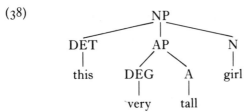

A key feature of the analysis (38) is that the string *very tall girl* does not form a constituent. But this seems to be wrong, for a number of reasons. Firstly, the sequence *AP – N* can be conjoined with another *AP – N* sequence, as in:

(39) (a)   These *very tall men* and *very short women* don't get on
     (b)   Mary is a *very pretty girl* and *very good cook*
     (c)   He is the *best writer* and *worst party-goer* that I know

And recall that one of our diagnostics for constituent structure was that a string is a constituent if it can be conjoined with another similar string. Secondly, the sequence *AP – N* can serve as the antecedent of the proform *one*: thus, in the sentence:

(40)   I like this very tall girl more than that *one*

the proform *one* can either 'stand for' the sequence *very tall girl*, so that (40) can be paraphrased as:

(41)   I like this very tall girl more than I like that *very tall girl*

or alternatively, *one* can 'stand for' the word *girl*, on which interpretation (40) can be paraphrased as:

(42)   I like this very tall girl more than I like that *girl*

On the interpretation (41), clearly the antecedent of *one* is the phrase *very tall girl*. But recall that one of the essential premises of constituent structure analysis is:

(43)   Only a *constituent* can serve as the antecedent of a proform

It follows therefore that the *AP – N* sequence *very tall girl* must be a constituent.

   We have now given two arguments to show that the *AP – N*

sequence in Noun Phrases of the form *DET – AP – N* is a constituent – i.e. that the structure of phrases like (37) *this very tall girl* must be along the lines, not of (38), but rather of (44):

(44)

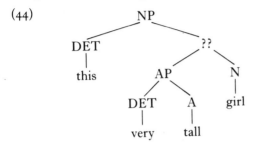

But what could be the category ?? which dominates the *AP – N* sequence? A reasonable guess might be that ?? is actually NP. But this cannot be right since phrases like *very tall girl* do not have the same distribution as a typical NP like *this very tall girl*, as we see from:

(45) (a) { This very tall girl / *Very tall girl } is my friend

(b) John can't stand { this very tall girl / *very tall girl }

(c) I spoke to { this very tall girl / *very tall girl }

Equally, it seems implausible to treat a phrase like *very tall girl* as representing simply an N (= Noun). So it seems that we reach the conclusion that a phrase like *very tall girl* represents some kind of 'intermediate' category, larger than an N, but smaller than an NP. But within the system of Phrase Structure Syntax, there are no categories intermediate between lexical and phrasal categories.

It is precisely this type of deficiency that X̄-Syntax ('X-bar Syntax') is designed to remedy. Within the X-bar framework, there may be more than one phrasal expansion of any given lexical category X: i.e. in an X-bar framework we find the following range of category-types:

(46) (i)   X (or X^0, 'X with no bars' = the lexical category X)

(ii) $\overline{X}$ (or X^1, 'X-bar' or 'X-single-bar')

(iii) $\overline{\overline{X}}$ (or X^2, 'X-double-bar')

(iv) $\overline{\overline{\overline{X}}}$ (or X^3, 'X-treble-bar')

(v)   Etc.

Each of the bar-categories corresponding to some lexical category X is called a *bar-projection* of X. One way of looking at the difference between Phrase Structure Syntax and X-bar Syntax is that Phrase Structure Syntax is a restricted version of X-bar syntax which imposes the condition that the maximum number of bar-projections of any category is 1 (because in Phrase Structure Syntax there is one and only one phrasal projection of any given category).

Given the alternative theory of categories proposed in (46), we might now reanalyse the structure of (37) along the following lines:

(47)

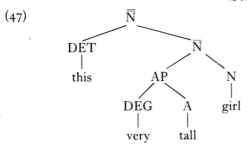

(though to be strictly consistent, we should also reanalyse the phrasal category AP (= Adjectival Phrase) as the corresponding bar-category, perhaps $\overline{\overline{A}}$; but linguists sometimes find it convenient to 'mix' the two systems, either for ease of exposition, or occasionally as a hedge against making precise claims about the exact number of bars over some category, so that AP then means 'an A with whatever the maximum number of bars that can appear over A is'). Given a structure like (47), we can provide a principled account of data like (39) and (40); in (39) coordination of phrases like *very pretty girl* and *very good cook* is possible precisely because both strings are constituents, and furthermore constituents of the same type ($\overline{N}$). Furthermore, we can account for the fact that in (40) – on the interpretation (41) – *one* has as its antecedent the phrase *very tall girl* by saying that *very tall girl* is an $\overline{N}$ constituent, and that *one* can function as a pro-$\overline{N}$.

There is, however, one additional complication which arises in the case of the pro-constituent *one*. Recall that we observed that *one* in (40) could 'stand for' either the phrase *very tall girl*, or the word *girl* on its own. Under the analysis proposed in (47), the phrase *very tall girl* would be an $\overline{N}$, whereas *girl* would be simply an N; this would mean that we would have to say that *one* can function *either* as a pro-$\overline{\text{N}}$, or as a pro-N. This in turn would imply that *one* has two distinct roles to play. Is there any way that we can avoid such an obviously undesirable conclusion? Indeed there is; since *one* is clearly a pro-$\overline{\text{N}}$ where it is construed with *very tall girl*, let us say that *one* functions uniquely as a pro-$\overline{\text{N}}$, so that whatever sequence serves as the antecedent of *one* must likewise be an $\overline{\text{N}}$. This would mean that on the interpretation (42) where *one* stands for *girl*, then *girl* too must be an $\overline{\text{N}}$: that is, the structure of (37) must not be (47) above, but rather (48) below:

(48)

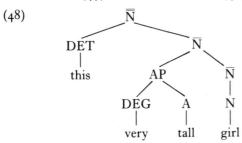

Given the structure (48), we could posit that on both interpretations of (40), *one* functions uniquely as a pro-$\overline{\text{N}}$, since *very tall girl* and *girl* are now both analysed as $\overline{\text{N}}$.

An obvious question to ask is whether we can find further supporting evidence in favour of the postulation of 'intermediate' categories like $\overline{\text{N}}$. One construction which might lend support to the postulation of just such a category, is the following:

(49) (a) *Tall girl* though she is, few people look up to her
  (b) *Short girl* though she is, few people look down on her
  (c) *Bad politician* though he is, everyone admires him

What is the constituent status of the italicised phrases in (49)? An obvious answer would be: NP. But notice that such phrases typically do not occur (at least, idiomatically or naturally) with the usual range of Determiner constituents which introduce Noun Phrases, like *a*, *the*, *this*, etc.:

(50) (a) ?**A** *tall girl* though she is, few people look up to her
  (b) ***The short girl** though she is, few people look down on her
  (c) ***This bad politician** though he is, everyone admires him

It may well be, then, that the constituent which appears immediately before *though* in sentences such as (49) is actually an N-bar, not an NP.

A further advantage claimed for X-bar Syntax (by Hornstein and
Lightfoot, Introduction to *Explanation in Linguistics* (1981) is that
it permits us to capture a more subtle range of *structural ambiguities* than its phrase structure counterpart. Hornstein and Lightfoot argue that a phrase such as:

(51)   the English king

is structurally ambiguous as between the two interpretations:

(52) (a)   the king who is English
     (b)   the king of England

These two interpretations, they argue, correspond to the respective
structures (53) (a) and (b):

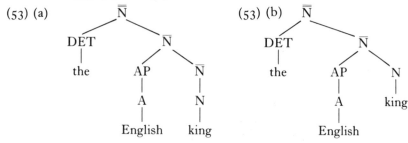

(53) (a)   = 'the king who is English'   (53) (b)   = 'the king of England'

The essential difference between the two analyses concerns the fact
that *king* has the status of N̄ in (53) (a) but not in (53) (b) where it
is only an N. If we assume that *one* functions uniquely as a pro-N̄,
then we should expect that the phrase *the English one* in:

(54)   I like the French king, but not the English one

can only have the interpretation (55) (a) below, not the interpretation (55) (b):

(55) (a)   = the king who is English
     (b)   ≠ the king of England

For those who share Hornstein and Lightfoot's intuitions about
this, the argument may seem a convincing one.
    But what of those who, like myself, feel that *the English one* can
have either of the interpretations in (55), contrary to what Hornstein and Lightfoot say? For these speakers, there are a number of
different ways of interpreting the relevant facts. One could deny
that there is any ambiguity at all in the expression *the English king*,

and say that instead it is just *vague*, meaning 'king connected in some way with England'; or, one could concede that the phrase is ambiguous, but maintain that the ambiguity is *lexical*, not structural (i.e. resides in the fact that *English* happens to have two senses). On either of these two analyses, there would be no justification whatever for claiming that the phrase (51) has two distinct structures. However, one way of maintaining Hornstein and Lightfoot's analysis for such speakers would be to argue that these speakers can use *one* both as a pro-$\bar{\text{N}}$ (hence interpretation (52) (a)), and as a pro-N (hence interpretation (52) (b)). Given the uncertainty both of the relevant judgements about the data, and of how exactly to interpret the data, Hornstein and Lightfoot's structural ambiguity argument seems far from compelling. In fact, it may even be that the whole empirical basis of arguments based on the proform *one* is questionable: see the Exercises at the end of this chapter for some material which might suggest this.

The essential point of Hornstein and Lightfoot's analysis is that Adjectival Phrases may be used to modify either an N, or an N-bar, thereby giving rise to potential cases of structural ambiguity. In a similar way, they also maintain that Prepositional Phrases (which might be analysed as P-double-bar in their framework) may modify either an N, or an N-bar. Thus, they argue that the two phrases:

(56) (a)   a student with long hair
     (b)   a student of physics

have the two distinct respective structures (57) and (58):

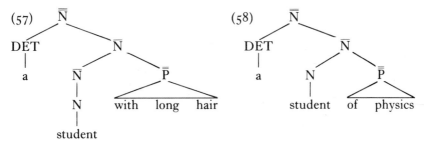

They argue that this distinction has considerable semantic plausibility:

> We also assume that syntactic constituent structure will play a
> role in determining the semantics of Noun Phrases such that
> each $\bar{\text{N}}$ specifies a semantic property. Therefore to attribute

(58) to John is to attribute one property to him, that he studies physics; to attribute (57) to John is to attribute two properties, that he studies, and that he has long hair. Hence it follows that *John is a student of physics*, meaning what it does, cannot be assigned a structure like (57); conversely, *John is a student with long hair*, meaning what it does, cannot have a structure like (58).

(Hornstein and Lightfoot, Introduction to *Explanation in Linguistics* (1981))

Notice that there is a simple way of testing their hypothesis: in (57), *student* is an N-bar, whereas in (58) it is only an N; we should therefore expect that in structures like (57) but not (58), *student* could be replaced by the pro-N-bar *one*: i.e. we should expect the following judgements:

(59) (a)   I like this student with short hair better than that one with short hair
     (b)   *I like this student of chemistry better than that one of physics

(60) (a)   I like the student with short hair better than the one with long hair
     (b)   *I like the student of chemistry better than the one of physics

(61) (a)   I'd prefer a student with short hair to one with long hair
     (b)   *I'd prefer a student of chemistry to one of physics

Do you agree with these judgements, or not?

There is also another, rather less obvious prediction made by the analysis (57) and (58); if *of physics* modifies an N, whereas *with long hair* modifies an N-bar, then given that an N is included inside an N-bar, we should expect that if both phrases are used to qualify the same expression, then the N-complement *of physics* will be included within (and hence *precede*) the N-bar complement *with long hair*: in other words, we should expect the pattern in (62) below:

(62) (a)   a student of physics with long hair
     (b)   *a student with long hair of physics

To see why (62) (b) would be expected to be 'impossible', consider the respective structures of the two phrases in (62), viz.

(63) (a)

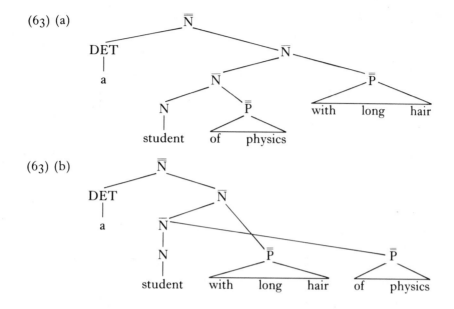

(63) (b)

It's quite clear that (63) (b) violates the 'no crossing of branches' restriction that we discussed earlier, and formulated as (6). Thus, given Hornstein and Lightfoot's assumptions about the structure of phrases like (56), a universal well-formedness condition on P-markers would rule out structures like (63) (b) as impossible in any language.

Some support for Hornstein and Lightfoot's analysis might come from coordination facts. Notice that we can coordinate two Prepositional Phrases which are both complements of an N, as in:

(64)   a student of physics and of chemistry

and we can also coordinate two Prepositional Phrases which are complements of an N-bar, as in:

(65)   a student with long hair and with short arms

But we cannot coordinate one type of Prepositional Phrase with the other:

(66) (a)   *a student of physics and with long hair
     (b)   *a student with long hair and of physics

Furthermore, it may well be that N-bar complements can be separated from their heads more freely than N-complements: cf.

(67) (a)   A student came to see me yesterday with long hair
     (b)   *A student came to see me yesterday of physics

In short, then, there do seem to be strong grounds for distinguishing two classes of prepositional complements: those which modify an N, and those which modify an N-bar. But of course this distinction presupposes in the first place that we recognise the existence of 'intermediate' categories like N-bar (intermediate between N, and NP).

While there is widespread agreement along linguists about the need to recognise the existence of such intermediate categories, what there is no agreement on is the question of just *how many* such intermediate categories there are, and whether this varies from one category to another. In our discussion of Noun Phrases above, we implicitly assumed just three nominal categories, namely N, N-single-bar, and N-double-bar. Joan Bresnan (in her 1976 article 'The form and function of transformations') suggests that this can be generalised across a number of categories, so that we have also P, $\bar{P}$, $\bar{\bar{P}}$; Q (= Quantifier), $\bar{Q}$, $\bar{\bar{Q}}$, A, $\bar{A}$, $\bar{\bar{A}}$; and so forth. Thus, for Bresnan, in a phrase like *very near the house*, *near* is a P, *near the house* is a $\bar{P}$, and *very near the house* is a P-double-bar, $\bar{\bar{P}}$.

However, it may well be that some categories have a greater range of bar-projections (= phrasal expansions) than others: take, for example, a sentence such as:

(68)   John ought to contact Mary

Here, we might conceivably propose that *contact* is a V, *contact Mary* is a V-single-bar, and *to contact Mary* is a V-double-bar. But we might go beyond this and argue that if *ought* is analysed as an AUX, and if AUX and the infinitive following it are analysed as a single constituent (corresponding to the PREDP – Predicate Phrase – constituent of Chomsky's *Aspects* (1965)), then the resultant phrase *ought to contact Mary* might be analysed as a V-treble-bar, and the whole clause *John ought to contact Mary* could then be analysed as a V-quadruple-bar (as indeed Bresnan proposes).

In short, the whole movement to extend the number of category-types in X-bar syntax raises two crucial theoretical questions:

(69) (i)   What is the range of categories which can have bar-projections? (E.g. does AUX have a corresponding constituent AUX-bar and, if not, why not?)

(ii)   What is the number of bar-projections associated with each such category? (E.g. do languages have an N-quadruple-bar constituent and, if not, why not?)

Some indication that these questions are far from settled can be gained from the following quotation (where n represents the maximum number of bars that can appear over a given category):

> In Chomsky's original formulation, n equals 2 for nouns and 3 for verbs (assuming the verb is the head of the sentence). Vergnaud (1974) and Siegel (1974) have n equal to 4, at least for nouns; Dougherty (1968) has n equal to 3 for nouns and 6 for verbs; Jackendoff (1969, 1974) has n equal to 2 for all categories. It now appears to me that . . . n equals 3 for all categories.
>
> (Jackendoff, 'Constraints on Phrase Structure Rules' (1977), p. 255)

Hitherto, we have been arguing that X-bar Syntax is a better theory than Phrase Structure Syntax because it recognises the existence of a wider range of categories in natural language. But surely this completely undermines our earlier methodological point that:

(70)   *The best theory is the most constrained theory*

Since Phrase Structure Syntax recognises only two types of category (lexical like N, and phrasal like NP), whereas X-bar Syntax recognises at least three types (N, $\overline{\text{N}}$, $\overline{\overline{\text{N}}}$, for example) and possibly as many as seven, then surely *in this respect* Phrase Structure Syntax is more constrained than X-bar Syntax, and hence should be preferred on general methodological grounds? This is indeed entirely true . . . or at least, it *would* be, if (70) were entirely accurate. But, in fact, (70) is rather carelessly formulated, and should instead read:

(71)   *The best theory is the most constrained theory consistent with the facts of natural language*

And of course, proponents of X-bar Syntax would argue that there are certain syntactic facts characteristic of natural language (facts concerning the use of proforms like *one* as in (59), facts concerning the relative order of constituents as in (62), and facts concerning coordination as in (65)) which cannot be explained without postulating a wider range of categories than are assumed in the framework of Phrase Structure Syntax.

This brief discussion of the need to *constrain* theories is particularly apposite here because although from one point of view X-bar syntacticians criticise Phrase Structure Syntax for being *too constrained* (in respect of not allowing a wide enough range of category types), from a different point of view they also criticise it for being *not constrained enough* (in respect of not restricting the class of possible sentence-formation rules in natural language). One important respect in which sentence-formation rules in Phrase Structure Syntax (i.e. Phrase Structure Rules) are excessively unconstrained was pointed out long before the advent of X-bar Syntax by John Lyons, in the following passage:

> Phrase Structure Grammars fail to formalise the fact that NP and VP are not merely mnemonically convenient symbols, but stand for sentence-constituents which are necessarily nominal and verbal, respectively, because they have N and V as an obligatory major constituent. What is required, and what was assumed in traditional grammar, is some way of relating sentence constituents of the form XP to X (where X is any major category: N, V, etc.). It would not only be perverse, but it should be theoretically impossible for any linguist to propose, for example, rules of the following form . . .:
>
> [72] NP → V – VP
> [73] VP → DET – N
>
> (Lyons, *Introduction* (1968), p. 33)

What is needed in order to disallow such 'impossible' rules as (72) and (73) is clearly a convention that will ensure that a Noun Phrase contain a head Noun, a Verb Phrase contain a head Verb, an Adjectival Phrase contain a head Adjective, a Prepositional Phrase contain a head Preposition, a Quantifier Phrase contain a head Quantifier, and so forth. In terms of Phrase Structure Rules, we want to ensure that only rules like the following are found universally, in any language:

(74) (a)   NP → . . . N . . .
     (b)   VP → . . . V . . .
     (c)   AP → . . . A . . .
     (d)   PP → . . . P . . .
     (e)   QP → . . . Q . . .

(where a rule like (74) (a) is interpreted as meaning 'An NP must contain an N, irrespective of whatever else (. . .) if anything at all, follows or precedes it'). If – following the convention used by Lyons and adopted by Chomsky – we use the category-variable X to denote 'any lexical category', then we want to restrict all PS (= Phrase Structure) Rules universally to being of the schematic form:

(75) $XP \rightarrow \ldots X \ldots$

And informally, (75) says 'Every X-Phrase must have an X as its head.'

But of course (75) is formulated within the framework of traditional Phrase Structure Grammar. How can we extend the insight it incorporates to the richer system of categories postulated within X-bar Syntax? An obvious suggestion would be to impose the following restrictions:

(76) (i)   An X-treble-bar must have an X-double-bar as its head
    (ii)   An X-double-bar must have an X-single-bar as its head
    (iii)   An X-single-bar must have an X as its head

In terms of rule-schemata, this means restricting our sentence-formation rules to being of the schematic form:

(77) (i) $\overline{\overline{\overline{X}}} \rightarrow \ldots \overline{\overline{X}} \ldots$
    (ii) $\overline{\overline{X}} \rightarrow \ldots \overline{X} \ldots$
    (iii) $\overline{X} \rightarrow \ldots X \ldots$

In fact, we can generalise the schema in (77) as:

(78) $X^n \rightarrow \ldots X^{n-1} \ldots$

to be interpreted as 'A phrase of category X with n bars must contain as its head (i.e. must immediately dominate) a constituent of category X with $n - 1$ bars, whatever else (. . .) if anything, precedes or follows that head.' If we further specify:

(79)   All sentence-formation rules in all languages must conform to the schema (78)

then we have imposed (in Chomsky's view) a very strong constraint on the form of syntactic rules, and thereby contributed substantially to the ultimate goal of maximally constraining grammars by constraining the form of the rules that may appear in them.

However, as we observed earlier, the obvious question that arises with any proposal to constrain grammars in some way is that of whether the proposed restriction is empirically adequate: i.e.

whether, if we impose the restriction concerned on all natural language grammars, those grammars will still be able to provide adequate descriptions of the full range of linguistic phenomena characteristic of natural languages. In the present case, the answer seems to be 'No', at least if we accept Hornstein and Lightfoot's analysis of structures like (53) (a), (57), or (63) (a): for each of those structures contains a substructure of the form:

(80)

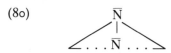

– a substructure which must have been generated by a rule of the form:

(81) $\overline{N} \rightarrow \ldots \overline{N} \ldots$

– a rule which would be excluded by (78). If we are to allow structures such as (80), then clearly the schema (78) will have to be replaced by:

(82) $X^n \rightarrow \ldots X^m \ldots$ (where m = n, or n−1)

Given the possibility of *recursion* in natural languages in any case, it would seem foolish to rule out intrinsically recursive rules like (81), which permit one category to be embedded within another category of the same type indefinitely; and one might argue that this is precisely the type of recursion (of N-bar) found in phrases like:

(83)   a tall, dark, handsome stranger

which might be argued to have the structure:

(84)

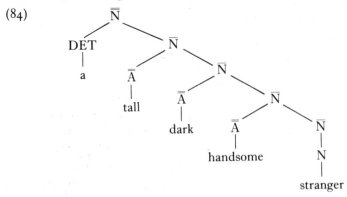

Even our weakened rule-schema (82) may still be far from adequate – and indeed it is easy enough to find examples of rules in the published literature which violate (82). A case in point is Chomsky's (1977) analysis of *topic* (TOP) and *complementiser* (COMP) constituents in 'On Wh-Movement' (p. 91). Chomsky assumes that the italicised *as*-phrase in a sentence like (85) (a) represent a TOP constituent, and that clause-introducing particles like *that* in (85) (b) represent a COMP constituent:

(85) (a)   *As for this book*, I think you should read it
     (b)   I told him *that* I was bored with X-bar syntax

To handle sentences like (86) below which contain both COMP and TOP:

(86)   I informed the students *that as far as this book is concerned*, they would definitely have to read it

Chomsky proposes a set of rules including the following:

(87) (i) $\bar{\bar{S}} \rightarrow TOP - \bar{S}$
     (ii) $\bar{S} \rightarrow COMP - \bar{\bar{S}}$

Which of these two rules violates our earlier schema (82), and in what respect? How would (82) have to be revised to accommodate (87)? Does the consequent weakening of (82) in this way reduce the proposed constraints on X-bar expansions to near-vacuity?

Another case where it seems likely that (78) would prove inadequate is in the case of *coordination*. In general, it seems that coordinated constituents have the same category status as their conjuncts: e.g. conjoining two Noun Phrases produces a Noun Phrase, conjoining two Prepositional Phrases produces a Prepositional Phrase, conjoining two Adverbial Phrases produces an Adverbial Phrase . . . and so on and so forth. Thus, the structure of a conjoined Noun Phrase like

(88)   *This tall boy and that short girl* (get on well together)

might well be:

(89) (a)

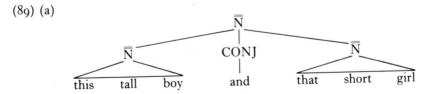

– a structure that might be generated by a rule like:

(89) (b) $\overline{\overline{N}} \rightarrow \overline{N} - CONJ - \overline{\overline{N}}$

– a rule which is again consistent with (82), but not with (78). So once again we see that although the ultimate goal is to constrain the class of possible grammars as much as possible, it occasionally turns out that proposed constraints (like (78)) are too *strong* (i.e. too restrictive), and must be abandoned in favour of *weaker* constraints (like (82)). We have to be conscious at all times of striking a balance between constraining grammars, and attaining empirical adequacy.

A couple of points where it is easy to be misled about X-bar Syntax should be noted. Firstly, as in the case of Phrase Structure Syntax, an unmodified constituent which has the same distribution as e.g. the corresponding double-bar constituent is assigned double-bar status (just as in our earlier model, it would have been assigned phrasal status). For example, in a sentence like:

(90)   John loves Mary

both *John* and *Mary* would be assigned the status of $\overline{\overline{N}}$ (assuming for the moment that this is the bar-category corresponding to NP), so that (90) would have the structure:

(91)

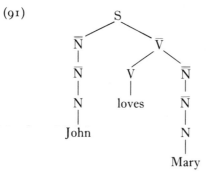

The reasons for this are essentially the same as those given earlier – i.e. to account for distribution, the possibility of serving as the antecedent of a typical pro-$\overline{\overline{N}}$ anaphor such as *he* or *she*, and so on and so forth.

A second point to bear in mind is that although it is generally the case within X-bar Syntax that a constituent containing an X is an X-bar, one containing an X-bar is an X-double-bar, and one containing an X-double-bar is an X-treble-bar (etc.), this does *not* mean that where we have a constituent of one type repeatedly embedded within another constituent of the same type, each successively larger containing constituent will have one more bar than the one it most immediately contains. To insist on this principle would be to deny the possibility of recursion, the very essence of which is that one constituent of a given type is embedded within another of exactly the same type: structures like (84) and (89) illustrate this point. Indeed, the desire to make provision for this type of recursion was the major motivation behind our proposal to replace (78) by (82). Hence, in a phrase like:

(92)   *out from under the bed* (came a tall dark handsome stranger)

we do not analyse *under the bed* as P-double-bar, *from under the bed* as P-treble-bar, and *out from under the bed* as P-quadruple-bar; rather we allow for the possibility of embedding one P-double-bar within another, so that (92) will have the structure:

(93)   [$_{\bar{\bar{P}}}$ out [$_{\bar{\bar{P}}}$ from [$_{\bar{\bar{P}}}$ under the bed]]]

in which *under the bed*, *from under the bed*, and *out from under the bed* are all P-double-bar constituents, recursively embedded one within the other.

Now let's turn to a different issue. We have already seen from (82) that it is convenient on occasions to have a *category variable* like 'X', which can be used to stand for 'any lexical category whatever' (and the corresponding variables '$\underline{X}$' standing for 'any single-bar category whatever', '$\overline{X}$' standing for 'any-double-bar category whatever', and so forth). Earlier, in (82), we made use of these category variables in imposing a universal condition on the form of possible sentence-formation rules. Chomsky (*Studies* (1972), pp. 30–1) argues that it may also be convenient to make use of such category variables in other cases: for example, he points out that using a category variable in the formulation of some sentence-formation rules would permit similarities between the types of complements permitted by the principal lexical categories to be handled in a fully general way: e.g. he notes, Nouns, Verbs, Adjectives and Prepositions all permit an immediately following clausal complement (e.g. an indirect question clause introduced by *whether*): cf.

(94) (a) the *question* whether John should leave
(b) He *asked* whether John should leave
(c) *curious* whether John should leave
(d) His query is *about* whether John should leave

Using the category variable X, the resultant symmetry in complement types can be captured in the obvious way in terms of a sentence-formation rule like:

(95) $\overline{X} \rightarrow X - S$

Yet a further use for the category variable X can be illustrated as follows. The most fundamental role of categories is to specify the *distribution* of words and phrases in a language, since those elements which have the same distribution are assigned to the same category. But very often, more than one category can occur in a given sentence position. For example, as Joan Bresnan notes in her 1976 article 'The form and function of transformations', in clause-initial position in so-called *wh*-questions we can find a variety of *wh*-phrases belonging to a variety of phrasal categories: e.g.

(96) (a) *What book* did you read? (= NP)
(b) *How long* is it? (= AP)
(c) *How quickly* did you read it? (= ADVP)
(d) *In what way* do you think he is wrong? (= PP)
(e) *How much* did it cost? (= QP)

In fact, it seems that just about any phrasal category in English can appear in this position. One way of specifying this would be simply to list all the phrasal categories that can occur in the relevant position: but this would obviously be to miss the generalisation that *any* phrasal category can occur in this position. How can we capture this generalisation? One way would be by the use of a *category variable*. Bresnan suggests that the right answer is:

(97) In *wh*-questions, any *wh*-phrase of category $\overline{\overline{X}}$ can occur in clause-initial position (where a *wh*-phrase is an interrogative phrase)

Thus, she is saying that any double-barred interrogative phrase can occur in the relevant position: the system of bars she presupposes is:

(98) NP = $\overline{\overline{N}}$; AP = $\overline{\overline{A}}$; PP = $\overline{\overline{P}}$; ADVP = $\overline{\overline{ADV}}$; QP = $\overline{\overline{Q}}$, etc.

So, it seems that a variety of uses can be found for a system of category variables.

Thus far, we have looked at two rather different systems of representing syntactic structure: Phrase Structure Syntax, and X-bar Syntax. Now we are going to look at a third, which we shall call *Feature-based Syntax*. Although this is in one sense a different system, it is in fact compatible with either of the other two; and indeed, in practice it is very often associated with X-bar Syntax, by virtue of the fact that all X-bar syntacticians make use of syntactic features. Let's begin our discussion by looking at one of the problems which Feature-based Syntax was designed to solve.

In some sentence-positions, as we have seen, a wide range of categories may appear: and the use of a category-variable provides a simple device for accounting for this. But in other positions, a much narrower range of categories can appear: e.g. consider the range of categories that can appear in the italicised position in the so-called *cleft sentences* illustrated below:

(99) (a)   It was *a car* that she bought (= NP)
   (b)   It was *in the shop* that I met her (= PP)
   (c)   *It is *very pretty* that she is (= AP)
   (d)   *It is *very conscientiously* that she works (= ADVP)
   (e)   *It is *very much* that he loves her (= QP)
   (f)   *It is *go home* that I will (= VP)

It appears that only NP and PP constituents can appear in the italicised *focus* position in cleft sentences. Of course, we can always specify this as a grammar of English by simply *listing* the set of categories that can occur in a given sentence-position – e.g. focus position in cleft sentences. But lists are arbitrary, and have no explanatory value since a list could in principle contain any random set of elements. A higher level of generality (and explanatory adequacy) could be attained if we could somehow capture the intuition that NP and PP form a natural distributional class. And Chomsky has suggested a way of capturing this type of generalisation (*Studies* (1972), pp. 48–61): he proposes that all syntactic categories be reanalysed not as unitary elements, but rather as sets (or complexes) of *syntactic features*. For example, he suggests, the four principal lexical categories V, N, A and P can be analysed as complexes of just two syntactic features (namely [±N] and [±V], i.e. nominal and nonnominal, and verbal and nonverbal) in the manner outlined in (100):

(100) $V = \begin{bmatrix} +V \\ -N \end{bmatrix}$ $N = \begin{bmatrix} -V \\ +N \end{bmatrix}$ $A = \begin{bmatrix} +V \\ +N \end{bmatrix}$ $P = \begin{bmatrix} -V \\ -N \end{bmatrix}$

Given the analysis in (100), we could then say that P and N together share the property of being $[-V]$ – i.e. nonverbal. If PP and NP are treated (as in Bresnan's analysis) as $\bar{\bar{P}}$ and $\bar{\bar{N}}$ respectively, then we could formulate the generalisation that:

(101)   Only $[\overline{\overline{-V}}]$ segments appear in focus position in cleft sentences (i.e. only double-barred nonverbal constituents)

Reanalysing categories as sets of features also provides a neat solution to the otherwise intractable problem of handling both the *similarities* and *differences* between distinct categories, in a unitary fashion. Consider, for example, the relation between the categories AUX and V (= Verb). They share certain common characteristics – e.g. morphologically they both inflect for present and past tenses, as we see from:

(102)   V   AUX

          work–worked   may–might
          like–liked   will–would
          play–played   can–could
          open–opened   shall–should
          etc.   etc.

But they also differ from each other in important ways: e.g. only AUX not V can appear in presubject position in direct questions:

(103) (a)   Will John leave?
      (b)   *Wants John to leave?

In a feature analysis, we can capture both the similarities and differences between the two if we say that both of them are verbal, non-nominal constituents, but that they differ in respect of a further feature $[\pm AUX]$: thus, under the proposed feature analysis, Verbs and Auxiliaries would be analysed as in:

(104) (a) $V = \begin{bmatrix} +V \\ -N \\ -AUX \end{bmatrix}$ (b) AUX $= \begin{bmatrix} +V \\ -N \\ +AUX \end{bmatrix}$

The supercategory of Verbs and Auxiliaries together would be identified as:

(105)   V & AUX = $\begin{bmatrix} +V \\ -N \end{bmatrix}$

Thus, any rule applying to Verbs only would be formulated as applying to the feature-set in (104) (a); any rule applying to Auxiliaries only would be formulated as applying to the feature-set in (104) (b); and any rule applying both to Verbs and Auxiliaries would be formulated as applying to the feature-set in (105).

Notice, too, that by introducing a feature [±PRO] we could handle both the similarities and differences between nonpronominal constituents and pro-constituents. For example, the similarities and differences between a nonpronominal NP like *the tall man*, and a pronominal NP like *he* might be dealt with by saying that nonpronominal NPs are feature complexes of the form (106) (a), pronominal NPs are of the form (106) (b), and the two together are identified as in (106) (c):

(106) (a) $\begin{bmatrix} \overline{-V} \\ +N \\ -PRO \end{bmatrix}$ (b) $\begin{bmatrix} \overline{-V} \\ +N \\ +PRO \end{bmatrix}$ (c) $\begin{bmatrix} \overline{-V} \\ +N \end{bmatrix}$

Features might also be a useful way of distinguishing between different types of Prepositions (or Prepositional Phrases). Thus, while both the verbs *live* and *go* can take PP-complements, they take different kinds of PP-complement: *live* takes a PP-complement indicating location: cf.

(107)   He lives in/near Dallas

whereas the verb *go* takes a PP indicating direction:

(108)   He went to/towards Dallas

Hence, it might be useful to subcategorise Prepositions into different types in terms of features like [±DIR] (directional/nondirectional), [±LOC] (locative/nonlocative), and so forth.

While the advantages of analysing categories as feature-complexes might be readily apparent, it nonetheless remains true that there is as yet no single unified framework of syntactic features which is accepted by a significant proportion of linguists. Instead, different individuals tend to evolve their own systems of features on a more or less ad hoc (= expedient) basis. Moreover, 'mixed' analyses using partly feature-complexes and partly traditional category symbols (N, $\overline{V}$, $\overline{\overline{P}}$, etc.) are also commonly used, either for clarity of exposition, or to avoid being side-tracked into a defence of one feature-system as opposed to another.

Summary

Phrase-markers are sets of *labelled nodes* interconnected by *precedence* and *dominance* relations; *terminal* nodes carry lexical items, but nonterminal nodes do not. In order to constrain the class of possible natural language sentence-structures, we impose the condition that *branches cannot 'cross'* in P-markers. There is some empirical evidence (from coordination, *one*-pronominalisation, etc.) in support of the existence of categories *intermediate* between lexical and phrasal categories, so that we might replace the Phrase Structure categories of X and XP by the richer system of *X-bar Syntax* in which more than one *phrasal projection* of lexical categories is recognised (i.e. X, X-single-bar, X-double-bar, etc.). In addition, in order to capture the similarities and differences between related sets of categories, it is useful to regard categories not as unanalyseable wholes, but rather as complexes of *syntactic features* like ±N, ±V, ±PRO, ±LOC, etc.

EXERCISES

Exercise I

Using the appropriate technical terminology (viz. 'dominates', 'precedes', 'immediately dominates', 'immediately precedes', 'is the mother/daughter/ sister of') describe the relations between at least *ten* pairs of nodes in the following Phrase-marker:

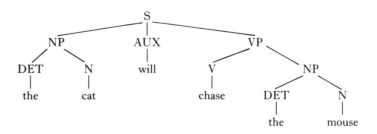

One type of recursive process found in English involves the possibility of *embedding* one clause internally within another: e.g. in (1) below the italicised clause (i.e. the *snores*-clause) is embedded within the *think*-clause:

(1)   I think *he snores*

Quite often, *embedded complement clauses* (i.e. clauses which are embedded in another clause as the complement of some verb, adjective, etc.) are introduced by a special clause-introducing particle called a *complementiser* (= COMP), as with the embedded complement clauses in (2) below, where the complementiser is italicised:

(2) (a)   I said *that* I was wrong
    (b)   I insist *that* he leave
    (c)   I don't know *whether* John fancies Mary
    (d)   I would prefer *for* you to leave [American English]

What we are interested in here is the constituent structure of embedded complement clauses: in particular, we are concerned with the question of whether a sentence like:

(3)   I wonder whether she snores

has the constituent structure (4) (a), (b), or (c):

(4) (a)

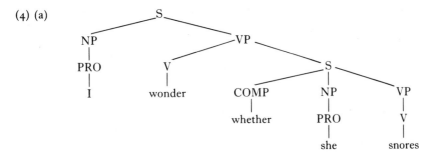

(4) (b)

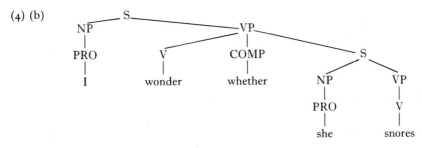

(4) (c)

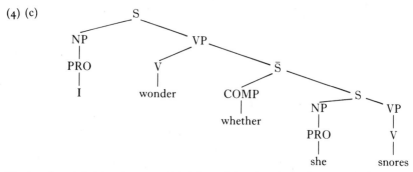

Notice that (4) (c) – but not (4) (a) or (b) – involves the postulation of a new category of *S-bar*. But is this justified?

Below are a set of sentences: decide for yourself which of them are grammatical, and which ungrammatical. Then, on the basis of familiar diagnostics for constituent structure, decide for yourself which analysis – (4) (a), (b), or (c) – is most compatible with your data.

(5) (a)   *Whether she snores*, I sometimes wonder
    (b)   *She snores*, I sometimes wonder whether

(6) (a)   I wonder *whether she snores*, and *whether he picks his nose*
    (b)   I wonder whether *she snores*, and *he picks his nose*

(7)   SPEAKER A: I wonder whether she snores
      SPEAKER B: You wonder *whether what*?
                 You wonder *what*?

(8) (a)   I don't actually know *whether she snores*, but I sometimes wonder ~~whether she snores~~
    (b)   I don't actually know whether *she snores*, but I sometimes wonder whether ~~she snores~~

Note: Analysis (4) (a) will be vindicated if there is evidence that the string *whether she snores* is a constituent, but *she snores* is not; (4) (b) will be the best analysis if *she snores* is a constituent, but *whether she snores* is not; and (4) (c) will be the preferred solution if both *she snores* and *whether she snores* are constituents (and hence behave as such with respect to distribution, coordination, anaphora, omissibility, etc.).

Exercise III

What would be the structure of the following Noun Phrases in an X-bar framework, and what kind of evidence might you use to establish this?

(1)   a specialist in fibreoptics from Paris

(2)   a woman from Paris in a trouser-suit

(3)   a book by Chomsky on Syntax

(4)   the presentation of their medals to the athletes

Exercise IV

The phrase *English student* can either mean:

(1) (a)   person who studies English

or

(1) (b)   person who comes from England

Following Hornstein and Lightfoot, let's assume that on interpretation (1) (a), *an English student* has the structure (2) (a) below, and on interpretation (1) (b) it has the structure (2) (b):

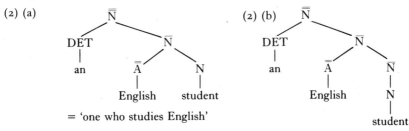

(2) (a)   (2) (b)

= 'one who studies English'

= 'one who comes from England'

Firstly, on what grounds might one justify such an analysis? And, secondly, given such an analysis, would one expect sentence (3) below to have the interpretation (4) (a), or (b), or both – and why?

(3)   He's the only French English student that we have on campus
(4) (a)   . . . the only person studying English who comes from France
    (b)   . . . the only person studying French who comes from England

*Exercise V

In their 1979 analysis of the English auxiliary system, Akmajian, Steele and Wasow propose a set of sentence-formation rules essentially of the form (1) below (slightly adapted):

(1) (a) $\underset{=}{S} \rightarrow NP - AUX - \overline{\overline{V}}$
    (b) $\overline{\overline{V}} \rightarrow (PERF) - \overline{V}$
    (c) $\overline{V} \rightarrow (PROG) - V$
    (d) $\overline{V} - V - NP$

AUX includes 'Modals' like *can, could, may, might, will, would, shall, should, must,* etc.
PERF represents the perfective use of *have*
PROG represents the progressive use of *be*

Show what constituent structure would be assigned *by these rules* to the following sentences:

(2) (a)   Bill may have been studying Spanish
    (b)   Bill may have studied Spanish
    (c)   Bill may be studying Spanish
    (d)   Bill may study Spanish

*Exercise VI

Many X-bar syntacticians would argue that a Noun Phrase like

(1)   these three rare books

has a structure along the lines of:

(2)

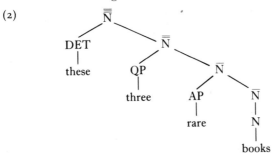

in which we posit the existence of an N-treble-bar constituent. Discuss
how the data given below might be argued to support such an analysis:

(3) (a)   these three rare books and manuscripts
    (b)   these three rare books and unpublished manuscripts
    (c)   these three rare books and four unpublished manuscripts
    (d)   these three rare books and those four unpublished manuscripts

(4) (a)   These three rare books are worth more than those
    (b)   These three rare books are like the others
    (c)   I like these three rare books, but not the other ones

**Exercise VII

In this chapter and the last, we use the traditional criterion of *coordination*
as one of our tests for constituency (i.e. we assume that only identical
constituents can be conjoined, idiomatically). In the light of the various
analyses proposed in the text and earlier exercises, show how this
assumption is called into question by data such as the following:

(1)   Mary is *very tired*, and *in a filthy mood*
(2)   *John will*, and *I may* go to the party
(3)   *these three* and *those four* rare manuscripts
(4)   John is *the author* and *the publisher* of three books
(5)   T. G. Mudslinger is *a great fan of*, and *secretly in love with*, Nim
           Chimpsky

Exercise VIII

Much of the justification for Hornstein and Lightfoot's analysis of the structure of Noun Phrases rests on the assumption that (i) the antecedent of *one* is always a unitary constituent, and (ii) it is an N-bar. Given their assumptions, a phrase like *a big black dog* will have the structure (1) below:

(1)

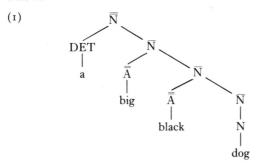

For speakers such as myself (and David Kilby, who first pointed out the problem to me), sentence (2) (a) below can have either of the interpretations (2) (b) or (2) (c), and sentence (3) (a) can have either of the interpretations (3) (b) or (3) (c):

(2) (a)   Jane has a big black dog, and Jean has a small one
    (b)   . . . a small black dog
    (c)   . . . a small dog

(3) (a)   Jane has a big black dog, and Jean has a brown one
    (b)   . . . a big brown dog
    (c)   . . . a brown dog

Which interpretation of which sentence proves problematic for Hornstein and Lightfoot's assumptions, and why?

FURTHER READING

Note: The books and articles below are all primary literature, and in many cases presuppose concepts and terminology which the beginner will not be familiar with at this stage. Hence, the reading material given here is advanced, and should not be tackled by beginners until they have also read chapters 4, 5 and 6.

Akmajian, Steele and Wasow (1979) 'Aux'
Hornstein and Lightfoot (1981) 'Introduction'
Jackendoff (1977) *Syntax*
Jackendoff (1977) 'Constraints'
Selkirk (1977) 'Structure'

4
The Lexicon

Thus far, we have been assuming that a *Grammar* contains three components:

(1) (i)   a set of *Categorial Rules* expanding phrasal categories into other (ultimately lexical) categories

    (ii)   a *Lexicon* (or dictionary) containing a list of the words in a language, together with a specification of the syntactic category(s) they belong to

    (iii)   a *Lexical Insertion Rule*, attaching lexical items (= words) under lexical category nodes (e.g. attaching *man* under N)

So, for example, our grammar might (simplistically) comprise the following:

(2)   Categorial Rules
    (i)   S → NP – AUX – VP
    (ii)   VP → V – NP
    (iii)   NP → DET – N

(3)   *Lexicon* (partial)
        bite = V; *cat* = N; *chase* = V; *dog* = N; *the* = DET; *will* = AUX; etc.

(4)   *Lexical Insertion Rule*
        For any terminal lexical category (i.e. one which is at the bottom of the tree), go to the Lexicon (3), and select from it at random any lexical item (= word) belonging to the same category, and insert it under the appropriate lexical category node

(2), (3) and (4) together will generate sentence-structures (Phrase-markers) like (5) below:

(5)

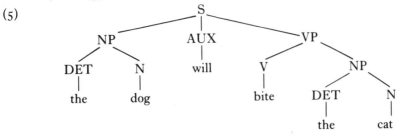

Our Lexicon (3) contains the Verbs *bite* and *chase*, and obviously either could have been inserted under the V-node in (5) above. But suppose that we extended our Lexicon to include other Verbs, e.g. those in (6) below:

(6)   *fall* = V; *pause* = V; etc.

Given that our existing Lexical Insertion Rule (4) allows us to insert any word which is a V under any V-node in a tree, then once we extend our Lexicon to include intransitive verbs like those in (6), we are wrongly going to predict that in place of *bite* in (5) we can insert any of the verbs in (6) – or indeed any other verb in English. But this is not the case at all, as we see from the ungrammaticality of:

(7) (a)   *The cat will pause the dog
    (b)   *The dog will fall the cat

Why has our grammar broken down at this point? It is not difficult to see why. For we have failed to make any provision for the fact that only *some* verbs in English (traditionally called *Transitive Verbs*) can be inserted into a VP (= Verb Phrase) which contains an NP (= Noun Phrase) following the Verb concerned, whereas others (traditionally referred to as *Intransitive Verbs*) cannot. There doesn't seem to be any general way in which we can predict which verbs can or cannot take a following NP complement (or 'object'), either: e.g. both *eat* and *devour* seem to have roughly the same meaning, but the former can be inserted in a VP which lacks any NP-object, whereas the latter cannot: cf.

(8) (a)   John ate/devoured the steak greedily
    (b)   I haven't eaten/*devoured yet

Since there doesn't seem to be any way in which we can predict whether a given verb does or does not permit a following NP-complement, it seems that this is the kind of idiosyncratic information which we shall have to include in the *Lexical Entry* (= dictionary specification) for each individual verb. This we might do by specifying in the Lexicon the types of Verb Phrases which a verb can be inserted into. One way of doing this would be in the manner indicated in (9):

(9) (a)   *chase*: V,   +[—NP]
            (i.e. *chase* is a verb which can (= +) be inserted in a VP (=

[. . .]) in the position marked by —, immediately preceding
an NP within the same VP)

(b)   *pause*: V,   −[—NP]

(i.e. *pause* is a verb which cannot (= −) be inserted in a VP
(= [. . .]) in the position marked —, where it is immediately followed by an NP within that VP)

What (9) (a) effectively says is that *chase* can take a direct object
NP, whereas (9) (b) says that *pause* cannot take a direct object NP.
To introduce some appropriate technical terminology, let us say
that *chase* is *subcategorised* as permitting a following NP-
complement, whereas *pause* is *subcategorised* as not allowing a
following NP-object; the information contained in square brackets
in (9) is called the *subcategorisation frame* of the item concerned,
since it specifies the range of complements a given verb is subcategorised as permitting, within the VP. More generally, the
subcategorisation frame of a Verb tells you what type of VP you can
or can't insert that Verb into. To handle a Verb like *eat* which – as
we see from (8) – can occur either with or without a following
NP-complement, we might adopt either of the conventions (10) (a)
or (b):

(10) (a)   *eat*: V,   +[— (NP)]
      (b)   *eat*: V,   ±[— NP]

Both conventions amount to saying that *eat* can be inserted into a
VP irrespective of whether that VP contains an NP-complement
following the V. That is, they both amount to saying that *eat* can be
used either transitively or intransitively.

Under the revised model presented here, lexical entries like (9)
and (10) contain not only *categorial* information (i.e. about
whether some item is a V or an N, etc.), but also *subcategorisation*
information about the kind of complements a given lexical item may
permit. It follows that we will now have to revise our earlier Lexical
Insertion Rule (4), perhaps along the lines suggested below:

(11)   *Lexical Insertion Rule*

Insert under any terminal category any word from the
Lexicon which (i) belongs to the same category, and (ii)
is subcategorised as permitting insertion into the kind of
sentence-structure it is being inserted into

To see how our revised lexical entries (9) and (10) work, consider the problem of choosing some word from the Lexicon which can be inserted under the V-node in a sentence-structure such as:

(12)

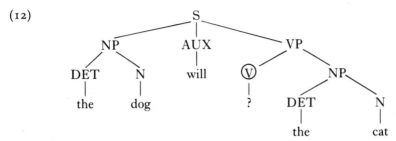

Suppose that our Lexicon includes the entries in (9) and (10) above. Can we insert *pause* under the encircled V-node in (12)? The answer is that we cannot, since although the lexical entry (9) (b) tells us that *pause* is a V, the subcategorisation frame associated with *pause* specifies that *pause* cannot be inserted into any VP where it is immediately followed by an NP; hence, *pause* cannot be inserted here. By contrast, there is nothing to prevent us from inserting *chase* under the encircled V-node in (12), since on the one hand *chase* belongs to the category V, and on the other hand it is subcategorised as permitting insertion under a V-node inside a VP where it is immediately followed by an NP-complement. Thus, by revising both the form of our lexical entries, and our Lexical Insertion Rule to take into account the subcategorisation restrictions associated with individual verbs, we manage to overcome the problem that only *some* verbs can be inserted into *some* types of sentence-structure.

By way of further illustration, consider how we might subcategorise the verb *put*. The range of complements which *put* permits are illustrated in (13) below:

(13) (a)   John put the book in the box/on the floor/near the table
     (b)   *John put the object
     (c)   *John put near the table

From (13), it appears that *put* must be subcategorised as requiring both a following NP-complement and a PP-complement. Thus, we might suggest that *put* will have a lexical entry like:

(14)   *put*: V,   +[— NP – PP]

A problem which arises with (14) is that it implicitly specifies that *put* can be followed by any type of PP; but, as (15) indicates, this is not the case:

(15)   *John put the book for/from/to the table

How can we account for the contrast between grammatical sentences like (13) (a) and ungrammatical ones like (15)? An obvious answer is that the PP-complement of *put* must indicate *location*. Using a feature like +LOC (= Locative) to indicate this, we might accordingly revise the lexical entry for *put* as:

(16)   *put*: V, + $\begin{bmatrix} — \text{NP} – \text{PP} \\ +\text{LOC} \end{bmatrix}$

Now consider how we might subcategorise a verb like *introduce*, for sentences such as:

(17) (a)   The butcher will introduce the baker to the candlestick-maker
     (b)   The butcher will introduce the baker
     (c)   *The butcher will introduce to the candlestick-maker
     (d)   *The butcher will introduce

As a first approximation, we might suggest:

(18)   *introduce*: V,   +[— NP – (PP)]

But (18) is clearly too general, in that it permits *introduce* to be followed by any type of PP-complement, thereby wrongly generating sentences such as the following as grammatical:

(19)   *The butcher will introduce the baker by/in/from the candle-stick-maker

But in fact *introduce* seems to require the preposition *to* introducing its PP-complement, not any other preposition. Accordingly, we might amend our earlier entry (18) as:

(20)   *introduce*: V,   +[— NP – (*to* – NP)]

To get some idea of how (20) works, consider the problem of choosing an item from the Lexicon to insert under the V-node in the following sentence-structure:

(21)

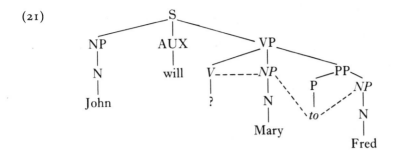

Since the italicised V-node in (21) is immediately followed by the italicised *NP – to – NP* sequence (linked by dotted lines marking precedence relations, i.e. left-to-right linear ordering), then we can indeed insert *introduce* under the V-node here. By the same token, we could not insert an item like *put* under the V-node in (21), because the lexical entry for *put* (16) specifies that *put* requires a locative PP as its complement, and *to Fred* is not a locative complement (e.g. we might argue that the PP-node in (21) carries the feature −LOC).

From the above discussion, we get some idea of the nature of the subcategorisation information that will have to be included in the Lexicon. The essential principle of subcategorisation is that items are subcategorised with respect to any idiosyncratic (i.e. not predictable from some general rule or principle) complements which they do or do not permit. So far, we have of course only considered the problem of subcategorising Verbs with respect to the types of Verb Phrases that they occur in. But similar problems arise with other categories: for example, Adjectives will have to be subcategorised with respect to the types of Adjectival Phrases they can occur in (i.e. with respect to the types of complements they permit within those Adjectival Phrases). Thus, in order to account for the restrictions in:

(22) (a)   Mary is fond of/*by/*with/*to John
     (b)   *Mary is fond

we might propose the following entry for *fond*:

(23)   *fond*: A, +[— *of* – NP]
       (i.e. '*fond* is an Adjective which can occur in an Adjectival Phrase where it is followed by *of* and an NP-complement')

By contrast, an Adjective like *sure* permits not only an *of-*

complement, but also an *about – NP* complement, and a *(that) – S* complement: cf.

(24) (a)   You're very sure of yourself
    (b)   I'm not sure about his temperament
    (c)   I'm sure (that) he will succeed

Accordingly, we might subcategorise *sure* along the following lines:

(25)   *sure*: A, +[— $\left\{ \begin{matrix} of \\ about \end{matrix} \right\}$ – NP], +[—*(that)* – S]

And in the same way that Adjectives have to be subcategorised with respect to the types of Adjectival Phrase they can occur in, so too Prepositions have to be subcategorised with respect to the types of Prepositional Phrase they can occur in (i.e. with respect to the types of complement they permit in the PPs in which they occur). For example, the preposition *before* permits either an NP or an S-complement: cf.

(26) (a)   I left before *the party* (= NP)
    (b)   I left before *the party started* (= S)

Accordingly, we might subcategorise *before* as follows:

(27)   *before*: P, +[— NP], +[— S]

By contrast, the preposition *because* takes either a PP-complement introduced by *of*, or an S-complement: cf.

(28) (a)   She left because *of a headache* (*of* – NP)
    (b)   She left because *she had a headache* (S)

Accordingly, our entry for *because* might be:

(29)   *because*: P,   +[— *of* – NP], +[— S]

In addition, we might argue that Nouns must also be subcategorised with respect to the types of Noun Phrases they can occur in. For example, a noun like *journey* can take two PP-complements, one introduced by *to* and the other by *from*: cf.

(30)   The journey *from Moscow to Peking* was arduous

But this is not true of a noun like *fact*:

(31)   *The fact from Moscow to Peking came as no surprise

In contrast, *fact* but not *journey* can take a following *that*-clause complement:

(32)   The fact/*journey that he was rude to her came as no surprise

Hence, we might propose to subcategorise these two nouns as follows:

(33) (a) *journey*: N, +[—(*from* – NP) – (*to* – NP)]
     (b) *fact*: N, +[—*that* – S]

Parentheses are added in (33) to indicate that the complements so enclosed are *optional* – hence alongside (30) we find:

(34) (a) The journey from Moscow was arduous
     (b) The journey to Peking was arduous
     (c) The journey was arduous

If we now summarise what we have said so far, it amounts to:

(35)   Verbs are subcategorised with respect to the Verb Phrases they occur in; Adjectives are subcategorised with respect to the Adjectival Phrases they occur in; Prepositions are subcategorised with respect to the Prepositional Phrases they occur in; Nouns are subcategorised with respect to the Noun Phrases they occur in

It seems a simple enough matter to extract a general principle of subcategorisation out of (35), perhaps along the lines of:

(36)   Any lexical item of category X will be subcategorised with respect to the type of X-phrase it can occur in

However, within the framework of X-bar Syntax, a natural question to ask is what exactly we mean by *X-phrase* in (36): do we mean X-bar, X-double-bar, or what? In order to try and answer this question, consider once more Hornstein and Lightfoot's claim about the different internal structures of *a student with long hair* on the one hand, and *a student of physics* on the other. This can be represented as in (37) below:

(37) (a)

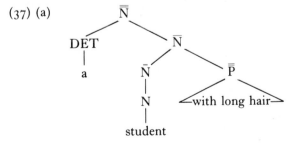

(37) (b)

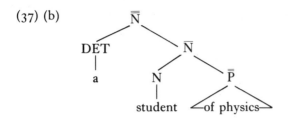

Notice that it doesn't seem to be the case that *student* will have to be subcategorised with respect to the type of P-double-bar complement it has in (37) (a), since virtually any noun can have this type of complement (subject to nonlinguistic constraints – hence the oddity of *!a theory with long hair*); cf.

(38) (a)   a boy with long hair
     (b)   a girl with long hair
     (c)   a cat with long hair
     (d)   a mouse with long hair
     (e)   a rabbit with long hair
     (f)   etc.

By contrast, the type of Prepositional Phrase complement found in (37) (b) cannot by any means be used to modify *any* head noun, as we see from:

(39) (a)   *a boy of physics
     (b)   *a girl of physics
     (c)   *a cat of physics
     (d)   *a mouse of physics
     (e)   *a rabbit of physics
     (f)   etc.

Thus, it seems that we would want to say that Nouns have to be subcategorised with respect to whether or not they permit complements like that in (37) (b), not that in (37) (a). What is the difference between the two types of Prepositional Phrase ($\overline{\overline{P}}$) complement? Notice that in (37) (b), the $\overline{\overline{P}}$-complement is a *sister* of the N *student*; whereas in (37) (a) this is not the case at all, but rather (to coin a new term) an *aunt* of the N *student*. This suggests the principle:

(40)   Items are subcategorised with respect to the range of *sister* constituents they do or do not permit

Let's see how principle (40) works out in some other cases:

consider a phrase like *very near the barn*, to which Bresnan would assign the structure:

(41)

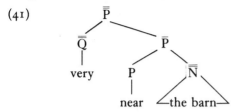

($\overline{\overline{Q}}$ = Quantifier Phrase; Bresnan assumes that DEG(ree) expressions like *very, somewhat, rather too, a little,* etc. are Quantifier Phrases; thus, for Bresnan, *very* has essentially the same quantifying function in *very near the barn, very fond of Debbie Harry, very slowly,* etc. that *much* and *many* have in *many foreign languages, not much sense,* etc. (and in Italian, for example, the same word *molto* would be used to quantify nominal, adjectival, adverbial and prepositional constituents).)

Here, the $\overline{\overline{N}}$ *the barn* is a sister of the P *near*; we should therefore expect that *near* will have to be subcategorised with respect to the type of complement it can take within the $\overline{P}$ immediately dominating it. And this does generally seem to be the case: for instance, we cannot replace *the barn* by a Clause, but can replace it by a Prepositional Phrase introduced by *to*: cf.

(42) (a)   *near (that) he was leaving
     (b)   near to the barn

By contrast, the $\overline{\overline{Q}}$ *very* in (41) is not a sister of the P *near*; hence we expect that *near* will not have to be subcategorised with respect to the range of $\overline{\overline{Q}}$-complements it permits, but rather will be free to take virtually any such complement. And this prediction seems to be borne out: cf.

(43) (a)   quite near the barn
     (b)   rather near the barn
     (c)   too near the barn
     (d)   fairly near the barn
     (e)   terribly near the barn
     (f)   etc.

Or, consider a different case, that of:

(44)   John ought to put the car in the garage

Let us assume – for the sake of argument – that (44) has the structure:

(45)

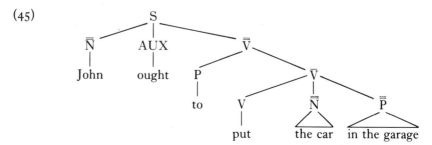

Principle (40) specifies that *put* will have to be subcategorised with respect to the range of sister-complements it permits – i.e. the range of complements which can occur within the V-bar dominating the V *put*: in (45), the $\overline{\overline{N}}$ *the car* and the $\overline{\overline{P}}$ *in the garage* are the only sisters of the V *put* – and as we have already seen, it is precisely in respect of these two complements that *put* has to be subcategorised. By contrast, the particle *to* introducing the $\overline{\overline{V}}$-complement is *not* a sister of *put* (nor would it be a sister of any verb in any infinitive expression). What this means is that we would expect that Verbs never have to be subcategorised with respect to whether or not they can occur in an infinitive expression introduced by *to*; rather all Verbs (though not of course Auxiliaries) can occur in an infinitive complement, so that this fact does not have to be recorded in the lexical entry for any verb. And this prediction is exactly correct.

   Thus far, we have assumed that items will be subcategorised with respect to the range of sister-complements which they *do and do not* permit: or, to put it more technically, that lexical entries will contain both *positive* and *negative* subcategorisation features. For example, we observed in (16) that *put* might be subcategorised as:

(46)   *put*: V,   + $\begin{bmatrix} - \text{ NP} - \text{PP} \\ +\text{LOC} \end{bmatrix}$

But of course (46) only specifies that *put* can be followed by an *NP – PP* sequence; it does not say e.g. that *put* cannot take an NP-complement alone, nor a PP-complement alone, nor indeed an AP (= Adjectival Phrase) complement, as we see from the ungrammaticality of:

(47) (a)   *John put the car
(b)   *John put in the garage
(c)   *John put very cheerful

Thus, a more complete entry for *put* might be:

(48)   *put*: V, $+\begin{bmatrix} -\text{NP} & -\text{PP} \\ & +\text{LOC} \end{bmatrix}$, $-[-\text{NP}]$, $-[-\text{PP}]$, $-[-\text{AP}]$, ..:

But given that the number of complements which a given verb does permit is usually fairly small, and that the number of complements which it doesn't permit is usually very large, entries like (48) are clearly going to contain a large number of *negative* subcategorisation features, and only a very small number of positive ones. Can we avoid this obviously undesirable situation? Chomsky, in *Aspects* (1965), suggests a way of doing this, and of thereby simplifying lexical entries. Suppose, he says, that we include in lexical entries only *positive subcategorisation features* – i.e. information about the range of sister complements which an item *does* permit or require. Suppose furthermore that we assume the following *Lexical Redundancy Rule:*

(49)   Any item not positively subcategorised with respect to a certain frame will be negatively subcategorised with respect to it

(49) can be paraphrased informally as:

(50)   Unless the dictionary entry for some word actually says that it can be followed by a particular type of complement, assume that it cannot be

A redundancy rule like (49) would enable us to get rid of complex lexical entries like (48), in favour of simpler ones like (46) which contain only *positive* subcategorisation information.

A Lexical Redundancy Rule like (49) provides an obvious way of simplifying lexical entries, and eliminating redundancy. Are there other types of redundancy that we can eliminate by the use of further Lexical Redundancy Rules? Some linguists have suggested that we may be able to eliminate further redundancy in our subcategorisation of items by positing redundancy rules of the schematic form:

(51)   If a given item occurs in construction X, it also occurs in construction Y

If this is so, then instead of subcategorising the items concerned as occurring in both construction X and construction Y, we can subcategorise them simply as permitting construction X, from which it will follow by the redundancy rule (51) that they will also permit construction Y. As a case in point, consider the two constructions illustrated in (52):

(52) (a)   John gave the book to Mary
     (b)   John gave Mary the book

Since *give* can be used in both constructions, we might propose to subcategorise *give* along the following lines:

(53)   *give*: V,   +[— NP – *to* – NP], +[— NP – NP]

But many other Verbs also take both constructions: cf.

(54) (a)   John handed the letter to Mary
     (b)   John handed Mary the letter
(55) (a)   John wrote a letter to Mary
     (b)   John wrote Mary a letter
(56) (a)   John sent a postcard to Mary
     (b)   John sent Mary a postcard

Thus it would seem that – for verbs of a certain type – we can predict that any verb which occurs in the *NP – to – NP* construction will also occur in the *NP – NP* construction. We might factor out the obvious redundancy here by proposing that verbs like those in (52) – (56) be subcategorised in the Lexicon solely as occurring in the *NP – to – NP* construction, i.e. as:

(57)   +[—NP – *to* – NP]

and then propose a lexical redundancy rule of the schematic form:

(58)   Any verb of a specified type which is subcategorised as
          +[— NP – *to* – NP] will also be subcategorised as
          +[— NP – NP]

As an example of a further type of redundancy which we might want to handle by a Lexical Redundancy Rule, consider active–passive alternations such as:

(59) (a)   A stranger might attack John
     (b)   John might be attacked (by a stranger)
(60) (a)   The police will arrest John
     (b)   John will be arrested (by the police)
(61) (a)   My car could overtake your car
     (b)   Your car could be overtaken (by my car)

(62) (a)   John may criticise Mary
(b)   Mary may be criticised (by John)

All of the verbs above (and many thousands more in English) occur both in transitive active structures like (a), and passive structures like (b). One way of describing this fact would just be to doubly subcategorise all the verbs in question as occurring both in active and in passive structures, so that each such Verb would have the subcategorisation features in (63):

(63) $+[— \text{NP}], +[be — -ed \ (by – \text{NP})]$

(*be* in (63) is the so-called 'passive auxiliary'; *-ed* represents the 'passive participle suffix' added to many verbs in the passive; and the parentheses round the *by*-phrase mean that it is optional in passive structures). But the 'double subcategorisation' solution in (63) fails to capture the obvious generalisation that for thousands of transitive verbs in English, they occur both in active and passive structures alike. Would not a more economical solution be to subcategorise each of the verbs in question as occurring in one of the constructions, and then have a redundancy rule from which it is predictable that the verbs concerned will also occur in the other construction?

However, one minor problem (which we ignored in the case of (52)–(56)) is: 'Which way round shall we state the relevant generalisation about subcategorisation?' One possibility would be:

(64)   Subcategorise the verbs concerned as occurring in active structures, and have a redundancy rule saying that verbs which occur in active structures can also occur in passive structures

But another possibility would be to state the generalisation 'the other way round', viz. as:

(65)   Subcategorise the verbs concerned as occurring in passive structures, and have a redundancy rule saying that verbs which occur in passive structures can also occur in active structures

Well, you might think there is nothing to choose between the two solutions. But if you think about it for a while, you'll see that (64) and (65) make rather different predictions: (64) predicts:

(66)   All active transitive structures have passive counterparts

whereas (65) predicts:

(67)   All passive structures have active counterparts

Unfortunately, there are well-known apparent counterexamples to both claims; for example, Bob Freidin, in 'Passives' (1975), notes that sentences like (68) and (69) appear to counterexemplify (64):

(68) (a)   Max resembles Harry
     (b)   *Harry is resembled by Max
(69) (a)   The kimono fits Dotty
     (b)   *Dotty is fit(ted) by the kimono

And sentences like (70) below cast doubt on the validity of (65):

(70) (a)   John is said/reputed/alleged to be a millionaire
     (b)   *People say/repute/allege John to be a millionaire

Thus, both rules have 'exceptions', so there is little to choose between them in this respect. Arbitrarily, we shall assume the traditional solution (64) in subsequent discussion. The question of how we deal with *exceptions* to rules, we shall deal with shortly.

   Thus far, we have made use of Lexical Redundancy Rules only to handle redundant subcategorisation features. But we might ask whether there are other types of redundancy which can be eliminated by the use of redundancy rules. It seems clear that there are. Consider the following paradigm:

(71)   *Adjective*   *Adverb*
         slow   slowly
         quick   quickly
         blunt   bluntly
         gruff   gruffly
         sad   sadly
         right   rightly
         etc.   etc.

Notice that all the adjectives on the left-hand side in (71) have a corresponding adverb ending in *-ly*; and this is in fact true for thousands of adjectives in English, namely that they all have corresponding *-ly* adverbs. Are we going to list each such Adjective–Adverb pair as unrelated entries in our Lexicon? To do so would seem to miss the obvious generalisation that it's entirely predictable that all such adjectives have corresponding adverbs in *-ly*, and lead to a great deal of redundancy. How can we eliminate this redundancy? One solution would be the following. Let's propose to list only the adjective form in the dictionary, and then propose a redundancy rule along the lines of (72) below which tells us how to form adverbs out of adjectives:

(72)   Given an Adjective of the form X, you can form the corres-
         ponding manner adverb (with the meaning of 'in an X
         manner') by adding the suffix -*ly* to give *X-ly*

Since the redundancy rule in (72) is of a type which tells us how to form one class of words (Adverbs) out of another class of word (Adjectives), we might follow Mark Aronoff in *Word-Formation* (1976) in calling such rules *Word-Formation Rules*. In terms of the notation Aronoff develops, our informal rule (72) might be stated more formally as:

(73) $[_A X] \rightarrow [_{ADV} [_A X] \text{-}ly]$
         Semantics (roughly): 'in an X manner'

All (73) says is that an Adjective of the phonetic form X can be formed into an Adverb containing the Adjective X by the addition of the phonetic sequence -*ly*, and that the resultant Adverb means (something like) 'in an X manner'. A Word-Formation Rule (WFR) such as (73) specifies how to form one type of word from another: the rule has three types of effect. Firstly, a *phonetic* effect (in the case of (73), this is to add -*ly*); secondly, a *syntactic* effect (in this case, to change the category of the compound form from that of its Adjective base to that of an Adverb); and thirdly a *semantic* effect (that is, the new word formed has a different meaning from that of the base word, and this new meaning has to be specified).

To make the concept of a *Word-Formation* (*Lexical Redundan-cy*) *Rule* clearer, let's look at another such rule. Consider the following alternations:

(74) | Adjective | Verb |
         |-----------|------|
         | rational | rationalise |
         | radical | radicalise |
         | international | internationalise |
         | local | localise |
         | individual | individualise |
         | visual | visualise |
         | formal | formalise |
         | etc. | etc.-ise |

It seems that from any adjective ending in -*al* we can form a corresponding verb by the addition of the suffix -*ise*, and the verb then has the sense of (roughly) 'make Adjective' (e.g. *international-*

ise means 'make international'). This generalisation we could express by a Word-Formation Rule such as the following:

(75) $[_A \text{X}al] \rightarrow [_V [_A \text{X}al] \text{-}ise]$
      Semantics: 'make Xal'

All rule (75) says is that from any adjective ending in *-al* we can form a verb ending in *alise*, and the verb will then mean 'make Xal'.

One important theoretical issue that we haven't touched on yet in relation to either Subcategorisation Redundancy Rules like (51), or Word-Formation Redundancy Rules like (73) and (75) is the question of *productivity*. What we have been rather naïvely assuming so far is that our two types of redundancy rule will be of the schematic form (76):

(76) (a) Any item which occurs in construction X occurs in construction Y
     (b) From any word of type X you can form a word of type Y

But the implicit assumption made in redundancy rules like (76) is that they are *exceptionless* – i.e. that the rules hold for all items of type X. Is this always, or even generally the case? Consider the following paradigm:

(77) | *Verb* | *Noun* |
      | --- | --- |
      | abandon | abandonment |
      | curtail | curtailment |
      | appease | appeasement |
      | develop | development |
      | assign | assignment |
      | advance | advancement |
      | abate | abatement |

Given such alternations, and hundreds of other similar ones, we might propose a Word-Formation Rule along the lines of:

(78) $[_V \text{X}] \rightarrow [_N [_V \text{X}] \text{-}ment]$
      Semantics: 'act of V-ing'

(78) says that from any verb we can form a corresponding noun (incorporating the verb) ending in *-ment*, with the meaning 'the act(ion) of V-ing' (so that *abandonment* means 'act(ion) of abandoning'). Now, given the paradigm in (77), this Word-Formation Rule looks quite productive. But if we look closer, we find that

there are hundreds of verbs in English which don't have corresponding -*ment* nouns: cf. e.g.

(79)   *Verb*   *Noun*
          repeal   *repealment
          design   *designment
          release   *releasement
          destroy   *destroyment
          arrive   *arrivement
          criticise   *criticisement

How are we to deal with this problem of 'exceptions' to rules? There are a number of possibilities open to us in the present case. One would be to say that the rule is *blocked* in cases where there already exists in the Lexicon some noun corresponding to the verb in question: i.e. the existence of nouns like *repeal, design, release, destruction, arrival* and *criticism,* 'blocks' the creation of -*ment* nouns. We might then say that the reason that the highly productive rule which forms adverbs in -*ly* from adjectives fails to apply with adjectives like *fast* (cf. **fastly*) is the fact that the Lexicon already contains the adverb *fast* (as in *He drives fast*) so that the existence of *fast* blocks the creation of **fastly*.

A second possibility would be to say that rules which have exceptions are *lexically governed*, and the items which undergo the rule must be so marked somehow in the Lexicon: to say that a rule is *lexically governed* is to say that only a specific subset of items (= words) are subject to the rule, not others (the opposite is a *lexically ungoverned* rule, one which applies irrespective of the actual choice of words). One way of marking which items undergo a lexically governed rule would be as follows: we might assign to each such rule a number: e.g. *ment*-Formation might be 'R27' (= rule 27). Let's also suppose that all verbs which undergo the rule are assigned the feature [+R27] (meaning 'undergoes rule 27') – hence *abandon* will be marked +R27, but *repeal* will not be. Finally, let's suppose that the rule is formulated in such a way as to apply only to verbs that are marked +R27, so that we reformulate our earlier rule (78) as:

(80) $[_v X] \rightarrow [_N [_v X] \text{ -}ment]$
          $+R27$

          Semantics: 'act of X-ing'

Yet a third possibility would be to deny that any rule which is so unproductive that it has a significant number of lexical exceptions can be a rule at all: i.e. we might deny that there is any *ment*-Formation rule at all, and simply *list -ment* nouns alongside their verb counterparts in the Lexicon.

So far, we have envisaged a Lexicon as being organised along the following lines: it contains:

(81) (a)   a set of lexical entries specifying for each such entry (= word) its category status, and its subcategorisation features (= the constructions it can occur in, where these are not predictable by some rule)

(b)   a set of Lexical Redundancy Rules of two types: Subcategorisation Redundancy Rules, and Word-Formation Redundancy Rules

The rules in (b) take the partially specified entries in (a) and convert them into fully specified entries (i.e. they fill in missing information which is predictable from redundancy rules). Two obvious questions – parallel to (81) (a) and (b) – to ask at this point are:

(82) (a)   Is there further information which must be contained in lexical entries, beyond that in (81) (a)?

(b)   Are there further types of lexical rules beyond those in (81) (b)?

Let's look at the second of these questions first – the question of what other types of lexical rules might operate within the Lexicon.

One further such class of rules which have been proposed in recent work are *Restructuring Rules*. Consider the following set of examples:

(83) (a)   They took a picture of John
     (b)   A picture was taken of John
     (c)   *John was taken a picture of

If we assume that *take a picture of someone* has the structure:

(83) (d) $[_V$ take] $[_{NP}$ a picture] $[_{PP}$ of someone]

and if we further assume that only an NP which is the object of a transitive verb can passivise in English, then it is easy enough to account for the contrast between (83) (b) and (c); we can passivise *a picture* in (83) (a) because it is the object of the verb *took*; we cannot passivise *John* in (83) (a) because *John* is not the object of the verb *took*, but rather the object of the preposition *of* (and we are assuming here that only the object of a verb, not the object of a preposition can passivise).

But now contrast (83) with (84):

(84) (a)   They took advantage of John
    (b)   Advantage was taken of John
    (c)   John was taken advantage of

This time, we find not just one, but *two* passive counterparts to our active sentence (84) (a). How can we account for this? If we assume that a VP like *take advantage of someone* has the structure:

(85)   [$_V$ take] [$_{NP}$ advantage] [$_{PP}$ of [$_{NP}$ someone]]

And if we continue to assume that only the object of a verb, not the object of a preposition can be passivised, then we have no principled way of accounting for passives like (84) (c) *John was taken advantage of*. It seems that what we want to say is that in sentences like (84) (c) the whole expression *take advantage of* can optionally be treated as some kind of complex verb, whose object (*John*) can passivise just like the object of any other transitive verb. One way of capturing this intuition would be to say that a sequence like (85) above can *optionally* undergo a lexical (i.e. in the Lexicon) Restructuring Rule, whereby the structure (85) is converted into:

(86)   [$_V$ take advantage of] [$_{NP}$ someone]

(84) (b) would then be the passive counterpart of (85), and (84) (c) would be the passive counterpart of (86). Optional Restructuring seems to be found with *take* and a number of semi-idiomatic NP-complements, as in 'double passive' structures like:

(87) (a)   (Great) care was taken of her
    (b)   She was taken care of
(88) (a)   No notice was taken of her
    (b)   She was taken no notice of
(89) (a)   Account was taken of his claim
    (b)   His claim was taken account of
(90) (a)   Note was taken of his ill-health
    (b)   His ill-health was taken note of

But it is by no means the case that *any* NP – P – NP complement of *take* (or indeed other verbs) can be restructured in this way: cf.

(91) (a)   Offence was taken at what she said
    (b)   *What she said was taken offence at

(92) (a)   A book was written about her
     (b)   *She was written a book about

Hence, the relevant Restructuring Rule must be heavily lexically governed in ways that are not immediately obvious. Notice that it doesn't appear to be the presence of the indefinite article *a* which blocks (92) (b), since we find e.g.

(93)   She was made a mockery of

where the sequence *make a mockery of* appears to have been restructured as a 'complex verb'.

So it may be that in addition to *redundancy rules* our Lexicon will also contain a set of somewhat idiosyncratic and highly lexically governed *restructuring rules* – as Chomsky has proposed in a number of works. But let's leave the question of how many different types of *lexical rules* our Lexicon will comprise, and return instead to the question raised in (82) (a) of the type of information that lexical entries must contain, in addition to categorial and subcategorisation information, plus a set of rule-feature markings where appropriate. Clearly, in addition to *syntactic* information of the type we have already looked at (category status, subcategorisation, etc.), lexical entries will also have to contain three other types of information – viz. phonological, morphological and semantic. Since we are concerned with *syntax* here, we shall have relatively little to say about these aspects of lexical entries. The phonological information contained in a lexical entry will have to specify the phonetic form of the item (= word) concerned, plus any phonological idiosyncrasies it may have. And the morphological entry for an item will have to specify its morphological structure, plus any idiosyncratic morphological features associated with it (e.g. irregular plurals or past tense forms, etc.).

What of the *semantic* information contained in lexical entries? What semantic information is to be included, and in what form? In the area of Semantics, there are more questions than answers. How would we represent the meaning of a verb like *kill* for example? Numerous linguists have suggested that the *sense* of words can be represented in terms of a primitive set of semantic primes ('meaning atoms', or *sememes*), so that the sense of *kill* would be 'CAUSE TO DIE'; others have objected that this amounts to little more than a rather unsophisticated kind of paraphrase, which *explains* nothing.

What else might we need to know about the meaning of a word like *kill*? Some linguists argue that dictionary entries should contain information about *selection restrictions*, so that we can specify that sentences like:

(94)   !John killed the corpse

are semantically anomalous: this we might do by saying (in traditional terms) that *kill* imposes a selection restriction on its object to the effect that it requires an *animate* object: this information we might incorporate into our entry for *kill* as in:

(95)   *kill*: V, $+[- [_{NP} +$animate$]$ $]$

Perhaps the best way to interpret (95) is as saying that the object of *kill* is *interpreted as being* animate: hence, when we come across a sentence containing a novel (= previously unencountered) object for a verb like *kill* as in:

(96)   John killed zombaluma

we immediately interpret the mystery object as being e.g. the name of some person or animate entity. (Of course, the discussion here is oversimplified for expository purposes; *kill* in 'figurative' uses can take inanimate objects: e.g. *Crowd disturbances are killing the sport*.)

Is there any further semantic information that lexical entries should contain? Some linguists (see e.g. Joan Bresnan's 'Realistic TG' (1978)) argue that the lexical entries for e.g. Verbs should specify also their *functional structure* (or 'logical argument structure'). This may in some cases be very different from the corresponding syntactic structure: for example, Bresnan notes that syntactically an expression like *rely on something* consists of an intransitive verb *rely* and a Prepositional Phrase *on something* – hence the fact that *on* can be separated from *rely* in sentences such as:

(97) (a)   *On that*, you can rely!
     (b)   He is someone *on whom* you can rely

But semantically, *on* seems to 'go with' *rely*, forming a complex expression *rely-on* meaning 'trust': hence

(98)   You can rely on John

means:

(99)   You can trust John

There is thus an obvious discrepancy between the syntactic structure of *rely on NP*, and its semantic (i.e. functional, or logical)
structure. Thus, in our lexical entry for *rely (on)*, we ought to
specify that *syntactically rely* is a verb subcategorised as taking a
PP-complement introduced by the Preposition *on*: but that *semantically rely on* is a 'single unit', a kind of 'composite predicate'. This
we might do by including in our lexical entries not only information
about the subcategorisation frame associated with a verb, but also
information about the functional structure associated with it.
Hence, our entry for *rely* might be along the lines of:

(100)   *Subcategorisation Frame*   *Functional Structure*
         rely: V, $+[— [_{PP} on — NP_2]]$ NP_1 RELY-ON NP_2

NP_1 in the functional structure in (100) represents the subject of
rely: we assume here that we do not need to subcategorise verbs like
rely as permitting an NP-subject, since this is predictable given an
appropriate redundancy rule specifying that all verbs of a given
class permit NP-subjects. RELY-ON is capitalised here in accordance
with the standard practice of capitalising *sememes* (i.e. 'meaning
atoms').

   Another group of linguists would argue that dictionary entries for
verbs should also contain a specification of what are known as
thematic relations. Consider sentences such as:

(101) (a)   The ball rolled to the bottom of the hill
      (b)   John rolled the ball to the bottom of the hill

In (101) (a) and (b) *the ball* has two entirely distinct syntactic
roles: in (a) *the ball* is the subject of *rolled*, whereas in (b) it is the
direct object of *rolled*. And yet one might argue that in the two
sentences, *the ball* in each case has the same semantic or *thematic*
role – namely that of the entity which undergoes motion. Hence we
might propose to develop a suitable set of terminology for describing the semantic role played by NPs which are the complements of
predicates. One such set of terminology is the system of *thematic
relations* developed by Gruber in *Lexical Structures* (dating back
to 1965, though published in 1976) and Fillmore in 'The case for
case' (1968), and first introduced (in a revised form) into an EST
framework by Ray Jackendoff in *Semantic Interpretation* (1972).

Within Jackendoff's system of thematic relations, *the ball* in both (101) (a) and (b) would have the role of THEME (= entity which undergoes motion, or suffers the effects of some action), *to the bottom of the hill* would fulfil the role of GOAL in both cases, and *John* in (101) (b) would have the role of AGENT (= entity instigating some action). Accordingly, we might propose to represent this information in our lexical entry for *roll* in the following way:

(102)   *roll*: V,   +[NP — [$_{PP}$ *to* – NP]]
                     THEME   GOAL
              +[NP — NP – [$_{PP}$ *to* – NP]]
                 AGENT   THEME   GOAL

The first line of our entry tells us that *roll* is a verb which can be used with an NP THEME subject, and a PP GOAL complement; the second line tells us that *roll* can also be used transitively, with an NP AGENT subject, and NP THEME object, and a PP GOAL complement.

As we noted above, there are more questions than answers in relation to the semantic properties of items which should be entered in the Lexicon: hence it is not surprising that each of the four proposals mentioned above (viz. decomposing the meaning of words into primitive 'meaning atoms' or *sememes*, specifying selection restrictions, indicating functional structure, and marking thematic relations) would be greeted with scepticism by many linguists. We are not primarily concerned with Semantics here, so we shall leave these questions to one side (though we shall return to some questions of Semantics in chapter 11).

Summary

A *Grammar* comprises a set of Categorial Sentence-Formation Rules, a Lexical Insertion Rule and a Lexicon. The Lexicon includes a list of all the words in the language, together with a specification of their idiosyncratic phonological, morphological, syntactic and semantic properties. Among the syntactic information which a lexical entry provides for a given item is its *subcategorisation frame*, specifying the range of sister constituents which the item takes. The semantic information about each item included in the Lexicon might comprise a specification of its sense, its functional and thematic structure and the selection restrictions associated with its complements. The Lexicon also comprises *redundancy rules* of various types (including Subcategorisation and Word-Formation Rules), and Restructuring Rules. Where these rules are *lexically governed*, each item which undergoes the rule must be so marked (e.g. by a positive rule-feature) in its lexical entry.

EXERCISES

Exercise I

Decide for yourself which of the examples below you regard as grammatical, and which as ungrammatical. On the basis of your decisions, discuss the question of how the verbs *tell*, *say* and *admit* should be subcategorised with respect to the choice of following complements that they permit; construct further examples if you need them.

(1) (a)   He tells the same story to all his friends
   (b)   He tells all his friends the same story
   (c)   He won't tell his friends that/whether he is ill
   (d)   He won't tell that/whether he is ill to his friends
   (e)   He won't tell (to) his friends
   (f)   He won't tell that/whether he is ill

(2) (a)   He says the same thing to all his friends
   (b)   He says all his friends the same thing
   (c)   He won't say that/whether he is ill to his friends
   (d)   He won't say his friends that/whether he is ill
   (e)   He won't say (to) his friends
   (f)   He won't say that/whether he's coming

(3) (a)   He won't admit his shortcomings to his friends
   (b)   He won't admit his friends his shortcomings
   (c)   He won't admit that/whether he is ill to his friends
   (d)   He won't admit his friends that/whether he is ill
   (e)   He won't admit his friends (where *admit* = CONFESS, not LET IN)
   (f)   He won't admit that/whether he is ill

Exercise II

The following sentences involve predicates (verbs and adjectives) which take complements introduced by prepositions: sometimes the prepositions can optionally be omitted. In the light of the problem of the 'omissibility' of Prepositions, discuss how the verbs and adjectives *sure*, *quarrel*, and *anxious* should be subcategorised in English with respect to the following complements that they permit (decide for yourself which sentences are, or are not, grammatical):

(1) (a)   I'm not sure of/about my facts
   (b)   I'm not sure of/about whether he'll turn up
   (c)   I'm not sure of/about that he will turn up

	(d)	I'm not sure the future
	(e)	I'm not sure whether he will turn up
	(f)	I'm not sure that he will turn up
(2)	(a)	They quarrelled over his behaviour
	(b)	They quarrelled over whether he should be sacked
	(c)	They quarrelled over that he had been sacked
	(d)	They quarrelled his behaviour
	(e)	They quarrelled whether he should be sacked
	(f)	They quarrelled that he had been sacked
(3)	(a)	He is anxious about her behaviour
	(b)	He is anxious about whether she will behave herself
	(c)	He is anxious about that she should behave herself
	(d)	He is anxious her behaviour
	(e)	He is anxious whether she will behave herself
	(f)	He is anxious that she should behave herself

**Exercise III

In the text, we proposed a Word-Formation Rule to the effect that:

(1) $[_A \text{ X }] \rightarrow [_{ADV} [_A \text{ X}] \text{ -}ly]$

Suppose we reverse the direction of the arrow in (1), so that instead we have:

(2) $[_{ADV} \text{X}ly] \rightarrow [_A \text{ X}]$

What is the difference between the two rules in the claims that they make? Which of the two rules would be more adequate to cope with examples like:

(3)
Adjective	Adverb
hard	hard/*hardly (not in same sense)
fast	fast/*fastly
well	well/*wellly
early	early/*earlily
late	late/*lately (not in same sense)

Can you think of other counterexamples to either or both of the proposed rules?

**Exercise IV

In the text, we proposed a Subcategorisation Redundancy Rule (58) to the effect that any verb which permits the *give something to someone* construction also permits the *give someone something* construction. Of course, we might alternatively have proposed the converse rule, to the effect that any verb which permits the *give someone something* construction also permits the *give something to someone* construction. Decide which of the following sentences you regard as grammatical; on the basis of your decisions, determine whether either of these rules would be adequate to handle your data, or whether they have exceptions, and if so what the significance of this fact is.

(1) (a)   I gave a clip round the ear/kick in the pants to him
    (b)   I gave him a clip round the ear/kick in the pants
(2) (a)   The postman delivered the parcel to him
    (b)   The postman delivered him the parcel
(3) (a)   I explained my theory to her
    (b)   I explained her my theory
(4) (a)   I told my secret to her
    (b)   I told her my secret
(5) (a)   I revealed the awful truth to her
    (b)   I revealed her the awful truth
(6) (a)   They presented a medal to her
    (b)   They presented her a medal

*Exercise V

What kind of redundancy rule might we formulate to handle the alternation between the (a) and (b) sentences below (assuming the grammaticality judgements given)? (Assume that *up* and *down* belong to the category P.)

(1) (a)   John picked up the book
    (b)   John picked the book up
(2) (a)   *John picked up it
    (b)   John picked it up
(3) (a)   John rang up his girlfriend
    (b)   John rang his girlfriend up
(4) (a)   *John rang up her
    (b)   John rang her up
(5) (a)   John threw away the magazines
    (b)   John threw the magazines away
(6) (a)   *John threw away them
    (b)   John threw them away

**Exercise VI

In the text, we suggested that rules like Adverb Formation and *ment*-Formation might be 'blocked' in cases where the Lexicon already has an adverb or noun of the type being created by the rule (hence we don't find *fastly* because of the existence of *fast* as an adverb). Can you think of cases where this 'blocking' solution breaks down – e.g. adjectives like *lovely* which have no -*ly* adverb (*lovelily*) in spite of the fact that there is no alternative adverb related to *lovely* – and can you think of any reasons for this? You might like to thumb through the pages of a dictionary checking a hundred or so adjectives and verbs to see whether they have -*ly* adverbs or -*ment* nouns.

**Exercise VII

In the text we assumed that rules like Adverb Formation and *ment*-Formation produce a uniform semantic effect: e.g. *-ly* adverbs always have the sense of 'in a . . . manner', and *-ment* nouns always have the sense of 'the act of . . . ing'. But is this always true? After all, *handsomely* means something a little different from the most usual sense of *handsome*. See if you can find (by going through a dictionary) other *-ly* adverbs (or *-ment* nouns) which diverge in meaning from the adjective or verb on which they are formed. If such differences of meaning are commonplace, what consequences do you think this might have for our proposed rules of Adverb Formation and *ment*-Formation?

FURTHER READING

Elementary

Keyser and Postal (1976) *Grammar*, pp. 159–92 (unconventional in parts)

Advanced

Note: It is not wise to tackle these until you have read chapters 5 and 6 as well.

Aronoff (1976) *Word-Formation* (on word-formation)

Bresnan (1978) 'Realistic TG' (on functional structure)

Jackendoff (1972) *Semantic Interpretation*, pp. 25–46 (on thematic relations)

Jackendoff (1975) 'Lexicon' (on redundancy rules)

Wasow (1977) 'Lexicon' (on lexical rules and transformations; not before chapter 6)

The following anthology is even more advanced, and contains a number of recent articles relating to the uses of the Lexicon; it should not on any account be tackled before you have read chapters 5–9:

Hoekstra (1980) *Lexical Grammar*

5
Transformations

So far, we have been assuming that there is only one level of structure in syntax; that is, the level of *Surface Structure* which represents the superficial syntactic structure of sentences. And we have been assuming that the task of any adequate Syntax of a language is to characterise (= generate) all the well-formed surface structures of the language. We have further assumed that this can be done by a set of categorial (i.e. phrase structure, or constituent structure) rules, supplemented by a Lexicon, and an appropriate Lexical Insertion Rule. In this chapter, we are going to argue that our existing types of rules are not adequate to handle certain characteristic constructions in natural languages, and that to handle these constructions we need to posit both a new level of structure (variously known as *Deep Structure*, *D-Structure*, *Underlying Structure*, *Base Structure*, *Remote Structure*, or *Initial Structure*), and a new type of rule called *Transformation* (= movement rule). We shall consider for purposes of illustration the syntax of *wh*-questions in English, and argue that to handle this we need to posit a transformation generally known as WH-MOVEMENT (also WH-PREPOSING, WH-FRONTING, etc.). But let's begin by establishing what a *wh*-question is.

Questions in natural languages can be classified into a number of types. One major typological division, for example, is between *yes–no questions* and *wh-questions*. *Yes–no questions* are so called because they permit 'Yes' and 'No' (or their counterparts in other languages) as appropriate replies – as in the following dialogue:

(1)   SPEAKER A: Are you going out tonight?
        SPEAKER B: Yes/No

Of course, speaker B does not have to reply *yes* or *no* to such a question: he might instead reply 'Maybe', 'I don't think so', 'That's right', 'Why do you ask?', 'Mind your own business', and so forth – but at least he has the option of answering 'Yes' or 'No'. *Wh-questions*, by contrast, are so-called because (in English) they typically involve the use of an interrogative word beginning with *wh-* (e.g. *who, why, what, when, where, which,* – but also *how*); in such questions, the speaker is requesting information about the identity of some entity in the sentence – for example, a *who*-question asks for information about the identity of a particular person, and an appropriate reply would therefore be a word, phrase, or sentence containing the requisite information: .cf. e.g.

(2)   SPEAKER A: Who won the big match?
         SPEAKER B: The All-Stars

Similarly, a *why*-question asks for the specification of a reason, a *where*-question asks for the specification of a place, and so forth.

A second typological division of questions (which is independent of the *yes–no/wh* distinction) is that between *echo questions* and *nonecho questions*. *Echo questions* are so-called because they involve one person echoing the speech of another, as in the following dialogue:

(3)   SPEAKER A: I bought a car
         SPEAKER B: You bought a car?

Here, speaker B is echoing a statement made by speaker A by using a yes–no echo question. He might instead have used a wh-echo question, as in:

(4)   SPEAKER A: I bought a car
         SPEAKER B: You bought what?

In both (3) and (4), speaker B is echoing a *statement* made by speaker A; but it is also possible to use an echo question to echo a *question* asked by another speaker, as for example in (5) below:

(5)   SPEAKER A: Did you buy a car?
         SPEAKER B: Did I buy a car?

In (5), a yes-no nonecho question by speaker A is echoed by a yes–no echo question from speaker B; speaker B might alternatively have used a wh-echo question, as in:

(6)   SPEAKER A: Did you buy a car?
         SPEAKER B: Did I what?

In both (5) and (6), speaker B echoes a yes–no question by speaker A. But we can echo not only questions and statements, but also other sentence-types – e.g. imperatives: cf.

(7)   SPEAKER A: Don't touch my projectile
        SPEAKER B: Don't touch your what?

Morphologically and syntactically, echo questions seem to have more in common with the sentence-types they are used to echo than with the corresponding nonecho questions.

In contrast to echo questions, *nonecho questions* are questions which do not echo the speech of others, but which can be used e.g. to initiate a conversation on some topic. So, for example, if a friend walks into a room, I can initiate a conversation with a nonecho question such as:

(8)   Where have you been?

but not with an echo question such as:

(9)   You have been where ?

since echo questions by their very nature can only be used to echo a previous sentence.

A third typological distinction which it is useful to make in discussing the syntax of questions is the traditional one between *direct questions* and *indirect questions*. Direct questions are questions in which the interrogative structure is an independent question – as e.g. in:

(10)   When did you get back?

Indirect questions, by contrast, are questions in which the interrogative structure is a dependent (i.e. embedded or subordinate) clause which is the complement of a verb like *ask*, *wonder*, etc., as with the italicised clause in:

(11)   He asked me *who I had talked to*

Note in particular the contrast between the italicised indirect question in (11) above, and the corresponding italicised direct question in (12):

(12)   He asked me: '*Who did you talk to?*'

Notice also from (11) and (12) that English spelling differentiates direct from indirect questions by enclosing direct – but not indirect – questions in quotation marks.

Having distinguished various different types of questions, let's now concentrate simply on *direct nonecho wh-questions* (for convenience, we'll use the term *wh-question* to mean *direct nonecho wh-question* unless otherwise specified, in what follows). For the sake of concreteness, let's start off by considering how we might generate a sentence like:

(13)   Which car will your father put in the garage?

Superficially, (13) consists of a sequence of an NP *which car*, an AUX *will*, another NP *your father*, and a VP *put in the garage*, with the VP in turn consisting of a V *put* and a PP *in the garage*. So, in order to generate the surface structure associated with (13), we might propose a set of Phrase Structure Rules (PS rules) including the following:

(14) (a)   S → NP – AUX – NP – VP
     (b)   VP → V – PP
     (c)   PP → P – NP
     (d)   NP → DET – N

(to mark the fact that the first NP in sentences like (13) is a *wh*-phrase – i.e. an interrogative NP – we might add to rule (14) the specification that the first NP introduced by rule (14) (a) must have the feature [+WH], but this is a complication which we ignore here for ease of exposition). Let's assume that we apply all the PS rules in (14), and insert appropriate items from the Lexicon under all the lexical category nodes except one, to give us:

(15)

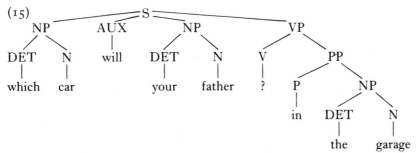

Let's now ask: which items from the Lexicon could we insert under the V-node in (15), in the position marked by '?'? An obvious answer would be that we can insert verbs like *put*.

But surprisingly, this is not the case at all. Why not? Recall that *put* is a verb which is subcategorised as requiring both a following NP-complement, and a following (locative) PP-complement, as we see from:

(16) (a)   John put the car in the garage (*put* – NP – PP)
     (b)   *John put the car (*put* – NP)
     (c)   *John put in the garage (*put* – PP)

On the basis of data like (16), we might subcategorise *put* as:

(17)   *put*: V,   + $\begin{bmatrix} \text{—NP – PP} \\ +\text{LOC} \end{bmatrix}$

But (17) says that *put* can only be inserted into a VP where it is immediately followed by both an NP and a PP; and yet in (15), the V-node is followed only by a PP, not by an NP. What does all this mean? It means that the way our grammar is presently constituted, it wrongly predicts that we cannot insert *put* under the V-node in (15); or, to be more concrete, it wrongly predicts that sentences like (13) *Which car will your father put in the garage?* are ungrammatical.

But worse is to come: for our existing grammar predicts that although we can't insert *put* in the vacant Verb slot in (15), we can insert a verb which is subcategorised to permit a following PP-complement on its own. Such a verb is *go*. On the basis of sentences like:

(18)   Will your father go in the garage?

in which *go* is followed solely by a locative PP, then *go* would be subcategorised as occurring in VPs of the schematic form indicated in (19) below:

(19)   *go*: V,   + $\begin{bmatrix} \text{— PP} \\ +\text{LOC} \end{bmatrix}$

But if *go* is subcategorised as permitting insertion into a VP where it is followed only by a locative PP, then we should expect it to be possible to insert *go* under the V-node in (15). However, this is not possible, since the resultant sentence is ill-formed: cf.

(20)   *Which car will your father go in the garage?

Thus, not only does our existing grammar wrongly predict that

(13) is ungrammatical, it also wrongly predicts that (20) is grammatical.

As if these two problems were not bad enough, we also face a further problem. Earlier on in (14), we suggested that one expansion of VP was into the sequence *V – PP*. But in the light of sentences such as:

(21)   Will your father *put the car in the garage?*

we clearly have to revise our earlier rule (14) (b) repeated below:

(14) (b)   VP → V – PP

in order to allow for the possibility of an NP between V and PP, as is the case with the italicised VP in (21), where the NP *the car* comes between the V *put* and the PP *in the garage*. This we might do by replacing rule (14) (b) above by the following rule:

(22)   VP → V – (NP) – PP

Rule (22) would then generate both types of VP italicised in:

(23)   Will you father *put the car in the garage?* (V – NP – PP)
         Will your father *go in the garage?* (V – PP)

So, if we replace rule (14) (b) by our revised rule (22), we now have the revised set of PS rules:

(24) (a)   S → NP – AUX – NP – VP
     (b)   VP → V – (NP) – PP
     (c)   PP → P – NP
     (d)   NP → DET – N

If we apply these rules (and in particular if we expand VP as *V – NP – PP)* and if – as before – we insert appropriate lexical items under all the lexical category nodes except the V-node, then we can generate a structure like:

(25)

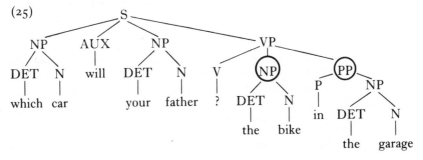

Notice that in (25), the V-node is immediately followed by the encircled NP- and PP-nodes: recall also from (17) that *put* is subcategorised as permitting insertion into a VP where it is followed by an *NP – PP* sequence. Such a sequence occurs in (25); therefore, our existing grammar predicts that we can insert *put* in (25). But this prediction is entirely false, since the corresponding sentence:

(26)   *Which car will your father put the bike in the garage?

is ungrammatical.

Thus, we see that our existing grammar faces three types of problem with *wh*-questions: (i) it wrongly predicts that sentences like (13) *Which car will your father put in the garage?* are ungrammatical; (ii) it wrongly predicts that sentences like (20) **Which car will your father go in the garage?* are grammatical, and (iii) it wrongly predicts that sentences like (26) **Which car will your father put the bike in the garage?* are grammatical. Thus, our present grammar fails even to attain *observational adequacy* in handling the syntax of *wh*-questions. But what exactly is the problem posed by *wh*-questions? And how can we modify our grammar so that it can handle them?

What's going on in all three types of sentence is that although the *wh*-phrase *which car* occurs at the beginning of the sentence, *for subcategorisation purposes it behaves as if it were actually positioned after the verb*. Notice that if indeed the *wh*-phrase *which car* in each case had been positioned after the verb (in the 'normal' position characteristic of direct objects of verbs), the subcategorisation problems that we faced in relation to sentences (13), (20) and (26) would never have arisen in the first place. Now if instead of looking at *wh-nonecho questions* we had been looking at *wh-echo questions*, it would indeed have been the case that an object phrase like *which car* would have occurred in typical object position after its verb, as we see from Speaker B's echo questions:

(27)   SPEAKER A: My father will put the Mercedes in the garage
         SPEAKER B: Your father will put *which car* in the garage?

(28)   SPEAKER A: Will my father put the Mercedes in the garage?
         SPEAKER B: Will your father put *which car* in the garage?

And, interestingly, echo questions like those asked by Speaker B would not have posed any problems for our existing grammar. To see this, consider the kind of verb that we might have been able to insert in place of the empty V-node in an echo-question structure like (29) below:

(29)

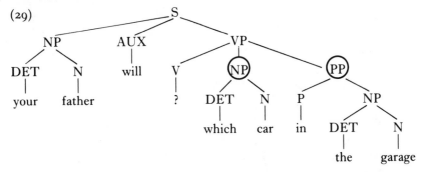

Suppose we ask whether or not *put* can be inserted under the V-node in (29)? The answer would of course be 'Yes', since we see from (17) that *put* is subcategorised as taking following NP and PP complements. And in (29), the empty V-node is indeed followed by an *NP – PP* sequence (encircled) within the VP. In other words, if only *which car* had occurred *after* the verb (as in (29)) rather than *before* the verb (as in (15)), we would never have run into the subcategorisation problems that we faced in respect of (15); and hence our grammar would not wrongly have predicted that (13) *Which car will your father put in the garage?* was ungrammatical.

And the same is also true of our second problem sentence, (20) **Which car will your father go in the garage?* If only the *wh*-phrase *which car* had occurred in postverbal position, then it would have been obvious why we could not insert *go* into a structure like (29): for recall from (19) that *go* is subcategorised as permitting a PP-complement, but not an *NP – PP*-complement. So we can't insert *go* in (29), because *go* doesn't permit both an NP and a PP complement, as we see from the ungrammaticality of:

(30)   *My father went the car in the garage

Furthermore, if only our problematic *wh*-phrase had occurred in the 'normal' postverbal position associated with direct objects in (26) **Which car will your father put the bike in the garage?*, then our existing grammar would have provided us with a simple account of why it is not possible to insert *put* in the slot marked — in a structure such as:

(31)   You father will — which car the bike in the garage?

For we could then only have inserted a verb which was subcategorised as taking a following *NP – NP – PP* sequence, since following
— in (31) we have an NP *which car,* another NP *the bike* and a PP
in the garage; and clearly *put* is not a verb subcategorised for
occurring in such a VP, as we see from our earlier subcategorisation
(17).

    In a fairly obvious sense, then, it seems as if the sentence-initial
wh-phrase in sentences like (13), (20) and (26) behaves for
subcategorisation purposes *as if it had actually occurred after the
verb*, rather than at the beginning of the sentence. But how can we
capture this intuition? Suppose that we postulate that the *wh*-
phrase in each case does actually originate (in a metaphorical sense)
after the verb, and only subsequently gets moved into initial
position by a rule which we shall call WH-MOVEMENT. More
concretely, we might propose an analysis along the following lines:

(32) (a)   Your father will put *which car* in the garage?

WH-MOVEMENT

    (b)   *Which car* will your father put — in the garage?

(— in (32) (b) just serves to indicate the position that *which car*
occupied before it was moved). An analysis like (32) presupposes
that we recognise *two levels of structure* in syntax; firstly, the
familiar *Surface Structure* (32) (b); but secondly an additional
level of abstract structure (32) (a) which underlies it, and which
Chomsky and others variously refer to as *Deep Structure, D-
structure, Base Structure,* or *Underlying Structure.* The underlying structure in this case is related to the surface structure by a
transformation (i.e. movement rule) called WH-MOVEMENT.

    An obvious question to ask is exactly how the revised *movement*
analysis of *wh*-questions like (13) *Which car will your father put in
the garage?* solves the subcategorisation problems that arose earlier.
Or indeed does it? The answer is that we only resolve the
subcategorisation problem if we assume that subcategorisation
restrictions are defined on the *underlying structure* of sentences,
not on their surface structure. That is, suppose that we propose
that the syntactic component of a grammar comprises two compo-

nents: (i) a *Base* comprising a set of categorial sentence-formation rules of the familiar format (S → NP – AUX – VP, etc.), a *Lexicon* which specifies the syntactic category that each lexical item belongs to and its subcategorisation restrictions, and an appropriate Lexical Insertion Rule; the *Base* generates sets of *Base Structures*; and (ii) a *Transformational Component* which contains movement rules like WH-MOVEMENT (and others). We might thus envisage a grammar organised along the following lines:

(33)   *Base*:   (i) Categorial (sentence-formation) Rules
                    (ii) Lexicon
                    (iii) Lexical Insertion Rule

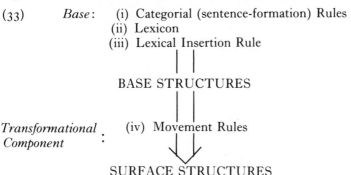

Consider how we might generate our sentence (13) *Which car will your father put in the garage?* in the revised model. Let us assume the familiar set of sentence-formation (categorial) rules:

(34) (a)   S → NP – AUX – VP
     (b)   VP → V – (NP) – PP
     (c)   PP → P – NP
     (d)   NP → DET – N

By applying these rules, and inserting appropriate items from the Lexicon under all the appropriate lexical categories except the V-node, we can generate the structure (35):

(35)

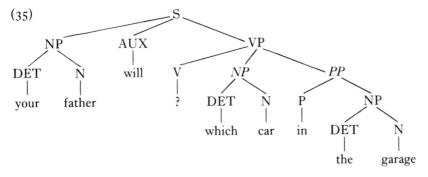

Can we now insert *put* under the V-node in (35)? To determine this, we must look at the subcategorisation of *put* in (17), which specifies that *put* can be inserted into a VP where it is immediately followed by an *NP – PP* sequence. And we note that (35) contains just such an *NP – PP* sequence (italicised). Hence, we can indeed insert *put*, which will give us:

(36)

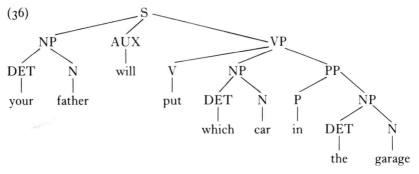

To derive from (36) the appropriate surface structure associated with (13) *Which car will your father put in the garage?*, we need to perform *two* movement operations; that is, we need to move *which car* to the front of the sentence, and we need to move the auxiliary *will* in front of the NP *your father* (or, equivalently, move the NP *your father* into a position where it follows the auxiliary *will*). If we perform these two movement operations, we will thereby *derive* the structure (37) below:

(37)

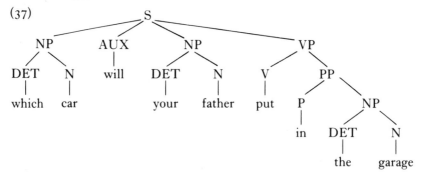

and (37) is precisely the surface structure associated with sentence (13). So it seems that a grammar containing movement rules like WH-MOVEMENT can cope with *wh*-questions, whereas our earlier grammar lacking movement rules could not.

As noted above, to derive (37) from (36), we need *two* movement operations, one involving the preposing of the *wh*-phrase, and another inverting the subject NP *your father* and the auxiliary *will*. An obvious question to ask is whether these two operations are both part of the same rule of WH-MOVEMENT, or whether they represent distinct rules of – say – WH-MOVEMENT and NP–AUX INVERSION. In fact, it seems clear that we must posit that two distinct movement rules are involved, for the following reasons. Firstly, inversion may take place in sentences not containing a *wh*-phrase: cf.

(38) (a)   Will your father put the car in the garage?
     (b)   Never again will your father put the car in the garage

Secondly, inversion may take place in sentences containing a non-preposed *wh*-phrase – e.g. in echo questions like that uttered by Speaker B:

(39)   SPEAKER A: Will your father put the Mercedes in the garage?
       SPEAKER B: Will my father put which car in the garage?

Thirdly, embedded *wh*-questions show preposed *wh*-phrases without inversion:

(40)   I don't know *which car* your father will put — in the garage

(where the italicised *wh*-phrase could be argued to have been moved out of the position marked — to the front of the embedded question clause). The same might also be argued to be true of relative clauses: cf.

(41)   the car *which* your father will put — in the garage

(though, of course, (41) involves a preposed *noninterrogative* *wh*-phrase). Thus, we see that on the one hand there are sentences like (38) and (39) which show inversion without *wh*-preposing, while on the other hand there are sentences like (40) and (41) which might be argued to show *wh*-preposing without inversion. For this reason, then, it seems clear that we must posit two distinct rules: (i) a rule of WH-MOVEMENT which moves *wh*-phrases into clause-initial position in certain clauses; and (ii) a rule of NP-AUX INVERSION which interchanges an NP and an immediately following AUX in particular types of clause. For the time being, we are going to be concerned only with the rule of WH-MOVEMENT, and in subsequent discussion therefore we shall largely ignore the (important) role played by NP–AUX INVERSION.

One question we might ask about WH-MOVEMENT is: 'What exactly is a *wh*-phrase, and what kind of *wh*-phrases can be moved to the front of a clause by WH-MOVEMENT?' By *wh-phrase*, we mean 'a phrase which contains a *wh*-word like *who, what, when, where, why, which, how,* etc.'. We see from (42) below that a Noun Phrase containing a *wh*-word can be moved out of the position marked — into the italicised position by WH-MOVEMENT:

(42) (a) *What* has he given — to Mary?
   (b) *How many parcels* will he send — to London?
   (c) *Which witch* might they burn — at the stake?
   (d) *Who* could she be talking to —?

And in (43) below, a Prepositional Phrase has undergone WH-MOVEMENT:

(43) (a) *To whom* can I send this letter —?
   (b) *About what* are they quarrelling —?
   (c) *In which book* did you read about it —?

In (44) an Adjectival Phrase has undergone WH-MOVEMENT:

(44) (a) *How anxious* will Mary be — about her exam results?
   (b) *How famous* has Nim Chimpsky become —?

And in (45) below, an Adverbial Phrase has undergone WH-MOVEMENT:

(45) (a) *How quickly* will he drink that beer —?
   (b) *How carefully* did he plan his campaign —?

So it seems that an NP, PP, AP, or ADVP containing a *wh*-word can undergo WH-MOVEMENT. This might suggest that *any phrasal category* can undergo WH-MOVEMENT. However, this is not the case, since e.g. neither a VP, nor a V-double-bar (= *to – VP*), nor an S, nor an S-bar can undergo WH-MOVEMENT, as we see from the ungrammaticality of (46) below:

(46) (a) **Read which book upside down* can he —? (VP, or $\bar{\bar{V}}$)
   (b) **To go where* does he want —? ($\bar{\bar{V}}$)
   (c) **She did what* does he think that —? (S)
   (d) **That she did what* does he think —? ($\bar{S}$)

So, it seems that only *nonverbal* phrasal categories can undergo WH-MOVEMENT in English.

Thus far, we have presented only one argument in favour of positing a transformation of WH-MOVEMENT – namely a *subcategorisation* argument to the effect that such a rule makes it possible to attain a relatively simple, unitary account of subcategorisation restrictions. But there are many other arguments which we might develop, lending support to the existence of such a rule. Let's look at a number of such arguments in turn.

Our first such argument is a morphological one, based on *case-marking* facts. In personal pronouns in English we find a morphological distinction between so-called *nominative* forms like *I/he/we/they*, and so-called *accusative* forms like *me/him/us/them*. Generally speaking (i.e. ignoring complications that are entirely irrelevant here), nominative forms are used *before* (i.e. as the subject of) verbs, and accusative forms are used *after* (i.e. as the object of) verbs and prepositions: cf.

(47) (a) *I/*me* fainted
    (b) John saw *me/*I*
    (c) Mary won't speak to *me/*I*

A rather similar alternation is found with the (interrogative and relative) *wh*-pronoun *who*, which – in conservative literary (i.e. pedantic) English – has the counterpart *whom*. In colloquial English, *who* is used as nominative and accusative alike, whereas in literary English the alternative accusative form *whom* is found. So, for example, in echo questions we find alternations such as the following:

(48)   SPEAKER A: I'm sure Nim Chimpsky admires Noam Chomsky
        SPEAKER B: You're sure *who/*whom* admires Noam Chomsky?

(49)   SPEAKER A: I'm sure Nim Chimpsky admires Noam Chomsky
        SPEAKER B: You're sure Nim Chimpsky admires *who/whom*?

Our earlier informal rule that the nominative for (= *who*) is used before the verb in a clause, and the accusative (colloquial *who*, literary *whom*) is used after a verb would of course handle the morphology of the *wh*-pronoun in cases like (48) and (49) above. But now consider the corresponding nonecho *wh*-questions:

(50) (a)   *Who/*Whom* are you sure — admires Noam Chomsky?
   (b)   *Who/Whom* are you sure Nim Chimpsky admires —?

How can we account for the fact that the italicised *wh*-pronoun must be nominative in (50) (a), but accusative in (50) (b)? It's not obvious how we could do this in terms of any *surface structure* difference between the two sentences, since in both sentences the *wh*-pronoun immediately precedes the verb *are* in the surface structure – and hence we might (wrongly) expect that in both cases a nominative pronoun should be used. By contrast, in a transformational grammar incorporating a rule of WH-MOVEMENT, no such problems arise: (50) (a) and (b) will derive from the respective base structures (= underlying structures):

(51) (a)   You are sure *who/*whom* admires Noam Chomsky?
   (b)   You are sure Nim Chimpsky admires *who/whom*?

Our earlier rule that only the nominative form *who* can be used preverbally, but the accusative form (*who*, literary *whom*) is used postverbally will then account for the fact that *whom* is possible (in certain styles of English) in (51) (b), but not (51) (a). Subsequently, the italicised *wh*-phrase in both cases in (51) will undergo WH-MOVEMENT, whereby it is repositioned sentence-initially. Provided that we assume that our case-marking rule which determines the choice between *who* and *whom* operates on some level of structure prior to the application of WH-MOVEMENT, sentences like (50) no longer pose any problem. But an essential part of the solution to the case-marking problem proposed here is the postulation of an abstract level of *underlying structure*, linked to (the technical expression is *mapped into*) the corresponding surface structure by a transformation of WH-MOVEMENT.

So far, we have looked at two arguments in support of having a rule of WH-MOVEMENT: (i) an argument from subcategorisation facts, and (ii) an argument from case-marking facts. Now we turn to a third argument, this time from *agreement* (= concord) facts. As is well-known, English has a rule of *person–number agreement* whereby a verb has to agree in person and number with the NP (Noun Phrase) immediately preceding it: hence alternations like:

(52) (a)   He might say this boy likes/*like Mary
     (b)   He might say those boys like/*likes Mary

The same agreement phenomenon is found in *wh*-echo questions like:

(53) (a)   He might say which boy likes/*like Mary?
     (b)   He might say which boys like/*likes Mary?

Of course, sentences like (53) pose no problem for our informal rule that verbs agree with the Noun Phrase immediately to their left. But now consider nonecho *wh*-questions like:

(54) (a)   Which boy might he say — likes/*like Mary?
     (b)   Which boys might he say — like/*likes Mary?

Our informal rule which says that a verb agrees with the NP immediately preceding it will not work here, because of course there is no NP immediately preceding *likes/like* in the surface structure of (54). Rather, it seems that what we want to say in order to handle cases like (54) is that the verb agrees with the NP that *used to* precede it. But this commits us to recognising that sentences like (54) derive from an underlying structure like (53) in which the *wh*-phrase *which boy(s)* occupies the position indicated by — immediately preceding the verb *like(s)*. In other words, it commits us to recognising the existence of an abstract level of structure (i.e. Base Structure) underlying the surface structure of sentences, with a transformation of WH-MOVEMENT *mapping* the base structure into the corresponding surface structure.

Now we turn to a fourth argument in support of postulating a rule of WH-MOVEMENT – an argument known as the *idiom chunk argument*. English has a class of Noun Phrases which are highly restricted in their distribution, in the sense that they generally occur only in conjunction with some specific verb: for example, the italicised expression in (55) generally occurs only immediately following the capitalised verb:

(55) (a)   John TOOK *advantage* of her generosity
     (b)   The government KEEP *tabs* on his operations
     (c)   I want you to TAKE *note* of what I say
     (d)   The soldiers PAID *homage* to their dead

For this reason, NPs like those italicised in (55) above are known as *idiom chunk NPs*. They do not have the same syntactic freedom of distribution as other NPs – for example, they cannot occur in typical NP-positions like those in (56) below:

(56) (a)   John is really interested in *tabs/*note/*heed/*advantage
     (b)   *Tabs/*advantage/*note/*heed really turn(s) me on
     (c)   Have you heard the one about *tabs/*note/*heed/*advantage?

The restrictions involved don't appear to be *semantic* in any obvious sense, since close synonyms of the items concerned are not subject to the same restrictions, as we can see from comparing *heed* with its close synonym *attention* (cf. *pay heed to* = *pay attention to*):

(57) (a)   You can't expect to have my attention/*heed all the time
     (b)   He's always trying to attract my attention/*heed
     (c)   He's a child who needs a lot of attention/*heed
     (d)   I try to give him all the attention/*heed he wants

Nor indeed are these restrictions *pragmatic* in nature: i.e. the ill-formedness of the *heed*-sentences in (56) and (57) is entirely different in kind from the oddity of sentences like:

(58)   That man will eat any jamjar which thinks he's stupid

which is purely *pragmatic* (i.e. lies in the fact that (58) describes the kind of bizarre situation which just doesn't happen in the world we are familiar with, where jamjars don't think, and people don't eat jamjars). Hence it seems implausible to analyse sentences like (56) and (57) as involving violations of selection restrictions (the latter being typically pragmatic in nature, i.e. relating to our ideas about the world). Instead, it seems that the restrictions in (55), (56) and (57) are essentially lexical–syntactic: i.e. it just happens to be an arbitrary syntactic fact about the subcategorisation of the item *heed* that in contemporary English it is virtually never used in any position save immediately following the verb *pay*.

In the light of the above generalisation that *idiom chunk NPs* are used only as the complements of certain specific predicates, consider how we are to handle sentences such as the following:

(59) (a)   *How much heed* do you think the committee will pay — to my proposals?
     (b)   *How much note* did you say you think she will take — of what I said?
     (c)   *How close tabs* do you think the FBI will keep — on the CIA?
     (d)   *How much advantage* does Reagan think he can take — of his opponents' misdemeanours?

If we say – as we did earlier – that idiom chunk NPs such as those above can only be used immediately following certain specific verbs, how are we to account for the grammaticality of sentences such as (59) above, in which the *idiom chunk NP* actually occurs sentence-initially? Once again, one way out of this dilemma is to posit that the idiom chunk NPs in sentences like (59) originate in the — position in underlying structure, and are subsequently moved from there into sentence-initial position by WH-MOVEMENT. We can then say that the sentences in (59) are grammatical precisely because the *wh*-idiom chunk phrase originated to the immediate right of the verb of which it is a complement in each case. But any such analysis presupposes both an abstract level of *underlying syntactic structure*, and a transformation of WH-MOVEMENT *mapping* (or *transforming*) that underlying structure into the corresponding surface structure.

Hitherto, we have argued that we need to appeal to an abstract Base Structure underlying *wh*-questions in order to provide a principled account of certain syntactic and morphological facts. Now we shall go on and argue that there are certain *phonological* facts which cannot be accounted for in any principled way without invoking both an abstract level of *underlying structure* in syntax, and a transformation of WH-MOVEMENT.

Under certain conditions, auxiliaries permit contracted forms such as those in (60):

(60)   *Full form*   *Contracted form*

Full form	Contracted form
is, has	's
had, would	'd
have	've
will	'll
am	'm
are	're
et cetera	etc.

In sentences like (61), we find that we can freely have either the full form or the contracted form of the italicised item:

(61) (a)   Mary is good at hockey, and Jean *is* good at volleyball
     (b)   Mary is good at hockey, and Jean*'s* good at volleyball

Notice, however, that if we omit the second occurrence of *good* in
(61), auxiliary contraction is no longer possible:

(62) (a)   Mary is good at hockey, and Jean is — at volleyball
     (b)   *Mary is good at hockey, and Jean's — at volleyball

(where — is used simply to mark the fact that *good* has been
omitted). Why should contraction be possible in (61), but not in
(62)? The answer seems to have something to do with the fact that
good has been omitted in (62), but not in (61). Informally, we
might suggest some rule along the lines of:

(63)   Contracted forms cannot be used when there is a 'missing'
           constituent immediately following

Thus, in (62), the adjective *good* is 'missing' from the position
marked —, and hence contraction is not possible here.

But now notice that contraction is also blocked in cases like:

(64) (a)   *How good* do you think Mary is — at Linguistics?
     (b)   **How good* do you think Mary's — at Linguistics?

How can we account for the impossibility of contraction in (64)?
Notice that if we postulate that the italicised *wh*-phrase originates in
the position marked — and is subsequently moved out of that
position by WH-MOVEMENT to the front of the sentence, then
there is an obvious sense in which we can say that there is a
'missing' constituent after *be* in (64). What is the missing constituent? Clearly, it is the preposed *wh*-phrase *How good?*

Having looked at one argument from *auxiliary contraction*, let's
now turn to look at a second argument to do with *wanna-*
contraction. In some varieties of (especially American) English,
want to can contract to *wanna* in sentences like:

(65) (a)   I *want to* win
     (b)   I *wanna* win

For some speakers of this type of dialect (including Chomsky),
wanna-contraction is possible in sentences like:

(66) (a)   Who do you *want to* beat —?
     (b)   Who do you *wanna* beat?

but not in sentences like:

(67) (a)   Who do you *want* — *to* win?
     (b)   *Who do you *wanna* win?

How can we account for the fact that contraction is possible in (66), but not in (67)? Once again, the notion *underlying structure* seems to be central to any account of what is going on here: for if we assume that in underlying structure *who* originates in each case in the position marked —, and is subsequently moved into initial position by WH-MOVEMENT, then we can say that contraction is blocked in (67) because *who* originates between *want* and *to*, thereby blocking contraction. By contrast, in (66) *who* originates after *beat* (in the position marked by —), and since it was not originally positioned between *want* and *to* does not block contraction. But of course for this account to be workable, we have to posit an abstract structure underlying sentences such as (66) (b) and (67) (b), and a rule of WH-MOVEMENT relating this underlying structure to the corresponding surface structure.

Having looked at a variety of morphological, syntactic, and phonological arguments in support of positing a rule of WH-MOVEMENT, we now turn to look at a *semantic* argument in favour of the same assumption – to be more precise, an argument to do with the interpretation of *reflexive pronouns*. Earlier, we suggested a rule of Reflexive Interpretation which determines what expression(s) a reflexive pronoun can be construed with in any given sentence. On the basis of sentences like:

(68)   John said that Harry spoke about himself to Fred

where *himself* can be construed only with *Harry* (not with *John* or *Fred*), we earlier proposed an informal rule along the lines of:

(69)   A reflexive is construed with some preceding NP in its own
         clause which has the same number, person and gender.

Given rule (69), consider the problem posed by *wh*-questions such as the following:

(70)   *Which witness* did you say you thought — perjured himself?

Clearly, *himself* must be construed with the italicised phrase *which witness* in (70); but this is in apparent violation of our rule (69), because *which witness* is not contained in the same clause as *himself*; thus, *which witness* is positioned at the front of the *say*-clause, whereas *himself* is contained in the *perjured*-clause. How can we deal with this apparent counterexample to our Reflexive Interpretation rule (69)? One simple answer would be to say that a reflexive pronoun can be construed with an appropriate NP which *used to be* in the same clause. If we then also posited that *which witness* in (70) originates in the position marked — as the subject of the *perjured*-clause, then since *himself* is also a constituent of the *perjured*-clause, we would have a principled account of why *himself* is construed with *which witness* in (70). But any such solution would commit us to the twin assumptions of (i) an abstract level of underlying structure, and (ii) a rule of WH-MOVEMENT mapping this abstract underlying structure onto the associated surface structure.

A further, similar type of argument supporting the same conclusion can be formulated in relation to facts about *selection restrictions*. Some predicates 'sound odd' with some types of complements: cf.

(71)   She was wearing a new dress/! a new theory

The same type of restrictions are found in echo questions such as:

(72)   He might think she was wearing which dress/!which theory?

and, more interestingly, in nonecho questions such as:

(73)   *Which dress/! which theory* might he think she was wearing —?

How can we account for the fact that sentence (73) is subject to exactly the same selection restrictions as (72)? If we posited that the italicised *wh*-phrase in (73) actually originates in the — position in underlying structure, then (73) and (72) would have essentially the same underlying structures, and if we further posited that selection restrictions are (in some way) determined by the underlying structure of sentences, then we could achieve a unitary account of the selection restrictions in cases like (72) and (73).

Notice, however, the kind of premises that would be involved in such an argument: these could be outlined informally as:

(74) (i)   If two sentences both sound 'odd' in the same way, then it is because they both express the same 'odd' idea
     (ii)   If they both express the same 'odd idea', they must have the same semantic structure ('meaning')
     (iii) If they have the same semantic structure, they must have the same underlying syntactic structure

Unfortunately, however, the type of reasoning sketched out in (74) is not strictly compatible with the general framework of *Auton-*

omous Syntax. In particular, the assumption that *if* two sentences have the same semantic structure, they *must* have the same underlying syntactic structure simply does not square with the central thesis of the *Autonomous Syntax* framework, namely that the question of what the syntactic structure (underlying or superficial) of a sentence is is *entirely independent of* the question of what its semantic structure may be. Thus, within this framework, (74) (iii) does not follow from (74) (ii). And indeed, there are those who would maintain that (74) (ii) does not follow from (74) (i) either. For this reason, many linguists regard arguments about syntactic structure based on evidence from selection restrictions as methodologically unsound; though it is no less true that the literature on Transformational Syntax is full of large numbers of arguments based on selection restrictions.

Having now given a number of morphological, syntactic, phonological and semantic arguments in support of postulating a rule of WH-MOVEMENT, let's look a little more closely at the operation of the rule. In particular, let's ask the question:

(75)   When a *wh*-phrase undergoes WH-MOVEMENT, where exactly does it get moved to?

Before we answer this question, let's digress a little to take a brief look at *embedded questions*. Embedded *wh*-questions show preposed *wh*-phrases, just like the corresponding direct questions: cf.

(76) (a)   I don't know *where* John went —
     (b)   I don't know *what* you think I was doing — to Mary
     (c)   I don't know *how many guests* he may have invited — to the party

The same arguments that we used in the case of direct questions can be put forward to suggest that in indirect questions too, initial *wh*-phrases originate internally within the sentence (i.e. in the position marked — in (76)) and are moved into initial position in the embedded interrogative structure by the familiar rule of WH-MOVEMENT. But what exactly do we mean by *initial position*? What position does the *wh*-phrase get moved into? In each case in (76) it's the position preceding the surface structure subject of the interrogative clause – i.e. the position immediately in front of *John/you/he*. But what kind of constituent occurs in presubject

position in a clause? The answer is: 'Complementisers (COMP)' –
i.e. clause-introducing particles like those italicised in (77):

(77) (a)   I said *that* I would go home
     (b)   I wonder *whether* he would go home

Notice that these complementisers are of two basic types: noninterrogative like *that*, and interrogative like *whether*. We might therefore suppose that the sentence-formation rules generating the
complement clauses in (77) would be:

(78) (a) $\overline{S} \rightarrow$ COMP – S
     (b)   COMP $\rightarrow$ ±WH
     (c)   Etc.

where +WH is the category of Interrogative Complementiser
(under which *whether* can be inserted), and −WH is the category of
Noninterrogative Complementiser (under which *that* would be
inserted in a tensed clause); we are assuming here that categories
are complexes of syntactic features, and that ±WH is one such
syntactic feature. Rule (78) (a) says that every clause (in the sense
of S-bar) has a complementiser introducing it, and rule (78) (b)
says that every complementiser is either interrogative or noninterrogative. Now, since complementisers typically occupy clause-
initial position, and since preposed *wh*-phrases also occupy clause-
initial position, it seems plausible to suggest that somehow
wh-phrases are 'attracted' to the initial COMP position; in the case
of *wh*-questions, preposed *wh*-phrases would clearly be attracted to
the position normally occupied by an initial interrogative (+WH)
complementiser.

But what exactly do we mean by saying that a *wh*-phrase is
'attracted' to the COMP position in a clause? There are two
possibilities we might explore here. One is that the *wh*-phrase
actually *occupies* the position normally held by the complementiser,
and hence *substitutes* for the complementiser: for obvious reasons,
we might refer to this as the *substitution* analysis of WH-
MOVEMENT. The second possibility is that the *wh*-phrase is
adjoined next to the complementiser: this we might call the
adjunction analysis. Now, if we look at what goes on in *wh*-
questions and *wh*-relative clauses (i.e. relative clauses involving

wh-relative pronouns like *who* and *which*) in modern English, it is virtually impossible to find any principled reason to prefer the one analysis to the other. But it turns out that if we look at relative clauses in earlier stages of English, and at *wh*-constructions in a number of other languages, there is considerable evidence that *wh*-phrases are *adjoined to the left of complementisers:* cf.

(79) (a)   a man *who that* he knew well (Middle English)
               WH COMP

      (b)   *Où que* tu vas? (Popular French)
            Where that you go? ('Where are you going?')
            WH COMP

      (c)   *M'amn lli* hdarti? (Colloquial Moroccan Arabic)
            With-whom that you-spoke? ('Who did you speak with/to?')
            WH   COMP

      (d)   *Che belle gambe che* hai! (Italian)
            What pretty legs that you-have! ('What pretty legs you have!')
            WH   COMP

Thus, it would seem that if we want to generalise WH-MOVE-MENT from modern English to other languages, the most likely candidate for a potentially universal formulation of the rule would be:

(80)   WH-MOVEMENT
          Adjoin a *wh*-phrase immediately to the left of COMP

But there still remains for us the problem of defining what we mean by the term *adjoin*: adjoin *how*? There are two types of possible *adjunction* operation we might envisage – called (i) *sister-adjunction*, and (ii) *Chomsky-adjunction*. To *sister-adjoin* one constituent A to another constituent B is to attach A immediately under the node C immediately dominating B; to *Chomsky-adjoin* A to B means to create a new B-node which immediately dominates both A and B; in either case, A can (in principle) be adjoined either to the left or to the right of B. We can represent the difference by taking a structure like (81) (a) (where C immediately dominates B), and seeing in (81) (b) the derived structure produced by sister-adjoining some other constituent A to B, and in (81) (c) the derived structure produced by Chomsky-adjoining A to B:

(81) (a)

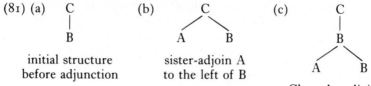

initial structure
before adjunction

sister-adjoin A
to the left of B

Chomsky-adjoin A
to the left of B

Now let's suppose that the underlying structure of a sentence such as *I don't know what he will do* is along the lines of (82) below, where the embedded interrogative clause is introduced by an abstract interrogative complementiser which is left 'empty' in modern English, but which could be filled in other languages by some appropriate lexical item (e.g. *lli* in Moroccan Arabic):

(82)

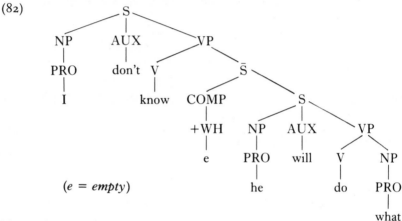

(*e = empty*)

Now, if the *wh*-NP *what* is sister-adjoined to the empty COMP introducing the embedded clause in (82), the resultant derived structure will be:

(83)   sister-adjunction of *wh*-phrase to COMP

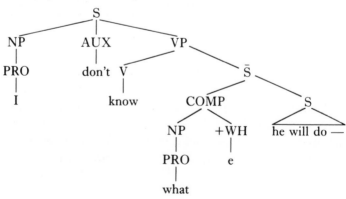

If on the other hand [$_{NP}$ *what*] is Chomsky-adjoined to COMP, we get:

(84)   Chomsky-adjunction of *wh*-phrase to COMP

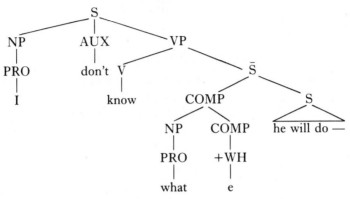

Which type of adjunction operation should be preferred, and why, is far from a settled issue. For the time being, suffice it to note that Chomsky assumes that *Chomsky-adjunction* is involved, so that WH-MOVEMENT in effect specifies:

(85)   WH-MOVEMENT
          Chomsky-adjoin *wh*-phrase immediately to the left of COMP

So much, then, for the mechanics of the rule. However, there is one complication to the COMP analysis which may not seem obvious at first sight. Embedded complement clauses like those in (77) above are typically introduced by overt complementisers in English, so it doesn't seem particularly implausible to say that they have a COMP introducing them, and that in embedded *wh*-questions the *wh*-phrase is adjoined to this COMP position. But what of main clauses (i.e. direct questions)? How are we to handle WH-MOVEMENT in direct questions like:

(86)   *What* will he do —?

Chomsky's answer is that we handle them in exactly the same way as embedded *wh*-questions like (81): i.e. we posit that main clauses have an abstract COMP (either interrogative or noninterrogative) introducing them, and that *wh*-phrases are adjoined to this COMP. Thus (86) will derive from the underlying structure (87):

(87)

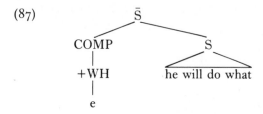

If we assume that WH-MOVEMENT is formulated as in (85) so as to Chomsky-adjoin *wh*-phrases to the immediate left of COMP, the result of applying WH-MOVEMENT (and NP–AUX INVERSION – but we ignore the details of this here) to (87) will be:

(88)

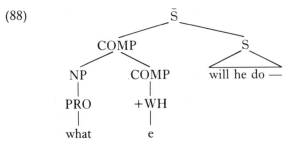

Notice that an essential part of this analysis is the assumption that not only embedded complement clauses, but main clauses too have abstract complementisers introducing them. But surely it is implausible to claim that all main clauses have an (interrogative or noninterrogative) complementiser introducing them? After all, main clauses in English do not typically have *overt* complementisers introducing them: cf.

(89) (a)   *That I am happy
     (b)   *Whether you are happy too?

One answer to this problem could be to argue that main clauses do indeed have abstract complementisers introducing them, but that these complementiser nodes are always left *empty* in main clauses in English (though not in all other languages), since *whether* and *that* are merely used as embedded-clause complementisers. The claim that main clauses too have complementisers introducing them begins to look rather less implausible once we start looking beyond English towards a universal account of the syntax of different clause-types in different languages: for we find that – for

example – many languages use an overt interrogative complementiser (usually called a *question particle* in traditional grammars) to introduce direct *yes–no* questions (i.e. they say 'Whether
you are leaving' instead of 'Are you leaving?'): some examples:

(90) (a)   *Vai* māte mājā? (Latvian)
            Whether mother at-home? ('Is mother at home?')
      (b)   *Kas* suitsetate? (Estonian)
            Whether you-smoke? ('Do you smoke?')
      (c)   *Aya* Ali ketab darad? (Persian)
            Whether Ali books has? ('Does Ali have any books?')
      (d)   *Waš* hdarti mʿah? (Moroccan Arabic)
            Whether you-spoke with-him? ('Did you speak with him?')
      (e)   *Nga* nin ndut-am e mɛnndɛ bɔ? (Duala)
            Whether this sorrow-my it will end? ('Will this sorrow of mine
            (ever) end?')
      (f)   *Czy* zamykacie okna? (Polish)
            Whether you-close windows? ('Are you closing the windows?')
      (g)   *Walay* sarai khaza khuwakhae? (Pashto)
            Whether man woman likes? ('Does the man like the woman?')

Still – we might argue – there is a difference between postulating
main clause complementisers (an interrogative one associated with
interrogative main clauses, a noninterrogative one associated with
noninterrogative main clauses) in a language like those in (90)
where they appear overtly on the one hand, and in a language like
English where they *never* appear overtly on the other. Postulating
an interrogative main clause complementiser introducing direct
questions is – we might argue – merely an unnecessary fiction, an
unwarranted abstraction. But is it really such a strange abstraction:
after all, the English spelling system makes use of just such an
abstract device for marking certain types of structure as interrogative . . . namely by the use of the *question mark*. One way of
thinking of +WH is simply as a device which fulfils exactly the
same role as the question mark; namely, it simply serves to mark
the fact that the clause concerned is interrogative rather than
noninterrogative. And of course, it is necessary to know whether or
not a clause is interrogative for syntactic, semantic and phonological reasons. Syntactically this information is important, since certain
rules (e.g. NP–AUX INVERSION) apply in interrogative but not
(generally) noninterrogative clauses: cf.

(91)   Is he leaving? (question only; not statement)

Semantically, it is important to know whether a clause is interrogative in order to know whether to interpret it as a question or not.
Likewise, the same is true phonologically, since questions are
usually assigned a different (rising) intonation contour from statements (falling). Thus, a sentence like:

(92)   You are leaving

can be either a statement or a question, and depending on which it
is will be assigned either a falling or a rising intonation contour. As
a statement, it will have the syntactic structure (93) (a) below, and
as a question (93) (b):

(93) (a)

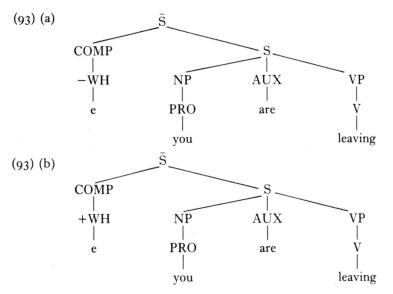

(93) (b)

Thus, within the framework within which we are working, *all
clauses* are assumed to be introduced by an (abstract or concrete)
COMP-node which marks the clause as interrogative or noninterrogative. WH-MOVEMENT then involves adjunction of *wh*-
phrases to the left of COMP.

   One final complication posed by WH-MOVEMENT should be
noted here. While saying that a sentence like (94) (a) derives from
the structure underlying (94) (b):

(94) (a)   What have you bought?
     (b)   You have bought what?

seems to pose few conceptual problems, making the parallel claim for embedded questions that a sentence like (95) (a) derives from the structure underlying the sentence (95) (b):

(95) (a)   I wonder what you have bought
     (b)   *I wonder you have bought what

poses the obvious problem that (95) (b) is *ungrammatical as a surface structure*. Isn't a WH-MOVEMENT analysis of sentences like (95) (a) therefore implausible? Unfortunately, this kind of question betrays a misconception of the nature of the construct *underlying structure*. In deriving a sentence from a particular underlying structure, we are *not* deriving one sentence from another (i.e. one surface structure from another). Rather, *underlying structure* is an *abstract* construct which we postulate in order to account for certain syntactic properties that sentences have. This abstract construct is not itself, nor ever could be a surface structure, since it requires the operation of various transformations to map it into a surface structure. It is thus a contradiction in terms to ask whether a particular underlying structure is a grammatical sentence, since by 'grammatical sentence' we normally mean 'syntactically well-formed *surface structure*'. Underlying structures can be well- or ill-formed *as underlying structures*; they cannot in principle be well- or ill-formed *as surface structures*. It thus makes little sense to object to a proposed analysis on the grounds that the underlying structure is *ungrammatical*. It would, by contrast, make perfect sense to object to an analysis on the grounds that given base rules which generate such underlying structures, and given the set of transformations assumed in that analysis, then from that underlying structure it is possible to generate one or more ungrammatical *surface structures*. Of course, confusion in such cases is made twice as easy by the fact that all too often linguists tend to make informal claims like '(95) (a) derives from (95) (b)' – which of course is inaccurate in that (95) (b) is a *sentence* (surface structure), and sentences don't derive from other sentences; rather, they derive from abstract structures. Hence the reasons why we earlier said '(95) (a) *derives from the structure underlying* (95) (b).' More accurately, we should have said that (95) (a) derives from the structure (95) (c) (informally):

(95) (c)   [COMP − WH] I wonder [COMP + WH] you have bought what

where −WH and +WH serve to mark the fact that the main (*wonder*-) clause is noninterrogative, and the embedded (*bought*-) clause is interrogative. Provided that we then stipulate (somehow: *how* is a question we return to later) that adjunction of *wh*-phrases like *what* to COMP is *obligatory* in embedded questions in English, then underlying structures like (95) (c) need not lead to the generation of any ungrammatical surface structures like (95) (b). Notice that although WH-MOVEMENT appears to be optional in main clauses and obligatory in embedded clauses in English, the same is not true of other languages; in Urdu, for example, it is *optional* in both types of clause, so that Urdu has embedded *wh*-questions without WH-MOVEMENT like (96) below:

(96) Mary nəhiŋ janti keh John mujhe *kia* dega
Mary not knows that John me what will-give
'Mary doesn't know John will give me what'
i.e. 'Mary doesn't know what John will give me'

Hence, also, the Urdu counterpart of the English sentence (95) (b) would be grammatical. The fact that there are languages in which abstract structures like (95) (c) have a direct surface structure counterpart might seem to lend further (universalist) support to the analysis.

Incidentally, for those who think it implausible to claim that in English *what* in a sentence like (95) (a) should originate internally within the *bought*-clause in the position it occupies in (95) (b), we should point out that this would indeed be possible as a well-formed English surface structure if the initial position were already filled by another *wh*-phrase, as in:

(97) I wonder where you bought *what*

So perhaps the proposed analysis is not quite as abstract as you thought!

Summary

On the basis of facts relating to subcategorisation, case-marking, agreement, idiom chunks, auxiliary contraction, *wanna* contraction, reflexives and selection restrictions, we argued that initial *wh*-phrases in *wh*-questions originate internally within the sentence in underlying structure, and subsequently get adjoined to the initial

(COMP) position by a transformation of WH-MOVEMENT. We therefore have to recognise two levels of structure in syntax – *Deep Structure*, and *Surface Structure*, related by transformations like WH-MOVEMENT. Our revised model of grammar thus has the schematic form of (98):

(98) 1. *Base*
(Phrase Structure Rules, Lexicon, Lexical Insertion Rule, Lexical Redundancy Rules, Word-Formation Rules, Restructuring Rules, etc.)
Output of Base: *deep structures*

2. *Transformations*
(movement rules like WH-MOVEMENT)
Output of Transformations: *surface structures*

EXERCISES

Exercise I

Discuss the Base rules and Transformations needed to generate the following sentences:

(1)   I don't know whether Mary will choose this book
(2)   Will Mary choose this book?
(3)   I don't know which book Mary will choose
(4)   Which book will Mary choose?

Assume that *this* and *which* = DET, and *don't* and *will* = AUX. Draw the underlying and superficial P-markers generated by your rules.

*Exercise II

For the purposes of this exercise, assume that the italicised *wh*-phrase in *wh*-exclamations like:

(1) (a)   *What a pretty dress* Mary is wearing —!
    (b)   *How tired* he looks —!

originates in the position marked —, i.e. in the position occupied by the corresponding *such/so*-phrase in sentences like:

(2) (a)   Mary is wearing such a pretty dress!
    (b)   He looks so tired!

Assume also that the *wh*-phrase in (1) is moved out of the — position into initial position by WH-MOVEMENT. Discuss how data such as (3) below might be used to justify this movement analysis:

(3) (a)   What a lot of cars he puts in the garage!
    (b)   How many girls he said were/*was coming to the party!

(c)   How little note he took of what I said!
(d)   *How good Mary's at Linguistics!
(e)   What a lot of people Mary said had hurt themselves in the accident!
(f)   What a nice dress/!theory Mary is wearing!

*Exercise III

How can data like (1) below be used to support the claim that the italicised relative pronoun originates in the position marked —, and is moved into the italicised position by WH-MOVEMENT?

(1) (a)   the car *which* he put — in the garage
    (b)   the car *which* he said — was/*were in the garage
    (c)   the flowers *which* she has/*she's — in the garden
    (d)   the car *which* I want — to (*wanna) skid
    (e)   the man *who* I think — perjured himself

*Exercise IV

Chomsky, in 'On Wh-Movement' (1977), argues that all of the sentences below involve an underlying *wh*-proform in the — position, which is subsequently preposed by WH-MOVEMENT, and thereafter deleted (as indicated by the slashes).

(1)   John is taller than w̷h̷a̷t̷ I thought —
(2)   John is easy w̷h̷o̷ to please —
(3)   I'm looking for something w̷h̷i̷c̷h̷ to write on —

What kind of arguments might be adduced to support the postulation of an underlying *wh*-proform in the position marked — in such cases? Invent other example sentences as you need them.

*Exercise V

Some linguists have argued in favour of positing a rule of THOUGH-MOVEMENT, whereby in a sentence like:

(1)   *Very tall* though she may be —, few people look up to her

the italicised AP (= Adjectival Phrase) originates in the position marked — and is subsequently moved in front of *though* by the transformation of THOUGH-MOVEMENT. But what kind of arguments could we put forward in support of postulating such a rule? Bearing in mind the arguments used in the text to support the postulation of WH-MOVEMENT, try and devise just such a set of arguments based on the data given in (2):

(2) (a)   Easy though she may be (*hard) to please, nobody likes her
    (b)   Bad politician (*-s) though everyone says he is, they all love him
    (c)   Pregnant though I know Mary/!my toothbrush is, I'm not worried

(d)   Proud of himself though we all know he is, he shouldn't boast
(e)   Easy though Mary is (*Mary's) to please, I can't stand her

*Exercise VI

Another movement rule suggested by a number of linguists is the rule of TOPICALISATION, whereby a constituent like that italicised in:

(1)   We all know he hates *Linguistics*

can be moved to the front of the sentence as a whole, giving:

(2)   *Linguistics*, we all know he hates —

What kind of arguments might be developed in support of such a rule?

*Exercise VII

Attempt to develop a set of arguments in support of a transformation of VP-PREPOSING, moving the italicised VP out of the position marked — into the italicised position in cases like:

(1)   I promised that I would mend the dishwasher, and *mend the dishwasher* I will —

FURTHER READING

Note: The discussions of WH-MOVEMENT in the works cited below are written in an earlier framework, and do not take account of more recent work relating to the role of COMP, etc.; hence they should be read with caution. A fuller bibliography of work on transformations is given at the end of chapter 6.

Akmajian and Heny (1975) *Principles*, pp. 372–8
Huddleston (1976) *Introduction*, pp. 135–46
Katz and Postal (1964) *Integrated Theory*, pp. 86–117 (to be read with care and scepticism; technical in parts)
Keyser and Postal (1976) *Grammar*, pp. 362–76
Perlmutter and Soames (1979) *Argumentation*, pp. 251–8, 587–90

The discussion in this chapter is largely based on the following article (which contains technical concepts the reader will not be familiar with until after reading chapters 6–9):

Chomsky (1977) 'On Wh-Movement'

6

More on transformations

In the last chapter, we looked at the motivation for, and operation of, the *adjunction* transformation of WH-MOVEMENT. In this chapter, we turn to look at a second, rather different type of movement rule posited by Chomsky – this time, a *substitution* rule called NP-MOVEMENT. This rule applies in a number of different constructions, including *passive* sentences like:

(1)   *The car* has been put — in the garage

where Chomsky would argue that the italicised NP has been moved out of the position marked — into the italicised position by operation of NP-MOVEMENT. But what evidence is there that the preverbal NP (italicised) in (1) originates in the postverbal position marked by —?

One such piece of evidence comes from *subcategorisation* facts. Recall that the verb *put* is subcategorised as taking following NP- and PP-complements, obligatorily. But in passive sentences such as (1), it would appear that *put* has been inserted into a VP containing only a following PP, but no following NP. If this is so, then our grammar will wrongly predict that sentences such as (1) are ungrammatical, since they (apparently) violate the subcategorisation restrictions on *put*. But of course that would be absurd, since (1) is in fact perfectly well-formed. How can we account for this? One possible answer is to posit that the preverbal NP in passive sentences like (1) originates in postverbal position in underlying structure – i.e. the italicised NP originates in the position marked — in (1): that is, we might posit that (1) derives from an abstract underlying structure which we could represent informally as:

(2)   [COMP −WH] — was put *the car* in the garage

(where — represents the position into which the italicised NP moves by NP-MOVEMENT). Notice that in (2), the verb *put* occurs in a VP where it is followed both by an NP *the car*, and by a PP *in the garage*. In other words, a sentence like (1) behaves for subcategorisation purposes as if it derived from an underlying structure like (2).

A second argument in support of an abstract underlying structure like (2) can be formulated in relation to *idiom chunk NPs*. Recall that NPs like *advantage, tabs, heed, note* and *homage* have an extremely restricted distribution, and are generally restricted to occurring immediately *after* specific verbs like *take, keep* and *pay*. But that being so, how are we to account for the grammaticality of sentences like:

(3) (a)   *Little heed* was paid — to her proposal
   (b)   *Close tabs* were kept — on all Thatcherites
   (c)   *Little note* was taken — of what I said
   (d)   *Due homage* was paid — to the dead
   (e)   *Little advantage* was taken — of the situation

For in (3), the idiom chunk NPs *precede* their associated verbs, not *follow* them as we earlier stipulated that they must do. How can we account for this apparent contradiction? Once again, if we posit that the italicised idiom chunk NPs originate in the position marked — and are only subsequently moved into the italicised preverbal position by NP-MOVEMENT, then we eliminate an apparent inconsistency in our grammar, and retain a simple generalisation about idiom chunk NPs – namely that they are restricted to occurring immediately after specific verbs *in underlying structure* (though of course they can subsequently be moved out of their underlying position by movement rules like NP-MOVEMENT or WH-MOVEMENT).

A third argument can be formulated in relation to *selection restrictions* (though recall that this type of argument has obvious methodological shortcomings within the framework of Autonomous Syntax). Recall that there are certain restrictions on the choice of following complement permitted by specific predicates – cf. e.g.

(4)   John cooked a new dish/!a new theory

But observe that precisely the same restrictions are found in passive sentences like:

(5)   *Not many new dishes//new theories* were cooked—at the Exhibition

How can we account for the apparently coincidental fact that passive subjects exhibit the same selection restrictions as active objects? An obvious answer would be to say that passive subjects originate as underlying (postverbal) objects – i.e. the italicised NP in sentences such as (5) originates in the postverbal position marked by — (i.e. the position characteristic of direct objects, in general), and is only subsequently moved into the italicised (preverbal, or subject) position by application of NP-MOVEMENT. We could then say that the restriction concerned holds between *cook* and *the* NP *which immediately follows it in underlying structure*.

    Thus far, we have considered only so-called *agentless passives* – i.e. passives which lack any agent-phrase introduced by the preposition *by*. But what about agent-passives like:

(6)   *The city* was destroyed — by the enemy

(where *by the enemy* is the *agent-phrase*)? Given the arguments above, we can maintain that the italicised NP *the city* originates in the position marked by —: thus, (6) might be analysed in the manner indicated schematically in (7) below:

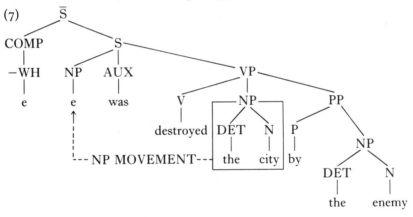

(the −WH complementiser in (7) serves to mark the fact that (7) is a statement). There is no evidence that either of the empty nodes ('e') contains any actual lexical item ('real word') in underlying structure, since only the words *was, destroyed, the, city, by, the* and *enemy* appear in the surface structure. In a fairly obvious sense, (7) is a sort of impersonal passive structure ('It was destroyed the city by the enemy') of the type found in languages like Welsh and Latin, for example. Application of NP-MOVEMENT to (7) results in the boxed NP *the city* moving into the 'empty' subject position to the immediate left of *was*, giving the superficial structure associated with (6) *The city was destroyed — by the enemy*.

One additional complication should be mentioned, however, and this concerns the source of the *agent-phrase* (*by the enemy* in (6)) in agent-passives. In (7) we assumed simply that the agent-phrase originates in the position inside the VP which it occupies in the corresponding surface structure (6). We should perhaps mention, however, that an alternative analysis – dating back to the earliest work in Transformational Grammar – has been proposed for agent-phrases in passives, under which the NP (*the enemy*) con-tained inside the agent-phrase originates not within the agent-phrase itself, but rather is the underlying subject of the whole passive sentence; under this revised analysis, the agent phrase underlyingly consists simply of *by* – [$_{NP}$ e] (i.e. *by* with an empty NP as its complement), and the underlying subject NP then moves into this empty NP position within the *by*-phrase by NP-MOVEMENT. We could represent this alternative (older) analysis of agent-phrases in passives in schematic terms as in (8):

(8)

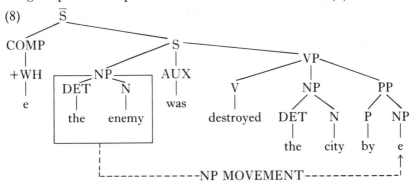

The result of applying NP-MOVEMENT to move *the enemy* into the *by*-phrase in (8) would be to produce a derived structure like (7); subsequently, NP-MOVEMENT could then reapply, this time to move *the city* into the vacant subject position, in the manner indicated schematically in (7).

In essence, the rule of NP-MOVEMENT discussed above in relation to passive sentences involves movement of a lexical NP (i.e. an NP containing 'real words') into an empty NP-position. Chomsky argues that there are a number of other constructions in which the same NP-MOVEMENT rule applies: one of these concerns sentences like:

(9)   *John* seems to me — to be unhappy

where Chomsky would argue that the italicised NP originates not as the main clause subject, but rather as the subordinate clause subject, in the position marked —. This would mean that the underlying structure of (9) is *similar* (though not identical) to that of:

(10)   It seems to me that *John* is unhappy

(the two underlying structures are not identical, since the subordinate clause is nonfinite (or *untensed*) in (9), but finite (or *tensed*) in (10)). Subsequently, in structures like (9), the NP *John* is moved out of the subordinate subject position marked by —, and *raised* out of the subordinate clause altogether and into the main clause, into the italicised main clause subject NP-position: hence the fact that the rule involved in this construction is sometimes known as (SUBJECT) RAISING.

What evidence is there that *John* originates as the subject of the subordinate clause in sentences like (9)? We'll look at a number of arguments supporting this claim, beginning with one which relates to facts about the interpretation of *reflexives*. Recall that – in general – a reflexive is construed with some preceding NP in the same clause which has the same number, gender and person. Notice, however, that in a sentence such as:

(11)   John seems to me — to have perjured himself

himself must be construed with *John*. But how can this be? After all, reflexives must be construed with some preceding NP in their own clause, and yet in (11) *himself* (which is the object of the *perjured*-clause) is construed with *John* (which is the subject of the *seems*-clause). Are we therefore to treat (11) as a *counterexample* to our earlier rule of REFLEXIVE INTERPRETATION, and accordingly revise the rule so as to allow a reflexive to be construed with any preceding NP in the same number, person, and gender, irrespective of whether it occurs in the same clause as the reflexive or not? Clearly, such a solution would simply not be workable, since it would wrongly predict that in sentences like:

(12)   John thinks Paul perjured himself

himself can be construed with either *Paul*, or *John*; but this is not the case, of course, since only *Paul* (not *John*) is a possible antecedent for *himself*; only if we retain our REFLEXIVE rule in its original formulation requiring that a reflexive have an antecedent *in the same clause as itself* can we handle (12) adequately. But if we retain our rule as it is, how are we to handle cases like (11)?

Notice that under the NP-MOVEMENT analysis of (11) on which *John* originates as the underlying subject of the *perjured*-clause, reflexive interpretation facts would present no real problems for us, since we could then say that the reflexive here is construed with the underlying subject of its clause. Subsequently, the rule of NP-MOVEMENT (alias (SUBJECT) RAISING) 'raises' the NP *John* out of subordinate subject position into main clause subject position, giving the superficial structure associated with sentence (11) *John seems to me — to have perjured himself*.

There is, however, one way in which we might seek to avoid this conclusion (and hence reject the RAISING analysis). Suppose we argue instead that sentence (11) doesn't actually contain two clauses at all, but rather consists of a single-clause structure in which *seems* functions as some kind of *quasi-auxiliary*. We could then argue that *John* is in the same clause as *himself* in surface structure, so we don't need any abstract underlying structure to explain the facts about reflexive interpretation in such sentences. Ah, but wait: it isn't that simple. If (11) does indeed really contain only one clause, then not only are *John* and the reflexive in the same clause, but so too are *me* and the reflexive; in which case, we'd expect to find that *me* could serve as the antecedent for an appropriate reflexive, in a sentence such as:

(13)   *John seems to me to have deceived myself

But this is not the case at all: *myself* cannot be construed with *me* here, and since there is no alternative antecedent for *myself* in the sentence, *myself* is uninterpretable, as is the sentence containing it. Why cannot *myself* be construed with *me* in (13)? The most obvious answer is that *myself* and *me* are in different clauses: i.e.

185

me is part of the *seems*-clause and *myself* is part of the *deceived*-clause. But if this is so, then sentences like (13) and (11) must have a two-clause structure – i.e. *John* cannot be in the same clause as *himself* in the surface structure of (11). But if *John* is not in the same clause as *himself* in (11), how can it be that *himself* is construed with *John*, bearing in mind that reflexives generally require a *clausemate antecedent* (i.e. an antecedent in the same clause as themselves)? The NP-MOVEMENT analysis provides the following answer to this mystery: although *John* is the main clause subject in surface structure, underlyingly he represents the subordinate clause subject. Because *John* is the underlying subordinate clause subject, he therefore occurs in the same clause as *himself* in underlying structure, and can be construed as the antecedent of *himself*. But if *John* is the underlying subordinate clause subject, how does he get to be the superficial main clause subject? By NP-MOVEMENT, of course. . .

Having looked at the *reflexive argument* in some detail, let's look more briefly at some other arguments which support the claim that the superficial subject of the *seem to VP* construction represents the underlying subject of the infinitive (*to-VP*) complement. A second such argument can be formulated in relation to *agreement* facts. Generally speaking, a *predicate nominal* (that is, an NP used as the complement of a *copula* verb like *be*) agrees in number with the subject of its own clause; thus in:

(14)   They consider John to be a fool/*fools

the predicate nominal (*a fool/fools*) agrees with the subject *John* of its own clause (the *be*-clause), not with the subject *they* of the main clause. In the light of this observation, consider number agreement in a sentence like:

(15)   *They* seem to me — to be fools/*a fool

Here, the predicate nominal *fools* agrees with the italicised NP *they*, in spite of the fact that (as we argued earlier) the two are contained in different clauses in surface structure. How can this be? Under the NP-MOVEMENT analysis of *seem-to-VP* sentences, sentences like (15) pose no problem; if we suppose that *they* originates in the — position as the subordinate clause subject, then we can say that the predicate nominal agrees with the *underlying* subject of its clause. How does *they* get from its underlying position as subordinate clause subject to its superficial position as main clause subject? By NP-MOVEMENT. . .

A third argument in favour of the NP-MOVEMENT analysis can be formulated in relation to *idiom chunk NPs*. There are a limited set of idiom chunk NPs in English (generally known as *subject idiom chunks*) which – in their idiomatic use – are restricted to occurring as the subject of certain specific expressions: cf.

(16) (a)   *The cat* is out of the bag
     (b)   *The fur* will fly
     (c)   *The shit* hit the fan (American idiom)

But notice that these subject idiom chunks also occur in sentences like:

(17) (a)   *The cat* seems – to be out of the bag
     (b)   *The fur* seems — to be flying
     (c)   *The shit* seems — to have hit the fan

How can it be that the italicised idiom chunk subjects can occur as the subject of *seems* in (17), when they are generally restricted to occurring only as the subjects of expressions like *be out of the bag*, *fly*, and *hit the fan*? The NP-MOVEMENT analysis provides a simple answer if we suppose that idiom chunk NPs are restricted to occurring as the subjects of specific predicates *in underlying structure*; for under the NP-MOVEMENT analysis, the italicised NPs in (17) originate in the position marked — as the subject of the idiomatic predicates concerned. How do they subsequently get into main clause subject position? By NP-MOVEMENT. . .

Having looked at just a handful of arguments in favour of the NP-MOVEMENT analysis of *seem*-sentences (Paul Postal in *On Raising* (1974) gives a couple of dozen such arguments, in detail), let's now turn to look at how NP-MOVEMENT works with predicates like *seem*. We can represent the operation of NP-MOVEMENT in a sentence like:

(18)   John seems — to like Mary

as being of the following schematic form:

(19)

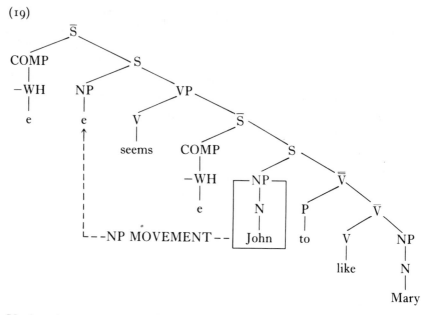

Under the conception of NP-MOVEMENT schematised above, the subordinate subject NP *John* moves into the empty NP-position in the main (*seems-*) clause, thereby becoming the superficial subject of the main clause.

If we now think back to the kind of NP-MOVEMENT operation we envisaged in our discussion of passive sentences in (7), we can see that the two different constructions involve essentially the same type of movement rule – a rule which we might outline informally as:

(20)   NP-MOVEMENT
        Move an NP into an empty NP-position

One aspect of (20) which might at first seem strange is the assumption that the moved NP moves into an *empty* NP-position. But what is the alternative? Suppose that we were to deny that the empty NP-subject of *seems* in (19) is underlyingly *empty*: then we are thereby committing ourselves to the assumption that the NP concerned is *filled* by some lexical expression (= set of words). But what lexical expression is it filled by? Well, I suppose the most likely candidate is *it*, by analogy with:

(21)   *It* seems that John likes Mary

But while *it* appears in the surface structure of (21), there is no *it* in
the surface structure of (18) *John seems to like Mary*. So, if *it* is
present in the underlying structure of (18), but not present in the
corresponding surface structure, where does the *it* disappear to?
Aha – you might say – the underlying *it* gets replaced by *John* as a
result of NP-MOVEMENT. But any such account would presuppose a rather odd view of the type of movement rule (substitution)
we are concerned with here, namely that:

(22)   A constituent can move into a position already held by another
          lexical constituent (i.e. a constituent filled with lexical mate-
          rial, i.e. 'real words')

This would allow for NP-MOVEMENT to replace an NP comprising *Margaret Thatcher* by another containing *Ronald Reagan*. But
that kind of movement operation is unprecedented in traditional or
any other kind of grammar, and intuitively we might feel that it is
an 'impossible' rule for any natural language to possess. Accordingly, we might want to 'ban' such rules from our theory of grammar.
But how can this be done? An obvious answer would be to propose
a constraint on possible movement (substitution) rules to the effect
that:

(23)   No rule in any natural language can replace a constituent
          containing lexical material by any other consituent

(23) would effectively ban rules like 'Replace *Margaret Thatcher* by
Ronald Reagan' from occurring in the grammar of any natural
language. (23) thus represents a strong constraint on the notion of
'possible substitution rule of natural language', and is in keeping
with Chomsky's programme to *maximally constrain rules*.
     Notice that if we adhere to principle (23), we would be barred
from proposing any analysis of either *raising* or *passive* sentences in
which the moved NP comes to replace another NP containing the
word *it*: this IT REPLACEMENT analysis would clearly violate
condition (23). By contrast, our original analysis of the *raising* and
passive constructions sketched out in (19) and (7) respectively does

not violate principle (23), since in both cases the moved NP (*John* and *the city*) moves into the empty NP occupying main clause subject position; and of course (23) allows an empty node to be filled by lexical material.

As we remarked earlier, the type of movement operation illustrated by the rule of NP-MOVEMENT is very different from that involved in WH-MOVEMENT; to be more precise, WH-MOVEMENT is an *adjunction* rule whereby one constituent is adjoined to another; by contrast, NP-MOVEMENT is a *substitution* rule, whereby one constituent is substituted for another (empty) one. NP-MOVEMENT has an interesting property, typical of other such substitution rules; under NP-MOVEMENT, one NP comes to occupy the position formerly held by another, empty NP. The constraint (23) offers us an explanation for why the moved NP comes to occupy a formerly *empty* node: but notice that (23) doesn't tell us what kind of empty node constituent can be replaced by a moved NP. Now it turns out – in both the raising and passive constructions – that the moved NP comes to occupy an empty NP-node, not e.g. an empty PP-, or VP-, or QP-, or AP-, or ADVP- (etc.) node. To achieve explanatory adequacy, a grammar of English must provide a principled account of why the NP in these cases moves into an empty *NP-position*, rather than into some other empty category position. This we might do – suggests Chomsky – if we were to impose on all substitution rules the constraint (24) below:

(24)   STRUCTURE-PRESERVING CONSTRAINT
         A constituent can only be moved by a substitution rule into
         another category of the same type

Thus, (24) specifies that NPs can only be substituted by other NPs, PPs can only be substituted by other PPs, APs can only be substituted by other APs, etc. – or, more generally, that a given category X^n (X with n bars) can only be substituted by another X^n. An attempt to develop a universal typology of transformations (in which structure-preserving transformations are a subset) is made by Joe Emonds in *English Syntax* (1976).

Thus far, we have looked at two (different kinds of) movement rules assumed by Chomsky in his recent work: WH-MOVEMENT, and NP-MOVEMENT. We have devoted a considerable part of our discussion to considering the question:

(25)   Where does the moved constituent get moved to?

– the answer being that it is adjoined to COMP in the case of
WH-MOVEMENT, and is substituted for an empty NP in the case
of NP-MOVEMENT. In concentrating on the question (25), we
have diverted attention away from another equally important
question – namely:

(26)   When a constituent moves out of a given sentence-position,
         what happens to the sentence-position it used to occupy?

For example, in (19) what happens to the boxed NP-position when
John moves out of the subordinate subject position into the main
clause subject position? Clearly, the lexical material *John* moves,
but does the NP-node immediately dominating *John* remain, or is it
somehow obliterated? Chomsky's answer is that the NP-node
does indeed remain behind, but it is of course *empty* of any lexical
material, since the material it used to contain has been moved
elsewhere in the sentence. To be more explicit, Chomsky assumes
that:

(27)   Any moved constituent of category X^n leaves behind in the
         position out of which it moves an empty category of the same
         type – $[_{X^n} e]$

At this point, when we are being asked to accept both that
constituents can move into empty node positions, and that they
leave behind empty nodes when they do move, we may begin to feel
that the whole theory is getting so abstract and elaborate that it
passes the comprehension of ordinary mortals (i.e. nonlinguists).
But perhaps a simple analogy will help to make things clearer. Just
think of the problems of moving house. You can't move into a
house unless it's *empty*; and when you move out of a house, you
don't take your old house with you – rather, you leave it behind,
empty. It's just the same with constituents: they too move into
empty nodes (in the case of substitution rules), and leave behind
them empty nodes. So what is going to be the derived structure that
we end up with if we apply NP-MOVEMENT to (19)? The answer
is:

(28)

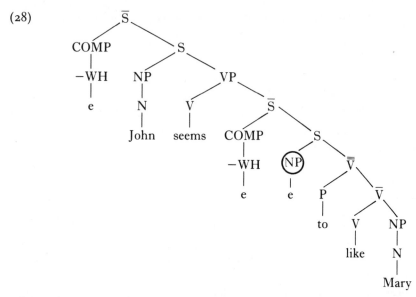

where the encircled NP is the empty NP-node left behind after
John moves out of subordinate subject position.

OK – we might say – I can see *what* Chomsky wants to do; but
what I can't see is *why* he insists on leaving abstract empty nodes all
over the place. Is this just abstraction for abstraction's sake? Not at
all: Chomsky would argue that there is strong *empirical motivation*
for the convention that moved constituents leave behind empty
categories: i.e. there are certain facts which you can't explain in any
obvious way unless you make this assumption, (27). Take, for
example, the *wanna*-contraction facts. In the case of a simple echo
question like:

(29)   You might want *who* to win?

if we asked why *want to* can't contract to *wanna* here, the answer
most of us would come up with would be: 'Because there's a *who*
between *want* and *to*, and contraction is only possible where *to*
immediately follows *want*.' But now suppose that we prepose *who*
in (29) by WH-MOVEMENT, and invert *you* and *might* by
NP–AUX INVERSION, to obtain:

(30)   Who might you want to win?
Here we find that contraction is not possible:

(31)   *Who might you wanna win?

But why isn't it possible? Earlier we said that the fact that prior to WH-MOVEMENT there *used to be* a *who* separating *want* from *to* somehow explained why contraction was not possible. But what kind of explanation is that? After all, once you've moved *who* out of the way by WH-MOVEMENT, *want* and *to* will surely become adjacent, and then we'd expect contraction to be able to apply, wouldn't we? Yes indeed. So the 'explanation' we gave earlier wasn't really an explanation at all.

Or was it? Suppose we now assume the convention (27) that we've just suggested, namely that moved constituents leave empty nodes behind them. In this case, the derived structure we get by preposing the *wh*-phrase in (29) is not (30), but rather:

(32)   [NP who] might you want [NP e] to win?

where [NP e] is the empty node NP left behind by movement of the NP *who*. Now let's ask the same question again: 'Why is contraction blocked in (32)?' This time, we can really answer the question: 'Contraction is blocked because *want* isn't immediately adjacent to *to*: there's an empty node NP separating the two.' Moral of the story: empty nodes aren't just there to make syntax harder to do; they're there because they help us to explain certain linguistic phenomena.

Now we're going to add a further refinement to the convention (27); but before we do, let's try and illustrate the motivation for the refinement. Let's go back to the rule of REFLEXIVE INTER-PRETATION that we considered earlier; and in particular, let's consider how it will work in cases like:

(33)   John seems to me to have perjured himself (formerly (11))

Remember that reflexives are construed with some preceding NP in their own clause, and that we argued earlier that *John* and *himself* are in different clauses in (33). Now how can it be that *himself* is construed with *John* if the two are contained in different clauses, and if our REFLEXIVE INTERPRETATION rule specifies that a reflexive requires a clausemate antecedent (an antecedent in the same clause)? Well, earlier we hinted that you could perhaps solve the problem by saying that *John* originates as the underlying subject of the *perjured*-clause, and that this fact somehow might account for the fact that *himself* is construed with *John*. Yet in one sense, it's not at all clear that we've really explained anything by saying what we said. After all, once *John* is moved out of the subordinate clause into the main clause by NP-MOVEMENT, he is no longer in the same clause as *himself*, and can't therefore be identified as the antecedent of *himself* by our REFLEXIVE INTERPRETATION rule – especially if, as we shall suggest subsequently, semantic interpretation rules operate on Surface Structure.

But once again, the convention (27) can help us; given such a convention, the structure which results from applying NP-MOVEMENT to the structure underlying (33) is:

(34)   John seems to me [$_{NP}$ e] to have perjured himself

(ignoring details, for ease of exposition) – a structure in which we have an empty NP-node as the subject of the infinitive. Given a structure like (34), our REFLEXIVE INTERPRETATION rule still won't be able to construe *himself* with *John*, because they aren't in the same clause: but what the rule *can* do is construe *himself* with the empty node subject of the *perjured*-clause. This then tells us that *himself* refers to whatever the empty node NP refers to. But here we meet a snag: how do we know what the empty node NP refers to? The answer is that the way we have set up our grammar at present, we don't, because *e* is just an empty node, the same as any other empty node. Somehow, we want to capture the fact that *e* 'stands for' *John* – i.e. [$_{NP}$ e] is the empty NP-node left behind by the movement of *John*, not of some other constituent. But we've no way of telling this by just looking at the structure (34).

How can we solve this problem? Chomsky's solution is as follows. Suppose we posit a convention whereby whenever a constituent is moved, the moved category and the empty category it leaves behind are coindexed – that is, assigned some unique subscript numeral which they share. That is, suppose we replace our earlier convention (27) by the revised convention:

(35)   TRACE THEORY CONVENTION (TRACE THEORY OF MOVEMENT RULES)
         Any moved category of type X^n leaves behind in the position out of which it moves any empty node 'trace' of itself [$_{X^n}$ e] which is coindexed with the moved constituent

Given the revised convention (35), the derived structure produced by applying NP-MOVEMENT to the structure underlying (33) will be:

(36)   [$_{NP_2}$ John] seems to me [$_{NP_2}$ e] to have perjured himself

Our REFLEXIVE rule can now construe *himself* with the empty NP-node which is the surface structure subject of the *perjured-*clause; and we can now recover the fact that the empty node 'stands for' *John* by virtue of the fact that the empty node NP is coindexed with the NP containing *John*. Thus if *himself* is anaphoric (i.e. refers back) to the empty node NP, and the empty node NP in turn is anaphoric to the NP *John*, then clearly *John* must be the antecedent of *himself*.

And finally, just one more piece of terminology, already introduced in (35). A coindexed empty node left behind by some moved constituent is called the *trace* of the moved constituent (hence the fact that Chomsky sometimes uses *t* rather than *e* to represent this type of empty node). Hence, the theory developed by Chomsky that movement rules leave behind a coindexed empty node *trace* of themselves is known as *(The) Trace Theory (of Movement Rules)*.

Given the trace-theoretic convention outlined informally in (35), the surface structure produced by the operation of NP-MOVEMENT in (19) will not be (28), but rather:

(37)

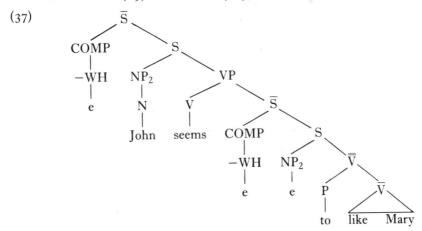

Notice that it is *categories* which carry indices (subscripts), not lexical items. Notice also that not only NP-MOVEMENT, but *all movement rules* (including WH-MOVEMENT) leave behind a

coindexed empty category when they move a constituent, given
(35). Thus, the surface structure of a sentence such as:

(38)   I wonder *what* he did —.

would be (informally, and omitting details):

(39)   I wonder [$_{NP_2}$ what] he did [$_{NP_2}$ e]

Finally, we should add a few brief words about the problem of
the *interaction of transformations*. Hitherto, we have – somewhat
artificially – limited ourselves largely to discussion of sentences
which involve only one application of one movement rule in their
derivation. But – we might ask – what happens in the derivation of
sentences which involve the application of more than one rule, or
indeed more than one application of the same rule? How do the
rules apply in such cases – *simultaneously* (i.e. all together at
once), or *sequentially* (one-after-another)?

Crucial to any attempt to answer such a question is the notion of
the *domain of application of a rule*. This we might define informally
as:

(40)   The domain of application of any rule is the minimal category
          dominating every constituent involved in the application of the
          rule

where *minimal* informally means 'lowest in the tree-structure'
(more formally, the minimal category dominating some constituent
X is that category dominating X which does not dominate any other
category dominating X). The role played by the domain of
application of a rule in the interaction of transformations can most
concretely be illustrated by an example. Let's consider how we
might derive the sentence:

(41)   How much heed seems to have been paid to your proposal?

Since *heed* is restricted to occurring underlyingly in the expression
pay (so much) heed, the idiom chunk argument tells us that the
underlying structure of (41) will be:

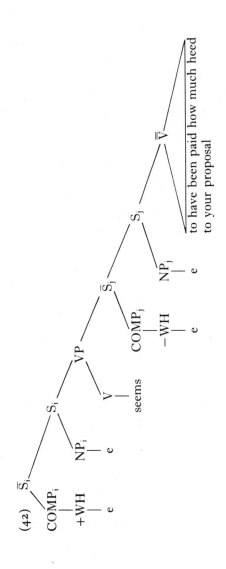

(42)

where *how much heed* occurs as the underlying object of the verb *paid* (*note*: the subscript letters in (42) are *not* of any theoretical significance (and, in particular, they have nothing to do with coindexing or traces); they are added merely to make it easy to identify and refer to particular nodes). In order to derive the surface structure associated with (41) from the underlying structure (42), the NP *how much heed* will have to undergo three successive (= sequential) movement operations; firstly, it will have to be substituted for the empty node under NP_j by NP-MOVEMENT; then it will subsequently be substituted for the empty node under NP_i, again by NP-MOVEMENT; and finally, it will be adjoined to the left of $COMP_i$ by WH-MOVEMENT. These three successive movements of the NP *how much heed* can be schematically represented as in (43) opposite.

But how do we know that the NP *how much heed* must undergo three successive movements, rather than e.g. being direct adjoined to $COMP_i$ at one go? The evidence that *how much heed* must at some stage have become the subject of S_i (the *seems*-clause) is quite convincing: namely, that the verb *seems* agrees in number and person (hence is in the third person singular form) with the NP *how much heed*; and verbs in English agree with their final *subjects*. The evidence that *how much heed* was at an earlier stage the subject of S_j (the *paid*-clause) is rather more oblique; it concerns the fact that the kind of *raising* operation found with verbs like *seem* typically only ever involves raising a subordinate clause *subject* into a position where it is subject of the superordinate *seem*-clause: in particular, it is not possible to raise a subordinate clause object in this way (for reasons we shall discuss later), as we see from the ungrammaticality of:

(44)   *John seems Mary to love — (cf. It seems that Mary loves John)

Thus, in order for *how much heed* to have become the subject of the *seems*-clause, it must first have become the subject of the *paid*-clause by a prior application of NP-MOVEMENT. For a language in which passive participles like *paid* agree with the final subject of their clause, agreement facts give us much more direct evidence in favour of the claim that *heed* must at some time have been the

(43)

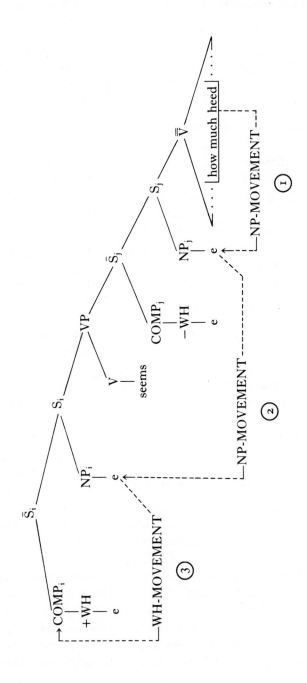

subject of the *paid*-clause. Italian is just such a language: as we see
from:

(45)   Quanta retta sembra esser stata data alla tua proposta?
          How-much heed (fem. sing.) seems to-be been (fem. sing.)
              paid (fem. sing.) to-the your proposal
          'How much heed seems to have been paid to your proposal?'

the fact that *data* 'paid' here agrees with *retta* 'heed' shows that
retta 'heed' must have been a sometime subject of *data* 'paid'. In
other words, before being adjoined to the main clause COMP by
WH-MOVEMENT, the NP *how much heed* must first have
become the subject of the *paid*-clause (by NP-MOVEMENT, alias
PASSIVISATION), and then have become the subject of the
seems-clause (by NP-MOVEMENT, alias SUBJECT RAISING).
Thus, the assumptions made in (43) seem to have a fair amount of
empirical support.

We have argued that the rules must apply in the manner
indicated in (43), in order to account for a variety of facts
(primarily to do with agreement). However, from the point of view
of our linguistic theory, we would hope to find that the way in
which the rules interact in (43) can be explained by some general
theoretical principle concerning the manner in which rules apply.
In order to establish just such a principle, it will be useful to return
to the notion we introduced in (40) of the *domain of application
of a rule*. Let's consider the domains of application of NP-
MOVEMENT and WH-MOVEMENT each time they apply in
(43). The first time that NP-MOVEMENT applies (to move *how
much heed* into NP_j) its domain of application is S_j. On the second
application of NP-MOVEMENT (whereby *how much heed* moves
from NP_j into NP_i), its domain of application this time is S_i; and
when WH-MOVEMENT applies to move *how much heed* from NP_i
and adjoin it to $COMP_i$, its domain of application is $\overline{S}_i$. Now if we
look at these three domains of rule application S_j, S_i, and $\overline{S}_i$, we
notice a fairly obvious fact; namely that of these three nodes, S_j is
the 'lowest' in the tree structure, S_i is the next lowest, and $\overline{S}_i$ is the
'highest'. This suggests that rules apply in Phrase-markers 'from
bottom to top' – i.e. starting at the bottom of the tree, and working
upwards. In other words, rules apply to subordinate constituents
(constituents 'lower' in the tree) before they apply to superordinate

('higher') constituents. This 'bottom-to-top' principle, we might state rather more formally as:

(46)   THE CYCLIC PRINCIPLE (OF THE APPLICATION OF TRANSFORMATIONS)
Any rule-application whose domain is D must precede any rule-application whose domain of application includes (= dominates) D

(46) simply states that 'smaller' (= 'lower' or subordinate) constituents undergo rules before 'larger' (= 'higher' or superordinate) constituents. *Note* that (46) imposes no restrictions on the way rules may apply in two circumstances, viz.

(47) (i)   where two or more rules have the *same* domain of application
(ii)   where two or more rules have *different but not mutually inclusive* domains of application

Let us assume that in the two cases in (47), the rules are free to apply in any random fashion (e.g. simultaneously, or sequentially in a random order, etc.). Just one more piece of terminology: when a rule is applying in some domain D, then node D is said to be *being cycled*. A complete set of rule-applications in some domain D is called a *cycle* (or, the *D-cycle*, or *the cycle on (node) D*). A node which can be the domain of application of at least some rules is called a *cyclic* node. To say that rules apply *cyclically* is to say that they apply 'from bottom to top' in accordance with the CYCLIC PRINCIPLE (46). Any transformation which obeys principle (46) is called a *cyclic transformation*. Any transformation which does not apply in accordance with principle (46) is called a *non-cyclic transformation*. We leave open here the question of whether any principled basis can be found for distinguishing between cyclic and noncyclic rules, and indeed the question of whether there are any noncyclic rules in natural language.

Let's now return to (43), and see whether the CYCLIC PRINCIPLE (46) makes the correct predictions about the order of application of our transformations here. Recall that the order of application we are presupposing for movement of *how much heed* is:

(48) (i)   NP-MOVEMENT into NP_j (in the domain S_j, i.e. *on the S_j cycle*)

   (ii)   NP-MOVEMENT from NP_j into NP_i (in the domain S_i = *on the S_i cycle*)

   (iii) WH-MOVEMENT from NP_i to be adjoined to $COMP_i$ (in the domain $\overline{S}_i$ = *on the $\overline{S}_i$ cycle*)

Furthermore, if we look at the Phrase-marker (tree-structure) in (43), we see:

(49) S_j is included in (= dominated by) S_i, which in turn is included in $\overline{S}_i$

That is, the rules have applied in *exactly* the manner predicted by the CYCLIC PRINCIPLE (46); that is, starting with the rule-application with the smallest domain, and ending with the rule-application with the largest (= most inclusive) domain. To be more precise: firstly, we have application of NP-MOVEMENT on the S_j cycle, moving *how much heed* into NP_j where it becomes subject of the *paid*-clause; then, we have another application of NP-MOVEMENT, this time on the S_i cycle, whereby *how much heed* moves into NP_i and thereby becomes subject of the *seems*-clause; finally, on the $\overline{S}_i$ cycle, application of WH-MOVEMENT moves *how much heed* out of NP_i and Chomsky-adjoins it to the immediate left of $COMP_i$.

   Our discussion of rule-interaction and the cyclic principle has been necessarily scanty: there are complex issues here which cannot easily be skated over. One important question which arises for linguistic theory is:

(50)   What is the set of *cyclic nodes* (= nodes which can constitute the domain of application of some rule(s)) in natural language?

Our discussion of (43) above assumed that both S and S-bar would be cyclic nodes. But what about other categories? Can PP ever be a cyclic node in any language – i.e. are there any rules which apply internally within a PP constituent, but not within any other kind of constituent? A number of linguists have suggested that NP is a cyclic category: for example, if we assume – following Chomsky – that in an NP such as:

(51)   [NP *the city's* destruction — by the enemy]

the italicised NP has been moved out of the position marked —
into the italicised position by application of NP-MOVEMENT,
then we are thereby committed to the assumption that NP-
MOVEMENT can reorder NPs not only within an S, but also
within an NP – i.e. that both S and NP are cyclic nodes for the rule
of NP-MOVEMENT. This in turn raises another general question:

(52)   Do different rules have different domains of application, and if
        so what principle determines what the domain of application of
        any given rule is? (Or, equivalently: Which nodes count as
        cyclic nodes for which rules, and why?)

Once again, these questions raise issues which are too complex to be
discussed here. Suffice it to say for the time being, questions like
(50) and (52) are still being hotly debated. As in any serious field of
enquiry, there are more questions than answers. But one final
comment: even if we accept the CYCLIC PRINCIPLE (46) as a
universal constraint on the manner of application of (at least *some*)
transformations in natural language, in order to achieve *explanatory adequacy* any linguistic theory must still try and explain
why – if they do – rules apply in a *cyclic* fashion, rather than e.g. in
an *anticyclic* fashion, i.e. 'from top to bottom'. Aha . . . another
unanswered question.

Our discussion has assumed that English has *two* distinct movement rules (at least; perhaps more) – namely WH-MOVEMENT
and NP-MOVEMENT. In his most recent work, Chomsky has
investigated the possibility that these two apparently distinct rules
may actually be one and the same rule. Indeed, he goes much
further and suggests the possibility that *all* movement rules in *all*
languages may actually be reflexes of one universal movement
metarule, which he terms α-MOVEMENT ('alpha-movement').
This metarule says simply:

(53)   ALPHA-MOVEMENT
        Move α (where alpha is a category variable, i.e. designates any
        random category you care to choose)

(53) amounts to the principle:

(54)   Move any category anywhere

Now, at first sight (53) might seem absurd: we all know that you
can't just move any constituent anywhere you like in a sentence.

But Chomsky's reasoning is essentially along the following lines. If we know that languages have rules moving constituents from one position into another in a sentence, then we ought to expect (as the simplest hypothesis) that in principle languages allow you to move any constituent anywhere, and if *in practice* this is not the case, then there must be a set of universal or language-specific principles which determine why it's not possible to move certain constituents into certain other positions. The task of *Universal Grammar* is then to discover what these conditions are that 'block' certain types of movement in language, that determine how movement rules apply, and so forth. Thus, the skeletal rule of ALPHA-MOVEMENT (53) will be 'fleshed out' by a set of (hopefully universal) *conditions on rule application* which will specify how movement rules can, and cannot, apply. Many of the relevant conditions we have already looked at. Recall, for example, the STRUCTURE-PRESERVING CONSTRAINT (24), which says:

(55)   STRUCTURE-PRESERVING CONSTRAINT
        A category can only be substituted for another category of the same type

Hence, by (55), an NP can be moved into an NP-position, but not into a V-position. Recall also that in (23) we proposed another condition which we might call the EMPTY NODE CONDITION, which says:

(56)   EMPTY NODE CONDITION
        A moved constituent can only be substituted for an empty category

This says in effect that moved constituents can only move into empty positions (just as people can only move into empty houses). (55) and (56) together specify that a moved NP can only be moved into an empty NP-position, and not e.g. into an empty VP-position, or a filled NP-position, etc. What happens to the position out of which a constituent moves? This again is determined by another universal principle which we looked at earlier, namely the TRACE THEORY CONVENTION (35), which specifies in effect that:

(57)   TRACE THEORY CONVENTION
        A moved constituent leaves behind in the position out of which it moves a coindexed empty node 'trace' of itself

So, when an NP moves, it leaves behind a coindexed empty node

NP, etc. Other universal principles may well determine the position to which a moved constituent is adjoined by *adjunction* operations: it may well be that universal principles determine that *wh*-phrases are adjoined to COMP, rather than e.g. to VP or PP. What these principles might be is a question which must remain unanswered pending much more detailed research. But the general conception of movement developed by Chomsky should be clear: let's start from the assumption that languages ought to allow anything to move anywhere, and if they don't, then let's try and establish what the principles might be that rule out certain types of movements as 'impossible'.

To end with: one more minor terminological complication. We have used various terms to refer to the abstract structures generated by the Base, including Deep Structure, Base Structure, and Underlying Structure; and we have referred to the output of the transformations as Surface Structures. In the past couple of years, however, Chomsky has preferred to use the terms D-structure, and S-structure for each of the relevant levels (for reasons which will become apparent later).

Summary

In addition to the adjunction rule of WH-MOVEMENT, English also has a substitution transformation of NP-MOVEMENT, operating in *passive* and *raising* constructions alike: both of these rules may be reflexes of a more general, perhaps universal, rule of ALPHA-MOVEMENT. Transformations may be subject to a number of general (putatively universal) principles of application, including the following:

(58) (i)   STRUCTURE-PRESERVING PRINCIPLE
A category can only be substituted for another category of the same type

(ii)   EMPTY NODE PRINCIPLE
A moved constituent can only be substituted for an empty category

(iii)   TRACE PRINCIPLE
A moved constituent leaves behind a coindexed empty node trace of itself

(iv)   CYCLIC PRINCIPLE
Cyclic rules apply to subordinate before superordinate constituents

6 More on transformations

Our revised overall model of grammar now looks something like this:

(59) (i) *Base*
     (a) Phrase Structure Rules (categorial rules)
     (b) Lexicon (lexical entries, lexical redundancy rules, word-formation rules, restructuring rules, etc.)
     (c) Lexical Insertion Rule
     Output of Base: *D-structures*

   (ii) *Transformational Component*
     (a) Transformations (WH-MOVEMENT, NP-MOVEMENT, etc. – or perhaps just ALPHA-MOVEMENT)
     (b) Conditions on the application of Transformations (STRUCTURE-PRESERVING CONDITION, EMPTY NODE CONDITION, TRACE CONDITION, CYCLIC CONDITION, etc.)
     Output of transformational component: *S-structures*

The Base Rules generate a set of *D-structures* which are transformed into *S-structures* by the Transformational Component.

EXERCISES

*Exercise I

Some linguists, in earlier work, argued in favour of positing a transformation of DATIVE-MOVEMENT which would have the effect of transforming an underlying structure like (1) (a) into the corresponding derived structure (1) (b):

(1) (a)

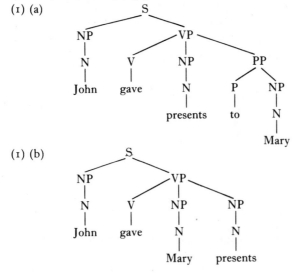

(1) (b)

In more recent work, however, a number of linguists have argued *against* the postulation of any such transformation, on the ground that it is incompatible with the restrictive typology of transformations allowed in the present framework. Show why DATIVE-MOVEMENT could not be analysed as a straightforward structure-preserving substitution. If such a rule did exist, could its domain of application be (i) NP only, (ii) VP only, (iii) S only? (*Note*: in (1) above we have omitted S-bar and its associated COMP for ease of exposition.)

Exercise II

In the following structure:

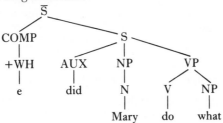

consider the effect of making either of the following two different assumptions

(1)   S-bar is a cyclic node for WH-MOVEMENT, but not S or any other node

(2)   S is a cyclic node for WH-MOVEMENT, but not S-bar or any other node

Would either or both of these assumptions prevent WH-MOVEMENT from applying to adjoin the *wh*-NP *what* to COMP in the above structure? Why?

Exercise III

In earlier work, a different analysis of passive sentences from the NP-MOVEMENT analysis proposed here was assumed: e.g. Akmajian and Heny, in *Principles* (1975, pp. 88–95), propose a single PASSIVE transformation which will directly map the structure (1) onto the corresponding derived structure (2) (we ignore the role of S-bar and COMP here, following their analysis):

(1)

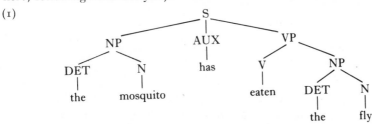

(2)

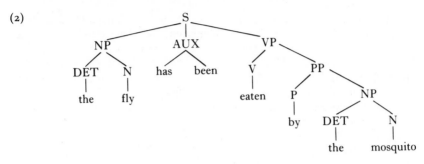

In what ways would such a rule be incompatible with the present framework? That is, why would such a PASSIVE rule be an impossible rule, given the assumptions made in the text?

Exercise IV

Discuss the syntax of the following sentences:

(1)   Who do you think shot himself?
(2)   Where/*Who do you wanna go?
(3)   John was arrested
(4)   John seems to have been arrested
(5)   Who seems to have been arrested?

*Exercise V

Another transformation proposed in earlier work is THERE-INSERTION – a rule which is supposed to map structures like (1) below onto (2):

(1)

(2)

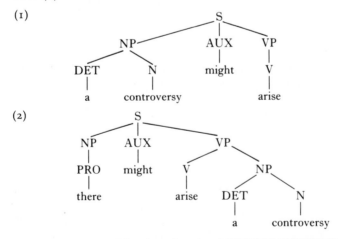

In what ways would any such rule of THERE-INSERTION (at least in the version given above) be incompatible with our present framework?

Exercise VI

In recent work in TG, it has been assumed that there are two types of subjectless infinitive clauses in English, represented respectively by the italicised subjectless infinitive clauses in (1) (a) and (b):

(1) (a)   John seems *to be successful*
    (b)   John tries *to be successful*

Since the italicised clause in either case lacks any overt COMP or subject, we might argue that in each case it has an empty COMP, and an empty subject NP; using the standard convention of representing empty constituents by lower case letters (hence *np* = empty node NP, i.e. [$_{NP}$ e]), and assuming that the main clause also has an empty COMP, we might represent the S-structure of (1) (a) and (b) as respectively:

(2) (a)   comp John seems [$_S$ comp np to be successful]
    (b)   comp John tries [$_S$ comp np to be successful]

But many linguists would argue that the superficial similarities between these two types of infinitive complements conceal important differences. To be more precise, they would argue that the empty *np*-subject of the infinitive after *seems* represents a *trace* of the underlying subject of the *be*-clause *John*, which is subsequently moved into main clause subject position by NP-MOVEMENT, in the manner indicated schematically in (19) in the text. But in the case of (2) (b), they would argue that *John* is not the underlying subject of *be*, but rather the underlying subject of *tries*, and that the underlying subject of the infinitive (*be*) clause is an empty pronominal NP (often designated PRO) which is interpreted as referring back to *John* by an appropriate semantic interpretation rule: i.e. they would argue that the *try*-complement has an 'invisible' pronominal subject both underlyingly and superficially. Thus, in *John seems to . . .* sentences, *John* is the underlying subject of the subordinate (*to*) clause, whereas in *John tries to. . .* sentences, *John* is the underlying subject of the main (*tries*) clause.

One obvious correlate of this supposed difference of underlying structure is the fact that verbs like *seem* (though not those like *try*) permit an idiom chunk subject: cf.

(3) (a)   The fur seems to fly every time they meet
    (b)   *The fur tries to fly every time they meet

If *seem* is a verb which takes SUBJECT RAISING (alias NP-MOVEMENT), but *try* is not, this difference would be simple enough to account for. We might then propose a simple diagnostic for whether a verb which takes an infinitive (*to*-VP) complement is a RAISING verb or not: namely that only RAISING verbs will permit idiom chunk subjects.

In much the same way, some adjectives seem to trigger RAISING and hence allow idiom chunk subjects – cf.

(4) (a)   *The fur* is certain — to fly
  (b)   *The shit* is certain — to hit the fan

(so that *certain* triggers RAISING), while others do not: cf. the oddity of:

(5) (a)   *The fur is anxious — to fly
  (b)   *The shit is anxious — to hit the fan

For convenience, let's use the term *predicate* to subsume *verbs* and *adjectives*. We might conclude from (3)–(5) that predicates like *seem* and *certain* are 'RAISING predicates' (i.e. trigger NP-MOVEMENT) in English, but those like *try* and *anxious* are not.

By devising a set of sentences parallel to those given above, decide for yourself which of the predicates listed in (6) below are 'RAISING predicates', and which are not.

(6)   *Verbs:* want; continue; hope; start; appear; decide; promise; threaten; need; desire; expect
      Adjectives: likely; keen; possible; probable; sure; bound; lucky; desperate; apt; silly; liable

**Exercise VII

In the text, we argued that in *seem – to – VP* structures, the superficial subject of *seem* is an NP which gets moved into its position as subject of *seem*, out of its underlying position as an NP-subject of the subordinate infinitive by a structure-preserving substitution rule of NP-MOVEMENT. Discuss the potential problems posed for this analysis by sentences such as the following:

(1) (a)   Rather plump seems to be how he likes his girlfriends
  (b)   Why she is leaving seems to be an obvious question to ask
  (c)   In Paris seems to be where they first met
  (d)   On Thursdays seems to be when she goes shopping at Harrod's
  (e)   A little too casually seems to have been how he addressed the judge
  (f)   For the Prime Minister to resign seems to be unthinkable

and by the parallel 'passive' sentences like:

(2) (a)   Rather plump is thought to be how he likes his girlfriends
  (b)   . . .etc. . . .

**Exercise VIII

Discuss the apparent problems posed for the Trace Theory account of TO-CONTRACTION (e.g. *want to* → *wanna*) by sentences such as the following, if we assume that the items *go*, *ought* and *have* are verbs which take an infinitival S-bar complement (with an empty COMP and an empty subject):

(1)	The shit is going to/gonna hit the fan
(2)	Tabs ought to/oughta be kept on the president
(3)	The fur has to/hasta fly before long

Suppose we generalise the Trace Theory account from TO-CONTRACTION to *all* types of contraction, so that contraction is always blocked by an intervening trace constituent. What problems would be posed for this generalised Trace Theory account of contraction by sentences such as:

| (4) | Who do you think'll win the competition? (*will* → *'ll*) |
| (5) | Which politician do you think's the best candidate? (*is* → 's) |

FURTHER READING

Note: The works cited below are written in an earlier framework, and hence may present analyses which are incompatible with the present framework, since they do not take account of e.g. the STRUCTURE-PRESERVING PRINCIPLE, the EMPTY NODE PRINCIPLE, the TRACE PRINCIPLE, and so forth.

Akmajian and Heny (1975) *Principles,* pp. 76–398
Bach (1974) *Syntactic Theory*, pp. 73–178
Grinder and Elgin (1973) *Guide*, pp. 69–108
Jacobsen (1978) *TG Grammar*, pp. 269–446
Keyser and Postal (1976) *Grammar*, pp. 193–400
Perlmutter and Soames (1979) *Argumentation*, pp. 1–590

The discussion in this chapter and the last is based on more recent works by Chomsky cited below: these, however, presuppose a number of technical devices that the reader is not yet familiar with, and so should not be tackled until after chapter 9:

Chomsky (1976) *Reflections*
Chomsky (1977) *Essays*
Chomsky (1977) 'On Wh-Movement'
Chomsky and Lasnik (1977) 'Filters and Control'

7
Constraints

Let's assume that English has a transformation of WH-MOVEMENT, whereby a *wh*-phrase (i.e. a constituent containing a *wh*-word like *who, what, which, where, when, why, how*, etc.) is adjoined to an appropriate COMP. For example, the rule operates to transform the underlying structure in each of the (a) sentences below into the corresponding derived structure in (b) (we ignore irrelevant details here):

(1) (a)   +WH you have bought *which car* = WH-MOVEMENT & NP–AUX INVERSION $\Rightarrow$

   (b)   *Which car* +WH have you bought —?

(2) (a)   +WH he might say that he saw *whose car?* = WH-MOVEMENT & NP–AUX INVERSION $\Rightarrow$

   (b)   *Whose car* +WH might he say that he saw —?

(3) (a)   +WH John could claim that you said that you saw *who?* = WH-MOVEMENT & NP–AUX INVERSION $\Rightarrow$

   (b)   *Who* +WH could John claim that you said that you saw —?

We can see from (2) and (3) that WH-MOVEMENT can move a *wh*-phrase out of a subordinate clause, and ultimately adjoin it to the COMP of the main clause; thus, in (2), *whose car* moves out of the *saw*-clause and is ultimately adjoined to the COMP of the *say*-clause; while in (3), *who* moves out of the *saw*-clause, across the *said*-clause, and is ultimately adjoined to the left of the abstract interrogative complementiser (+WH) introducing the *claim*-clause.

Given that – as we have just seen – WH-MOVEMENT can generally extract *wh*-phrases out of subordinate clauses, we should expect to be able to move the italicised *wh*-phrase in (4) (a) out of the (subordinate) relative clause containing it, to be adjoined to the main clause COMP: but in fact, such movement is impossible, since the resultant structure (4) (b) is ungrammatical:

(4) (a)   +WH you have met the man that invented *what* = WH-
            MOVEMENT & NP–AUX INVERSION $\Rightarrow$

     (b)   *What +WH have you met the man that invented —?

One way in which we might seek to handle cases such as (4) would
be by adding the following *rule-specific* exception statement to our
rule of WH-MOVEMENT:

(5)   WH-MOVEMENT can extract a *wh*-phrase out of any type of
            subordinate clause, except a relative clause

However, a problem that arises with a rule-specific condition
such as (5) is that it isn't just *wh*-phrases which can't be extracted
out of relative clauses. For instance, English might be argued to
have a TOPICALISATION transformation which allows certain
types of constituents in a sentence to be fronted (= moved to the
front of a sentence – though not necessarily adjoined to COMP;
this question we leave aside here) in order to mark it as the *topic* of
the sentence – as with the italicised Noun Phrase in:

(6) (a)   I don't think I'd ever do *that kind of thing* = TOPICALISA-
            TION $\Rightarrow$

     (b)   *That kind of thing*, I don't think I'd ever do —.

But it turns out that TOPICALISATION too is blocked from
moving elements out of relative clauses: cf.

(7) (a)   I know a man who does *that kind of thing* = TOPICALISA-
            TION $\Rightarrow$

     (b)   **That kind of thing*, I know a man who does —

Yet a third movement rule which might be proposed for English is
THOUGH-MOVEMENT – the rule which preposes the italicised
AP (= Adjectival Phrase) in (8) (a), and moves it in front of *though*
(once again, for simplicity, we ignore the question of exactly where
the AP is attached to):

(8) (a)   Though I think she is *very pretty*, I don't like her =
            THOUGH MOVEMENT $\Rightarrow$

     (b)   *Very pretty* though I think she is —, I don't like her

But once again, THOUGH-MOVEMENT cannot be used to
extract APs out of relative clauses: cf.

(9) (a)   Though I've met someone who is *very kind*, I don't want to
            marry him = THOUGH MOVEMENT $\Rightarrow$

     (b)   **Very kind* though I've met someone who is —, I don't want to
            marry him

Another movement rule which might be proposed for English is $\overline{\text{V}}$-PREPOSING (alias VP-PREPOSING), which fronts the italicised $\overline{\text{V}}$ in sentences such as:

(10)   I suspected that he would be playing cricket, and *playing cricket* he was —

But this rule too is unable to move constituents out of relative clauses:

(11)   *They said they were looking for a man who was wearing pink tights, and *wearing pink tights* they found a man who was —

A fifth movement transformation which has been widely proposed in the relevant literature is the rule of ADVERB PREPOSING, which fronts the italicised ADVP (= Adverbial Phrase) in:

(12) (a)   I think I'll go to a disco *tomorrow* = ADVERB PREPOS-ING $\Rightarrow$
     (b)   *Tomorrow*, I think I'll go to a disco —

But as with our earlier rules, ADVERB PREPOSING too is blocked from extracting any ADVP out of a relative clause: cf.

(13) (a)   I know someone who's going to a disco *tomorrow* = ADVERB PREPOSING $\Rightarrow$
     (b)   *Tomorrow*, I know someone who's going to a disco —

   To summarise: we have looked at five movement transformations, each of which can generally extract constituents out of subordinate clauses, but none of which can extract any element out of a relative clause. What are we to do? One possibility would be to build rule-specific exception conditions into our formulation of each separate movement rule, along the lines of (14):

(14) (a)   WH-MOVEMENT cannot extract elements out of relative clauses
     (b)   TOPICALISATION cannot extract elements out of relative clauses
     (c)   THOUGH-MOVEMENT cannot extract elements out of relative clauses
     (d) $\overline{\text{V}}$-PREPOSING cannot extract elements out of relative clauses
     (e)   ADVERB PREPOSING cannot extract elements out of relative clauses

But somehow in (14), we seem to be missing an obvious generalisation, since the same exception condition is being stated separately for each of the five rules. To avoid the obvious redundancy and lack of generality in (14), clearly we need some more general condition that is not *rule-specific*, to the effect that:

(15)   No movement rule can extract constituents out of a relative clause

(15) is more general than (14) in an obvious sense; it therefore has greater predictive power. For (14) amounts to saying that it is an accidental property of the particular movement rules listed in (14) that they are subject to the 'no-extraction-out-of-relative-clauses' condition; (14) would thus lead us to expect (implicitly) that we might find some other movement rule of English which is *not* subject to the condition, and *can* extract elements freely out of relative clauses. (15) by contrast stipulates that it is an inherent property of *all* movement rules that they are subject to the 'no-extraction-out-of-relative-clauses' condition, and (15) thus predicts that *no* movement rule in English could ever extract any element out of a relative clause. (14) has *less* predictive power in the sense that it cannot tell us whether other movement rules not listed in (14) will or will not be subject to the relevant condition, whereas (15) tells us that they will be.

A general condition on the application of rules like (15) is called a *constraint*: (15) is thus a constraint on the application of transformations. (*Note*, however, that Chomsky prefers the term *condition on rules*, rather than *constraint*.) The seminal work on *constraints* (on transformations) is J.R. Ross's (1967) MIT PhD thesis *Constraints on Variables in Syntax* (circulated in mimeographed form by the Indiana University Linguistics Club in 1968; the most important parts of it are reprinted and published in a much-shortened version in G. Harman (ed.) *On Noam Chomsky: critical essays* (1974), pp. 165–200). Ross calls conditions like (15) *island constraints*; because in the picturesque metaphorical terminology he introduces, another way of stating (15) informally is:

(16)   Relative Clauses are islands

– the general idea being that once you are marooned on an island, you're stuck there, and can't be got off the island by any movement rule at all. Thus, we might define an island as:

(17)   An island is a construction out of which no *subpart* can be
            extracted by any movement rule (though the *whole island* may
            be moved as one unit)

Many other structures also form *islands* – for example, *Noun
Complement Clauses*: these are clauses which are complements of
head nouns like *fact*, *idea*, *claim*, *theory*, etc: i.e. the *that*-clause in
expressions like:

(18) (a)   the fact *that he has left*
     (b)   the idea *that the world is round*
     (c)   the claim *that you are wrong*
     (d)   the theory *that rules apply cyclically*

Noun complement clauses look superficially rather similar to
relative clauses: there are, however, clear syntactic differences
between the two; for example, relative clauses can either be
introduced by a complementiser (e.g. *that*), or a *wh*-word like *who*
or *which*, whereas Noun Complement Clauses are always introduced by a complementiser, never by a *wh*-word:

(19) (a)   the claim *that/which you made* (Relative Clause)
     (b)   the claim *that/*which you made a mistake* (Noun Complement
            Clause)

Furthermore, a complementiser (e.g. *that*) introducing a relative
clause can often be omitted in English, but omitting the complementiser in a noun complement clause tends to result in a
relatively unidiomatic structure: cf.

(20) (a)   the theory *Chomsky developed* (Relative Clause)
     (b)   ?the theory *rules apply cyclically* (Noun Complement Clause)

Finally, Relative Clauses can be used to modify any head noun,
whereas Noun Complement Clauses are only found after a restricted set of head nouns: cf.

(21) (a)   the car *that you bought* (Relative Clause)
     (b)   *the car *that the world is round* (Noun Complement Clause)

In other words, nouns have to be *subcategorised* for whether they
take a Noun Complement Clause or not, but no nouns have to be
subcategorised for whether they can be modified by a relative clause
or not. This might suggest that there are clear structural differences
between Relative Clauses and Noun Complement Clauses, bearing
in mind that constituents are generally subcategorised in respect of

the range of *sister* constituents they permit. A natural suggestion to this effect within the framework of X-bar syntax would be the following:

(22)   *Relative Clause*

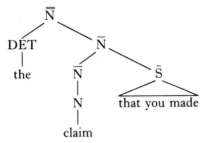

(23)   *Noun Complement Clause*

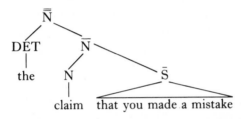

under which Relative Clauses would be complements (= sisters) of an N-bar, whereas Noun Complement Clauses would be complements (= sisters) of an N.

But, to return to Noun Complement Clauses: why did we suggest earlier that they are islands? Well, observe, for example, that WH-MOVEMENT cannot extract a *wh*-phrase out of a Noun Complement Clause: cf.

(24)   **What* can't you explain the fact that he bought —?

Nor can TOPICALISATION:

(25)   **Bananas*, I don't believe the rumour that he hoards —

Nor THOUGH-MOVEMENT:

(26)   **Very intelligent* though I believe your claim that she is—, the fact remains that she can only count up to 5

Nor V̄-PREPOSING:

(27)   *Some say that he was playing cricket, but *playing cricket* I don't believe the unfounded allegation that he was —

Nor ADVERB PREPOSING:

(28)   **Tomorrow*, I have already rejected the possibility that there
         will be a strike —

On the assumption that the italicised constituent in each case
originates in the position inside a noun complement clause marked
by —, and is moved into the italicised position by some movement
rule, then we might account for the ill-formedness of sentences
such as (24)–(28) by a constraint such as the following:

(29)   No rule can move any element out of a Noun Complement
         Clause

This might equivalently be expressed as

(30)   Noun Complement Clauses are islands

Thus far, we have seen that two different types of clauses form
islands – (i) Relative Clauses, and (ii) Noun Complement Clauses.
An obvious question to ask is whether this is just coincidental, or
whether there is some common property which the two types of
clause share. We can see from (22) and (23) above that this is
indeed the case: i.e. in both cases, there is a constraint against
moving any element X out of the bracketed clause in structures of
the type:

(31) $[_{NP} . . .N - [_{\bar{S}}. . .X. . .]. . .]$

Following Ross, we might call structures like (31) *Complex Noun
Phrases – complex* in the sense that they contain a head nominal
modified by a clause. We might then propose to conflate our earlier
RELATIVE CLAUSE CONSTRAINT (15) with our NOUN
COMPLEMENT CLAUSE CONSTRAINT (29), and replace
them both by a single constraint, which – following Ross – we
might call the COMPLEX NOUN PHRASE CONSTRAINT
(often abbreviated to CNPC):

(32)   COMPLEX NOUN PHRASE CONSTRAINT
         No rule can move any element out of a Complex Noun Phrase
         Clause (i.e. no rule can move any constituent X out of the
         bracketed clause in any structure of the type (31))

We might call clauses like that bracketed in (31) *Adnominal Clauses*
(because in a fairly obvious sense, they modify some nominal
constituent). Accordingly, we could paraphrase (32) as:

(33)   No constituent can be moved out of an Adnominal Clause

Let's now turn to look at another type of subordinate clause which is also an *island*. It is not unusual in English (or other languages) for one clause to function as the *subject* of another: for example, in (34), the italicised embedded (= subordinate) clause in each case functions as the subject of the main clause:

(34) (a)   *For you to give up Linguistics* would be a pity
     (b)   *That the world is round* is obvious

But notice that WH-MOVEMENT cannot extract a *wh*-phrase out of a clausal subject:

(35)   **What* would for me to give up — be a pity?

Nor can TOPICALISATION move a constituent out of a clausal subject:

(36)   **Linguistics*, for you to give up — would be a wise move

Nor THOUGH-MOVEMENT:

(37)   **Extremely attractive* though that Mary is — may seem obvious, not everyone thinks so

Nor V̄-PREPOSING:

(38)   **Unzipping his banana*, for him to be — while Mary was talking to him would be extremely rude

Nor ADVERB PREPOSING:

(39)   **Tomorrow*, for him to leave — would be a pity

On the basis of examples such as those above, we might propose (following Ross) the following constraint:

(40)   SENTENTIAL SUBJECT CONSTRAINT
          No constituent can be moved out of a sentential subject (i.e. out of a clause which is itself the subject of another clause)

Alternatively, we might express (40) as:

(41)   Sentential subjects are islands

Thus far, we have seen two types of subordinate clause that form islands: (i) Complex Noun Phrase Clauses, and (ii) Sentential Subject Clauses. Now let's look at a third. As we have already discussed, English has a class of *embedded questions* introduced by a +WH (interrogative) complementiser, which may either be filled by *whether*, or be left empty and have a preposed *wh*-phrase adjoined to it: these two possibilities are illustrated in:

(42) (a)   I wonder *whether* he saw her
     (b)   I wonder *who* he saw —

Notice, however, that WH-MOVEMENT cannot extract a *wh*-phrase out of an embedded question clause (of either type):

(43)   *What* might he ask where/whether I hid —?

Nor can TOPICALISATION:

(44)   *Pornolinguistics*, he asked me when/whether we teach —

And the same is true of THOUGH-MOVEMENT:

(45)   *Popular*, I sometimes wonder why/whether she is —

And of V̄-PREPOSING:

(46)   *Playing cricket*, I don't know where/whether he is —

And of ADVERB PREPOSING:

(47)   *Tomorrow*, I don't know how/whether he's leaving —

On the basis of the above examples, we might follow Chomsky (in a 1962 paper presented to the Ninth International Congress of Linguists) in proposing the following constraint:

(48)   WH-ISLAND CONSTRAINT
          Clauses introduced by a *wh*-phrase (*who*, *whether*, etc.) are
          islands

In the light of more recent work we might express (48) alternatively as:

(49)   No constituent can be moved out of any clause containing a
          wh-phrase in COMP

So far, we have looked at three types of subordinate clause which form islands: (i) Adnominal Clauses, (ii) Sentential Subject Clauses and (iii) *Wh*-clauses. But it isn't just *clauses* of certain types that are islands: on the contrary, other constituents may also be islands. For example, Ross suggests that *coordinate structures* (i.e. structures of the type *X and Y, X or Y*, etc.) are also islands. Thus, WH-MOVEMENT is blocked from *who* out of the coordinate structure *naughty Nelly and who?* in:

(50)   *Who* have you just met naughty Nelly and —?

And TOPICALISATION is similarly blocked from extracting *Mildred* out of the coordinate structure *George and Mildred* in:

(51)   **Mildred*, I really like George and —

And much the same is true of THOUGH-MOVEMENT:

(52)   **Handsome* though he's tall, dark and —, she doesn't fancy him

And of V̄-PREPOSING:

(53)   *The police always suspected that he was sniffing glue and smoking grass, and sure enough, *smoking grass* he was sniffing glue and —

And of ADVERB PREPOSING:

(54)   **Tomorrow*, I might go to a disco today or —

To handle data like (50)–(54) we might – following Ross – posit a constraint along the lines of:

(55)   COORDINATE STRUCTURE CONSTRAINT
          No element can be moved out of a coordinate structure

which in turn can equivalently be expressed as:

(56)   Coordinate structures are islands

Once again, however, we emphasise that to call a given type of structure an *island* is to say that no *subpart* of the island can be moved off the island; this does not of course block movement of the island as a whole: hence the contrast between:

(57) (a)   **What* did you see who and —?
     (b)   *Who and what* did you see —?

In (57) (a), part of the coordinate structure *who and what* has been moved, leading to ungrammaticality; in (57) (b) by contrast, the whole coordinate structure has been moved – and that does *not* violate the constraint (56).

Now we move on to a fifth constraint – the A-OVER-A CONSTRAINT (again suggested by Chomsky in the early 1960s). Consider the following paradigms

(58) (a)   He will emerge out of which tunnel?
     (b)   *Which tunnel* will he emerge out of —?
     (c)   *Out of which tunnel* will he emerge —?
     (d)   **Of which tunnel* will he emerge out —?

(59) (a)   You can study Linguistics up to what age?
     (b)   *What age* can you study Linguistics up to —?
     (c)   *Up to what age* can you study Linguistics —?
     (d)   **To what age* can you study Linguistics up —?

Let us suppose – as seems by no means implausible – that the structure of Prepositional Phrases like *out of which tunnel* and *up to what age* is essentially:

(60) (a)   (b)

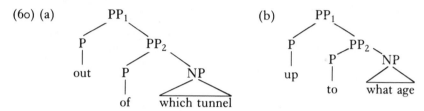

These two structures can equivalently be represented as:

(61) (a)   [$_{PP_2}$ out [$_{PP_2}$ of [$_{NP}$ which tunnel]]]
     (b)   [$_{PP_2}$ up [$_{PP_2}$ to [$_{NP}$ what age]]]

(*Note*: the numerical subscripts used here and below are added solely for ease of identification, and have no special theoretical significance: i.e. PP_1 and PP_2 are both the same type of category, viz. Prepositional Phrase.) How is it that we can prepose NP and PP_1 in structures like those above, by WH-MOVEMENT, but not PP_2? We might seek an answer to this question in terms of the following constraint proposed by Chomsky:

(62)   A-OVER-A CONSTRAINT
            No constituent of category A can be moved out of a larger
            containing constituent of category A (= of the same type)

Notice that PP_2 in (60) and (61) is contained within the larger PP_1 – hence extraction of PP_2 by WH-MOVEMENT is blocked by the A-OVER-A CONSTRAINT. By contrast, the AOAC (= A-OVER-A CONSTRAINT) does not prevent WH-MOVEMENT from preposing either the NP *which tunnel/what age*, or PP_1 *out of which tunnel/up to what age*. Predictably, other movement rules like TOPICALISATION are subject to the same constraint: cf.

(63) (a)   The players will emerge out of this tunnel before long
     (b)   *This tunnel*, the players will emerge out of — before long

(c)   *Out of this tunnel*, the players will emerge — before long
(d)   **Of this tunnel*, the players will emerge out — before long

Before we look at some further applications of the A-OVER-A CONSTRAINT, we pause to consider an important methodological point which arises in connection with the question of *real* and *apparent counterexamples* to constraints. Consider the following paradigm:

(64) (a)   They might fall out over what?
    (b)   *What* might they fall out over —?
    (c)   **Out over what* might they fall —?
    (d)   *Over what* might they fall out —?

Now, if we were to assume that (64) has essentially the same structure as (58), we might then assume that the phrase *out over what* has the structure:

(65) $[_{PP_1}$ out $[_{PP_2}$ over $[_{NP}$ what]]]

In such a case, (64) would be a counterexample to the proposed A-OVER-A CONSTRAINT, since in (64) PP_2 can be moved, but not PP_1. So have we managed to counterexemplify the constraint?

Of course, we have not. Why not? Because our discussion *assumes* without justification that (65) is the constituent structure of the phrase: if, by contrast, we reject this assumption and propose instead that the Verb Phrase *fall out over what* has the structure (simplified):

(66) $[_{VP}$ $[_V$ fall out] $[_{PP}$ over $[_{NP}$ what]]]

in which *fall out* is treated as a 'complex' or 'phrasal' verb, then a principled account can be given of *all* the data in (64). Thus, *what* can be preposed freely in (64) (b) without violating AOAC, because it is an NP not immediately contained within another NP, but rather contained within the PP *over what*. Likewise the PP *over what* can be preposed freely without violating AOAC, because it is not contained within another PP, but rather within the VP *fall out over what*. And finally, the string *out over what* cannot be preposed in (64) (c) because it is neither a PP, nor indeed a constituent (*out* is part of the complex verb *fall out*); and the most fundamental constraint of all on transformations which has been assumed in all transformational work (and much traditional work) is what

Schwartz (1972) termed the UNIT MOVEMENT CON-STRAINT: viz.

(67)   UNIT MOVEMENT CONSTRAINT
        No single application of any transformation can move a string
        of elements which do not form a *continuous constituent*

By contrast, if we were to assume that in (64) the phrase *out over what* is a constituent, and a PP moreover, then we would be left with no principled explanation of why the alleged PP *out over what* cannot be preposed at all, as we see from (64) (c) **Out over what might they fall?*

We can underline this most important point in relation to the following paradigm:

(68) (a)   You don't look up to who?
     (b)   *Who* don't you look up to —?
     (c)   **Up to who* don't you look —?
     (d)   **To who* don't you look up —?

For speakers who share my judgements about (68) (especially (d)), it seems that we have no reason to suppose that either *up to who* or *to who* forms a Prepositional Phrase; it may well be, therefore, that for these speakers *look up to* is a complex phrasal verb, with an NP *who* as its object.

The foregoing discussion highlights the crucial theoretical point that *apparently* similar superficial sequences of categories – in our present cases, sequences of $V - P - P - NP$ – may have *very different* constituent structures. Any discussion of whether a given type of sentence is or is not a counterexample to such-and-such a constraint (or, equally, any discussion of whether certain data are *consistent with* a given constraint) must therefore be prefaced by a discussion of the constituent structure of the sentence concerned, and a justification of the structure assumed.

Just one further complication: bearing in mind the possibility of *structural ambiguity* in natural language, one should also bear in mind the possibility that a given string of words (e.g. a $V - P - P - NP$ sequence) might have more than one possible constituent structure. In this regard, consider the following sentences (my judgements again; others may disagree):

(69) (a)   He was running away from who?
     (b)   *Who* was he running away from —?

(c)   *Away from who* was he running —?
(d)   *From who* was he running away —?

There seem to be two equally plausible analyses of a VP like *running away from who* in (69):

(70) (a)   [$_{VP}$ running [$_{PP_1}$ away [$_{PP_2}$ from [$_{NP}$ who]]]]
    (b)   [$_{VP}$ [$_V$ running away][$_{PP}$ from [$_{NP}$ who]]]

If (70) (a) were uniquely the right structure, then we should expect to be able to *wh*-prepose the NP *who*, and PP$_1$ *away from who*, but not PP$_2$ *from who*, since extraction of PP$_2$ out of PP$_1$ would violate the A-OVER-A CONSTRAINT. If (70) (b) were uniquely the right structure, then we should expect to be able to prepose the NP *who* and the PP *from who*, but not the sequence *away from who* since the latter is not a constituent, and the UNIT MOVEMENT CONSTRAINT (67) forbids movement of nonconstituent sequences. But in actual fact we can prepose both *from who* and *away from who*: the only assumption we can make here which would be consistent with the A-OVER-A CONSTRAINT would be that (69) (a) is *structurally ambiguous*, and hence that *running away from who* can have either of the structures in (70). Of course, if we are to avoid the danger of *circularity* in the argument, we must find independent evidence that this is in fact so.

The essential methodological point which arises from our discussion is one which Chomsky has repeatedly emphasised – e.g. in the following passage:

(71)   Linguistics would perhaps profit by taking to heart a familiar lesson of the natural sciences. Apparent counterexamples and unexplained phenomena should be carefully noted, but it is often rational to put them aside pending further study when principles of a certain degree of explanatory power are at stake.
                    Chomsky, 'On Binding' (1980)

That is, very often *apparent counterexamples* may turn out not to be *real counterexamples*, either because some crucial assumption made in the discussion turns out to be untenable, or because the phenomenon in question is the result of some further, independent principle (perhaps one of a poorly understood nature).

After this brief methodological digression, let's return to the A-OVER-A CONSTRAINT. Consider the following paradigm:

(72) (a)   They might burn which politician's book about China?
    (b)   *Which politician's book about China* might they burn —?
    (c)   **Which politician's book* might they burn — about China?
    (d)   **Which politician* might they burn — 's book about China

Suppose we assume that the phrase *which politician's book about China* has the structure:

(73)   [[[which politician $_{NP_3}$] 's book $_{NP_2}$] about China $_{NP_1}$]

(in which *which politician* is an NP, *which politician's book* is an NP, and *which politician's book about China* is also an NP). Can we then explain why NP$_1$ but not NP$_2$ can undergo WH-MOVEMENT in (72)? Indeed we can; for notice that the A-OVER-A CON-STRAINT will block extraction of NP$_3$ out of its containing NP$_2$; and will also block extraction of NP$_2$ out of the containing NP$_1$. In other words, the A-OVER-A CONSTRAINT makes entirely correct predictions about (72) – provided that we assume that (72) incorporates the structure (73).

Hitherto, we have been looking at a number of *constraints* proposed by Ross and Chomsky during the 1960s. Now we are going to move on to consider some of the more recent constraints (or *conditions on rules*, as he prefers to call them) proposed by Chomsky in the 1970s. Chomsky himself has been one of the sternest critics of his own and Ross's early work on constraints, in more recent times. He argues that while early work on constraints managed to attain a certain degree of *descriptive adequacy* it did not approach (or take seriously enough) the ultimate goal of *explanatory adequacy*. Thus, merely to label a set of constituents as *islands* in a grammar overlooks the fundamental theoretical question of explaining 'Why are *these* constructions, and not others, islands? And why do islands exist at all?' Grammars which simply list an apparently heterogeneous set of constructions as islands lack both *generality* and *naturalness* (i.e. psychological plausibility), Chomsky argues. In place of the essentially idiosyncratic constraints devised in work in the 1960s, he seeks more general and natural constraints with greater genuine explanatory force.

One of the most important of these more general constraints (developed by Chomsky in a number of papers dating from 1971) is the SUBJACENCY CONDITION. For the purposes of our discussion, let's assume without argument that English has a transformation called EXTRAPOSITION (FROM NP) whereby a (certain type of) complement of a (generally indefinite) nominal can be detached from the NP containing it, and *extraposed* (= moved to clause-final position). For example, we might say that the italicised postnominal Prepositional Phrase in (74) (a) can be moved into clause-final position in (74) (b) by application of EXTRAPOSITION:

(74) (a)   A critical review *of his latest book* has just appeared

‖

EXTRAPOSITION FROM NP

⇂⇂

(b)   A critical review — has just appeared *of his latest book*

Perhaps too the same rule operates to extrapose the italicised postnominal clause in cases like:

(75) (a)   A book *which deals with Constraints* has just appeared

‖

EXTRAPOSITION FROM NP

⇂⇂

(b)   A book — has just appeared *which deals with Constraints*

Now consider a more complex case of EXTRAPOSITION FROM NP: observe that in (76) below, the extraposed Prepositional Phrase (italicised) can be positioned after *appeared*, but not after *worrying*:

(76) (a)   The fact that a critical review *of his latest book* has just appeared is very worrying = EXTRAPOSITION FROM NP
⟹

(b)   The fact that a critical review — has just appeared *of his latest book* is very worrying

(c)   *The fact that a critical review — has just appeared is very worrying *of his latest book*

If EXTRAPOSITION FROM NP simply involves rightward movement of some constituent to the end of some clause, why is movement to the end of the *appeared*-clause possible, but not movement to the end of the *worrying*-clause? Chomsky's answer is to propose the following constraint (= *condition on rules*):

(77)   SUBJACENCY CONDITION
        No constituent can be moved out of more than one containing NP- or S-node (in any single rule-application)

(NP and S are thus *bounding nodes* in respect of (77), since they limit the number and nature of the constituent *boundaries* that any moved constituent may cross in any single movement.)

How the SUBJACENCY CONDITION blocks extraposition of the PP in (76) (c) but not (76) (b) should be apparent from:

(78)   The fact that [[a critical review
         of his latest book_{NP}] has appeared_S] is worrying

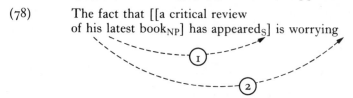

Notice that moving the PP *of his latest book* after *appeared* as in ① above will only move it out of the bracketed NP originally containing it, *a critical review of his latest book*; this does not violate the SUBJACENCY CONDITION (77), since the latter permits movement out of *one* NP (or S). By contrast, repositioning *of his latest book* after *worrying* in (78) as in ② does indeed violate the SUBJACENCY CONDITION, since this time *of his latest book* has moved not only out of the bracketed NP *a critical review of his latest book*, but also out of the bracketed S *a critical review of his latest book has appeared*; this second movement thus involves movement out of *both* an NP *and* an S, thereby leading to violation of the SUBJACENCY CONDITION, which allows only movement out of *one* containing NP- or S-node.

Before we go on to consider how some of the earlier Ross–Chomsky constraints might be subsumed under SUBJACENCY, let's first look at a potential *counterexample* to the SUBJACENCY CONDITION. Consider the possibility of adjoining the *wh*-NP *what* to the main clause COMP in the manner indicated in (79), by application of WH-MOVEMENT:

(79)   COMP[_{S₁} he will think [_{S̄} that [_{S₂} you were doing *what*]]]

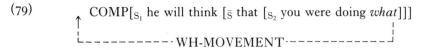

thereby deriving ultimately (assuming application of NP–AUX INVERSION):

(80)   *What* will he think that you were doing —?

Notice that the analysis proposed in (79) contains an obvious violation of the SUBJACENCY CONDITION (77), in that the *wh*-phrase *what* has been moved out of both the S-nodes S_2 and S_1: this violates the condition that no constituent can be moved out of more than *one* containing S- (or NP-) node. Thus, the derivation outlined in (79) violates the SUBJACENCY CONDITION. It might therefore seem that sentence (80) is a *counterexample* to the proposed condition, since the condition appears to wrongly predict that (80) is ungrammatical.

But closer reflection shows that this is not the case at all. For, in actual fact, there is an alternative way of deriving (80) from the same underlying structure as before, without violating the SUB-JACENCY CONDITION. Recall that WH-MOVEMENT in its most general form is formulated as:

(81)   Move *wh*-phrase

and that given putatively universal conditions on the way move-ment rules apply, this amounts to:

(82)   Chomsky-adjoin *wh*-phrase to the left of COMP

Now, we assumed in (79) that the only way in which *what* could be adjoined to the main clause COMP would be if WH-MOVEMENT applied in such a way as to adjoin *what* directly (i.e. in a single movement) to the main clause COMP. But notice that (82) would be equally consistent with an alternative derivation for sentence (80), on which *what* was first adjoined to the subordinate clause COMP by one application of WH-MOVEMENT, and then subse-quently moved from there to be adjoined to the main clause COMP by a second application of the same rule of WH-MOVEMENT, in the manner indicated schematically in (83):

(83)

$[\bar{s}_1 \uparrow$ COMP $[s_1$ he will think $[\bar{s}_2 \uparrow\uparrow [_{COMP}$ that$] [s_2$ you were doing what$]]]]$
└────── ②──────────┘ └───────── ①────────┘

Under the revised analysis in (83), *what* is adjoined to the subordinate clause COMP on the $\bar{S}_2$ cycle, and then moves from there to be adjoined to the main clause COMP on the $\bar{S}_1$ cycle; i.e. *what* moves from the subordinate COMP to the main clause COMP on successive cycles; for this reason, the revised analysis is known variously as the *successive cyclic analysis of* WH-MOVEMENT, or as the COMP-*to*-COMP *analysis of* WH-MOVEMENT. Notice that neither of these two movements of *what* in itself violates SUBJACENCY; on the first movement *what* moves out of S_2, which is allowed by SUBJACENCY which permits movement out of one S-node; on the second movement, *what* moves out of $\bar{S}_2$ and S_1; but this does not lead to any violation of SUBJACENCY, since only S, not S-bar is a *bounding node for* SUBJACENCY; so only one *bounding node* has been crossed.

So, we see that there are in principle two possible ways of deriving (80) from an underlying structure in which *what* originates as a following (sister) complement of *doing*: under the analysis (79) (advocated by a number of linguists, including Joan Bresnan), we have to say that WH-MOVEMENT is not subject to the *bounding* restriction imposed by the SUBJACENCY CONDITION, and hence that WH-MOVEMENT (and other rules like it, for instance TOPICALISATION) is an *unbounded movement rule*, by which a *wh*-phrase can move indefinitely far to the left, across an unbounded number of clause boundaries, into initial position in some sentence (or clause). Under the alternative *successive cyclic* analysis proposed by Chomsky, WH-MOVEMENT is formulated simply as in (82), and is therefore free to apply either in the manner indicated in (79) (unboundedly) or in the manner indicated in (83): *but only if the rule applies successive cyclically* (i.e. in the manner of (83)) *will the resultant derivation be well-formed*. The SUBJACENCY CONDITION, in the case of WH-MOVEMENT, then does not simply rule out particular sentences as ill-formed; rather, it rules out *particular derivations of particular sentences*. But here we shall leave the Chomsky–Bresnan debate about whether rules like WH-MOVEMENT apply in a bounded or unbounded fashion; for the time being, we shall assume – with Chomsky – that the rule *is* in fact subject to the SUBJACENCY CONDITION.

And what about our earlier transformation of NP-MOVEMENT; is this subject to SUBJACENCY, or not? Here, there seems little doubt (or disagreement among linguists) that it must be. Consider a (skeletal) underlying structure such as the following:

(84)   COMP [$_{S_1}$ np is thought COMP [$_{S_2}$ John to want COMP [$_{S_3}$ Mary to win]]]

(where lower case 'np' represents an *empty* NP-*node*; cf. *It is thought that John wants (for) Mary to win*). Let's now ask which of the two lexical NPs in the sentence, *John* and *Mary* could move into the empty main clause subject NP-position? The answer is *John*, not *Mary*: cf.

(85) (a)   John is thought — to want Mary to win
    (b)   *Mary is thought John to want — to win

Why should this be? The SUBJACENCY CONDITION provides an obvious answer; for, movement of *John* into the empty node NP-position 'np' on the S_1 cycle would involve movement across only one *bounding node*, namely S_2; by contrast, movement of *Mary* into *np* on the S_1 cycle would involve movement across *two bounding nodes*, namely S_3 and S_2; but SUBJACENCY permits movement across only one such node.

Thus, sentences like (85) lend clear support to the view that NP-MOVEMENT is subject to the SUBJACENCY CONDITION; failure to apply the rule in a successive cyclic fashion will result in a derivation which is filtered out as ill-formed by the SUBJACENCY CONDITION. Notice, incidentally, that NP-MOVEMENT could not have applied successive cyclically in (84); i.e. it would not be possible for *Mary* to move from subject position in S_3 to subject position in S_2 on the S_2 cycle, and then from subject position in S_2 to subject position in S_1 on the S_1 cycle. One reason is that movement of *Mary* into S_2 subject position would be blocked by virtue of the fact that the S_2 subject position is already filled by *John* (and substitution rules can only move constituents into *empty* nodes).

The same is also true, naturally enough, of the type of NP-MOVEMENT found in so-called 'Subject Raising' (or 'Raising') sentences, such as:

(86)   The fur seems to be likely to fly

Given the classic *idiom chunk argument*, (86) will derive from an underlying structure along the lines of:

(87)   COMP [$_{S_1}$ np seems COMP [$_{S_2}$ np to be likely COMP [$_{S_3}$ *the fur* to fly]]]

(cf. *It seems that it is likely that the fur will fly*). Any movement of the italicised NP *the fur* directly into the empty *np* main clause (S_1)

subject position will involve movement across the two *bounding nodes* S_3 and S_2, and will therefore violate SUBJACENCY; but if *the fur* moves first into the empty *np* position in the *likely*-clause (crossing S_3) on the S_2 cycle, and then moves from there into the empty *np* position in the *seems*-clause (crossing S_2) on the S_1 cycle, then neither of these movements will violate the SUBJACENCY CONDITION, and we thus correctly predict that (86) will be well-formed. But once again, there is no need to stipulate in our formulation of the rule of NP-MOVEMENT itself that the rule is inherently bounded; rather, the rule is allowed to apply freely in either bounded or unbounded fashion, but with the SUBJACEN-CY CONDITION filtering out any derivation of any sentence in which NP-MOVEMENT has applied in an unbounded fashion. To build into our formulation of the NP-MOVEMENT rule itself the condition that the rule apply only in a successive cyclic (bounded) fashion would of course simply be to duplicate in an individual rule-formulation a condition which is already imposed indepen-dently by a general *constraint* (= the SUBJACENCY CONDI-TION) on all rules of a specified type.

As we noted earlier, Chomsky maintains that the SUBJACEN-CY CONDITION is a more *general* and *natural* constraint than those proposed in earlier work in the 1960s; more particularly, he argues that many of the earlier constraints are subsumed in the SUBJACENCY CONDITION. Consider, for example, the im-possibility of extracting a *wh*-phrase out of a relative clause in sentences like:

(88)   *Who are you reading a book that criticises —?

In earlier work, the ill-formedness of such sentences was attributed to violation of Ross's COMPLEX NOUN PHRASE CON-STRAINT (32); but (88) can equally be handled in terms of the SUBJACENCY CONDITION, as we see from (89):

(89)

There are in principle two ways in which *what* could be adjoined to the main clause COMP. One possibility – illustrated in ③ – would be for *who* to be adjoined directly to the main clause COMP; but this would mean that *who* thereby crosses three bounding nodes – S_2, NP_1, and S_1. The second possibility would be for *who* to be adjoined firstly to the subordinate clause COMP on the S_2 cycle (thereby crossing only one bounding node, S_2) and thereafter to be adjoined to the main clause COMP on the S_1 cycle; but this second movement would be across two bounding nodes, NP_1 and S_1, and would therefore violate SUBJACENCY. In short, there is no way of deriving (88) without violating the SUBJACENCY CONDITION. So, in other words, the SUBJACENCY CONDITION obviates the need for the COMPLEX NOUN PHRASE CONSTRAINT.

Chomsky further argues that the same SUBJACENCY CONDITION also obviates the need for the SENTENTIAL SUBJECT CONSTRAINT (40) – a constraint originally designed to account for the ill-formedness of sentences like:

(90)   **What* would for me to do — annoy you?

The only special provision that needs to be made in this case is to assume that all sentential subject complements have the status not only of $\overline{S}$ (clause), but also of NP – so that such complements are, in traditional terms *noun clauses* (or less inaccurately, *nominal clauses*). Given this assumption, then (90) would derive from the underlying structure (91) below:

(91)

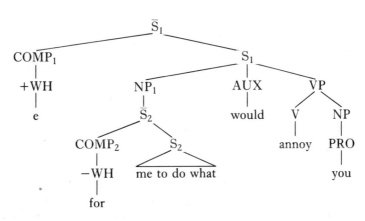

There are then two ways in which *what* might be adjoined to the main clause $COMP_1$, indicated schematically in (92) below:

(92)

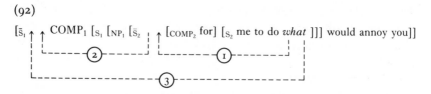

The first is for *what* to be adjoined directly to COMP₁ in a single application of WH-MOVEMENT, as in ③; but this would mean that *what* moves out of three bounding nodes – namely S₂, NP₁, and S₁ – thereby violating SUBJACENCY. The second possibility is for *what* to be adjoined first to the subordinate clause COMP₂ on the $\bar{S}_2$ cycle (thereby moving across only one bounding node S₂), and then subsequently to move from there to be adjoined to COMP₁ on the $\bar{S}_1$ cycle as in ②; but of course this second movement violates the SUBJACENCY CONDITION, in that it involves movement out of the two bounding nodes NP₁ and S₁. Thus, there is no way of deriving sentences like (90) without violating the SUBJACENCY CONDITION; or, in other words, the SUBJACENCY CONDITION obviates the need for the SENTENTIAL SUBJECT CONSTRAINT.

Yet another constraint which can – so Chomsky argues – be subsumed under SUBJACENCY is the WH-ISLAND CON-STRAINT (48) – a constraint designed to account for the ungram-maticality of sentences like:

(93)   *What might he ask whether I hid —?

There are two ways in which *what* might get from its underlying position following *hid* to its superficial sentence-initial position, indicated schematically in:

(94)

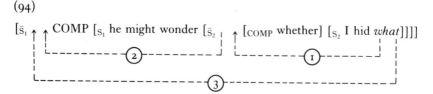

One possibility would be for *what* to be adjoined directly to the main clause COMP₁, as in ③; however, this would involve movement out of two containing bounding nodes, namely S₂ and S₁, thereby violating SUBJACENCY. The second possibility is for *what* to be adjoined first to the subordinate clause COMP as in ①, and then to the main clause COMP as in ②; the first movement crosses S_2, and the second movement crosses S_1. In each case, only *one* bounding node is being crossed in ① and ②, so we might ask *why* (93) should be ill-formed, since there appears to be no violation of SUBJACENCY if WH-MOVEMENT applies successive cyclically. The answer is that there is indeed no violation of SUBJACENCY here; but that adjunction of *what* to the subordinate clause COMP *whether* violates another, independent constraint, viz.

(95)   WH-COMPLEMENTISER CONSTRAINT
No constituent can be adjoined to a COMP which already contains a *wh*-constituent (i.e. a *wh*-complementiser like *whether*, a *wh*-NP like *who, what, which*, a *wh*-adverb like *how*, etc.)

Since the constraint (95) blocks *what* from being adjoined to the complementiser *whether*, *what* cannot be adjoined to the main clause COMP successive cyclically; the only alternative route is – as in ③ – direct attachment to the main clause COMP, and this is of course blocked by the SUBJACENCY CONDITION. Thus, the ill-formedness of (93) is attributable in part to the SUBJACENCY CONDITION (which blocks one way of deriving the sentence), and in part to the WH-COMPLEMENTISER CONSTRAINT which blocks the only other way of deriving it.

But surely – we might object – invoking a new constraint (95) is an entirely *ad hoc* move (i.e. a move designed solely to get us out of this particular difficulty, and lacking any independent motivation)? In actual fact, however, it does seem that there is some independent support for the constraint (95), from paradigms like (96) below:

(96) (a)   He might give what to who?
   (b)   *Who* might he give what to —?
   (c)   *What* might he give — to who?
   (d)   *Who what might he give — to —?
   (e)   *What who might he give — to —?

Notice that in (96), we can adjoin either of the *wh*-phrases *who* and *what* to the (empty) main clause COMP individually; but we cannot adjoin them both to COMP. Why not? A constraint such as (95) would provide a natural explanation for this, provided we assume in addition the UNIT MOVEMENT CONSTRAINT

(67), the latter ensuring that *who* and *what* cannot be adjoined in one movement together to COMP, since they do not form a single constituent. Overall, then, SUBJACENCY provides a *partial* account of the ill-formedness of (93), insofar as it blocks one way of deriving such sentences (other ways are blocked by other constraints).

Overall, then, it seems that the SUBJACENCY CONDITION has considerable generality, since it obviates the need for a number of earlier constraints proposed in the literature. Essentially, what the condition says is:

(97)   No constituent can be moved out of more than one containing bounding node in any single rule-application

So far we have assumed that S and NP are bounding nodes with respect to SUBJACENCY. An important question to ask, however, is whether other nodes might also be bounding nodes, and what the effect of alternative assumptions about bounding nodes might be, for SUBJACENCY.

Suppose we assume, for example, that S-bar is a bounding node with respect to SUBJACENCY. Consider the effect of this assumption on a sentence such as

(98)   *What* did he say that he didn't like —?

Underlying (98) would be the structure:

(99) $[_{\bar{S}_1}$ COMP$_1$ $[_{S_1}$ he did say $[_{\bar{S}_2}$ $[_{COMP_2}$ that] $[_{S_2}$ he didn't like *what*]]]]

If WH-MOVEMENT applies on the $\bar{S}_2$ cycle to adjoin *what* to the left of *that*, the result will be:

(100) $[_{\bar{S}_1}$ COMP$_1$ $[_{S_1}$ he did say $[_{\bar{S}_2}$ *what* $[_{COMP_2}$ that] $[_{S_2}$ he didn't like —]]]]

But if we now try and apply WH-MOVEMENT again on the $\bar{S}_1$ cycle, to adjoin *what* to the left of COMP$_1$, and if we continue to assume that both S and S-bar (as well as NP) are bounding nodes, we find that the resultant move is blocked by SUBJACENCY, since *what* thereby moves across (= out of) two containing bounding nodes, namely S_2 and S_1. Thus, if we assume that S-bar is a bounding node as well as S and NP, our grammar wrongly predicts that sentences such as (98) *What did he say that he didn't like?* are ungrammatical. This is clearly false. The effect of making S-bar a bounding node with respect to SUBJACENCY is effectively to make all movement rules clause-bound (i.e. restricted to reordering elements within clauses, and unable to move elements out of one clause into another). There are languages (e.g. Russian) where WH-MOVEMENT does appear to be clause-bound (at least for certain types of clauses); for such languages, it is appropriate to take S-bar as a bounding node with respect to SUBJACENCY.

But surely not in English. After all, WH-MOVEMENT in English is never clause-bound . . . is it? Well, perhaps there are some cases where it is: consider the following data, from Chomsky's 'On Wh-Movement' (1977) (the judgements are Chomsky's, not mine):

(101) (a) *What did John complain that he had to do — this evening?
      (b) *What did John quip that Mary wore —?

Data like (101) suggest that WH-MOVEMENT cannot extract *wh*-phrases out of the complement of certain types of verbs. But of course, the judgements in (101) would exactly be predicted if we assumed that in English S-bar, S and NP are all three bounding nodes with respect to SUBJACENCY. Let us assume tentatively that this *is* indeed the case – i.e. that S-bar is also a bounding node.

Now we are faced with the converse of our earlier problem: namely that our grammar now predicts that WH-MOVEMENT can never extract a *wh*-phrase out of the complement of any verb at all in English; but this is falsified by examples like (98) *What did he say that he didn't like?* How can we overcome this problem? What Chomsky proposed in 'On Binding' (1980) is that we assume that *universally* S-bar is a bounding node for SUBJACENCY. This then predicts that no *wh*-phrase can ever be extracted out of the complement of any verb. For those languages where specific verbs allow elements to be extracted out of their complements we then 'state that with certain matrix verbs, S-bar does not count as a bounding node for Subjacency' (Chomsky, 'On Binding' (1980)). For example, the lexical entry for *say* would stipulate that *say* is subcategorised as permitting a following noninterrogative tensed (= finite) S-bar complement, and would indicate that this S-bar is not a bounding node. By contrast, the entry for *quip* would state only that *quip* permits a following noninterrogative S-bar complement; since no mention is made of this S-bar not being a bounding node, then it will of course count as a bounding node for SUBJACENCY, so that WH-MOVEMENT will not be able to extract elements out of the complement of verbs like *quip*. Nor will any other movement rule.

If we now stipulate that S-bar, S and NP are bounding nodes for SUBJACENCY, and if we maintain our earlier position that S-bar, S and NP are also CYCLIC nodes, then the question arises of whether we can identify the set of bounding nodes with the set of cyclic nodes. This is a complex theoretical issue which we cannot deal with here; but suffice it to say that many linguists have sought to identify the two (i.e. *cyclic nodes = bounding nodes*).

Let's now move on to another of the more recent constraints proposed by Chomsky: the TENSED S CONDITION. We have already observed that in the 'Raising' construction found with verbs like *seem*, an NP can be moved out of subject-position in a subordinate infinitive complement, to become the subject of the *seem*-clause – schematically:

(102) (a)   comp np seems [$_{\bar{S}}$ comp [$_S$ *John* to like Bill]] $==$ NP-MOVEMENT $\Rightarrow$

(b)   comp *John*$_2$ seems [$_{\bar{S}}$ comp [$_S$ np$_2$ to like Bill]]

(c)   John seems to like Bill

(*comp* in lower case letters represents an empty COMP node; *np* in lower case letters means an empty NP-node; subscripts represent coindices; hence *np*$_2$ represents the trace left behind by movement of *John*). Notice here, however, that the verb in the bracketed subordinate clause is *untensed* (that is, nonfinite – i.e. it cannot carry present or past tense inflections like -*s* and -*d*). By contrast, if the subordinate clause is *tensed* (i.e. contains a verb or auxiliary inflected for tense), then NP-MOVEMENT is blocked, as we see from (103) below:

(103) (a)   comp np seems [$_{\bar{S}}$ comp [$_S$ *John* likes Bill]] $==$ NP-MOVEMENT $\Rightarrow$

(b)   comp John$_2$ seems [$_{\bar{S}}$ comp [$_S$ np$_2$ likes Bill]]

(c)   *John seems likes Bill

So, it seems that NP-MOVEMENT can 'raise' an NP out of an untensed clause, but not out of a tensed clause. How can we account for this asymmetry between these two types of complement clauses? Chomsky proposes that we do so in terms of the following constraint (adapted from a version given in 'On Wh-Movement' (1977), p. 74):

(104)   TENSED S CONDITION
          No rule can involve X and Y in structures of the type:
          $\ldots X \ldots [_{\bar{s}} \ldots Y \ldots] \ldots X \ldots$
          where S-bar is *tensed*

In the case of a *movement rule*, for a rule to *involve* two constituents X and Y means for the rule to move some constituent from position X to position Y, or conversely from position Y to position X. Thus, in respect of movement rules, (104) amounts to:

(105)   No rule can move any element out of (or into) a tensed clause

Consider why the constraint (104) will block 'Raising' in cases like (103); notice that in the underlying structure (103) (a), *John* is contained within the bracketed tensed S-bar *comp John likes Bill*; and that in the derived structure (103) (b), *John* has moved outside this tensed S-bar, thereby violating the TENSED S CONDITION (104). By contrast, in (102) (a), *John* is contained within an *untensed* (infinitival) S-bar *comp John to like Bill*, so that movement of *John* out of this subordinate clause is not blocked here. In consequence, a grammar incorporating the constraint (104) correctly predicts that (102) (c) is grammatical, but not (103) (c).

Let's look at another case where the rule of NP-MOVEMENT is again subject to the TENSED S CONDITION. Observe that NP-MOVEMENT can apply to 'passivise' the italicised subordinate subject NP *the fur* in cases such as (106) below – or more precisely, to move it out of subordinate subject position into the empty main clause subject NP-position, giving (106) (b), which is the derived structure associated with the sentence (106) (c):

(106) (a)   comp np is expected $[_{\bar{s}}$ comp $[_{s}$ the fur to fly]] $=$ NP-MOVEMENT $\Rightarrow$
      (b)   comp the fur$_2$ is expected $[_{\bar{s}}$ comp $[_{s}$ np$_2$ to fly]]
      (c)   The fur is expected to fly

Of course, there is no violation of the TENSED S CONDITION (104) in (106), since *the fur* has been moved out of an *untensed* clause (S-bar). But now consider what happens if we try and move the subordinate subject into the empty main clause subject NP-position in (107) below: this time, the resultant sentence (107) (c) is ungrammatical:

(107) (a)   comp np is expecteds[$_{\bar{S}}$ comp [$_S$ the fur will fly]] = NP-MOVEMENT ⇒
      (b)   comp the fur$_2$ is expected [$_{\bar{S}}$ comp [$_S$ np$_2$ will fly]]
      (c)   *The fur is expected will fly

This time, we do indeed violate the TENSED S CONDITION, by virtue of the fact that *the fur* originates within the bracketed tensed S-bar (which is *tensed* by virtue of the fact that it contains the auxiliary *will* which is inflected for present rather than past (= *would*) tense), and has been moved out of that S-bar. Once more, the TENSED S CONDITION provides a principled account of why the subject of an untensed clause (e.g. the subject of an infinitive) can be passivised, but not the subject of a tensed clause.

Of course, as we have already had occasion to remark, the essence of a *constraint* is that it governs the application not just of *one* rule like NP-MOVEMENT, but rather of a whole class (or even various classes) of rules. So we might ask: Does the TENSED S CONDITION apply to rules other than NP-MOVEMENT? Chomsky argues that it does; and furthermore that not only does it apply to all *movement rules*, but also to certain types of *semantic interpretation rule*, as well. To see this, let's go back to our earlier REFLEXIVE RULE, which we formulated informally as:

(108)   A reflexive pronoun is construed with any preceding NP in the same clause which has the same number, person and gender as the reflexive

Notice that what we have done in (108) is to build into our formulation of the reflexive rule a number of idiosyncratic conditions (viz. (i) the antecedent must *precede* the reflexive, and (ii) the antecedent must be *in the same clause as* the reflexive) which are specific to that particular rule. But the whole programme of Chomsky's research is to eliminate *rule-specific* conditions of application in favour of general *constraints* on whole classes of rules. In keeping with this programme, we might propose to 'strip' rule (108) of all its idiosyncratic (rule-specific) conditions of application, and thereby reduce it to something along the lines of:

(109)   A reflexive can be construed with any other appropriate NP in the Phrase-marker (= Sentence) containing it

(We leave aside the complex question of what counts as an

appropriate antecedent for a reflexive; a naive (and fallacious) view would be that an *appropriate* antecedent is one with the same number, gender, and person as the reflexive.) Having stripped down our REFLEXIVE RULE to a skeletal form like (109), we might now ask whether general constraints like the TENSED·S CONDITION might be used to stop the rule from *overgenerating* (i.e. wrongly construing a reflexive with an NP which cannot be interpreted as its antecedent). In this respect, it is interesting to note the contrast between:

(110) (a)   I consider myself to be right
     (b)   *I consider (that) myself am right

Let us assume that underlying (110) are the respective structures (informally)

(111) (a)   comp I consider [$_{\bar{s}}$ comp myself to be right]
     (b)   comp I consider [$_{\bar{s}}$ comp myself am right]

Recall that the TENSED S CONDITION specifies:

(112)   No rule can involve X and Y in structures of the type:
          . . . X . . . [$_{\bar{s}}$ . . . Y . . .] . . . X . . .
          where S-bar is tensed

In the case of a semantic interpretation rule like the REFLEXIVE RULE, for a rule to *involve* two constituents X and Y means for the rule to *construe* X with Y, or vice-versa. Thus, in the case of semantic interpretation rules, (112) might be paraphrased informally as:

(113)   No rule can construe an anaphor inside a tensed S-bar with an antecedent outside that tensed S-bar (or vice-versa)

Armed with our revised REFLEXIVE RULE (109), and the TENSED S CONDITION (113), let's see how we can deal with the contrast between (110) (a) and (b). Assuming the structure (111), we see that in (111) (a), the REFLEXIVE RULE (109) is quite free to construe the anaphor *myself* with the antecedent *I*, since although they are in different clauses, *myself* is contained within an *untensed* clause and the constraint (113) allows an anaphor in an untensed clause to be construed with an antecedent outside that clause. But now consider (111) (b): here the anaphor *myself* is contained within a *tensed* clause, so that the RE-FLEXIVE RULE is blocked from construing *myself* with *I* by virtue of the fact that *I* lies outside the bracketed tensed S containing *myself*, and the TENSED S CONDITION specifies that no anaphor inside a tensed clause can be construed with an antecedent outside that clause. In other words, if we assume a general REFLEXIVE RULE like (109), the TENSED S CONDITION will correctly predict the contrast between (110) (a) and (b), if we assume the structure (111). Notice, by contrast, that the traditional 'clausemate' formulation of the REFLEXIVE RULE given earlier in (108) could *not* handle the contrast in (110), assuming the structure (111), since we would expect that as *myself* is the subordinate clause subject in both cases, and therefore not in the same clause as *I*, that *myself* cannot be construed with *I* in either case; this is, of course, simply wrong. Thus, if the structure (111) is correct, then sentences like (110) constitute strong counterexamples to the CLAUSEMATE account of reflexives, and evidence in support of the TENSED S CONDITION account. They also show that semantic interpretation rules are also subject to some constraints, as well as movement rules.

But let's return now to movement rules again. Earlier, we noted that NP-MOVEMENT is subject to the TENSED S CONDITION; so a natural question to ask is whether the same is also true of WH-MOVEMENT? Here we run into certain difficulties, which can be illustrated in relation to:

(114)   What will she say that she did?

Given our earlier comments on the successive cyclic application of WH-MOVEMENT, (114) would be derived in the manner indicated schematically in (115) below (where we ignore NP–AUX INVERSION and other irrelevant details):

(115)

$$[_{\bar{S}_1} \text{ COMP}_1 \ [_{S_1} \text{ she will say } [_{\bar{S}_2} \ [_{\text{COMP}_2} \text{ that}] \ [_{S_2} \text{ she did } \textit{what}]]]]$$

WH-MOVEMENT$_2$ WH-MOVEMENT$_1$

On the $\bar{S}_2$ cycle, *what* is adjoined to the left of COMP$_2$, inside $\bar{S}_2$ since *what* has not (on this movement) yet moved outside its tensed S-bar ($\bar{S}_2$), there is no violation of the TENSED S CONDITION on this movement. Then, on the $\bar{S}_1$ cycle, *what* is adjoined to the left of COMP$_1$ by a second application of WH-MOVEMENT. But this second movement of *what* *does* violate the TENSED S

CONDITION, for this time *what* moves out of the tensed $\overline{S}_2$ to be adjoined to the left of COMP$_1$ inside $\overline{S}_1$. Thus the derivation (115) violates the TENSED S CONDITION; furthermore, it should be easy enough to see that the same would be true if *what* moved directly from its underlying position in (115) following *did* to its surface structure position to the left of COMP$_1$, since this derivation too would involve movement of *what* out of the tensed clause $\overline{S}_2$. In other words, there is no way of deriving (114) without violating the TENSED S CONDITION. Or, to put the same thing a different way, our present analysis wrongly predicts that sentences like (114) are ungrammatical: i.e. sentences like (114) are counterexamples to our present formulation of the TENSED S CONDITION.

In this situation, we are faced with two choices: either abandon the TENSED S CONDITION altogether, or modify it in some way so that it becomes consistent with examples like (114). To abandon the condition entirely would seem unfortunate, since the condition appears to have genuine explanatory value in cases like (102), (103), (106), (107) and (110). Hence, it seems more sensible to modify the condition in some way such that it can then handle counterexamples like (114). One possibility – suggested by Chomsky in 'On Wh-Movement' (1977), p. 85, ex. 46 – would be to modify the TENSED S CONDITION by adding the italicised condition in (116) below:

(116)   TENSED S CONDITION (revised version)
No rule can involve X and Y in structures of the type:
$\ldots$ X $\ldots$ [$_{\overline{S}}$ $\ldots$ Y $\ldots$] $\ldots$ X $\ldots$
where $\overline{S}$ is tensed, and *where Y is not in COMP*

Consider now the effect of the revised formulation on our derivation (115); on its first movement, *what* is not in COMP, and does not move out of the tensed $\overline{S}_2$, but rather is Chomsky-adjoined to the left of COMP$_2$, giving the substructure in (117) below:

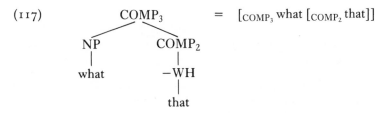

(117)   COMP$_3$ =   [$_{COMP_3}$ what [$_{COMP_2}$ that]]

Thus, on this first movement, there is clearly no possible violation of the TENSED S CONDITION. But now consider the second movement of *what*: this time it does indeed move out of a tensed S-bar, namely $\overline{S}_2$, so once again it appears that this second movement violates the TENSED S CONDITION. But closer reflection shows this is not the case, since our revised condition (116) stipulates that movement out of a tensed S-bar is permitted just in case the moved constituent is contained in COMP prior to its movement; and this is precisely the case with the second application of WH-MOVEMENT in (115), for *what* immediately prior to movement is contained within COMP in the manner detailed in (117). To see this, consider the rather more detailed outline of the *second* application of WH-MOVEMENT in (115) given below:

(118)

$[_{\overline{S}_1}$ COMP$_1$ $[_{S_1}$ she will say $[_{\overline{S}_2}$ $[_{COMP_3}$ *what* $[_{COMP_2}$ that$]]$ $[_{S_2} \ldots]]]]$

└ ─ ─ ─ ─ WH-MOVEMENT$_2$ ─ ─ ─ ─ ─ ┘

It should be clear from (118) that although *what* does indeed move out of the tensed S-bar $\overline{S}_2$ on this second movement, it is being moved out of a containing COMP-node (namely COMP$_3$), and since the revised condition (116) permits movement of an element in COMP out of a tensed S-bar, then there is no longer any violation of the TENSED S CONDITION in (118). In other words, sentences like (114) are no longer counterexamples to the (revised) TENSED S CONDITION. The effect of the proposed revision is thus to ensure that WH-MOVEMENT need not violate the TENSED S CONDITION (provided it applies successive cyclically).

Now let's move on to consider one final constraint proposed by Chomsky in his more recent work, namely the SPECIFIED SUBJECT CONDITION. In the version given in 'On Wh-Movement' (1977), p. 74, this says:

(119)   No rule can involve X and Y in structures of the type:
          $\ldots X \ldots [_\alpha \ldots Y \ldots] \ldots X \ldots$
          where α is an S-bar or NP which contains a specified subject
          (i.e. a subject not containing Y and not controlled by X)

Bearing in mind that *involve X and Y* in the case of movement rules means move some constituent from Y to X (or vice-versa), and ignoring for the sake of ease of exposition the complex condition in parentheses in (119), we can say that in the case of movement rules, (119) amounts to:

(120)   No rule can move a nonsubject constituent out of a clause (S-bar) or NP with a (specified) subject (where by *nonsubject constituent* we mean a constituent which is neither a subject, nor part of a subject)

Let's first of all see how the constraint (119) deals with potential cases of overgeneration by the rule of NP-MOVEMENT. Let's go back to our earlier underlying structure (102) (a), repeated here in more skeletal form as (121):

(121)   comp np seems [$_{\bar{S}}$ comp John to like Bill]

Earlier, we saw that NP-MOVEMENT can apply to move *John* into the empty NP subject-position in the *seems*-clause, giving (102) (c) *John seems to like Bill*; this derivation violates neither the SUBJACENCY CONDITION, nor the TENSED S CONDITION. But what prevents NP-MOVEMENT from moving not *John*, but rather *Bill* into the empty main clause subject-position, giving the derived structure (122) below:

(122)   comp Bill$_2$ seems [$_{\bar{S}}$ comp John to like np$_2$]

The answer is that neither the SUBJACENCY CONDITION nor the TENSED S CONDITION will prevent this, since neither are thereby violated. If we look at (119) – and its more informal counterpart (120) – we see however that the SPECIFIED SUBJECT CONDITION is indeed violated by the movement of *Bill* into main clause subject position, since *Bill* is a nonsubject constituent of an S-bar (bracketed) which has the subject *John*; movement of the nonsubject *Bill* across the subject *John* thus violates the SPECIFIED SUBJECT CONDITION, so that our grammar correctly predicts that the resulting sentence:

(123)   *Bill seems John to like

is ungrammatical. In contrast, movement of the subject *John* in (121) *is* allowed, since *John* is a subject, and the constraint only blocks movement of nonsubjects.

Now let's see whether the SPECIFIED SUBJECT CONDITION also avoids overgeneration by the rule of NP-MOVEMENT in the case of passive sentences. Consider an underlying structure like:

(124)   comp np is expected [$_{\bar{S}}$ comp John to help Mary]

If NP-MOVEMENT applies to move the subordinate subject *John* into the empty main clause subject-position here, there is no violation of the SPECIFIED SUBJECT CONDITION, since *John* is a subject constituent, and the constraint only blocks movement of nonsubjects: thus, the resultant sentence:

(125)   John is expected to help Mary

is well-formed. But consider now what happens if we apply NP-MOVEMENT to move the object *Mary* into the empty main clause subject-position. The result is then an ungrammatical sentence, viz.

(126)   *Mary is expected John to help

Why is this? Clearly, the SPECIFIED SUBJECT CONDITION (119/120) provides the answer: for in (126) a nonsubject constituent (*Mary*) has been moved out of a clause with a subject (*John*), thereby violating the constraint.

As before with the TENSED S CONDITION, we might ask whether the SPECIFIED SUBJECT CONDITION generalises from movement rules to semantic interpretation rules. There is some evidence that it does: consider the following contrast:

(127) (a)   Mary considers herself to have outwitted John
      (b)   *Mary considers John to have outwitted herself

Let us suppose that the sentences (127) have the respective structures:

(128) (a)   comp Mary considers [$_{\bar{S}}$ comp herself to have outwitted John]
      (b)   comp Mary considers [$_{\bar{S}}$ comp John to have outwitted herself]

Recall that in the case of an interpretation rule, for a rule to *involve* two constituents X and Y means for it to construe X with Y, or vice-versa; thus (again ignoring details), we might paraphrase the constraint (119) informally along the lines of (129) below, with respect to its effect on semantic interpretation rules:

(129)   No rule can construe a nonsubject anaphor contained within a clause (S-bar) or NP which has a subject with some constituent outside that clause or NP

Notice that the condition (129) does not prevent the REFLEXIVE RULE from construing *herself* with *Mary* in (128) (a), since *herself* is a subject anaphor, and the constraint only applies to *nonsubject* anaphors. But in (128) (b) by contrast, the constraint *does* prevent the REFLEXIVE RULE from construing *herself* with *Mary* since *herself* is a nonsubject constituent of a (bracketed) clause with a subject (*John*), and the potential antecedent *Mary* lies outside that clause. But if *herself* in (128) (b) cannot be construed with *Mary*, and if there is no other appropriate antecedent for *Mary* in the sentence, then the resultant sentence (127) (b) is simply uninterpretable by virtue of the fact that the anaphor *herself* cannot be assigned an antecedent.

So it seems that just like the TENSED S CONDITION, the SPECIFIED SUBJECT CONDITION constrains the application not only of movement rules, but also of semantic interpretation rules. However – again, just as with the Tensed S Condition – the Specified Subject Condition runs into apparent problems with respect to WH-MOVEMENT. Consider again our earlier problem sentence (114) *What will she say that she did?*, and the schematic derivation outlined for it in (115) above. Notice that the second movement of *what*, out of $\overline{S}_2$ to be adjoined to COMP$_1$ on the $\overline{S}_1$ cycle involves movement of a nonsubject constituent (*what*) out of an S-bar ($\overline{S}_2$) which has a specified subject (*she*), thereby violating the SPECIFIED SUBJECT CONDITION. In other words, our present version of the SPECIFIED SUBJECT CONDITION (119) wrongly predicts that (114) *What will she say that she did?* is ungrammatical. Clearly, then, we need to revise (119), perhaps along the familiar lines suggested by Chomsky in 'On Wh-Movement' (1977), p. 85, by adding the condition '*where Y is not in COMP*'. The revised version thus becomes:

(130)   SPECIFIED SUBJECT CONDITION (revised)
No rule can involve X and Y in structures of the type:
$$\ldots X \ldots [_\alpha \ldots Y \ldots] \ldots X \ldots$$
where α is an S-bar or NP with a specified subject, and where Y is not in COMP

If we now return to the second movement of *what* in (115) or (118), we see that although *what* is moving out of an S-bar (namely $\overline{S}_2$) with a subject (namely *she*), there is no violation of the SPECI-FIED SUBJECT CONDITION here because *what* is actually in

COMP$_3$ (see (118)) immediately prior to the second application of WH-MOVEMENT, and our revised condition (130) allows constituents to 'escape' out of COMP, since in the case of movement rules, (130) amounts to:

(131) No rule can move a nonsubject constituent not in COMP out of a clause (S-bar) or Noun Phrase with a specified subject

Thus, as before with the TENSED S CONDITION, a simple modification of our original formulation of the condition, by adding the phrase 'where Y is not in COMP' will ensure that WH-MOVEMENT can continue to extract constituents out of tensed clauses, or clauses which have specified subjects. This COMP CONDITION is sometimes referred to as the COMP *escape hatch*, because its effect is to ensure that constituents can only 'escape' out of a tensed clause, or a clause with a specified subject, if they are first moved into COMP. Rather inaccurately we might then say that the only rules which are – in effect – not subject to Tensed Subject Condition or Specified Subject Condition are rules which adjoin elements to COMP – e.g. WH-MOVEMENT.

Having looked at a wide variety of constraints which have been proposed in the relevant literature, we should add one final comment on how such constraints are to be understood. One possible interpretation is the *absolute* interpretation, namely that no rule in any language can ever under any circumstances violate *any* of the constraints applicable to that type of rule. A second interpretation (and the one supported by Chomsky) is the *relative* interpretation under which all rules in all languages would be expected to obey the relevant constraints *in the unmarked case* (i.e. 'normally'), but particular *marked* (i.e. exceptional) rules might have built into their formulation the condition that they do in fact violate one or more of the constraints. This allows for the possibility that particular rules in English or other languages may violate particular constraints.

Summary

The Transformational Component of a grammar includes as well as transformations like WH-MOVEMENT, NP-MOVEMENT, and others (or perhaps ALPHA-MOVEMENT), a number of general

CONSTRAINTS or CONDITIONS ON TRANSFORMA-
TIONS such as those mentioned in chapter 6 (e.g. the STRUC-
TURE-PRESERVING CONSTRAINT, etc.), and those dealt
with in this chapter, which we might summarise informally as in
(132) below:

(132) (i)   *COMPLEX NOUN PHRASE CONSTRAINT* (CNPC) – Ross
(32)
No element can be extracted out of an adnominal clause

(ii)   *SENTENTIAL SUBJECT CONSTRAINT* (SNSC) – Ross
(40)
No element can be moved out of a clause which is the subject
of another clause

(iii)   *WH-ISLAND CONSTRAINT* (WHIC) – Chomsky (48)
No element can be moved out of a clause containing an overt
wh-complementiser or *wh*-phrase in COMP

(iv)   *COORDINATE STRUCTURE CONSTRAINT* (CSC) – Ross
(55)
No element can be moved out of a coordinate structure

(v)   *A-OVER-A CONSTRAINT* (AOAC) – Chomsky (62)
No constituent of category A can be moved out of a larger
containing constituent of category A

(vi)   *UNIT MOVEMENT CONSTRAINT* (UMC) – Schwartz (67)
Only a string of elements which form a constituent can be
moved together in any single application of any movement rule

(vii)   *SUBJACENCY CONDITION* (SC) – Chomsky (77)
No constituent can move across more than one bounding node
in any single rule application (bounding nodes = S & NP, and
perhaps also S-bar)

(viii)   *COMPLEMENTISER CONSTRAINT* (CC) – Chomsky (95)
No constituent can be adjoined to a COMP which already
contains a *wh*-constituent

(ix)   *TENSED S CONDITION* (TSC) – Chomsky (116)
No constituent of a tensed clause (= S-bar) not in COMP can
be moved outside that tensed clause, or construed with any
element outside that tensed clause

(x)   *SPECIFIED SUBJECT CONDITION* (SPSC) – Chomsky
(130)
No nonsubject constituent of a clause or NP with a specified
subject can be moved (or construed with any constituent)
outside that clause or NP, unless it is in COMP

Our overall model of grammar now looks something like this:

(133) (i)   *Base*
(a) Phrase Structure Rules (categorial rules)

(b) Lexicon (lexical entries, lexical redundancy rules, word-formation rules, restructuring rules, etc.)
(c) Lexical Insertion Rule
Output of Base: *D-structures*
(ii) *Transformational Component*
   (a) Transformations   (WH-MOVEMENT,   NP-MOVE-MENT, etc. – or perhaps just ALPHA-MOVEMENT)
   (b) Conditions (= Constraints) on Transformations (e.g. STRUCTURE-PRESERVING CONDITION, EMPTY NODE CONDITION, TRACE CONDITION, CYCLIC CONDITION, COMPLEX NOUN PHRASE CONSTRAINT, SENTENTIAL SUBJECT CONSTRAINT, WH-ISLAND CONSTRAINT, COORDINATE STRUCTURE CONSTRAINT, A-OVER-A CONSTRAINT,   UNIT   MOVEMENT   CONSTRAINT, SUBJACENCY CONDITION, COMPLEMENTISER CONSTRAINT, TENSED S CONDITION, SPECIFIED SUBJECT CONDITION, etc.)
Output of Transformational Component = *S-structures*

EXERCISES

Exercise I

Discuss the ways in which WH-MOVEMENT might apply in the following sentences, and which constraints – if any – might be violated, assuming in each case that the italicised *wh*-phrase originates in the position marked —.

(1)   *Who* will he claim that you said you saw —?
(2)   *What* won't he believe the allegation that Mary did —?
(3)   *Who* are you anxious about whether you'll get a Valentine card from —?
(4)   *What* would for Harry to read — be a good idea?
(5)   *Who* won't he talk to Mary or —?
(6)   *To which stranger* did she walk up — in the street?

Exercise II

Discuss the ways in which NP-MOVEMENT might apply in the following structures to move the italicised NP out of the position marked — into the italicised position, and what constraint(s) – if any – might thereby be violated.

(1) (a) $[_{\bar{S}_1}$ *John* seems $[_{\bar{S}_2}$ to be unlikely $[_{\bar{S}_3}$ — to win the prize]]]
   (b) $[_{\bar{S}_1}$ *John* seems $[_{\bar{S}_2}$ is unlikely $[_{\bar{S}_3}$ — to win the prize]]]
   (c) $[_{\bar{S}_1}$ *John* seems $[_{\bar{S}_2}$ to be unlikely $[_{\bar{S}_3}$ — will win the prize]]]
   (d) $[_{\bar{S}_1}$ *The prize* seems $[_{\bar{S}_2}$ to be unlikely $[_{\bar{S}_3}$ John to win —]]]

Exercise III

Assume that in a Noun Phrase like *Mary's pictures of John*, *Mary* is the *subject* of that Noun Phrase; but that a Noun Phrase like *pictures of John* or *those/these/the/some pictures of John* is *subjectless*. Assume also a very general formulation of the REFLEXIVE RULE along the lines of:

(1)   A reflexive can be construed with any appropriate antecedent in the same sentence

Now discuss which constituents can serve as the antecedent of the reflexive in the examples below, and which constraints block overgeneration by the rule (1):

(2)   John knows that Fred admires himself
(3)   John likes Fred's pictures of himself
(4)   John collects pictures of himself
(5)   John told Fred that himself was wrong
(6)   John told Fred about Mary's photos of himself
(7)   Photos of himself never flatter Fred
(8)   John's photos of himself annoy Fred.

*Exercise IV

In sentences such as:

(1)   John wrote/destroyed a book about Nixon

there could in principle be two distinct structures which the sequence *a book about Nixon* might have: either *a book about Nixon* might form a single NP constituent, along the lines of:

(2)   John wrote/destroyed [NP a book about Nixon]

Or alternatively, *a book* might be a separate NP constituent, and the sequence *about Nixon* a separate PP constituent (so that the sequence *a book about Nixon* is not one constituent but two), so that we have the structure:

(3)   John wrote/destroyed [NP a book] [PP about Nixon]

There is of course a third possibility, namely that the sequence *a book about Nixon* might be structurally ambiguous, and therefore might have either of the analyses in (2) or (3) above.
In the light of these three possibilities, consider the following sentences:

(4) (a)   How many books about Nixon did John write?
    (b)   How many books did John write about Nixon?
    (c)   Who did John write a book about?
    (d)   A book about Nixon was written
    (e)   A book was written about Nixon
(5) (a)   How many books about Nixon did John destroy?
    (b)   *How many books did John destroy about Nixon?

(c)   *Who did John destroy a book about?
(d)   A book about Nixon was destroyed
(e)   *A book was destroyed about Nixon

Assuming the grammaticality judgements given above, which structure(s) would be appropriate for *write a book about Nixon*, andswhich for *destroy a book about Nixon*? (Assume that the three possibilities are (i) only (2); (ii) only (3); (iii) either (2) or (3).)

Given the structure(s) you assume, discuss whether or not the SUB-JACENCY CONDITION would be sufficient to account for the ungrammaticality of *all* the asterisked examples.

Exercise V

Discuss which of the following sentences (if any) are ungrammatical in your idiolect:

(1)   Who do you regret that John insulted?
(2)   Who does she realise that they have arrested?
(3)   What is it true/false/likely that John did?
(4)   Where did he grunt that he was going?
(5)   Where is it strange that you met her?
(6)   What did he stammer that he had seen?
(7)   What did he snap that he would never do?
(8)   Which type of breakfast cereal did he mutter that he couldn't stand?

In the light of your judgements, discuss the possibility that WH-MOVEMENT might be lexically governed. If it is, what implications follow from this in relation to SUBJACENCY, lexical entries, etc.?

*Exercise VI

There are a class of subordinate clauses sometimes known as 'adverbial clauses' which are introduced by so-called 'subordinating conjunctions' like *when, while, because, before, after, if*, etc. These 'conjunctions' can take tensed clause complements, but we might wonder whether their clausal complements have the status of S, or S-bar: i.e. we might ask whether a phrase like *when I came home* has the structure (1) (a) or (1) (b):

(1) (a)   when [$_S$ I came home]
    (b)   when [$_{\bar{S}}$ comp [$_S$ I came home]]

Show that the SUBJACENCY CONDITION, TENSED S CONDITION, and SPECIFIED SUBJECT CONDITION would make different predictions about the possibility or otherwise of WH-MOVEMENT applying to move the italicised wh-phrase out of the — position in the sentences below, depending on which analysis we choose. Which analysis makes the right predictions?

(2)   *Which film* did you fall asleep when you were watching —?

(3)   *Which film* did the Arabs get annoyed because the TV companies showed —?

(4)   *Which film* did you feel sick after you'd seen —?

(5)   *Which film* do you get angry if they show —?

*Exercise VII

What kind of constraint might be proposed to block overgeneration in the ungrammatical sentences below (assume the judgements given):

(1) (a)   *Who* do you think (that) he saw —?
    (b)   *Who* do you think (that) he spoke to —?
    (c)   *Who* do you think — will come to the party?
    (d)   **Who* do you think that — will come to the party?

(2) (a)   *What* would you like (for) me to do —?
    (b)   *Who* would you like (for) me to talk to —?
    (c)   *Who* would you like — to come to the party?
    (d)   **Who* would you like for — to come to the party?

Show how this constraint you propose, together with the WH-ISLAND CONSTRAINT might provide a principled account of the relative ill-formedness of sentences like the following:

(3) (a)   ?*Who* do you wonder whether he met —?
    (b)   ?*Who* do you wonder whether he talked to —?
    (c)   **Who* do you wonder whether — is coming to the party?

**Exercise VIII

In the text, we argued that sentences like:

(1)   I consider myself to be right

are consistent with an analysis in terms of Chomsky's *conditions* (e.g. the TENSED S CONDITION, and the SPECIFIED SUBJECT CONDITION), and inconsistent with the *clausemate* analysis of reflexives, provided that we assume that (1) has the structure:

(2)   comp I consider [$_{\bar{S}}$ comp myself to be right]

so that *myself* is the subject of the *be*-clause. But an alternative analysis of V–NP–to–VP structures with verbs like *want*, *consider*, etc. which was proposed in earlier work (cf. e.g. Postal, *On Raising* (1974)) is that in such cases the preinfinitival NP represents the underlying subject of the infinitive, but the superficial object of the main clause, having been 'raised' into the main clause by the rule of SUBJECT-TO-OBJECT RAISING. If we adapt the RAISING analysis to our present framework, this would mean that we might propose that (1) has the S-structure (3) below:

(3)   comp I consider *myself*$_2$ [$_{\bar{S}}$ comp np$_2$ to be right]

where *myself* has been moved out of subordinate subject into main clause object position by NP-MOVEMENT, and np_2 is the trace left behind by this movement. Assuming that the rule of REFLEXIVE INTERPRETATION operates on S-structure not on D-structure, discuss whether either the *clausemate* account, or the *conditions* account, or both, would be compatible with the alternative analysis (3). Given the NP-MOVEMENT analysis (3), how could we account for the ill-formedness of:

(4)   *I consider myself is right?

(You should be able to come up with at least *two* different reasons why (4) is ill-formed.) Which of the two accounts (the *clausemate* account and the *conditions* account) could best handle cases like:

(5)   I arranged for myself to be woken up early

**Exercise IX

Discuss the problems posed for the COORDINATE STRUCTURE CONSTRAINT by sentences such as the following

(1)   Noam Chomsky, I've always admired – and Nim Chimpsky, too
(2)   What did you go and do that for?
(3)   Which of your televisions did he try and mend?
(4)   Which of your students did you take an axe and kill?

Can you think of any ways of overcoming at least some of these problems?

**Exercise X

In earlier work in TG in the mid 1960s, a distinction was drawn between two types of movement transformation: *chopping* and *copying* transformations. A *chopping* rule moves a constituent from position X to position Y without leaving any overt constituent behind in position Y; a *copying* rule moves a constituent from X to Y, and simultaneously inserts a pronoun in position Y which agrees with the moved constituent in person, number, gender, etc. To see the difference between the two types of rule, take a D-structure like:

(1)   I can't stand *John*

By applying the *chopping* transformation of TOPICALISATION to the italicised constituent, we can prepose *John* to give:

(2)   *John*, I can't stand —

and notice that here the position out of which *John* has moved (marked by —) is left empty. But by applying the corresponding *copying* rule of LEFT DISLOCATION to *John*, we end up instead with the S-structure:

(3)   *John*, I can't stand *him*

where not only has *John* been preposed, but in the position out of which he has moved, a copy pronoun (*him*) is left behind.

More recently, linguists have cast doubt on the claim that copying rules exist, and have treated structures such as (3) as *base-generated* (i.e. not involving any movement of any constituent). If we assume that movement rules are subject to constraints such as those in (132), what problems would be posed for the *movement* analysis of *dislocation* structures like (3) by sentences such as the following (assume that they are all grammatical):

(4)   *John*, I know someone who can't stand *him*
(5)   *John*, I sometimes wonder why nobody likes *him*
(6)   *John*, Mary has invited Paul and *him* to her party

If we further assume that copying rules are supposed to involve a copy pronoun being left behind which agrees in person, number and gender with the moved constituent, what problems are posed for this assumption (and hence more generally for the assumption that copying rules exist at all) by sentences such as:

(7)   *The man next door*, I can't stand *her*
(8)   *The little brat across the road*, I can't stand *it*
(9)   *John*, I can't stand *the bastard*
(10)   *John*, *the silly fool* gives me the creeps
(11)   *John*, *the silly, incompetent, arrogant fool* gives me the creeps

Exercise XI

In the text, we argued that (76) (c) is ungrammatical because it violates the SUBJACENCY CONDITION, in that it involves movement of the PP *of his latest book* across both an NP-node and an S-node (hence across more than one bounding node). The tacit assumption made here (cf. (78)) is that the rule concerned (EXTRAPOSITION FROM NP) cannot apply successive cyclically in the manner indicated below:

(1)

The fact that [[a critical review *of his latest book* NP] has appeared S] is worrying S]

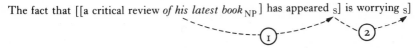

Consider the following two alternative formulations of the relevant EXTRAPOSITION rule:

(2)   Extrapose PP
(3)   Extrapose a PP contained in a structure of the form [NP NP – PP]

Which formulation of the rule would prevent successive cyclic application of the rule in (1), and why?

FURTHER READING

Ross's constraints

Note: These works are written in an earlier framework.

Ross (1968) *Constraints on Variables in Syntax*
Ross (1974) 'Excerpts'
Perlmutter and Soames (1979) *Argumentation*, pp. 277–319.

Chomsky's conditions

Note: These works are primary literature and difficult to follow.

Chomsky (1976) *Reflections*, pp. 78–118
Chomsky (1977) *Essays*, pp. 81–210
Chomsky (1977) 'On Wh-Movement'

8

Deletion

English is traditionally assumed to have three types of relative clause construction, viz.

(1) (a)   Restrictive Relative Clauses
    (b)   Appositive Relative Clauses
    (c)   Free Relative Clauses.

Restrictive Relative Clauses include the italicised in:

(2) (a)   I met the man *who lives next door* in town
    (b)   The book *that you lent me* was interesting
    (c)   I enjoyed the meal *you made us*

They are so called because in an expression such as *the man who lives next door*, the relative clause *who lives next door* restricts the class of men referred to to the one who lives next door. As we see from (2), restrictive relative clauses can be introduced by a *wh*-pronoun like *who*, a complementiser like *that*, or they may contain *no wh*-pronoun or complementiser. As we see from (3), restrictive relative clauses can sometimes be extraposed and separated from their 'heads':

(3)   A MAN came to see me *who said he was from the Gas Board*

Thus in (3) the italicised restrictive relative clause is separated from the 'head' NP that it modifies (capitalised).

    Appositive Relative Clauses are those such as the italicised in:

(4) (a)   John – *who used to live in Cambridge* – is a good friend of mine
    (b)   Yesterday I met your bank manager, *who was in a filthy mood*
    (c)   Mary has left home – *which is very unfortunate for her parents*

They generally serve as 'parenthetical comments' or 'afterthoughts' set off in a separate intonation group from the rest of the sentence

(this being marked by a comma, or hyphen, or brackets in writing);
unlike restrictives, they can be used to qualify unmodified proper
nouns (i.e. proper nouns not introduced by a Determiner like *the*,
as with *John* in (4) (a)). They are always introduced by a
wh-pronoun, never by the complementiser *that*, or by an empty
COMP: cf.

(5) (a)   John – *who you met last week* – is a good friend of mine
    (b)   *John – *that you met last week* – is a good friend of mine
    (c)   *John – *you met last week* – is a good friend of mine

And, generally speaking, they cannot be extraposed (i.e. separated)
from their head; cf.

(6) (a)   *John came to see me – *who you met last week*
    (b)   *Mary is living at home – *who is very nice*

Free Relative Clauses are those such as the italicised in:

(7) (a)   *What you say* is true
    (b)   This is *who I spoke to*
    (c)   I will go *where you go*

They are characterised by the fact that they are apparently
antecedentless – i.e. they don't appear to refer back to any constituent in their own or any other sentence.

Henceforth, we shall confine our discussion (unless otherwise
specified) to *restrictive relative clauses* (so the term *relative clause*
can be equated with *restrictive relative clause* in most of what
follows). One type of Relative Clause found in English is what we
shall call *wh*-relatives – illustrated by NPs like the following:

(8) (a)   the man *who(m)* I met
    (b)   the book *which* I read
    (c)   the day *when* we went to Paris
    (d)   the place *where* we stayed
    (e)   the reason *why* I went there

In each case, the superficial structure of these '*wh*-relatives' seems
fairly clear: an expression like *the man who I met* is clearly an NP (it
can undergo NP–AUX INVERSION, as in *Is the man who I met
at home?*) which comprises a 'head NP' modified by an S-bar
complement which contains a *wh*-pronoun in COMP. That is, the
structure of an expression like *the man who I met* would be along
the lines of:

(9)   [$_{NP}$ [$_{NP}$ the man] [$_{\bar{S}}$ [$_{COMP}$ who] [$_{S}$ I met]]]

Alongside *wh*-relatives like those in (8), we find a corresponding set of *that*-relatives in English: cf.

(10) (a)   the man *that* I met
     (b)   the book *that* I read
     (c)   the day *that* we went to Paris
     (d)   the place *that* we stayed
     (e)   the reason *that* I went there

An NP such as *the man that I met* would seem to have much the same structure as *the man who I met* save that the COMP introducing the relative clause contains the complementiser *that* rather than a relative pronoun. Hence the structure of (10) (a) might be along the lines of:

(11)   [$_{NP}$ [$_{NP}$ the man] [$_{\bar{S}}$ [$_{COMP}$ that] [$_{S}$ I met]]]

In addition, we find a third type of Relative Clause in English, parallel to the other types illustrated in (8) and (10), save for the fact that the COMP introducing the relative clause is left empty: cf.

(12) (a)   the man I met
     (b)   the book I read
     (c)   the day we went to Paris
     (d)   the place we stayed
     (e)   the reason I went there

Since the type of relative clause in (12) has an empty COMP, let's call them *e*-relatives (*e* = 'empty'). The structure of (12) (a) we assume to be parallel to that of (8) (a) and (10) (a) – i.e. to be essentially:

(13)   [$_{NP}$ [$_{NP}$ the man] [$_{\bar{S}}$ [$_{COMP}$ e] [$_{S}$ I met]]]

Let's refer to *e-relatives* and *that-relatives* together as *non-wh-relatives*. We thus divide (restrictive) relative clauses into two types: *wh-relatives* and *non-wh-relatives*; and within *non-wh-relatives* we distinguish *that-relatives* from *e-relatives*. In this chapter, we shall be especially concerned with the syntax of non-*wh*-relatives.

In a nutshell, what we shall be arguing is that non-*wh*-relatives contain an underlying *wh-relative pronoun*, which is adjoined to COMP by WH-MOVEMENT, and subsequently deleted by a rule of *WH-DELETION* when in COMP. In more concrete terms, we shall be claiming that an NP like *the man that I met* is derived as follows:

(14) (a)   the man [$_\bar{s}$ [$_{COMP}$ that] [$_S$ I met *who*]] = D-structure
     =WH-MOVEMENT ⟹

(b)   the man [$_\bar{s}$ [$_{COMP}$ *who* that] [$_S$ I met —]] = S-structure
     =WH-DELETION ⟹

(c)   the man [$_\bar{s}$ [$_{COMP}$ that] [$_S$ I met —]] = Surface Structure

That is, in D-structure *met* has a *wh*-relative pronoun object *who*; this is then adjoined to COMP by the WH-MOVEMENT transformation, giving the S-structure (14) (b); subsequently the rule of WH-DELETION applies to delete *who* in COMP, giving the Surface Structure (14) (c). Notice here that we distinguish between *S-structure* (the output of the transformations), and *Surface Structure* (the output of the deletion rules). The reason for the terminological innovation *S-structure* should now be clear. We shall similarly propose to analyse *e*-relatives in a parallel fashion, so that *the man I met* will be derived as follows:

(15) (a)   the man [$_\bar{s}$ [$_{COMP}$ e] [$_S$ I met *who*]] = D-structure
     =WH-MOVEMENT ⟹

(b)   the man [$_\bar{s}$ [$_{COMP}$ *who* e] [$_S$ I met —]] = S-structure
     =WH-DELETION ⟹

(c)   the man [$_\bar{s}$ [$_{COMP}$ e] [$_S$ I met —]] = Surface Structure

We shall now attempt to justify the *deletion* analysis proposed for non-*wh*-relatives. Let's start by asking: What evidence is there that non-*wh*-relatives contain an underlying *wh*-pronoun in D-structure – i.e. what evidence is there in favour of D-structures like (14) (a) and (15) (a) for relative NPs like (10) (a) and (12) (a)? One piece of evidence in support of this claim comes from familiar *subcategorisation* facts. Recall that on the basis of examples such as:

(16) (a)   John put the book on the table
     (b)   *John put the book
     (c)   *John put on the table

we earlier argued that *put* should be subcategorised as requiring a following NP-object and (locative) PP-complement – i.e. as:

(17)   put: V,   +[— NP – PP]
                       +LOC

But in the light of (16) and (17), consider the italicised relative clause in an NP such as:

(18)   the book *John put on the table*

Unless we posit that the verb *put* has an NP-object *which* in D-structure in (18), the italicised clause will fail to satisfy the subcategorisation restrictions in (17), since we see from the un-grammaticality of (16) (c) **John put on the table* that the verb *put* cannot generally be followed by a locative PP alone. But if we posit that (18) derives from a D-structure containing *which* in the NP-position following *put* – i.e.

(19)   the book John put *which* on the table

then since *which* is a pronoun and hence also an NP, we thereby satisfy the subcategorisation restrictions for *put*. Naturally, the same argument holds for *that*-relatives, as well as *e*-relatives.

Another version of the same *subcategorisation* argument can be formulated in relation to prepositions. A subset of prepositions – sometimes referred to as *transitive prepositions* – cannot generally be used without a following NP-complement (or '-object'): two such prepositions are *to* and *from*: cf.

(20) (a)   He travelled to Moscow from Paris
     (b)   *He travelled to from Paris
     (c)   *He travelled to Moscow from

Hence, both *to* and *from* will be subcategorised as:

(21)   +[—NP]

i.e. as requiring an NP-object. But in the light of this subcategorisation restriction on 'transitive prepositions', consider the italicised relative clauses in:

(22) (a)   the town *he travelled to from Moscow*
     (b)   the town *he travelled to Moscow from*

In (22) (a) *to* apparently lacks an NP-complement; and in (22) (b), *from* apparently lacks an NP-complement; both sentences appear to violate the restriction (21) which specifies that both prepositions require an NP-object. We should therefore expect that both structures will be ungrammatical: but they are not. How can we account for this paradox? Notice that if we posit that the relative clauses in (22) have an underlying relative pronoun *which* as the

NP-complement of *to/from*, so that (22) (a) and (b) derive from the respective D-structures:

(23) (a)   the town he travelled to *which* from Moscow
     (b)   the town he travelled to Moscow from *which*

then we no longer run into subcategorisation problems, since *which* is a relative pronoun and hence also an NP, and the two preposi- tions *to* and *from* both have NP-complements in the D-structures (23) (a) and (b) (and recall that subcategorisation restrictions hold at D-structure). Once again, the same argument can be extended to *that*-relatives to argue that they too have an underlying *wh*-pronoun in their D-structures.

A second argument leading to the same conclusion can be formulated in relation to *agreement* facts. Recall that a finite verb agrees in number and person with the subject of its own clause, and not e.g. with any NP outside its own clause: cf.

(24)   He told me [that *they are*/*is/* am wrong]

In the light of this observation, consider a relative clause like the (*that-*) clause in

(25)   a film (that) I think [$_\bar{S}$ *is* very entertaining]

Here, the italicised verb is third person singular: we should expect therefore that it is agreeing with a third person singular subject of its clause. But there is (apparently) no subject for the bracketed clause. We cannot say that *is* agrees 'directly' with *the film*, because we have already seen from (24) that verbs never agree with NPs outside their own clause. How can we resolve this problem? A simple answer is to say that (25) derives from an abstract D- structure containing a *wh*-pronoun, viz.

(26)   a film (that) I think [$_\bar{S}$ comp [$_S$ which is very entertaining]]

and that *which* here is a third person singular form, which is adjoined first to the left of the empty comp, then to the left of *that*, and is then deleted by WH-DELETION.

A third argument in support of positing underlying *wh*-pronouns in non-*wh*-relatives can be formulated in relation to AUXILIARY CONTRACTION facts. For all speakers of English, *is* can be contracted to *'s* in a sentence like:

(27) (c)   It *is* that kind of book
     (d)   It*'s* that kind of book

And for many speakers, the same is also true of *has* in a sentence such as:

(28) (a)   He *has* a book in his hand
     (b)   He*'s* a book in his hand

But contraction of both forms is blocked in relative NPs like:

(28) (a)   the kind of book (that) it *is*
     (b)   *the kind of book (that) it*'s*
(29) (a)   the book (that) he has in his hand
     (b)   *the book (that) he*'s* in his hand

How can we account for the fact that contraction is not possible in these two cases? Recall, in chapter 5 we made the following informal generalisation about contraction:

(30)   Contraction is blocked if there is a 'missing constituent' after the item concerned

Now if we say that underlyingly (28) and (29) contain a *wh*-pronoun after *is/has* so that they derive respectively from the D-structures:

(31) (a)   the kind of book (that) it is *which*
     (b)   the book (that) he has *which* in his hand

then we can say that it is the fact that there is a constituent following *is/has* which is *wh*-moved into COMP (and leaves behind a trace) that blocks contraction: i.e. the presence of the trace of the *wh*-phrase after *is/has* (marking the 'missing' *wh*-phrase) blocks contraction. To be more precise, application of WH-MOVEMENT to (31) will produce the S-structures:

(32) (a)   the kind of book [$_{\bar{S}}$ [$_{COMP}$ which$_2$ (that)] [it is np$_2$]]
     (b)   the book [$_{\bar{S}}$ [$_{COMP}$ which$_2$ (that)] [$_S$ he has np$_2$ in his hand]]

The trace then counts as a 'missing constituent' in the sense of (30), and therefore blocks contraction. The S-structure (32) is then converted onto the corresponding Surface Structure by application of WH-DELETION to erase the *wh*-pronoun *which* in either case.

   A number of other arguments can be given in support of positing an underlying *wh*-pronoun in non-*wh*-relatives: these are essentially parallel to the types of argument used to motivate transformations, so there is little point in reiterating them here.

Let's assume that we can motivate the postulation of underlying *wh*-relative pronouns in non-*wh*-relatives. Since these *wh*-pronouns do not appear in Surface Structure in non-*wh*-relatives, clearly they must undergo deletion. But do they undergo deletion before or after they can be moved into COMP? We have been tacitly assuming so far that *wh*-phrases are *first* moved into COMP, and *then* deleted once they are in COMP: hence a derivation like (15) for *the man I met*. But a second possibility would be to say that these *wh*-pronouns undergo deletion in the S containing them, and are never moved into COMP at all (so that non-*wh*-relatives involve WH-DELETION without WH-MOVEMENT). This second possibility is illustrated schematically in (33) below:

(33) (a) the man [$_\bar{S}$ [$_{COMP}$ e] [$_S$ I met *who*]]
                  =WH-DELETION ⟹
       (b) the man [$_\bar{S}$ [$_{COMP}$ e] [$_S$ I met]]

So, we have two competing analyses for non-*wh*-relatives in English: (i) WH-MOVEMENT + WH-DELETION; and (ii) WH-DELETION.

But how on earth can we tell whether non-*wh*-relatives undergo movement as well as deletion, or not? In fact, there is a fairly obvious test that we can apply here. Earlier, we discussed in detail a number of *constraints on movement rules* proposed by Ross, Chomsky and others – generally known as *island constraints*. Now if non-*wh*-relatives do in fact involve movement as well as deletion, then we should expect that they will be subject to island constraints. So let's test whether they are.

One such constraint we discussed was the COORDINATE STRUCTURE CONSTRAINT, which says (informally)

(34)   No element can be moved out of a coordinate structure

The constraint (34) accounts for the impossibility of moving the italicised phrase out of the position marked — in:

(35)   **Which boy* did you meet which girl and —?

But are non-*wh*-relatives subject to the same constraint? Consider the ill-formedness of:

(36)   *the man (that) I met Mary and

How can we account for the ill-formedness of (36)? The *movement* analysis proposed here provides us with an obvious answer. (36) derives from the D-structure:

(37)   the man (that) I met Mary and *who*

and under the *movement* analysis, *who* will then be adjoined to the COMP of the relative clause, giving:

(38)   the man *who* (that) I met Mary and —

But this movement will clearly violate the COORDINATE STRUCTURE CONSTRAINT (34): subsequent WH-DELETION of *who* will give the ill-formed (36). But (36) is of course ill-formed because of the illicit movement of the *wh*-phrase prior to deletion.

A similar kind of argument can be formulated in relation to the WH-ISLAND CONSTRAINT, which specifies (informally):

(39)   No element can be moved out of a clause beginning with a
         wh-phrase

Given (39), we have a simple account of the oddity of:

(40)   ?*Who* do you wonder where he met —

since *who* has been moved out of the embedded question clause introduced by *where*. In the light of (39), consider:

(41)   ?a book (that) I wonder where he read

How can we account for the oddity of (41)? Under the *movement* analysis, this is straightforward: (41) derives from:

(42)   a book (that) I wonder where he read *which*

Application of WH-MOVEMENT will move *which* to the front of the relative clause to be adjoined to COMP, giving:

(43)   a book which (that) I wonder where he read —

and this movement will violate the WH-ISLAND CONSTRAINT (39). Subsequently the *wh*-pronoun *which* will be deleted by WH-DELETION, giving the Surface Structure (41). But (41) is ill-formed because movement of *which* in (43) violates the WH-ISLAND CONDITION.

In short, since it seems clear that non-*wh*-relatives obey the constraints on movement rules that we discussed earlier, it is plausible to claim that non-*wh*-relatives in English must involve WH-MOVEMENT prior to WH-DELETION. This in turn means that it is likely that deletion rules must operate *after* transformations like WH-MOVEMENT. In other words, it suggests that we might envisage a grammar organised along the lines of:

(44) 1.   Base Rules
       2.   Transformations
       3.   Deletion Rules

So far, we have been assuming a deletion rule along the lines of:

(45)   WH-DELETION
          Delete *wh*-phrase in COMP

But isn't there a snag to such a rule? If we posit that *wh*-phrases in COMP can freely undergo deletion, then surely we should expect that not only *relative wh*-phrases, but also *interrogative wh*-phrases can undergo deletion in COMP? So, if we take a D-structure like:

(46)   COMP you have bought what?

and apply WH-MOVEMENT to adjoin *what* to COMP, and also apply NP–AUX INVERSION, we will obtain the S-structure:

(47)   [$_{COMP}$ what] have you bought —?

Since we now have a *wh*-phrase contained within COMP, we might expect that it can undergo deletion by the WH-DELETION rule (45). But in fact this is not the case at all, as we see from the ungrammaticality of:

(48)   *Have you bought —?

So it seems that we need some way of ensuring that *wh*-relative phrases can be deleted in COMP, but not *wh*-interrogative phrases. But how?

The answer proposed by Chomsky and Lasnik in 'Filters and Control' (1977) is to posit that deletion of interrogative *wh*-phrases is blocked by a universal condition on deletion rules, which we can outline informally as:

(49)   RECOVERABILITY CONDITION (ON DELETION)
          Only elements which do not have semantic content can be
          deleted

Such a condition seems to be required in order to prevent there being rules which can randomly delete any arbitrary set of elements – e.g. *John*, or *loves*, or *Mary* in a sentence like:

(50)   John loves Mary

and thereby give rise to such ill-formed sentences as:

(51)   (a) *Loves Mary   (b) *John Mary   (c) *John loves

But how can a condition such as (49) prevent the deletion of *interrogative wh*-phrases in COMP, while still permitting the deletion of *relative wh*-phrases in COMP? Chomsky and Lasnik's answer is that in interrogatives 'the wh-word has semantic content. It is in fact a kind of quantifier. In relatives, however, the wh-word has no semantic content . . . We may assume, then, that the appropriate form of the RECOVERABILITY CONDITION will prevent deletion of the quantifier-like wh-word [in interrogatives], with its intrinsic semantic content, but not the wh-form that appears in relatives' ('Filters and Control', p. 447). But what does Chomsky mean by saying that an interrogative *wh*-word is 'a kind of quantifier'? What he is in effect saying is that the Logical Form of a sentence like:

(52)   Who came?

is along the lines of:

(53)   For which person x (is it the case that): x came?

where *who* corresponds to the quantifier expression *For which person x*. In short, he is arguing that *wh*-relatives have no intrinsic meaning and hence can be deleted without violating the condition (54), whereas *wh*-interrogatives have intrinsic meaning, and hence cannot undergo deletion because of the RECOVERABILITY CONDITION (49).

   Chomsky and Lasnik also argue that the RECOVERABILITY CONDITION provides a principled explanation of why prepositions cannot be deleted along with *wh*-relative pronouns. Consider a D-structure along the lines of:

(54)   the man COMP I spoke *to whom*

Adjoining the italicised *wh*-phrase to COMP by WH-MOVEMENT will give:

(55)   the man [_{COMP} to whom] I spoke —

(which is a perfectly well-formed S-structure, of course). But now, what is to prevent us from deleting the *wh*-phrase *to whom* in COMP, to derive the ungrammatical Surface Structure:

(56)   *the man I spoke —

Chomsky and Lasnik's reply is that deletion of *to whom* will violate the RECOVERABILITY CONDITION (49) by virtue of the fact that the preposition *to* has semantic content. By this they mean that *to* (like other prepositions) has inherent meaning – a meaning different from that of other prepositions like *from*, *by*, *with*, *on*, etc. Since the RECOVERABILITY CONDITION (49) says that we cannot delete items that have inherent meaning, and since prepositions have inherent meaning, it therefore follows that we can never delete prepositions – hence the impossibility of deleting *to whom* in (55), since this would entail not only deleting *whom*, but also *to*.

Thus far, we have only looked at tensed (= finite) relative clauses in English. But English also has a class of untensed (= nonfinite) relative clauses, known generally as *infinitival relatives*. Consider, for example:

(57)   He was looking for a screwdriver *with which to mend the lock*

In (57), the italicised relative clause is infinitival, and contains a *wh*-phrase (*with which*) in COMP: hence we might refer to this type of relative clause as an *infinitival wh-relative*. But alongside (57), we also find the parallel construction:

(58)   He was looking for a screwdriver *to mend the lock with*

In this second type of infinitival relative, we find no overt *wh*-phrase; hence we might refer to this second type as *infinitival non-wh-relatives*. Exactly the same types of argument put forward earlier in relation to tensed (= finite) non-*wh*-relatives can be advanced in support of the claim that infinitival non-*wh*-relatives also involve an underlying *wh*-pronoun in D-structure, which is moved into COMP by WH-MOVEMENT, and there deleted by WH-DELETION. For example, infinitival relatives are subject to the COORDINATE STRUCTURE CONSTRAINT (34), as we see from:

(59)   *He was looking for a screwdriver to mend the lock with a chisel and

a fact which can be accounted for easily enough if we suppose an underlying *wh*-pronoun (*which*) that is moved into COMP (out of a coordinate structure, thereby violating the COORDINATE STRUCTURE CONSTRAINT) by WH-MOVEMENT, and there deleted by WH-DELETION.

Let's look a little more closely at the syntax of infinitival relatives. Underlying an NP like *a screwdriver with which to mend the lock* (given standard arguments) we might posit the D-structure:

(60)   a screwdriver COMP PRO to mend the lock *with which*

with PRO here being the 'understood' empty NP-subject of the infinitive. Application of WH-MOVEMENT to the italicised *wh*-phrase would adjoin it to COMP, giving:

(61)   a screwdriver [$_{COMP}$ with which] PRO to mend the lock —

If we now try to apply WH-DELETION to the *wh*-phrase *with which* in COMP in (61), we see that we cannot because the RECOVERABILITY CONDITION does not allow the deletion of prepositions (since the latter have semantic content): hence we correctly predict the ungrammaticality of:

(62)   *a screwdriver to mend the lock —

(which cannot mean 'a screwdriver with which I can mend the lock', though irrelevantly it can mean 'a screwdriver which will mend the lock').

But now, suppose that instead of preposing the *wh*-PP *with which* in (60), we prepose simply the *wh*-NP *which* instead: the result will be the following S-structure:

(63)   a screwdriver [$_{COMP}$ which] PRO to mend the lock with —

If we now apply WH-DELETION to delete the *wh*-phrase *which* in COMP, the result will be the grammatical Surface Structure:

(64)   a screwdriver to mend the lock with (cf.(58))

And yet there is an unforeseen complication here. Hitherto, given the optionality of relative pronouns in relative NPs like:

(65)   the book (which) I read

we have been assuming that WH-DELETION is an optional rule. But if the rule is optional, then we should expect to have the option of *not* applying the rule in (63), and thus ending up with the Surface Structure:

(66)　　*a screwdriver which to mend the lock with

But relative constructions like (66) are ungrammatical in modern English. Somehow, we have got to avoid generating structures like (66), while still permitting structures like (64) and (65). How can we do this? As a first approximation, we might try revising our WH-DELETION rule along the lines of:

(67)　　WH-DELETION
　　　　Delete *wh*-phrase in COMP; optionally in tensed clauses, obligatorily in untensed (= infinitival) clauses

A rule like (67) would account for the following contrasts:

(68) (a)　　He wants someone *who he can talk to*
　　(b)　　He wants someone *he can talk to*
(69) (a)　　*He wants someone *who to talk to*
　　(b)　　He wants someone *to talk to*

In (68) the italicised relative clause is tensed, hence deletion of the *wh*-pronoun *who* in COMP is optional. But in (69), the italicised relative clause is untensed (= infinitival), and hence deletion of the *wh*-pronoun *who* is obligatory. All of which is exactly what we predict from rule (67).

But so far we have only considered *wh*-pronouns which are the object of prepositions. What about a *wh*-pronoun which is the object of a verb? Here again we find the same paradigm:

(70) (a)　　She is looking for something *which she can wear for the party*
　　(b)　　She is looking for something *she can wear for the party*
(71) (a)　　*She is looking for something *which to wear for the party*
　　(b)　　She is looking for something *to wear for the party*

Once again, deletion of the *wh*-pronoun *which* is optional in the tensed relative clause (70), but obligatory in the infinitival relative (71). So, all in all, it seems that we have considerable empirical support for the proposal to make WH-DELETION obligatory in infinitives, but optional in finite clauses.

However, the observant reader will already have noticed a complication (have you?!). If we say that *wh*-phrases in COMP are obligatorily deleted in infinitival relatives, how can we account for the nondeletability of *wh*-PPs in COMP in cases like:

(72) (a)   He's looking for someone [_{COMP} *in whom*] to put his trust
(b)   *He's looking for someone to put his trust
(73) (a)   He searches for things [_{COMP} *about which*] to complain
(b)   *He searches for things to complain

(cf. also (62), in the sense intended). It seems clear that although deletion of *wh*-phrases in COMP in infinitival relatives is generally obligatory, it is neither obligatory nor even possible with *wh*-PPs in COMP. Why should this be? In 'On Binding' (1980), Chomsky suggests that the nondeletability of *wh*-PPs in COMP is predictable from the RECOVERABILITY CONDITION (49), given the assumption that Ps have 'semantic content' and hence cannot be deleted. He therefore suggests that the rule of WH-DELETION be reformulated along the following lines:

(74)   Delete *wh*-phrase in COMP obligatorily (up to Recoverability) in infinitives, optionally in untensed clauses

To delete a constituent obligatorily *up to Recoverability* means to delete it obligatorily if deletion does not violate the RECOVERABILITY CONDITION, but not to delete it at all if deletion would violate the RECOVERABILITY CONDITION (e.g. if a Preposition would thereby get deleted also). In the light of (74), now consider the following paradigm for infinitival relatives:

(75) (a)   *He's looking for someone *who to fix the sink*
(b)   He's looking for someone *to fix the sink*
(76) (a)   *He's looking for something *which to do*
(b)   He's looking for something *to do*
(77) (a)   *He's looking for something *which to complain about*
(b)   He's looking for something *to complain about*
(78) (a)   He's looking for something *about which to complain*
(b)   *He's looking for something *to complain*

In (75) *who* is obligatorily deleted, in accordance with (74); the same is true of *which* in (76) and (77). But in (78), the *wh*-phrase *about which* is not deleted because to do so would violate the RECOVERABILITY CONDITION (49); hence, deletion here is impossible, and the rule therefore does not apply, leaving an undeleted *wh*-PP *about which*. Since the rule seems to make the correct predictions about *wh*-pronouns which are (i) subjects, (ii) objects of verbs, and (iii) objects of prepositions, it seems to be adequate to handle all the data we have looked at.

Thus far, we have discussed the applicability of WH-

DELETION in two types of relative clause construction – tensed relatives, and infinitival relatives. But are there other constructions in which WH-DELETION applies? In 'On Wh-Movement' (1977) Chomsky argues that there are in fact many other related constructions in which WH-DELETION (and prior to it, WH-MOVEMENT) applies. That is, he argues that there are many constructions which contain underlying abstract *wh*-phrases which are moved into COMP by WH-MOVEMENT, and there deleted by WH-DELETION. One such construction is comparatives like:

(79)   Mary is more talkative than Fred is

Chomsky would argue that underlying (79) is a D-structure along the lines of:

(80)   Mary is more talkative than [$_{\bar{S}}$ COMP Fred is *what*]

Application of WH-MOVEMENT then adjoins the *wh*-phrase to COMP, giving:

(81)   Mary is more talkative than [$_{\bar{S}}$ [$_{COMP}$ what] Fred is —]

an S-structure which corresponds to the dialectal surface form:

(82)   %Mary is more talkative than what Fred is

Subsequently, WH-DELETION applies to the S-structure (81) to erase (= delete) the *wh*-phrase *what*, yielding the Surface Structure:

(83)   Mary is more talkative than Fred is (= (79))

But – we might ask – what evidence is there, other than the occurrence of *what* in some dialects of English – for the WH-MOVEMENT + WH-DELETION analysis of comparatives proposed by Chomsky? Chomsky's main argument is the by now familiar one that comparatives obey constraints on movement rules, and hence must involve movement (e.g. of a *wh*-phrase). Consider, for example, the oddity of:

(84)   *Mary is more talkative these days than I wonder whether she
         was five years ago

We have a simple account of the ill-formedness of such sentences if we posit that underlyingly (84) contains a *wh*-pronoun like *what*, so that (84) derives from a D-structure which we can represent informally as:

(85)   Mary is more talkative these days than I wonder whether she
          was *what* five years ago

Application of WH-MOVEMENT to adjoin *what* to the initial
COMP in the comparative clause will give the S-structure:

(86)   Mary is more talkative these days than *what* I wonder whether
          she was — five years ago

But this movement will be in violation of the WH-ISLAND
CONSTRAINT (39), since *what* has been moved out of the
whether-clause. Subsequently, *what* is deleted by WH-
DELETION in (86). But the derivation as a whole is ill-formed
because it violates the WH-ISLAND CONSTRAINT, and so the
resultant sentence (84) is also ill-formed.

   Yet another construction argued by Chomsky (in 'On Wh-
Movement') to involve an underlying *wh*-moved, *wh*-deleted relative pronoun are *topic* structures such as:

(87)   This book, I really like

In earlier work in Transformational Grammar, it was assumed that
(87) derived from a D-structure like

(88)   I really like *this book*

by a rule Chomsky-adjoining the italicised (topicalised) phrase to
the left of the whole clause. But Chomsky's analysis is very
different. Yes, you've guessed it: an underlying *wh*-phrase. More
specifically, Chomsky proposes an analysis which we can represent
schematically as:

(89) (a)   [$_{\bar{\bar{s}}}$ [$_{TOPIC}$ this book] [$_{\bar{s}}$ COMP [$_{S}$ I really like *what*]]]
            =WH-MOVEMENT $\Rightarrow$

     (b)   [$_{\bar{\bar{s}}}$ [$_{TOPIC}$ this book] [$_{\bar{s}}$ [$_{COMP}$ what] [$_{S}$ I really like —]]]
            =WH-DELETION $\Rightarrow$

     (c)   [$_{\bar{\bar{s}}}$ [$_{TOPIC}$ this book] [$_{\bar{s}}$ COMP [$_{S}$ I really like —]]]

Once again, the same types of argument are used to motivate the
analysis – e.g. the fact that *topic* structures are subject to constraints on movement rules like the COORDINATE STRUC-
TURE CONSTRAINT – hence the ill-formedness of:

(90)   *This book, I really like that magazine and

or indeed the WH-ISLAND CONSTRAINT – hence the fact
that sentences like (91) are relatively unidiomatic:

(91)   ?This book, he asked me where I had read

In actual fact, Chomsky goes beyond comparative and topic structures to argue that many other types of construction also involve an underlying *wh*-relative pronoun which undergoes WH-MOVEMENT, and then WH-DELETION. For further details, see 'On Wh-Movement'.

We have devoted the whole of our discussion of deletion to just one rule: WH-DELETION. This is partly because the rule plays a central role in nearly all Chomsky's more recent work; and partly also because many deletion rules proposed in earlier work have subsequently been abandoned. Let's conclude our discussion by looking at two theoretical problems which arise from any discussion of deletion. One of these is concerned with the RECOVERABIL-ITY CONDITION (49), which specifies that no element with semantic content can be deleted. In all our discussion so far, we have assumed that in non-*wh*-relatives there is an underlying *wh*-relative-pronoun (*who* or *which*) which gets moved into COMP by WH-MOVEMENT, and then deleted in COMP by WH-DELETION. The obvious assumption made by such an analysis (an assumption explicit in Chomsky and Lasnik 'Filters and Control' (1977)) is that the *wh*-pronouns *who* and *which* in English do not have semantic content. That is, we might argue that their function is simply to serve as anaphors, and hence refer back to some appropriate antecedent in the sentence containing them, but that they themselves have no intrinsic meaning of any sort. This assumption, however, might be questioned, e.g. in relation to the following contrast:

(92) (a)   the Christian which we threw to the lions
     (b)   the Christian who we threw to the lions

Here, there is a clear difference in meaning between the two examples: (92) (a) conveys a contemptuous attitude to Christians which (92) (b) does not. And yet the only overt correlate of this meaning difference is the choice of *which* versus *who* as the relative pronoun introducing the relative clause. Are we therefore to conclude that *wh*-pronouns like *who* and *which* in English *do* have semantic content?

If we do accept that *who* and *which* have semantic content, then clearly the RECOVERABILITY CONDITION (49) will determine that *who* and *which* can never be deleted in English. This in turn means that we can no longer argue that non-*wh*-relatives involve deletion of *who* or *which*. Does this mean that we must therefore abandon our movement + deletion analysis of non-*wh*-relatives? Not necessarily. For one possibility that we might suggest is that non-*wh*-relatives have an underlying abstract, invisible pronoun which we might designate as WH-PRO, which has certain syntactic features (e.g. number, gender, case), but no 'semantic content'. This abstract WH-PRO form would then be the relative counterpart of the abstract PRO form which we posited to represent the 'understood' subject of certain apparently subjectless infinitive complements. Given the postulation of such an abstract WH-PRO form, we might then say that a phrase like *a man I know* derives from the D-structure:

(93)   a man COMP I know WH-PRO

Application of WH-MOVEMENT will then adjoin the abstract WH-PRO to COMP, giving:

(94)   a man [$_{COMP}$ WH-PRO] I know —

Subsequent application of WH-DELETION will then erase this abstract pro-form, giving the surface form:

(95)   a man I know

It may be that there is some support for such a proposal from other languages: in Chinese, for example, non-*wh*-relatives are subject to (certain) island constraints associated with movement rules, and yet it is implausible to derive them by movement and deletion of overt *wh*-relative pronouns, since *Chinese has no overt relative pronouns* (i.e. no equivalent of English *who* or *which*). Hence, the only way of defending Chomsky's movement + deletion analysis in Chinese would be to posit movement and deletion of an abstract 'invisible' *wh*-pro-form.

If we say that overt *wh*-pronouns can never be deleted because they have semantic content, then the question arises of whether in fact there ever are any lexical items (= words) in language which have absolutely no semantic content whatever. After all, we might say, what use would a language have for a contentless word? If in fact it is the case that all words have some semantic content, then the RECOVERABILITY CONDITION in effect amounts to the condition that:

(96)   No lexical item(s) (= real word(s)) can ever be deleted in any natural language

Or, equivalently, to the condition that:

(97)   Only 'invisible' pro-forms (= empty categories) can be deleted

This position seems to be hinted at in Chomsky's remarks in the *Pisa Lectures* (1980) that 'If you have a phonetic matrix you can't delete' (pp. 5–6), and 'You never delete a phonetic matrix': what he is saying here is that no item with an overt phonetic form (= no 'real word') can ever be deleted. If this is so, then clearly WH-DELETION will involve deletion of an abstract *wh*-pro-form, not deletion of a 'real' *wh*-word like *who* or *which*. The theoretical issues involved here are extremely complex; hence we leave aside the question of whether deletion rules can delete 'real words' or not.

A second, no less problematic issue raised by *deletion* is the question of the fate that befalls a deleted category. 'What happens to a constituent that gets deleted?' we might ask. Once again, the issues involved here are extremely complex, so let me just summarise two recent positions taken on this issue. The position adopted by Chomsky and Lasnik in 'Filters and Control' (1977) is that deletion erases 'a category and its contents': e.g. when you delete an NP, there is no 'empty NP' left behind. A different position adopted by Kayne in his unpublished paper 'ECP extensions' (1980, p. 17) is that deletion involves deletion of the *contents* of a category (syntactic, semantic, phonetic features, etc.), but not of the category itself, which remains as an empty node. The theoretical issues raised by these two alternatives are complex, and so we shall do no more than merely mention the possibilities here. To attempt to resolve the issues would require certain assumptions about the organisation of other components of the grammar that we have not looked at yet.

Summary

There are a number of constructions in English which do not show any overt *wh*-phrase in Surface Structure, and yet which can be argued to have an underlying *wh*-phrase which subsequently undergoes WH-MOVEMENT to COMP, and then WH-DELETION; evidence from subcategorisation facts, susceptibility to movement constraints and so forth provides some support for the proposed WH-MOVEMENT + WH-DELETION analysis. Deletion is subject to a universal RECOVERABILITY CONDITION. If we incorporate deletion rules into our Grammar, our revised model is along the lines of (98) below:

(98) (i) *Base*
      (a) Phrase Structure Rules
      (b) Lexicon (lexical entries, lexical redundancy rules, word-formation rules, restructuring rules, etc.)
      (c) Lexical Insertion Rule
      Output of Base: *D-structures*
  (ii) *Transformational Component*
      (a) Transformations (WH-MOVEMENT, NP-MOVE-MENT, etc. – or perhaps just ALPHA-MOVE-MENT)
      (b) Conditions on Transformations (STRUCTURE-PRESERVING CONDITION, SUBJACENCY, etc.)
      Output of Transformational Component: *S-structures*
  (iii) *Deletion Component*
      (a) Deletion Rules (WH-DELETION, etc.)
      (b) Conditions on Deletion (RECOVERABILITY CONDITION, etc.)
      Output of Deletion Component: *Surface Structures*

EXERCISES

Exercise I

Discuss the significance of the following data on WANNA-CONTRACTION for the analysis of non-*wh*-relatives like those italicised below:

(1) (a)   Reagan is the man *I want to beat*
  (b)   Reagan is the man *I wanna beat*
(2) (a)   Reagan is the man *I want to win*
  (b)   *Reagan is the man *I wanna win*

Exercise II

Discuss the significance of the following examples for the analysis of non-*wh*-relatives (it might be useful to remind yourself of some of the CONSTRAINTS we discussed earlier)

(1)   *the man I talked to Mary and

(2)   *the man I met someone who knows

(3)   *the man I don't believe the rumour that a gunman killed

(4)   *a man that I am doubtful about whether I have met

(5)   *a man that for me to help would be unthinkable

*Exercise III

In earlier work in TG, a number of linguists argued in favour of a deletion rule called GAPPING, which would erase the slashed material in (1) below under identity to (= if it were identical to) the italicised material:

(1)   John *ate* an apple, and Mary ̶a̶t̶e̶ a pear

The rule leaves a 'gap' in the sentence containing the deleted constituent – hence the name GAPPING. Try and formulate arguments in support of the claim that 'gapped' sentences involve a deleted constituent using arguments parallel to those developed in the text in support of a rule of WH-DELETION. For example, what is the significance of the fact that AUXILIARY CONTRACTION is blocked in cases like:

(2) (a)   Jean will write to Mary, and Jim will ̶w̶r̶i̶t̶e̶ to Joan
     (b)   *Jean will write to Mary, and Jim'll to Joan

*Exercise IV

Another deletion rule posited in earlier work in TG is the rule of VP-DELETION, which erases the slashed material under identity to the italicised material in sentences such as:

(1)   John won't *wash the dishes*, but Fred will ̶w̶a̶s̶h̶ ̶t̶h̶e̶ ̶d̶i̶s̶h̶e̶s̶

Given such a rule, how could we account for the noncontractability of *will* to *'ll* in sentences such as:

(2)   *John won't wash the dishes, but Fred'*ll*

Might we suggest a similar explanation for why *want to* can be contracted to *wanna* in:

(3)   I won't go to the cinema because I don't *wanna* go to the cinema

but not in:

(4)   *I won't go to the cinema because I don't *wanna*

**Exercise V

In Chomsky's *Essays* (1977), it is argued that sentences like:

(1)   I want to win

are derived from an underlying structure along the lines of:

(2)   comp I want [s comp *myself* to win]

by a rule of REFLEXIVE DELETION, which applies to delete the italicised reflexive pronoun. Show how such an analysis would provide a simple account of agreement restrictions in sentences such as:

(3) (a)   I want to be a politician
    (b)   *I want to be politicians

Now go on and suggest how we could obviate the need for any rule of REFLEXIVE DELETION if we assumed instead that the bracketed infinitive complement in (2) has an empty (pronominal) NP subject, which we might represent as PRO – cf.

(4)   comp I want [s̄ comp PRO to win]

If we adopt the PRO solution instead of the REFLEXIVE DELETION solution, what stipulation would we have to make about the difference between PRO on the one hand and traces on the other in order to account for contrasts like:

(5) (a)   I wanna win
    (b)   *Who do you wanna win?

   **Exercise VI*

In 'Filters and Control' (1977), Chomsky and Lasnik posit not a rule of WH-DELETION, but rather a more general rule of COMP-DELETION, which allows for *any* element contained in COMP to be deleted, subject to the RECOVERABILITY CONDITION being satisfied. The generalised rule of COMP-DELETION will delete not only *wh*-phrases in COMP, but also overt complementisers like *that* and *for* in sentences such as:

(1) (a)   I said *that* I was tired
    (b)   I said I was tired
(2) (a)   I would prefer *for* you to stay at home
    (b)   I would prefer you to stay at home

Show how this more powerful rule of COMP-DELETION is unnecessary in a framework which assumes a Base Rule of the form:

(3) $\alpha \rightarrow e$ ('Any category can be left empty')

How can we account for sentences like (1) (b) and (2) (b) without invoking COMP-DELETION?

   Exercise VII

In 'On Wh-Movement' (1977), Chomsky suggests that a sentence like

(1)   John is easy to please

represents an infinitival relative construction, and so derives from the D-structure:

(2)   John is easy COMP PRO to please whom

WH-MOVEMENT then adjoins *whom* to COMP giving the S-structure:

(3)   John is easy [COMP whom] PRO to please —

Subsequent WH-DELETION of *whom* then gives (1) *John is easy to please*. What kind of arguments might be used to support such a claim?

**Exercise VIII

Given the analysis of *easy to please* constructions in Exercise VII, discuss the problems posed for the analysis by sentences such as the following (deciding for yourself which are grammatical):

(1)   John is easy (who) to commit suicide
(2)   John is easy (who) to beat
(3)   John is easy (who) to talk to
(4)   John is easy (to who(m)) to talk

**Exercise IX

In the text, we assumed that in sentences like:

(1)   This is *who I spoke to*

the italicised constituent is a free relative NP. But an alternative possibility might be that it is an embedded interrogative clause. Under the relative analysis, *who* in sentences like (1) would be a relative pronoun, whereas under the interrogative analysis it would be an interrogative pronoun. What predictions would either analysis make about the deletability of the bracketed *wh*-phrase in sentences like those below – and which prediction is the correct one?

(2) (a)   This is (who) will help you
    (b)   This is (who) to help you
(3) (a)   This is (who) you should see
    (b)   This is (who) to see
(4) (a)   This is (who) you should talk to
    (b)   This is (who) to talk to
(5) (a)   This is (to whom) you should talk
    (b)   This is (to whom) to talk

**Exercise X

Consider the following examples:

(1) (a)   I'm looking for a place *in which* to stay
    (b)   I'm looking for a place to stay

(2) (a) I'm looking for a way *in which* to help you
   (b) I'm looking for a way to help you
(3) (a) I'm trying to find the best way *by which* to get to Calais
   (b) I'm trying to find the best way to get to Calais

Suppose we argue that in each case, the (b) example is derived from the (structure underlying the) (a) example by WH-DELETION. What problems would this pose for the RECOVERABILITY CONDITION? Is there an alternative analysis for the (b) sentences consistent with the RECOVERABILITY CONDITION – can you suggest one?

**Exercise XI*

If we adopt the suggestion at the end of the text that the RECOVER-ABILITY CONDITION blocks the deletion of 'real words' like *which* and *who*, then show that our formulation of WH-DELETION in (74) which says:

(1) Delete *wh*-phrase in COMP obligatorily (up to Recoverability) in infinitives, optionally in tensed clauses

will no longer account for the ungrammaticality of sentences like:

(2) (a) *He's looking for someone who to help him
   (b) *He's looking for something which to do
   (c) *He's looking for someone who to talk to

**Exercise XII*

In the text, we assumed that island constraints are applicable uniquely to *movement* rules, and are hence of the schematic form:

(1) No rule can move a constituent from position X to position Y in a specified type of structure (e.g. where X is inside a coordinate structure, *wh*-clause, adnominal clause, etc. and Y is outside it)

Suppose we now abandon the assumption that only movement rules are subject to island constraints, and argue that other types of rules (especially deletion rules) may also be subject to island constraints. That is, suppose we assume that all constraints are of the schematic form:

(2) No rule can involve X and Y in certain types of structures (where for a rule to involve X and Y means in the case of movement rules 'move from X to Y (or vice-versa)', and in the case of deletion rules 'delete X under identity to Y or vice-versa')

To be more precise, we might reformulate our familiar island constraints along the lines of:

(3) No rule can involve X and Y where Y is inside and X outside an island — i.e. (i) a coordinate structure, (ii) an indirect question clause, (iii) a sentential subject clause, (iv) a complex NP, etc.

In the light of (3) above, show how, if we assume that WH-DELETION involves deletion of a *wh*-pronoun (whether 'real' or 'abstract' is not important here) under identity to its 'head' NP, we can account for the fact that non-*wh*-relatives like those in (4) below obey island constraints, *without the need to posit that they involve* WH-MOVEMENT.

(4) (a)   *the man I saw Mary and
    (b)   ?the man I'm curious about whether you like
    (c)   *a man that for me to see would be a mistake
    (d)   *a man that I know someone who has met

FURTHER READING

For a look at the types of deletion rule posited in earlier work in TG, see:

Akmajian and Heny (1975) *Principles*, pp. 233–59
Keyser and Postal (1976) *Grammar*, pp. 67–112

The discussion in this chapter is based largely on more recent work by Chomsky discussed in the following:

Chomsky and Lasnik (1977) 'Filters and Control'
Chomsky (1980) 'On Binding'
Chomsky (1980) *Pisa Lectures*
Chomsky (1977) 'On Wh-Movement'

However, the last three of these presuppose knowledge of a number of concepts that the reader will not be familiar with at this stage; hence they should not be tackled until you have finished the rest of the book.

9
Filters

Earlier, we saw that *constraints* (or conditions on transformations) are one of the devices used by Chomsky to prevent overgeneration by the base rules and transformations. A second such device are *filters* (alias *output constraints*, or *surface structure constraints*). These were first developed by Ross in *Constraints on Variables in Syntax* (1967).

Let's look at one of the filters developed by Ross: the INTERNAL CLAUSE FILTER. Ross observes that if we apply NP–AUX INVERSION to sentences such as:

(1) (a)   *That the world is round* is obvious
   (b)   *For Mary to climb the fence* would surprise Bill

the result of permuting the italicised clause with the following auxiliary is a very awkward and unidiomatic structure:

(2) (a)   *Is *that the world is round* obvious?
   (b)   *Would *for Mary to climb the fence* surprise Bill?

How can we account for the difference in grammaticality between sentences like (1) and (2)? Ross suggests that we might do so in terms of a *filter* like the following:

(3)   INTERNAL CLAUSE FILTER
       Any surface structure containing one clause embedded internally within another is ungrammatical

Notice that in both (1) and (2) the italicised clause is embedded as a complement of (= 'the subject of') the main clause: but whereas in (1) the italicised clause is flanked only on the right by material belonging to the main clause, in (2) it is flanked on both the left and the right by material from the main clause: thus, if we define 'embedded internally' to mean 'flanked by overt material to both the left and right', then in this sense the italicised clause is embedded internally within the main clause in (2) but not (1). Since (2) but not (1) violates the INTERNAL CLAUSE FILTER (3), then (2) is ill-formed, and (1) well-formed.

How plausible is the filter (3)? At first sight, it might appear that we can find some fairly simple counterexamples to it. Consider:

(4) (a)　Would *overthrowing the government* be a good idea?
   (b)　Would someone *who tries to overthrow the government* be executed?

In (4) (a) we have a gerund complement embedded internally within the main clause, while in (4) (b) it might appear that the italicised relative clause is also embedded internally within the main clause, in the sense of (3). How can we deal with such apparent counterexamples? Take the case of gerund complements first. Notice that in (3), we avoided the question of what exactly we meant by the term 'clause': do we mean S-bar, or just S? At the time that Ross was writing (1967) this would not have been a meaningful question, since X-bar Syntax had not yet been developed. But let's try and interpret his proposed filter in terms of more recent theoretical developments. Let's suppose that *clause* in (3) is to be identified with *S-bar*, i.e. a COMP – S structure. If so, then there are serious reasons to doubt that gerund complements have the status of S-bar. The primary reason for saying this is that gerund complements appear to have no COMP position: thus, whereas tensed and infinitival interrogative complements can be introduced by the complementiser *whether*, this is *never* the case with gerunds: cf.

(5) (a)　I have my doubts about *whether* I should go there
   (b)　I have my doubts about *whether* to go there
   (c)　*I have my doubts about *whether* going there (OK without *whether*)

(Notice incidentally that in a sentence like:

(6)　　　I don't know whether *going there* would be a good idea

whether is not a COMP introducing the gerund phrase (italicised), rather it is the COMP introducing the *would*-clause: hence (6) is not a counterexample to the claim that gerund complements never have complementisers.) Likewise, whereas tensed and infinitival

interrogative clauses can have a *wh*-moved *wh*-phrase in their
COMP, this is never the case with gerund complements:

(7) (a)   I'm thinking about *where* I should go —
    (b)   I'm thinking about *where* to go —
    (c)   *I'm thinking about *where* going — (OK *about going there*)

Thus, since gerunds appear to lack COMP, they cannot have the
status of S-bar: they are probably best analysed as NPs containing
an internal VP. Now, if we restrict the filter (3) so that by *clause* we
mean 'S-bar', then clearly sentences like (4) (a) are no longer a
problem for us, since although (4) (a) contains an internal gerund
complement, gerunds do not have the status of S-bar, and hence are
not subject to the filter (3).

But what of our 'internal' relative clause in (4) (b)? Here there
can surely be no doubt that the relative clause has the status of
S-bar, since it contains a *wh*-phrase (*who*) in the initial COMP
position. However, what we would probably want to say about
relative clauses is (in informal terms) that they are not complements
of clauses, but rather of NPs: i.e. the relative clause in (4) (b) is
embedded within the NP *someone who tries to overthrow the
government* – an NP which has the internal structure:

(8)   [$_{NP}$ someone [$_{\bar{S}}$ who tries to overthrow the government]]

That is, relative clauses are *adnominal* complements (= they serve
to modify nominals). By contrast, the types of clauses we were
talking about in (1) and (2) are *predicate complement clauses* – i.e.
clauses which are themselves the subject or object of some predicate
expression (the predicate is usually a verb, but might alternatively
be an adjective, or even certain types of NP). To be more strictly
correct, since both the italicised clauses in (1) are *subjects*, all we
have actually shown at the moment is that clauses which are the
subjects of other clauses cannot be embedded internally within
them. However, the same filter seems to hold for nonsubject
clauses, as the following contrasts illustrate:

(9) (a)   I told *the story* to my mother
    (b)   *I told *that I was leaving* to my mother
    (c)   I told her *the story*
    (d)   I told her *that I was leaving*

(10) (a)   I said to her *that I couldn't stand spaghetti*
    (b)   *I said *that I couldn't stand spaghetti* to her

(11) (a)   It seemed to everyone *that he ought to retire*
    (b)   *It seemed *that he ought to retire* to everyone

So, to summarise: it seems that we must tighten up our INTERNAL CLAUSE FILTER (3) in at least two ways: firstly, we must restrict the term *clause* to S-bar; and secondly, we must add the qualification that the filter holds for predicate complement clauses, not for adnominal clauses. The first modification is trivial; the second can be achieved in structural terms, but the relevant structural definitions become quite complex, so we shall not go into the details here. For our purposes, it will be sufficient to modify (3) as:

(12)   INTERNAL S-BAR FILTER
        Any surface structure containing an S-bar embedded within another clause, and flanked to the left and right by overt lexical material from that clause, is ill-formed

(12) needs to be tightened up in various ways that are not of concern to us here: for some discussion, see Kuno's 'Constraints on internal clauses and sentential subjects' (1973) (though this is a technical work, not recommended for the beginner).

One important theoretical distinction which should be drawn is that between *constraints* like the COORDINATE STRUCTURE CONSTRAINT, SUBJACENCY CONDITION, etc., and *filters* like the INTERNAL CLAUSE FILTER (3). Constraints are *conditions on derivations* (more precisely, conditions on pairs of successive phrase-markers in a derivation), a *derivation* being the sequence of phrase-markers (beginning with D-structure, and ending with Surface Structure) which represents the syntactic structure of a sentence. *Constraints* are of the schematic form:

(13)   If at one stage of derivation you have a constituent C inside an island, and if at the next stage of derivation (after some rule has applied) C lies outside the island, then the resulting derivation (and with it, the resulting surface structure, i.e. sentence) is ill-formed

We can illustrate this in relation to the COORDINATE STRUC-TURE CONSTRAINT: consider the following partial derivation:

(14) (a)   the man [₅ that I saw [ₐ John and who]]

‖

　　　　　WH-MOVEMENT

‖

(b)   the man [₅ who that I saw [ₐ John and —]]

‖

　　　　　WH-DELETION

⇓

(c)   the man [₅ that I saw [ₐ John and —]]

which might be argued to be the derivation (ignoring details) of:

(15)   *the man that I saw John and

What's wrong with (15)? The answer is that in the course of the derivation (14), we have violated the COORDINATE STRUC-TURE CONSTRAINT; more particularly, in (14) (a) *who* is contained within the bracketed *island* coordinate structure α, and in the next stage of derivation (14) (b), *who* lies outside the bracketed coordinate structure island α. Hence, even though no further constraint is violated in getting from (14) (b) to (14) (c), the resultant derivation is ill-formed. But notice what we did here to check for violations of the COORDINATE STRUCTURE CON-STRAINT: we compared *two successive stages of a derivation*. In this sense, constraints are *conditions on (successive stages of) derivations* (i.e. conditions on successive pairs of structures in a derivation). By contrast, filters are *conditions on (single) structures* – and, furthermore, on structures which serve as the output of a particular component of the grammar. They are of the schematic form:

(16)   Any structure of type X is ill-formed

For example, our surface structure filter (3) said that any surface structure containing an internal S-bar is ill-formed. To check for violations of this type of filter, all you need to do is look at the surface structure which is the final output of a given syntactic derivation: you don't need to compare the surface structure with any preceding stage of derivation. In short, constraints *compare two successive levels of structure* in a derivation; a filter merely checks the output of a given rule-component, and hence scans only a *single level of structure*. Or, even more succinctly: constraints require you to compare the *input and output* of a rule; filters require you only to check the *output* of a given set of rules.

After Ross's early work, the next significant contribution to the development of a Theory of Filters was Perlmutter's *Deep and Surface Structure Constraints in Syntax* (1971; written around 1968). The main theoretical interest of the book was to demonstrate that the possible orderings of unstressed ('clitic') pronouns in Spanish and French were best dealt with in terms of a *filter*. But Perlmutter also developed one important filter for English: let's look at this. But first, some background information.

In English, as we already know, constituents can be moved out of embedded tensed clauses, irrespective of whether or not the embedded clause is introduced by an overt complementiser: thus, in the following examples *who* has been extracted from the position marked — out of the bracketed embedded complement clause into the italicised COMP position by WH-MOVEMENT:

(17) (a)   *Who* did he say [that he met —]?
     (b)   *Who* did he say [he met —]?

But notice, however, that when *who* is the subject of the embedded bracketed complement clause, we find a different situation:

(18) (a)   **Who* did he say [that — was coming]?
     (b)   *Who* did he say [— was coming]?

In (18) we see that a *wh*-phrase which is the subject of a clause can be extracted out of that clause if the clause has no overt complementiser, but not where the clause has an overt complementiser like *that*. How can we account for this? Perlmutter proposes to do so in terms of the following filter, to which he gives no name, but which we shall call the SUBJECT FILTER:

(19)   SUBJECT FILTER
       Any surface structure containing a nonimperative clause without an overt subject is ungrammatical (in English)

(Bear in mind that this was written prior to the development of X-bar Syntax, so there is no sense asking whether he means S or S-bar by 'clause'.) However, in order to handle the contrast between (18) (a) and (b) in terms of the filter, Perlmutter has to resort to the artificial expedient of claiming that the bracketed complement has the status of a Clause in (18) (a), but not in (18) (b).

There are a number of difficulties which arise from Perlmutter's treatment of the contrast between (18) (a) and (b). For one thing, the whole solution is circular. How do we know that the bracketed complement is a clause in (18) (a) but not (18) (b)? Because extraction of a *wh*-subject is possible in (18) (a) but not (18) (b). How do we know that extraction is possible in (18) (a) but not (18) (b)? Because the bracketed complement has the status of a Clause in (18) (a) but not (18) (b).

Quite apart from the vicious circularity of Perlmutter's solution, there are also considerable empirical shortcomings to it. For example, it wrongly rules out the italicised clauses as ungrammatical in English (unless, of course, we resort to the circular solution of saying that they are not clauses):

(20) (a) What shall I do? *Go home?*
    (b) 'What are you doing tonight?' – *'Washing my hair'*
    (c) 'Hm, *must remember to post this letter'*, he thought to himself

In each case, the italicised constituent in (20) is arguably a clause, and is certainly nonimperative, and yet lacks an overt subject.

A very different solution to the problem of the ungrammaticality of sentences like (18) (e) is proposed in Chomsky and Lasnik's important paper 'Filters and Control' (1977): theirs is the first attempt to develop a systematic *Theory of Filters* since Perlmutter's work almost a decade before. Exploiting the use of empty nodes, they suggest (ibid. p. 456) that sentences like (18) (a) should be ruled out by a filter which we give an informal initial approximation of in (21) below:

(21)   EMPTY SUBJECT FILTER
    Any Surface Structure containing a clause introduced by the complementiser *that*, where the complementiser is immediately followed by an empty NP, is ill-formed

How will (21) account for the ungrammaticality of (18) (a)? The answer is that movement of the *wh*-phrase *who* out of its initial position marked by — will leave behind an empty NP trace in subordinate subject position, so that the sequence *that was coming* in (18) (a) **Who did he say that was coming?* would have the structure:

(22) $[_{COMP}$ that$]$ $[_{NP_2}$ e$]$ was coming

in which we find the prohibited sequence *that – np* (where we use *np* to represent 'empty node NP').

Chomsky and Lasnik go on to suggest that our *that – np* filter should be extended to include *whether*, given contrasts like:

(23) (a)   ?*Who*$_2$ did you wonder whether Bill saw *np*$_2$?
    (b)   *Who$_2$ did you wonder whether *np*$_2$ saw Bill?

(the italicised *np* here is, of course, the trace of the moved *wh*-phrase). Both sentences in (23) violate the WH-ISLAND CONSTRAINT, since both involve movement out of an embedded interrogative clause introduced by *whether*. And yet, (23) (b) is far less acceptable than (23) (a). How can we explain this? Well, if we extend the *that – np* filter (21) to include *whether* as well as *that*, so that our revised filter becomes (informally):

(24)   *(that   ) – np
        (whether)

      i.e. 'Any sequence of *that* or *whether* immediately followed by an empty NP is ill-formed'

then we can handle the contrast easily enough: (23) (a) violates only the WH-ISLAND CONSTRAINT, not the filter (24), whereas (23) (b) violates both the WH-ISLAND CONSTRAINT and the filter (24); since (23) (b) violates two conditions, and (23) (a) only one, clearly (23) (b) is going to be expected to be less acceptable than (23) (a).

Even (24) is not general enough, however, since it fails to account for contrasts like:

(25) (a)   ?*Who*$_2$ do you wonder when Bill saw *np*$_2$?
    (b)   *Who$_2$ do you wonder when *np*$_2$ saw Bill?

Clearly, the filter (24) has to be generalised from *that* and *whether* to include any interrogative (= +WH) complementiser containing overt material, whether this be a complementiser (*whether*), or a preposed *wh*-phrase (*when*, *who*, *which boy*, etc.). Hence, following Chomsky and Lasnik (p. 456, example 83), we might replace (24) by:

(26)   *(that) – np
        (+WH)

      Informally: 'No *that*-clause or interrogative clause can have an empty NP subject'

We might also ask whether the EMPTY SUBJECT FILTER (26) should be extended to include relative clauses introduced by a *wh*-pronoun in COMP like *who*, or *which* (the filter obviously already covers relative clauses introduced by *that*, but does not generalise to *wh*-relatives, since relative clauses are noninterrogative, i.e. −WH). The answer to this question depends on whether sentences like (27) (b) are felt to be discernibly worse than those like (27) (a):

(27) (a)   **Which book$_2$ did you meet the man who wrote np$_2$?*
     (b)   ***Which author did you read a book which np$_2$ wrote?*

For me, at any rate, there is a marked difference between the two: both sentences are unidiomatic, since both involve violation of the COMPLEX NOUN PHRASE CONSTRAINT (or SUBJACENCY), which forbids extraction out of relative clauses. But (27) (b) is much worse. One way of accounting for this, would be to extend Chomsky and Lasnik's filter along the following lines:

(28)   EMPTY SUBJECT FILTER
       **[$_{\bar{S}}$ [$_{COMP}$ φ] [$_{NP}$ e] . . .] where $\bar{S}$ is tensed, and φ is non-null
       i.e. 'No tensed clause can be introduced by a nonempty COMP immediately followed by an empty NP'

So far, all the examples that we have looked at involve *tensed clauses*. How do untensed clauses (i.e. infinitives) behave in this respect, we might ask? That is, are infinitives containing a non-empty COMP followed by an empty subject ungrammatical? Consider the following contrast:

(29) (a)   I would prefer for Bill to stay here
     (b)   **Who$_2$ would you prefer for np$_2$ to stay here?*

The ill-formedness of (29) (b) suggests that we cannot have *for − np,* and hence that (28) should be expanded to include untensed as well as tensed clauses: this we might do by revising (28) as:

(30)   EMPTY SUBJECT FILTER
       **[$_{\bar{S}}$ [$_{COMP}$ φ] [$_{NP}$ e] . . .] where φ is non-null
       i.e. 'No clause can contain a nonempty COMP immediately followed by an empty NP'

(30) is intended to say that no clause with an overt COMP can have an empty subject.

However, a problem for the proposed more general formulation of the EMPTY SUBJECT FILTER is that – as Chomsky and Lasnik note (1977, p. 455) – there are dialects of English in which we find sentences such as:

(31)   *Who$_2$* are you going to try for *np$_2$* to go to the church social with you?

i.e. dialects in which the complementiser *for* can indeed be followed by an empty NP. For such dialects, it is clear that the more general formulation given in (30) does not hold. One solution to this dilemma (essentially that proposed by Chomsky and Lasnik) is to argue that all dialects of English have a more restricted filter along the lines of (26) – perhaps expanded to (28) – and that only *some* (= most) dialects of English also have an additional filter, (32) below:

(32)   FOR–TO FILTER (Chomsky and Lasnik, 1977, p. 450, example 61)
        **for – to*
        i.e. Any clause containing the complementiser *for* followed by *to with no overt constituent separating them* is ungrammatical

The italicised phrase is added here because of course *for* is separated from *to* by an empty trace NP in ungrammatical examples like (29) (b). To make this clearer, we might reformulate (32) as:

(33)   **for – φ – to*, where φ is null

Whichever version of the EMPTY SUBJECT FILTER we settle on ((26), (28), or (30)), we face problems in respect of relative clause constructions like:

(34)   the book *that fell on the floor*

To see why, consider the derivation of (34); underlying (34) would be the D-structure:

(35)   the book [$_{\bar{S}}$ [$_{COMP}$ that] [$_S$ which fell on the floor]]

Application of WH-MOVEMENT to adjoin *which* to the left of *that* would give the S-structure (36)

(36)   the book [$_{\bar{S}}$ [$_{COMP}$ which$_2$ that] [$_S$ np$_2$ fell on the floor]]

Subsequent application of WH-DELETION to erase *which* would give the Surface Structure:

(37)   the book [$_{\bar{S}}$ [$_{COMP}$ that] [$_S$ np$_2$ fell on the floor]]

And in (37), we have the prohibited sequence *that – np*, but without the sequence being ungrammatical. All the versions of the

EMPTY SUBJECT FILTER we have suggested so far wrongly predict that the resultant phrase (34) *the book that fell on the floor* is ungrammatical. But this is simply wrong. Hence, we clearly have to revise our formulation of the filter, to exclude relative clauses from it. The simplest way of doing this would be, e.g.:

(38)   EMPTY SUBJECT FILTER
          *[$_{\bar{S}}$ COMP – np . . .] where COMP is non-null, where $\bar{S}$ is tensed, and where $\bar{S}$ is not a relative clause

The condition 'where $\bar{S}$ is not a relative clause' can be reformulated in structural terms in the manner proposed in Chomsky and Lasnik (1977, p. 456), but this additional complication need not concern us here.

Once we add a condition excluding relative clauses from the filter (i.e. allowing relative clauses introduced by *that* to have empty subjects) it should become clear why we would want to restrict the resultant filter (38) to tensed clauses; for if we extend it to untensed clauses, then we would expect that while nonrelative infinitives introduced by *for* cannot have empty subjects, infinitival relatives introduced by *for* – i.e. structures like the italicised in:

(39)   He's looking for a book *for me to read*

can indeed have an empty subject after *for*. But this is not the case, as we see from the ungrammaticality of:

(40)   *I'm looking for a man *for to fix the sink*

Underlying (40) would be the D-structure:

(41)   I'm looking for a man [$_{\bar{S}}$ for who to fix the sink]

WH-MOVEMENT will then give:

(42)   I'm looking for a man [$_{\bar{S}}$ who$_2$ for np$_2$ to fix the sink]

And WH-DELETION then yields the Surface Structure:

(43)   I'm looking for a man [$_{\bar{S}}$ for np$_2$ to fix the sink]

We then predict that (43) is well-formed, since although it contains the sequence *for – to*, this is in a relative clause, and relative clauses are excluded from the filter. To be more precise, we predict that – for the majority dialect of English – the sequence *for – np – to* will be ungrammatical in nonrelative clauses like (29) (b), but grammatical in relative clauses like (40), since relative clauses are excluded from the filter. But this is quite wrong: both are equally ungrammatical in the majority dialect. In other words, a grammar of the majority dialect which attempts to amalgamate the *for – to* filter with the *COMP – np* filter will wrongly predict that sentences like (40) are well-formed. By contrast, a grammar which restricts the *COMP – np* filter to tensed nonrelative clauses – as in (38) – will correctly predict that (43) is ill-formed, since it contains the prohibited *for – to* sequence, and the FOR–TO FILTER holds for relative and nonrelative clauses alike. Overall, then, the optimum solution appears to be to have an EMPTY SUBJECT FILTER along the lines of (38) restricted to tensed nonrelative clauses, and a separate, dialect-specific FOR–TO FILTER like (32) or (33), holding for all infinitives (irrespective of whether they are relative or nonrelative clauses).

Let's move on now to consider another, less complex filter developed by Chomsky and Lasnik (1977). By way of introduction, consider relative clause structures of the type:

(44)   the man that I saw

Recall that Chomsky would argue that (44) derives from a D-structure along the lines of:

(45)   the man [$_{\bar{s}}$ [$_{COMP}$ that] [$_S$ I saw who]]

Application of WH-MOVEMENT would adjoin the *wh*-phrase *who* to COMP, giving the S-structure:

(46)   the man [$_{\bar{s}}$ [$_{COMP}$ who that] [$_S$ I saw —]]

We can now apply WH-DELETION to the S-structure (46); recall that the rule is optional in tensed relatives, in order to account for the optionality of *which* and *who* in structures like:

(47) (a)   the book (*which*) I read about
     (b)   the man (*who*) we met

If we apply our optional rule of WH-DELETION to (46), we get the Surface Structure:

(48)   the man [$_{\bar{s}}$ [$_{COMP}$ who] [$_S$ I saw —]]

and (48) is of course perfectly well-formed. But since WH-DELETION is *optional* in tensed clauses, we also have the option of *not* applying the rule, in which case the output of our grammar will be a Surface Structure like (46): but (46) is not well-formed as a Surface Structure, since we don't have relative structures like:

(49)   *the man who that I saw

in English. Clearly, we need some way of blocking Surface Structures like (49): an obvious solution would be to propose a *filter* which disallows any sentence containing more than one overt constituent in COMP. Thus (adapting the proposal made by Chomsky and Lasnik somewhat), we might propose the following:

(50)   MULTIPLY FILLED COMP FILTER
         *[$_{\text{COMP}}$ . . . α . . . β . . .] where α and β are nonempty
         i.e. 'No COMP can contain more than one overt constituent'

The filter (50) will naturally rule out Surface Structures like (46), since (46) contains two overt constituents *who* and *that* both in COMP, and (50) disallows this configuration.

The filter (50) also generalises to other cases. Consider, for example, an underlying structure such as:

(51)   COMP he has left what where?

Notice here that we can adjoin either of the *wh*-words to COMP, giving us (assuming application of NP–AUX INVERSION) the grammatical sentences:

(52) (a)   *What* has he left — where?
     (b)   *Where* has he left what —?

But if either of the *wh*-phrases can be adjoined to COMP, what is to prevent us from adjoining *both* of them to COMP, giving the ill-formed structures:

(53) (a)   *[$_{\text{COMP}}$ What where] has he left —— ?
     (b)   *[$_{\text{COMP}}$ Where what] has he left —— ?

The answer is, of course, that the MULTIPLY FILLED COMP FILTER (50) will rule out structures such as (53) as ill-formed Surface Structures, because they contain two overt constituents *what* and *where* in COMP.

In much the same way, we can show that the filter (50) also operates in infinitival relatives. Consider a sentence such as:

(54)   I'm looking for *a book for John to talk about*

The NP here would derive from the D-structure:

(55)   a book [COMP for] [S John to talk *about which*]]

Application of WH-MOVEMENT would adjoin the italicised *wh*-PP to COMP, giving:

(56)   a book [COMP *about which* for] [John to talk —]]

Recall that WH-DELETION is 'obligatory up to Recoverability' in infinitives; but here we cannot delete the italicised *wh*-phrase, because it contains the preposition *about*, and prepositions have semantic content, and the RECOVERABILITY CONDITION disallows deletion of elements with 'semantic content'. In other words, were we not to find some way of preventing this, our grammar would generate (56) as a well-formed Surface Structure. How can we avoid this? The answer is that the MULTIPLY FILLED COMP FILTER (50) will filter out structures like (56) as ill-formed, since COMP in (56) contains both the *wh*-PP *about which* and the complementiser *for*, and the filter marks as ungrammatical any surface structure with more than one overt constituent in COMP.

Let's now turn to look at another filter. We have assumed hitherto that Clauses have the status of S-bar and comprise an abstract COMP and an S, with the S expanded in the usual way. This assumption is clearly justified for embedded clauses, since they do indeed have overt complementisers, as we see from:

(57) (a)   I said [S̄ [COMP that] [S John loves Mary]]
     (b)   I wonder [S̄ [COMP whether] [S John loves Mary]]

Recall also that *wh*-phrases get moved into COMP by WH-MOVEMENT, as in the example in (58), where *who* has moved out of —:

(58)   I wonder [S̄ [COMP who] [S John loves —]

The assumption that WH-MOVEMENT involves adjunction of *wh*-phrases to COMP commits us to accepting the additional assumption that main clauses have abstract COMPs associated with them: hence we posit that a sentence like:

(59)   Who will Charles marry?

involves movement of the *wh*-phrase into an abstract COMP, giving the S-structure:

(60)   [comp who] [s will Charles marry —]]

Hence, there is clear motivation for suggesting that even nonembedded clauses have a COMP-node introducing them. Now recall that given the Base Rule (61) which Chomsky assumes:

(61) $a \to e$ (= 'Any category can be left empty')

then we should expect that the COMP introducing a clause can either be left empty, or filled by an appropriate complementiser at D-structure: and indeed in cases like (62) this does indeed seem to be the case, since the complementiser (italicised) introducing the embedded clause is optional:

(62) (a)   I think (*that*) he is leaving
     (b)   I would prefer (*for*) you to stay

Now, if COMP-nodes can generally be left empty (optionally) in the base, then we should expect that since main clauses contain a COMP-node, this node can also be left empty in the base: and indeed this is the case with direct statements like (63) (a), or direct questions like (63) (b) – *comp* in lower case letters here indicates an empty COMP:

(63) (a)   comp it is raining
     (b)   comp is it raining?

But since all categories can optionally be *filled* as well as left empty in underlying structure, our rules will also generate main clauses with appropriate overt COMPs – i.e. they will generate alongside (63) structures like (64) below:

(64) (a)   *That it is raining
     (b)   *Whether it is raining?

But such sentences are ungrammatical as nonembedded (= *root*) clauses (though they are grammatical if interpreted as (elliptical) embedded clauses, e.g. as a reply to a question like 'What did he say/ask?'). So apparently we need some kind of filter to rule out sentences like (64) as ungrammatical as root (i.e. main) clauses.

Before we look at this filter, let's turn to a second, apparently unrelated problem, which will turn out to be directly relevant. We have already mentioned a number of times the rule of NP–AUX INVERSION which applies in direct *yes–no* and *wh*-questions alike. The rule is optional in most types of questions – e.g. in *yes–no*-questions like:

(65) (a)   You're leaving already?
     (b)   Are you leaving already?

and perhaps in echo-questions like:

(66) (a)   He has bought what? (echo of statement)
     (b)   Has he bought what? (echo of question)

Notice, however, that in direct questions containing a preposed *wh*-phrase in the COMP of the main clause, we find a different situation, viz.

(67) (a)   What has he bought?
     (b)   *What he has bought?

(though again (67) (b) is OK as an elliptical embedded question, in a context like: 'What did you ask him – *what he has bought?*'). Thus, if we say that NP–AUX INVERSION is *optional* (as sentences like (65) suggest that it must be) then our grammar is going to *overgenerate* in cases like (67) (b) – i.e. it will wrongly predict that (67) (b) is grammatical as a main clause.

So now we have two apparently unrelated problems: overgeneration in cases like (64) on the one hand, and overgeneration in cases like (67) on the other. Have these two cases got anything in common? What we are concerned with essentially is main clauses like the following:

(68) (a)   *That it* is raining
     (b)   *Whether it* is raining
     (c)   *What he* has bought

What have such sentences got in common? Well, notice that in each case the sentence begins with a nonempty COMP followed by an NP. This observation prompts Chomsky and Lasnik (1977, p. 486) to propose the following filter:

(69)   ROOT CLAUSE FILTER
           *[$_{\bar{S}}$ COMP – NP . . .] where $\bar{S}$ is a root (= nonembedded)
                                   clause, and COMP is nonempty
           i.e. 'A root sentence containing a nonempty COMP im-
           mediately followed by an NP is ill-formed'

How will the filter block sentences like (68)? Well, in (68) (a) we have an overt complementiser *that* immediately followed by the NP *it*; in (68) (b) we have the overt complementiser *whether* again immediately followed by the NP *it*; and in (68) (c) we have an overt COMP containing the *wh*-phrase *what*, immediately followed by an NP *he*. So in all three cases, we have a violation of the ROOT CLAUSE FILTER (69). Thus, a grammar incorporating the filter (69) will correctly predict that all the sentences in (68) are ungrammatical as root (= nonembedded, or nonsubordinate) clauses.

Let's move on now to a further filter discussed in Chomsky and Lasnik (1977, pp. 479–82). They note that verbs like *hope* and *long* typically take a PP-complement introduced by *for*: cf.

(70) (a)   They are hoping *for* victory
      (b)   She is longing *for* his return

They also take an infinitive complement introduced by *for*: cf.

(71)   What she is longing for is *for him to return*

We would thus expect to find that *long for* can be immediately followed by a *for* + *infinitive* complement: but this is not so: cf.

(72)   *She is longing for *for him to return*

(the first *for* here is the preposition that goes with the verb *long for*, and the second one is the complementiser *for* that introduces infinitives with overt subjects). But of course (72) is ungrammatical: its grammatical counterpart is:

(73)   She is longing for him to return

In (73), it seems likely that *for* is the preposition associated with *long for* and that the infinitive has an empty COMP introducing it – i.e. (73) has the structure:

(74)   She is longing for comp him to return (comp = empty COMP)

If our base rules generate *long for* followed by an infinitival S-bar complement, then we should expect to find that the infinitive can have either an empty COMP – as in (73/74) – or a *for* COMP, as in (72). But (72) is ungrammatical. Why? Chomsky and Lasnik's solution to the problem is to suggest the following filter:

(75)   FOR–FOR FILTER (Chomsky and Lasnik, 1977, p. 481)
           **for – for*
           i.e. 'Any Surface Structure containing the sequence *for – for* is
           ungrammatical'

As our final example of a filter, let's turn to a rather different type of problem. Consider a D-structure of the form:

(76)   comp they don't think comp he will talk to who

Let's assume that WH-MOVEMENT applies successive cyclically, and that on the subordinate clause cycle, it attaches the *wh*-phrase *to who* to the subordinate COMP, giving:

(77)   comp they don't think [comp to who] he will talk

Now let's also assume that on the main clause cycle, WH-MOVEMENT applies this time to prepose only the *wh*-NP *who*, not the whole *wh*-PP *to who*; let's also assume that NP–AUX INVERSION applies: the resultant Surface Structure will then be:

(78)   [comp who] don't they think [comp to] he will talk

(we are omitting traces here, to simplify discussion). But of course the corresponding sentence:

(79)   *Who don't they think to he will talk?

is entirely ungrammatical. Why? One suggestion might be that it is because we have *stranded* the preposition *to* (i.e. left it without its NP-complement *who*) internally within the sentence in (79). But this cannot be the right explanation, since the same has happened in the grammatical sentence (80) below:

(80)   Who did he talk *to* in the pub?

However, there is an interesting difference between (78) and (80): in (78), the preposition has been stranded internally within COMP, whereas in (80) the preposition is stranded internally within S. Accordingly, we might propose a filter along the lines of:

(81)   STRANDED PREPOSITION FILTER
         *[comp . . . [pp P − φ] . . .] where φ is null
         i.e. 'Any COMP containing a PP which contains a P without an
             overt complement is ill-formed'
         Or (informally) 'You can't strand a preposition in COMP'

The filter (81) will neatly handle the contrast between the ungrammatical (79) where *to* has been stranded in the subordinate COMP, and the grammatical (80) where *to* has been stranded, but not in COMP.

Furthermore, the filter (81) also proves useful in the case of infinitival relatives. Consider a D-structure like:

(82)   a book [s̄ comp [s PRO to talk about which]]

Adjunction of the *wh*-PP *about which* to COMP will give:

(83)   a book [s̄ [COMP about which] [s PRO to talk —]]

Suppose we now apply WH-DELETION to delete simply the *wh*-NP *which*: the resulting Surface Structure will be:

(84)   a book [s̄ [COMP about] [s PRO to talk —]]

But the structure (84) is ill-formed, as we see from:

(85)   *I'm looking for a book about to talk (* in intended sense)

Why is (85) ill-formed? The STRANDED PREPOSITION FILTER (81) provides an obvious answer, since (84) and (85) contain the preposition *about* stranded internally within COMP. Thus, our filter not only accounts for why WH-MOVEMENT leads to ungrammaticality in (78), but also accounts for why WH-DELETION leads to ungrammaticality in (83/84).

Having looked at some specific filters, let's turn now to look at some more general theoretical questions. The overall organisation of a grammar that we have envisaged hitherto comprises essentially:

(86) (i)   A very general set of Base Rules, Transformations, and Deletion Rules which massively *overgenerate*: i.e. they generate not only well-formed sentence structures, but also ill-formed ones

   (ii)   A set of *constraints* and *filters* which mark the overgenerated sentences as ungrammatical

A natural question to ask is: 'Why assume a very general set of sentence-formation rules in the first place which massively overgenerate, and then resort to devices like filters to deal with the overgeneration?' Why not revise the rules (86) (i) in such a way that they *never* overgenerate? Surely then we would have a more 'natural' grammar of English?

There are a number of answers to this question, ranging from the metatheoretical to the purely practical. But before we look at these, perhaps we should first clear up a certain conceptual confusion in the notion of *overgeneration*. Intuitively, we tend to interpret the notion as meaning something along the lines of:

(87)   A set of rules *overgenerates* if it wrongly generates as well-formed, sentence-structures which are actually ill-formed

Behind the conception embodied in (87) is the hidden assumption (88):

(88)   A set of sentence-generation rules like (86) (i) should constitute a set of *necessary and sufficient* conditions for sentences to be well-formed in English

But this is clearly not the case: on the contrary, rules like (86) (i) constitute a set of necessary *but not sufficient* conditions for sentences to be well-formed in English. Only an *overall grammar* complete with Base Rules, Transformations, Constraints on Transformations, Deletion Rules, Constraints on Deletion, Surface Structure Filters, Semantic Interpretation Rules, and so forth can (if adequately formulated) constitute a necessary and sufficient set of conditions for a sentence to be well-formed. In other words, there's nothing intrinsically 'wrong' with rules that overgenerate – provided that the overgeneration is taken care of elsewhere in the grammar. We only need get worried if the *overall grammar* overgenerates in non-trivial ways.

But even if, from a metatheoretical perspective, there is nothing 'wrong' with rules that overgenerate, isn't it still the case that *overgeneration* is a result of having a set of sentence-generation rules that are excessively general, or just badly formulated? Wouldn't it be better to give the rules concerned a 'tighter' formulation so that they don't 'leak' (i.e. overgenerate) in the first place? Well, to do that, we would need to build in to our formulation of each of the rules concerned a number of conditions of application which are specific to that rule – i.e. a number of *rule-specific applicability conditions*. But in an obvious sense, filters are more *general* than rule-specific applicability conditions. That is, filters take the general form 'Any structure of type X is ill-formed, *irrespective of whatever set of rules might be used to generate X*': but rule-specific applicability conditions are less general, since they say in effect 'Rule R must not produce structures of type X.' The *filter* states that no rules at all can produce an (overall) output X; the rule-specific applicability condition says that rule R can't, *but says nothing about whether other rules can produce structures of type X*. Therefore, a rule-specific applicability condition is less general, and has less predictive power than a *filter*. So, on considerations of *generality* alone, filters are to be preferred to rule-specific applicability conditions.

By way of illustration, consider our STRANDED PREPOSITION FILTER (81): this filter ruled out certain outputs from the rule of WH-MOVEMENT in cases like (78), and from the rule of WH-DELETION in cases like (84). If instead of a filter, we had used rule-specific applicability conditions, we would have had to build in one set of conditions to WH-MOVEMENT, and another set of conditions to WH-DELETION, thereby needing two sets of conditions, instead of *one* filter. Clearly the *filter* is the more general solution.

Thus one reason for preferring filters to rule-specific applicability conditions is their greater *generality*. Chomsky would add to this considerations of *universality* as well. Consider the rule of WH-MOVEMENT. If we build into our formulation of this rule idiosyncratic language-specific (or even dialect-specific) conditions of application, then it is self-evidently impossible to attain any *universal* formulation of WH-MOVEMENT valid across languages. As a very simple illustration of this point, consider the following contrast between English and French:

(89) (a) Who was he talking to?
    (b) *Qui parlait-il à?
        Who talked-he to? = 'Who was he talking to?'

This illustrates the point that WH-MOVEMENT can strand prepositions internally within an S (though not in COMP) in English, but not in French. Of course, one could handle this difference between the two languages by building rule-specific applicability conditions into our formulation of the rule of WH-MOVEMENT itself, with different conditions holding for each language: e.g. along the (informal) lines of:

(90) (a) DÉPLACEMENT DE QU (French)
        Adjoin a *wh*-phrase *not immediately contained in PP* to COMP
    (b) WH-MOVEMENT (English)
        Adjoin a *wh*-phrase to COMP

We would then end up with two entirely distinct rules, as their names suggest: one for French, and a different one for English. Under this analysis, there would be no possibility of a universal rule of WH-MOVEMENT. The two rules in (90) would be *similar*, but not *the same rule*.

By contrast, under the *filters* account, WH-MOVEMENT would be given a universal formulation along the lines of:

(91)   Adjoin *wh*-phrase to COMP

(NB: saying that (91) is *universal* does not mean that every language has (91): it means that *if* a language has a rule of WH-MOVEMENT, it will take the form of (91) and move *wh*-phrases to be adjoined to COMP, and not e.g. to PP.) The differences between French and English could then be handled by language-specific Surface Structure Filters. More precisely, whereas English would be subject to the STRANDED PREPOSITION FILTER (81) which forbids a preposition from being stranded inside COMP, French would be subject to the more general filter (92) below:

(92)   FILTRE DES PRÉPOSITIONS EN RADE
            *$[_{PP} P - \varphi]$ where φ is null
            i.e. you can't have a PP containing a Preposition without an
            overt complement: = You can't strand a preposition

The filters approach has a number of advantages: firstly, it enables us to maintain a very general, putatively universal formulation of WH-MOVEMENT; secondly, it permits a revealing comparison of the similarities and differences between French and English, insofar as both languages have filters forbidding prepositions from being stranded, but the French filter is more general than the English one. And thirdly, since filters of the kind we are talking about operate at Surface Structure, relegating the differences between French and English to a difference of *filters* is in effect saying that the differences between French and English (two historically closely related languages) is merely a *superficial* one, concerned with certain minor Surface Structure differences – but these differences do not affect the 'common core' of syntactic rules like WH-MOVEMENT which the languages share.

To considerations of the added generality and universality achieved by the use of filters, Chomsky would add a further metatheoretical consideration: namely that a theory which stipulates that:

(93)   No rule may be subject to a rule-specific condition of application

is far more *constrained* than a theory which stipulates that:

(94)   Every individual rule may be subject to its own rule-specific idiosyncratic conditions of application

A theory which maintains position (94) – Chomsky would argue – is far less constrained (in the sense that it permits a much larger class of potential grammars) than a theory which – like Chomsky's – adopts position (93). And the more constrained a theory is (Chomsky would maintain), the more plausible it is as a model of language and language acquisition.

Now let's turn briefly to another question – the question of the place of filters (of the type we have talked about here) in a grammar. We have referred to them a number of times as *Surface Structure Filters*, the clear implication being that they operate at Surface Structure, on the output generated by successive application of the Base Rules, Transformations, and Deletion Rules. Why should filters *follow* the application of Deletion Rules, we might ask? We can answer this in relation to the MULTIPLY FILLED COMP FILTER (50) discussed earlier. Consider a D-structure like:

(95)   the book [COMP that] I dislike *which*

Application of WH-MOVEMENT to adjoin the italicised *wh*-phrase to COMP will give the S-structure:

(96)   the book [COMP which that] I dislike

(ignoring traces, for simplicity). Applying the optional rule of WH-DELETION will give us the Surface Structure (97) (a), whereas taking the option of not applying the rule will give us the Surface Structure (97) (b):

(97) (a)   the book [COMP that] I dislike
     (b)   the book [COMP which that] I dislike

Now let's consider three alternatives:

(98) (a)   The MULTIPLY FILLED COMP FILTER (saying that no COMP can contain more than one overt constituent) operates at D-structure
     (b)   It operates at S-structure
     (c)   It operates at Surface Structure

(98) (a) would clearly give the wrong results: both (97) (a) and (b) have the D-structure (95), and (95) does not violate the filter (50), hence we would wrongly predict that both (97) (a) and (b) are well-formed. (98) (b) also gives the wrong results, since both phrases in (97) have the same S-structure (96), and (96) violates the filter, so that our grammar wrongly predicts that both (97) (a) and (b) are ill-formed. But (98) (c) *does* give the right predictions: (97) (a) is OK because it contains only one overt element in COMP, whereas (97) (b) is ill-formed because it contains two overt constituents – *which* and *that* – in COMP. In other words, we have empirical evidence that filters of the type we have discussed here must operate at *Surface Structure* – after application of the deletion rules.

Summary

In addition to *constraints*, a second device used to block overgeneration by syntactic rules are *filters*: whereas constraints monitor the input and output of a given rule in a derivation, filters by contrast scan the surface structures produced by the grammar as a whole. Thus, the revised overall model of grammar that we are envisaging takes the form:

(99) (i)　*Base*
　　　　　(a) Phrase Structure Rules (= categorial rules)
　　　　　(b) Lexicon (lexical entries, Lexical Redundancy Rules, Word-Formation Rules, Restructuring Rules, etc.)
　　　　　(c) Lexical Insertion Rule
　　　　　Output of Base = D-Structures
　　　(ii)　*Transformational Component*
　　　　　(a) Transformations
　　　　　(b) Conditions (= Constraints) on Transformations
　　　　　Output of Transformational Component = S-structures
　　　(iii)　*Deletion Component*
　　　　　(a) Deletion Rules
　　　　　(b) Conditions on Deletion
　　　　　Output of Deletion Component = Surface Structures
　　　(iv)　*(Surface Structure) Filters*
　　　　　Output of Filters = filtered Surface Structures

Among the filters we discussed in this chapter are the following:

(100) (i) INTERNAL CLAUSE FILTER (Ross, adapted)
Any Surface Structure containing an S-bar embedded within another clause, and flanked to the left and right by overt lexical material from that clause, is ill-formed

(ii) EMPTY SUBJECT FILTER (Chomsky and Lasnik, adapted)
No tensed nonrelative clause with a nonempty COMP can have an empty NP immediately following COMP

(iii) FOR–TO FILTER (Chomsky and Lasnik)
Any clause containing the complementiser *for* followed by *to* with no overt constituent separating them is ungrammatical

(iv) MULTIPLY FILLED COMP FILTER (Chomsky and Lasnik)
No COMP can contain more than one overt constituent

(v) ROOT CLAUSE FILTER (Chomsky and Lasnik)
Any root clause containing an overt COMP immediately followed by NP is illformed

(vi) FOR–FOR FILTER (Chomsky and Lasnik)
Any clause containing the sequence *for – for* is ungrammatical

(vii) STRANDED PREPOSITION FILTER (English)
No preposition can be stranded internally within COMP

EXERCISES

Exercise I

For the purposes of this exercise, make the following assumptions:

(1) An interrogative COMP (= +WH) can either be left empty in D-structure, or filled by *whether – optionally*

(2) WH-MOVEMENT is always optional

(3) NP–AUX INVERSION is always optional

Given these assumptions, our grammar will generate all of the examples below as well-formed Surface Structures. Which ones are actually ill-formed, and what filters will be needed to account for their ill-formedness?

(4) (a) John will choose who? (no *whether*, no INVERSION, no WH-MOVEMENT)

(b) Will John choose who? (no *whether*, INVERSION, no WH-MOVEMENT)

(c) Who will John choose? (no *whether*, INVERSION, WH-MOVEMENT)

(d) Who John will choose? (no *whether*, no INVERSION, WH-MOVEMENT)

(5) (a) Whether John will choose who? (*whether*, no INVERSION, WH-MOVEMENT)

(b) Whether will John choose who? (*whether*, INVERSION, no WH-MOVEMENT)

(c) Who whether will John choose? (*whether*, INVERSION, WH-MOVEMENT)

(d) Who whether John will choose? (*whether*, no INVERSION, WH-MOVEMENT)

Do any of these sentences require us to posit additional filters, over and above the ones in the text (see (100))?

Exercise II

Discuss the status of the following sentence with respect to the MULTIPLY FILLED COMP FILTER:

(1) You wonder *whether who* will come?

*Exercise III

For the purposes of the exercise, assume that NP–AUX INVERSION is an optional rule which can apply in root and embedded clauses alike. Assume also the grammaticality judgements given below. What kind of filters will we need to block the ungrammatical sentences (i) in the dialects where the sentences marked % are grammatical, and (ii) in the dialects where the % sentences are ungrammatical:

(1) (a) He asked me where she had gone
(b) %He asked me where had she gone
(c) He asked me whether she had gone
(d) *He asked me whether had she gone
(e) *He asked me she had gone
(f) %He asked me had she gone

*Exercise IV

Assume for the purposes of the exercise that adjectives like *sure* are subcategorised as permitting an S-bar complement optionally introduced by the preposition *about*: viz.

(1) *sure*: A, $+[— \text{(about)} − \bar{S}]$

Given this assumption, consider the following sentences, and decide what filter(s) might be needed to filter out any you regard as ungrammatical:

(2) (a) I'm not sure about whether he's coming
(b) I'm not sure whether he's coming

(3) (a) I'm not sure about where he's going
(b) I'm not sure where he's going

(4) (a) I'm sure about that he's leaving
(b) I'm sure that he's leaving

(5) (a)   I'm anxious about for you to help me
   (b)   I'm anxious for you to help me
(6) (a)   I'm undecided about whether to interfere
   (b)   I'm undecided whether to interfere

*Exercise V

Chomsky and Lasnik suggest a **for–for* filter for English. Assuming the grammaticality judgements given below, could this filter be generalised in any way?

(1) (a)   I don't know if she's coming back tomorrow yet
   (b)   *I don't know if she's come back yet yet
(2) (a)   Mary wanted to see the prisoners, so I showed her them
   (b)   *Mary wanted to see the prisoner, so I showed her her
(3) (a)   I think that for Napoleon to slight Josephine would be disgraceful
   (b)   *I think that that Napoleon slighted Josephine was disgraceful
(4) (a)   I didn't know where to put it, but finally I decided on under the table
   (b)   *I didn't know where to put it, but finally I decided on on the table
(5) (a)   He's more famous as an actor than as a sculptor
   (b)   *He's just as famous as an actor as as a sculptor

Exercise VI

The following data contrast children's sentences (at the age of 2–3 years) with that of the corresponding sentences in adult speech. If we assume that NP–AUX INVERSION is optional in both child and adult speech, what filter could we say that the adult has which the child has not yet incorporated into his grammar? (Ignore minor morphological errors.)

	CHILD	ADULT
(1) (a)	What did you doed?	What did you do?
(2) (a)	Where's his other eye?	Where's his other eye?
(3) (a)	Why kitty can't stand up?	Why can't kitty stand up?
(4) (a)	Which way they should go?	Which way should they go?
(5) (a)	Where the other Joe will drive?	Where will the other Joe drive?

**Exercise VII

Decide whether the following sentences are grammatical, and what problems – if any – they pose for any of the filters proposed earlier.

(1)   Who do you think that, in all probability, would make a good chairman?
(2)   Who would you prefer for not to be present?
(3)   What a nice pear Mary's got!
(4)   Whether perhaps it is raining? (= direct question)
(5)   He admitted that he had been drinking both to me and to his mother

***Exercise VIII**

Given the development of Trace Theory, many constraints on movement rules can instead be reformulated as filters of the schematic form

(1)   ISLAND FILTER
        Any structure of the schematic form below is ill-formed:
        $\ldots X_2 \ldots [\alpha \ldots t_2 \ldots] \ldots X_2 \ldots$
        where t_2 is a coindexed empty node trace of X_2 and where α is an
        island (i.e. a coordinate structure, an embedded question, a complex
        NP, a sentential subject, etc.)

Show that given this reinterpretation of many of the constraints we looked at earlier, it would still be possible to account for the ill-formedness of sentences like those in (2) below, but *only if these particular filters apply at S-Structure* (prior to Deletion), *not if they apply at Surface Structure*:

(2) (a)   *a man that I know Mary and
    (b)   ?a man that I'm curious about whether you met
    (c)   *a man that for me to criticise would be unfair
    (d)   *a man that I know someone who knows

Assume that *deletion* involves erasure of a category and its contents (i.e. doesn't leave an empty node behind).

FURTHER READING

For earlier work on the Theory of Filters, see:

Perlmutter (1971) *Constraints*

For more recent work, see:

Chomsky and Lasnik (1977) 'Filters and Control'

10

Case

Personal pronouns in English may have as many as three distinct forms – cf. the paradigm:

(1)   he – him – his

These three forms are traditionally referred to as different *cases* (or case-forms) of the pronoun: thus, *he* might be called the *nominative* case-form of the pronoun, *him* the *objective* form, and *his* the *genitive* form. These different case-forms are typically used in different sentence-positions, as we see from:

(2) (a)   *He* lives here (= *nominative*)
    (b)   I can't stand *him* (= *objective*)
    (c)   *His* car has·broken down (= *genitive*)

Other personal pronouns in English also have the same three case-forms, as we see from the paradigm:

(3)   *nominative*   I   we   he   they
       objective   me   us   him   them
       genitive   my   our   his   their

We could argue that a parallel case-system operates in more literary registers of English with the relative and interrogative pronoun *who* (= *nominative*), which has the objective form *whom*, and the genitive form *whose*.

In all the five pronouns we have looked at so far, each case-form is phonetically distinct from any other case-form; this is not always so, however. For example, with the pronoun *she* (= *nominative*), we find no overt distinction between the objective and genitive forms, both being *her*. And the pronouns *you* and *it* share a common nominative–objective form, though have distinct genitive forms (*your* and *its*). The same is true of relative–interrogative *who* in colloquial English, where *who* is used as a nominative and objective form alike, with the distinct genitive form *whose*. Overall, then, we may say that pronouns in English have three distinct case-forms – *nominative, objective* and *genitive* (though these distinctions are not always phonetically marked). The case-system found in English pronouns can thus be represented more completely as:

(4)

nominative	I	we	he	they	she	you	it	who
objective	me	us	him	them	her	you	it	who(m)
genitive	my	our	his	their	her	your	its	whose

So far, we have only looked at case in *pronouns*: but bearing in mind that pronouns are NPs in English, we might ask whether *case* is not so much a property of pronouns, but rather of NPs in general. And indeed, it does seem that this is the case, since typical NPs like *John* and *the man next door* can enter into the same case-paradigm as we find in (2): cf.

(5) (a)   *John* lives here (= *nominative*)
    (b)   I can't stand *John* (= *objective*)
    (c)   *John's* car has broken down (= *genitive*)

We might therefore say that it is a general property of NPs in English that they have three case-forms: *nominative, objective* and *genitive*. In the case of nonpronominal NPs, however, we find that there is no overt phonetic distinction between nominative and objective case-forms (just as there is no overt phonetic distinction between the nominative and objective forms of pronouns like *you, it* and (colloquially) *who*). We shall continue to assume (following Chomsky) that all NPs in English have three distinct case-forms (*nominative, objective* and *genitive*), even though some case-distinctions may not be phonetically realised in modern English.

As we noted earlier in relation to (2), different case-forms are appropriate to different NP-positions in a sentence: e.g. we couldn't have used the objective form in place of the nominative in (2) (a), nor in place of the genitive in (2) (c); and we couldn't have used the nominative in place of the objective in (2) (b): cf.

(6) (a)   **Him* lives here (= *objective*)
    (b)   **I can't stand *he* (= *nominative*)
    (c)   **Him* car has broken down (= *objective*)

Another way of putting this is to say that NPs in English are assigned a case (*nominative*, or *objective*, or *genitive*) in virtue of their position in a sentence. We might therefore propose that any adequate grammar of English must contain a set of *case-marking rules* which assign to NPs some case appropriate to their sentence-position. Let's consider how these case rules might work for English.

We'll begin by looking at the case-marking of prepositional objects – i.e. of NPs which are the complement of a preposition. As we see from (7), such NPs are assigned *objective* case:

(7)   He ran towards *me/*I/*my*

Traditional grammars speak of a preposition *governing* its object: informally, then, we might propose a case-marking rule such as the following:

(8)   NP is assigned the case-feature [+OBJECTIVE] if it is governed by a Preposition

Of course, *objective* case is not only used in English to mark the object of a preposition; it is also assigned to an NP which is the object of a transitive verb: cf. e.g.

(9)   John hit *me/*I/*my*

Once again traditional grammars often speak of a verb as *governing* its object; so we might propose for sentences like (9) an informal case-marking rule such as:

(10)   NP is assigned the case-feature [+ OBJECTIVE] if it is governed by a transitive verb

Clearly we can conflate our two rules (8) and (10) into a single rule as:

(11)   NP is assigned the case-feature [+OBJECTIVE] if it is governed by a transitive verb or preposition

Is it merely a coincidence that both transitive verbs and prepositions assign objective case to their complements in English? Within the theory of syntactic features developed by Chomsky, this is not a coincidence, since V = [−N, +V] and P = [−N, −V], so that V and P share in common the fact that they are both non-nominal, i.e. [−N]. Thus, greater generality would be achieved if we reformulated (11) as:

(12)   NP is assigned the case-feature [+OBJECTIVE] if it is governed by a transitive [−N]

But the difficulty that we face with a rule like (11) or (12) is that we haven't defined what we mean by the term *govern*. What we want to say is that in a PP like (13) (a) below [p *towards*] governs [NP *me*], and that in a VP like (13) (b) below, [v *hit*] governs [NP *me*]:

(13) (a)   (13) (b)

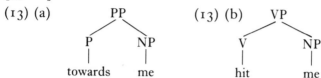

As a first approximation (to be revised later), we might try to define the relation *governs* in the following terms:

(14)   A Preposition or Verb governs any constituent which it c-commands

where *c-commands* (= constituent commands) is defined as:

(15)   X c-commands Y iff (= if and only if) the first branching node dominating X dominates Y, and X does not dominate Y, nor Y, X.

Let's see whether in terms of the above definitions, the preposition *towards* c-commands the NP *me* in the structure (13) (a). It seems clear that it does, since the first branching node dominating the preposition *towards* is the PP-node, and this dominates the NP *me*. Likewise, in (13) (b) the verb *hit* again c-commands the NP *me*, since the first branching node above the verb *hit* is the VP-node, and this dominates the NP *me*. Hence it might seem plausible at first sight to equate the relation *governs* with *c-commands*.

However, closer reflection shows that this cannot be so. For consider the structure of the VP *ran towards me* in a sentence like (7) *He ran towards me*. This might be:

(16)

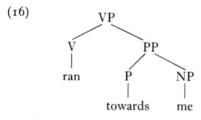

In (16), we want to say that the NP *me* is governed by (i.e. is the object of) the preposition *towards*, not by the verb *ran*. Now while it is true (as we have just seen in relation to (13) (a)) that the preposition *towards* c-commands the NP *me*, it is also true that the verb *ran* c-commands the NP *me* in (16). For notice that the first branching node above the V *ran* is the VP-node, and that this VP-node dominates the NP *me*. Thus if we (wrongly) equate the traditional notion *govern* with the structural notion *c-command*, we find that both the verb *ran* and the preposition *towards* actually c-command the NP *me*. In informal terms, this amounts to saying that *me* is the object of both *towards* and *ran* in (16). This is clearly counterintuitive, since we want to say that the NP *me* is the object of (and hence governed by) only the preposition *towards*, not the verb *ran*.

Incidentally, similar problems would arise with complex PPs like that italicised in:

(17)   The noise came *from inside the house*

If the italicised phrase is assumed to have the structure:

(18)

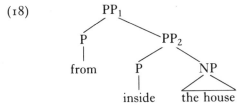

then it turns out that not only the preposition *inside* c-commands the NP *the house* (since the first branching node above the preposition *inside* is PP$_2$, and PP$_2$ dominates the NP *the house*), but in addition the preposition *from* also c-commands *the house* (by virtue of the fact that the first branching node above *from* is PP$_1$, and PP$_1$ also dominates the NP *the house*). In other words, if we equate *governs* with *c-commands*, we will be saying in effect that both *inside* and *from* govern *the house*, and hence that *the house* is both the object of *inside*, and the object of *from*. But this is counterintuitive, since what we want to say is that the NP *the house* is governed only by the preposition *inside*, not by the preposition *from*.

But – we might object – does it really matter if we say that a given NP can be governed both by a verb and by a preposition, or by more than one preposition? After all, since verbs and prepositions in English both assign the same case to their objects (i.e. *objective* case), the worst that can happen is that a given NP will be assigned the same case twice: e.g. in (18) the NP *the house* will be marked objective once by virtue of being c-commanded by *inside*, and a second time by virtue of being c-commanded by *from*. And does it really matter if a given NP is assigned the same case more than once?

Well, we might object to multiple assignment of the same case to a given NP on the grounds of its morphological implausibility: e.g. we don't find NPs in English carrying two genitive inflections (i.e. two occurrences of the possessive –*'s* morpheme: hence the ill-formedness of **John's's*), and hence there is no reason to assume that any NP in English can be multiply marked for the same case. But the problem is not just that identifying *govern* with *c-command* leads to some NPs being assigned the same case more than once; rather, it is more serious, since we can show that it leads to NPs being assigned the *wrong* case in certain situations. Consider, for example, the case-marking of the italicised NP in a sentence such as:

(19)   I think that *John* left

We might assume that the VP *think that John left* has the structure:

(20)

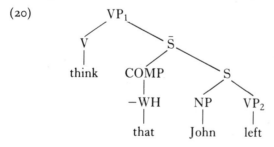

Notice here that the transitive verb *think* actually c-commands the NP *John* since the first branching node above *think* is VP_1, and VP_1 dominates the NP *John*. Since *think* is a transitive verb, then if we say that transitive verbs assign *objective* case to NPs which they c-command, the NP *John* will wrongly be marked [+OBJECTIVE] in (20). *Wrongly*, because we see if we replace

John by an appropriate pronoun that we must have a nominative NP here, not an objective one: cf.

(21) (a)   I think that *he* left (= *nominative*)
     (b)   *I think that *him* left (= *objective*)

So it seems clear that we cannot define the relation *governs* in terms of *c-command*.

The problems for any attempt to identify *governs* with *c-commands* are multiplied in languages with richer case-systems than English. Take the case-system of Latin, for example. Whereas in English both the object of a verb and the object of a preposition are assigned the same case (*objective*), this is not so in Latin; in Latin, the direct object of a transitive verb is assigned a case known traditionally as *accusative*; the complements of certain prepositions are also assigned accusative case; but Latin also has a subset of prepositions which assign to the NPs they govern a different case (with no correlate in English) called the *ablative* in traditional Latin grammar (the *ablative* case is morphologically distinct from the *accusative* case). One such preposition which 'takes' the ablative case is *de*, meaning 'about'. In the light of this, consider the problems posed by case-marking of the italicised NP in a sentence like:

(22)   Caesar de *bellis* scripsit
        Caesar (*nominative*) about wars (*ablative*) wrote
        = 'Caesar wrote about (the) wars'

Let's assume for the sake of exposition that the phrase *de bellis scripsit* is a VP with the structure:

(23)

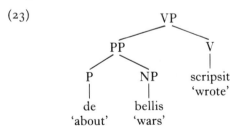

If we look closely at (23), we see that both the preposition *de* 'about' and the transitive verb *scripsit* 'wrote' c-command the NP *bellis* 'wars'. Since *de* is a preposition which 'takes' the ablative case, then if we say that verbs and prepositions assign case to NPs that they c-command, *bellis* will be assigned *ablative* case. But since the verb *scripsit* 'wrote' also c-commands the NP *bellis* 'wars', and since it is a transitive verb, and transitive verbs assign *accusative* case, then the NP *bellis* 'wars' will also be assigned *accusative* case. The net result will thus be that the NP *bellis* is assigned both *ablative* and *accusative* case. But this is simply *wrong*: the NP *bellis* is morphologically *ablative* (the corresponding accusative form being *bella*, entirely distinct), and is not in any sense accusative. In other words, the c-command analysis would wrongly produce instances of *case conflict*, where a given NP is assigned more than one distinct case. But there is no evidence that this situation arises in natural languages: i.e. it is typically the case that NPs in natural language are morphologically marked for only one case.

How can we avoid the situation in which a given NP is multiply marked for case (e.g. either assigned the same case more than once, or assigned more than one distinct case)? Clearly, what we want to do is define the notion *govern* in such a way that no NP can have more than one *governor*, and of course in such a way as to ensure that an NP is assigned the right governor. To be more concrete, we want to specify that in (16) it is the P *towards* and not the V *ran* that governs the NP *me*; that in (18) it is the P *inside* and not the P *from* that governs the NP *the house*; and that in (23) it is the P *de* and not the V *scripsit* that governs the NP *bellis*. How can we do this? Thinking rather more carefully about these structures, it seems that what we want to be able to do is to pick out the *minimal* (= 'least inclusive', 'smallest', or 'lowest in the tree', in informal terms) potential governing node which c-commands the NP in question as the governor of that NP. Thus, in our earlier structure (16) – repeated here as (24) for convenience –

(24)

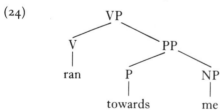

although both the verb *ran* and the preposition *towards* c-command the NP *me*, *towards* is the *minimal* potential governor of *me* in the sense that (informally) it is the 'lower' of the two. This suggests that a more promising definition of *governs* would be along the following lines (adapted from Chomsky, 'Markedness and Core Grammar' (1980), p. 12):

(25)   X governs Y iff X is the minimal governing node c-commanding Y

A *governing node* is simply a node which can act as a governor: we have already seen that V and P can be governors: Chomsky argues that the same is also true of N and A; the resultant set of governing nodes (V, P, N and A) he calls *lexical categories* in more recent work (employing the term in a very different sense from that we have met so far, where by *lexical category* we have meant *non-phrasal category*). What (25) amounts to in more formal terms is the following (extremely complex) condition:

(26)   X governs Y just in case
             (i) X is a governing node c-commanding Y
         & (ii) there is no other governing node Z such that:
                     (a) X c-commands Z
             & (b) Z c-commands Y
             & (c) Z does not c-command X

(For the definition of c-command, see (15); recall that we are assuming that only lexical categories (V, P, N, A) are governing nodes.) Let's see whether our revised definition of *govern* in terms of *minimally c-command* will produce the desired result of saying that e.g. in a structure like (24) the verb *ran* does not *govern* the NP *me*. Let's assume the following values for X, Y and Z:

(27)

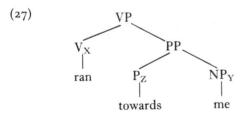

Referring back to the complex definition in (26), let's now ask whether the verb *ran* (= X) governs the NP *me* (= Y) in the sense of (26). Condition (26) (i) is certainly met, since X c-commands Y by virtue of the fact that the first branching node above the verb *ran* (= X) is the VP-node, and this does indeed dominate the NP *me* (= Y). But notice that condition (ii) is *not* met, because there is indeed a governing node Z (= the Preposition *towards*) which has the properties specified in (a), (b) and (c) in (26) (ii); for notice that firstly *towards* satisfies (26) (ii) (a) because X (= the verb *ran*) c-commands Z (= *towards*) by dint of the fact that the first branching node above X (= VP) dominates Z (= *towards*). And secondly, the preposition *towards* satisfies condition (26) (ii) (b), since the first branching node above *towards* is the PP-node, and this dominates Y (= *the house*). And thirdly, *towards* satisfies (26) (ii) (c) since Z does not c-command X by virtue of the fact that the first branching node above the preposition *towards* is the PP-node, and this does not dominate the verb *ran*. Thus, the verb *ran* does not govern the NP *me* because although condition (26) (i) is met, condition (26) (ii) is not.

So far, we have shown that if we define *govern* in terms of *minimally c-command* (cf. (25)), we reach the correct conclusion that the verb *ran* does not govern the NP *me* in (24). But given the revised definition of *govern*, will it turn out (as we want) that the preposition *towards* governs the NP *me*? To see this, let's change the values of X, Y and Z to the following:

(28)

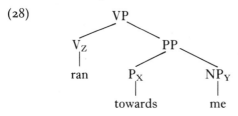

and let's now ask whether *towards* governs *me* in the sense of (26). Notice that condition (26) (i) is met, because X (= *towards*) c-commands Y (= *me*) in the sense that the first branching node over *towards* is PP, and PP dominates the NP *me*. But is the complex negative condition (26) (ii) met? Let's see. The only plausible candidate for Z here is the V *ran*; but *ran* does not satisfy the conditions for Z in (26) (ii): e.g. X (*towards*) does not c-command Z (*ran*) in (28), since the first branching node above the preposition *towards* is PP, and PP does not dominate Z (= the verb *ran*). Hence, *ran* cannot be Z; since there is no other plausible source of Z in (28), we conclude that there is in fact no Z satisfying the conditions laid down in (26) (ii) (a), (b) and (c); hence, both conditions (26) (i) and (ii) are met, and the preposition *towards* does indeed govern the NP *me*. We have thus reached the situation we wanted: namely that in terms of the definition in (26), the preposition *towards* governs the NP *me*, but the verb *ran* does not. So, it looks like (26) may be a more adequate definition of the term *govern*.

Although (26) proves adequate to handle the cases we have looked at so far (provided we make certain additional assumptions which we will deal with shortly about cases like (20)), there are some structures where (26) seems to produce the wrong results. Consider, for example, the structure of the italicised phrase in:

(29)   Many people are baffled *by linguists' theories*

Let's assume that the structure of the italicised phrase is:

(30)

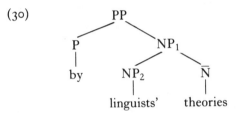

In terms of the definition of *govern* given in (26), it turns out (as you can verify for yourself) that the preposition *by* governs not only (correctly) NP_1, but also (incorrectly) NP_2. The net result of this is that NP_2 *linguists'* is assigned objective case, by virtue of being governed by the preposition *by*. Clearly, however, this is wrong, since NP_2 must be marked *genitive*, not objective, since if we replace *linguists'* in (29) by a pronoun which is morphologically marked for case, we need a genitive, not an objective pronoun:

(31) (a)   Many people are baffled by *their* theories (= *genitive*)
     (b)   *Many people are baffled by *them* theories (= *objective*)

Our problem, then, is to tighten up the definition of *govern* in (26) so that we can exclude the possibility of the preposition *by* governing (and assigning objective case to) NP_2 in (30), while still allowing *by* to govern (and assign objective case to) NP_1 (that NP_1 is objective can be seen from the fact that you can replace the phrase *linguists' theories* by the objective pronoun *them*). How can we do this?

The solution proposed by Chomsky in his more recent work is to stipulate:

(32)   NP is an absolute barrier to government (i.e. one category cannot govern another across an intervening NP boundary)

Returning now to our structure:

(33)   [$_{PP}$ by ([$_{NP_1}$) [$_{NP_2}$ linguists'] theories]]

we see that the reason why the preposition *by* cannot govern NP$_2$ *linguists'* is because of the presence of the intervening encircled NP-boundary, NP$_2$. Thus, if we tighten our definition of *govern* in (26) to include the condition (32) that NP is an absolute barrier to government, we reach the correct conclusion that *by* in (30) governs NP$_1$, not NP$_2$. Hence only NP$_1$ is marked *objective*, not NP$_2$.

A natural question to ask is whether other categories also form an absolute barrier to government. There is some evidence that this may be true of clause boundaries (e.g. S-bar) as well. Consider e.g. the ungrammaticality of:

(34)   *John tried Mary to leave

How can we account for the fact that (34) is ungrammatical? One possible answer might be formulated in terms of case-marking. Let's assume that the VP *tried Mary to leave* has the structure:

(35)

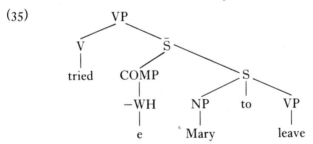

Now, if we assume for the moment that only lexical categories (V, P, N, A) can be governing nodes (and hence the empty complementiser introducing the infinitival clause in (35) is not a governing node), then it turns out that the verb *tried* in (35) actually governs the NP *Mary*, and hence (unless we do something to prevent this) will assign *objective* case to *Mary*. But if *Mary* gets assigned objective case, then how come that sentences like (34) are ungrammatical?

Now consider an alternative approach to (35). Suppose we stipulate:

(36)   S-bar is an absolute barrier to government (i.e. no category can
govern another category across an intervening S-bar)

This would mean that the verb *tried* in (35) cannot govern *Mary*,
for reasons which are obvious if we represent (35) in more skeletal
fashion as:

(37)   tried [$_{\bar{S}}$ Mary to leave]

Clearly, *tried* cannot govern *Mary* in (37), because of the intervening S-bar. Hence, *Mary* fails to be assigned objective case; in fact,
it turns out that *Mary* receives no case at all – i.e. is unmarked for
case. If we now propose the following CASE FILTER:

(38)   CASE FILTER
Any sentence containing an overt (i.e. phonetically non-null)
NP is ill-formed if the NP has no case-marking

then we now have a principled account of the ill-formedness of
sentences like (34): i.e. (34) is ill-formed because it contains an
overt NP *Mary* which has no case, so that the sentence falls foul of
condition (38). Furthermore, condition (38) has obvious morphological motivation, in the sense that it's hard to imagine how an NP
could exist in English without case-marking: what would be the
uncase-marked form of the third person masculine singular personal pronoun in English? Would it be '*h*'? The question is
meaningless, since all pronouns (hence also NPs) have intrinsic
case-marking: e.g. *he* is nominative, *him* objective, and *his* genitive.

If we accept that not only NP, but also S-bar counts as an
absolute barrier to case-marking, then we can conflate the twin
conditions (32) and (36) as:

(39)   BARRIER CONDITION
NP and S-bar are absolute barriers to government (i.e. one
category cannot govern another across an intervening NP or
S-bar boundary)

The BARRIER CONDITION (39) can of course be directly
incorporated into our earlier definition (26) of *governs* (i.e. we can
revise (26) so as to subsume (39)). For the sake of intelligibility,
however, we shall leave (39) as a separate condition.

So far, we have looked only at *objective* case-marking in English,
and seen that the complex relation *governs* plays a central role in its
description. Let's now turn to look at the assignment of nominative

case in English, and see whether here too the relation *govern* is an important one. Consider first the conditions under which an NP is assigned *nominative* case. Traditionally, it is often said that nominative case is assigned to an NP which is the subject of its clause. However, this is inaccurate, as we see from the following paradigm:

(40) (a)　I think that *he/*him* will read the book
    (b)　I wonder whether *he/*him* will read the book
    (c)　I will read the same book that *he/*him* will read

(41) (a)　I want *him/*he* to read the book
    (b)　It would be a good idea for *him/*he* to read the book
    (c)　I'm looking for a book for *him/*he* to read

We see from (40) and (41) above that the subject of the *read*-clause is assigned nominative case in (40), but not in (41). How come? Somehow, this difference appears to correlate with the fact that the *read*-clause in (40) is *tensed* (i.e. finite, or marked for tense by the presence of the TENSE auxiliary *will*), whereas the *read*-clause in (41) is *untensed* (i.e. nonfinite, containing no TENSE auxiliary like *will, would, shall, should, can, could, may, might*, etc.). Following Chomsky (e.g. *Rules and Representations* (1980), p. 170), we might assume that clauses are of two types in English, *tensed* (= finite), and *untensed* (= infinitival), with tensed clauses containing a TENSE constituent (which we earlier called AUX), and untensed clauses containing instead the infinitive marker *to*. That is, let's assume that the Phrase Structure rule expanding clauses (in the sense of S, not S-bar) is:

(42)　　　S → NP − $\left\{ \begin{array}{l} \text{TENSE} \\ to \end{array} \right\}$ − VP

We might then propose the following informal rule of *nominative* case-marking:

(43)　　　NP is marked nominative if the subject of a tensed S (i.e. an S containing a TENSE auxiliary)

Consider how this might work in a simple case like (40) (a); let's assume that the subordinate clause in (40) (a) has the structure:

(44)

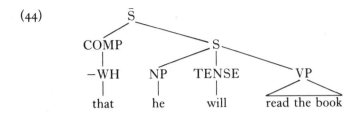

What is particularly interesting about (44) is that, if we extend the class of governing nodes to include a TENSE auxiliary, we find that the TENSE auxiliary *will* actually governs (in the sense of (26) and (39)) the subject NP *he*. This opens up the interesting possibility that *government* may play a key role not only in *objective* case-marking, but also in *nominative* case-marking as well. Accordingly, we might follow Chomsky (*Pisa Lectures* (1980), p. 9) and suggest the following formulation of the relevant rule:

(45)   NP is assigned the case-feature [+NOMINATIVE] if governed by TENSE

Of course, if we adopt (45), we have to allow not only lexical categories (V, P, N, A), but also TENSE to be a governing node.

A minor complication to the *government* account of nominative case-marking is posed by tensed sentences which appear to contain no overt tense-marking auxiliary like *will*, etc. – e.g. by sentences like:

(46)   He quit

How can *he* in (46) be governed by a TENSE auxiliary, since the sentence appears to contain no such auxiliary? One possibility which we might explore here would be to say that auxiliariless tensed clauses contain an empty TENSE constituent. More specifically, we might assume that TENSE is expanded by the Base Rules into ±PAST, where −PAST would be lexicalised e.g. as *will*, *can*, *may*, etc., and +PAST would be lexicalised as e.g. *would*, *could*, *might*, etc. Bearing in mind the possibility of leaving any category empty in the Base, we might then expect to find tensed clauses containing an empty +PAST auxiliary, and we could argue that sentences like (46) *He quit* are just such a case. Under this analysis, (46) would have the D-structure and S-structure (47) below:

(47)

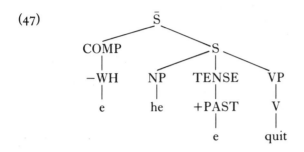

Given such an analysis, the subject NP *he* is indeed governed by TENSE, and will therefore correctly be marked nominative by rule (45).

Thus far, we have looked briefly at nominative and objective case-assignment, and seen that in both cases the relation *govern* appears to play a key role. Let's now turn to look briefly at the assignment of *genitive* case to NPs in English, and see if here too *government* is important. Chomsky has devoted relatively little space to discussion of genitive case-marking, so that his proposals in this regard are clearly somewhat sketchy and tentative. What we want to be able to say is that in a structure such as:

(48) $[_{NP_2}$ $[_{NP_1}$ the soldiers'] $[_{\bar{N}}$ sudden departure]]

the 'inner' NP, NP_1 *the soldiers'*, is assigned genitive case (hence the pronominal counterpart '*their* departure', with genitive *their*). One rather artificial way of ensuring this (outlined in a rather sketchy form in the *Pisa Lectures*, p. 24) is to suppose that English has a rule adjoining an abstract morpheme POSS(essive) to the italicised NP in structures of the schematic form:

(49) $[_{NP}$ NP_1 – $\bar{N}]$

giving (presumably) the structure:

(50) $[_{NP}$ $[_{NP_2}$ NP_1 – POSS] – $\bar{N}]$

We might then propose the following case-marking rule:

(51)   NP is assigned the case-feature if governed by POSS

Since NP_1 in (50) is governed by POSS, it will be assigned genitive case by rule (51). Hence also in (48), POSS-INSERTION will lead to a structure in which NP_1 *the soldiers'* is governed by POSS, and then marked genitive by rule (51). If indeed we do adopt the government account of genitive case-marking in (51), then the result is that we can handle all case-marking in English in terms of *government* – i.e. as:

(52) (a)　　NP is nominative if governed by TENSE
　　　(b)　　NP is objective if governed by a transitive V or P (= −N)
　　　(c)　　NP is genitive if governed by POSS

While the account of *objective* case-marking in terms of government seems fairly well motivated, the account of nominative case-marking in terms of government by TENSE is less convincing, and the proposed account of genitive case-marking in terms of government by an abstract POSS morpheme is clearly no more than a flight of fancy. This is not a matter of any importance, however: for Chomsky's purposes (which we shall come to shortly), it would be of no consequence if one were to reformulate along more adequate lines the rules of nominative and genitive case-marking. For example, Chomsky would be quite happy with replacing (52) (a) by e.g.

(53)　　　NP is nominative if the subject of a tensed clause

– provided that the notions *subject* and *tensed clause* were structurally defined. So, too, he would be equally happy with a rule which simply stipulates that in structures like (49) NP$_1$ is assigned genitive case. In no sense does any part of the 'Case Theory' he seeks to develop rest on the assumption that *all* case-marking must be handled in terms of the relation *govern*.

　　Thus far, we have looked at case-marking in a variety of NP-positions, including the subject of a tensed clause, the object of a verb, and the object of a preposition. However, we have not yet considered the case-marking of an NP which is the subject of an infinitive (other than our brief discussion of infinitives after *try* in relation to (34)). Let's begin by looking at infinitive complements which are introduced by the complementiser *for* – i.e. let's consider the case-marking of the italicised infinitive subject in a sentence such as:

(54)　　　For *him* to resign would be a pity

We might assume that the infinitive complement in (54) has the structure in (55):

(55)

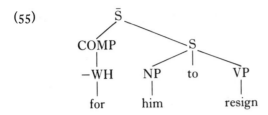

Notice here that if we say that *for* is a *prepositional* complementiser, then *for* will govern (and assign *objective* case to, by rule (52) (b)) the NP *him*. Notice that government here is across an S, not across an S-bar, as (56) below makes clearer (visually):

(56)   [s̄ for [s him to resign]]

Hence the BARRIER CONDITION (39) does not block government of *him* by *for*. Thus, provided we say that *for* is a prepositional complementiser, our existing rules (52) handle case-marking of the subject of an infinitive introduced by *for* without any difficulty.

Although the subject of an infinitive introduced by the prepositional complementiser *for* is assigned objective case in English, the same is not true of the subject of infinitives introduced by the interrogative complementiser *whether*: cf.

(57)   *I don't know [s̄ whether [s John to leave]]

But this we can account for in terms of our existing rules. Let us suppose that *whether* is not a prepositional complementiser, and in fact is not a lexical category (V, P, N, A) at all, and hence not a possible governor. If so, then *whether* (not being a governor) cannot govern (and hence cannot assign case to) the infinitive subject *John*. Furthermore, the NP *John* cannot be governed (and assigned objective case) by the transitive verb *know* either, since there is an intervening S-bar barrier (cf. (39)) in between the two, and S-bar acts as an absolute barrier against case-assignment, given the BARRIER CONDITION (39). In short, our existing case-rules fail to assign any case at all to *John* in (57). But this means that sentences like (57) fall foul of the CASE FILTER (38), since the latter throws out any sentence containing a caseless overt NP. So, not only do our existing rules handle *for*-infinitives, they also handle interrogative infinitives.

So far, we have looked at the case-marking of the subjects of infinitives introduced by overt complementisers like *for* and *whether*. But what about the subject of a 'bare' infinitive complement (i.e. an infinitive complement which lacks any overt complementiser)? In fact, we have already seen in relation to (34) **John tried Mary to leave* that the subject of a bare infinitive will fail to be assigned any case by rules (52), which in turn means that bare infinitive complements would be expected never to permit overt subjects in English: this is also true of constructions like:

(58)　　*[s̄ him to leave] would be a mistake

Him in (58) cannot be governed (and assigned nominative case) by the TENSE auxiliary *would*, since *him* lies inside and *would* outside the bracketed S-bar, and S-bar is an absolute barrier against government, given the BARRIER CONDITION (39). So, *him* in (58) fails to be assigned any case at all, with the result that the structure (58) falls foul of the CASE FILTER (38), which disallows overt caseless NPs.

Thus, one of the predictions made by the rules (52) would appear to be that bare infinitive complements never permit overt subjects in English (since such subjects fail to be assigned case by the rules in (52)). Unfortunately, however, this prediction is not *quite* correct. There are in fact a handful of verbs in English which permit a following bare infinitival complement with an overt subject: cf. e.g.

(59) (a)　I consider *him* to be a fool
　　(b)　I want *him* to leave
　　(c)　I expect *him* to win
　　(d)　I saw *him* leave

In each of the sentences above, it seems plausible to follow Chomsky in assuming that the italicised NP is the subject of the following infinitive (though to argue this would take us far astray). If this is so, then how can we provide a principled account of the fact that such verbs permit bare infinitive complements with overt *objective* subjects? A number of different possibilities might be envisaged, but we shall mention only two.

Kayne, in his unpublished paper 'On certain differences between French and English' (1980), has suggested that we posit that verbs like those above in (59) take an S-bar infinitive complement introduced by an invisible (= phonetically null) prepositional complementiser which he designates by the symbol Ø. Under Kayne's analysis, (59) (a) would have the structure:

(60)   I consider [s̄ [COMP Ø] [s him to be a fool]]

Given such a structure, the 'invisible' prepositional complementiser Ø would govern (in the sense of (26) and (39)) the NP *him* and hence assign objective case to *him* by rule (52) (b). There would then be three types of verb taking noninterrogative infinitive complements in English: those subcategorised as taking an infinitive introduced by *for*, those subcategorised as taking an infinitive introduced by Ø, and those subcategorised as taking an infinitive introduced by an empty (nonlexical, and hence nongovernor) complementiser *e*: i.e. Kayne posits three noninterrogative infinitival complementisers in English: *for*, Ø and *e*.

Chomsky, by contrast, proposes (*Pisa Lectures*, 1980) a very different analysis. He proposes that bare infinitive complements with overt subjects should be analysed as having the status of S and not S-bar at the level at which case-marking applies: he suggests that such bare infinitives underlyingly have the status of S-bar with an empty COMP, but that they undergo a rule of S-BAR DELETION which erases both the S-bar and the empty COMP prior to case-marking at S-structure. Under Chomsky's analysis, the input structure to the case-marking rules (52) in the case of a sentence like (59) (a) will be:

(61)   I consider [s him to be a fool]

Given the structure (61), the verb *consider* actually governs the NP *him*, and since *consider* is a transitive verb, assigns objective case to *him*. Notice that *consider* governs *him* only across an S (not across an S-bar), so that there is no violation of the BARRIER CONDITION (39) here. And since *him* has been assigned case, there is no violation of the CASE FILTER (38) either. Hence, sentences like (59) are well-formed.

Of course, neither analysis is particularly inspired or inspiring; both are clearly *circular* in obvious ways. For if we ask 'Why can you have an overt subject to infinitive complements like those in (59)?', the answer provided is 'Because they have a Ø complementiser (or no S-bar).' And if we ask 'How do you know they have a Ø complementiser (or no S-bar)?', the answer is 'Because they permit overt subjects.' Circular solutions have no explanatory power; but it may be that certain facts of language are so idiosyncratic and unpredictable that it is not possible to provide a principled (noncircular) account of them.

So far, we have noted that some infinitives can, and others cannot have an overt lexical NP subject in English, and we see that Chomsky tries to handle such differences in terms of the Case Theory he develops. But an obvious question to ask is how we are to deal with infinitives which underlyingly have empty NP-subjects (NB we are not talking about the infinitive complements found after 'Raising' verbs like *seem* here, since these underlyingly have an overt subject which subsequently undergoes NP MOVE-MENT). Chomsky assumes that in sentences like:

(62)   John tried *to frighten Mary*

the italicised infinitive complement has an empty pronominal NP subject which he designates as PRO: given this assumption, (62) would have the D-structure and S-structure:

(63)   comp John tried [$_{\bar{s}}$ comp PRO to frighten Mary]

He further maintains that PRO, although abstract, must contain inherent person, number and gender features – e.g. in (64) below PRO must be third person masculine singular in order to account for contrasts such as:

(64)   John tried [$_{\bar{s}}$ PRO to be a good soldier/*good soldiers]

How can we account for the fact that the 'predicate nominal' *good soldier(s)* must be singular here, not plural? If we assume that PRO is a third person masculine singular form, then we can handle such cases in terms of the independently motivated rule of SUBJECT–PREDICATE AGREEMENT: i.e. we can say that *good soldier* is singular because it agrees with the singular subject of its clause, PRO.

Although empty pronouns (i.e. PRO) carry person, number and gender, Chomsky argues (*Pisa Lectures*, 1980, p. 22) that PRO never carries case, and furthermore that PRO can never be governed. To underline the importance of this, let's reiterate it as:

(65)   PRO-CONDITION
          Any sentence containing PRO in a position where it is governed (or case-marked) is ill-formed

By contrast, recall that overt lexical NPs can only occur in NP-positions where they are both governed and case-marked: it follows, therefore, that in general terms PRO and overt lexical NP will be in complementary distribution – i.e. where we find the one, we don't find the other, and vice-versa. We can illustrate this complementarity in terms of the following paradigm (adapted from Chomsky, 'Markedness and Core Grammar', 1980, p. 11):

(66) (a) It is unclear [$\bar{\text{s}}$ [$_{\text{COMP}}$ how] [$_{\text{S}}$ PRO to solve the problem]]
    (b) *It is unclear [$\bar{\text{s}}$ [$_{\text{COMP}}$ how] [$_{\text{S}}$ John to solve the problem]]
    (c) It is unclear [$\bar{\text{s}}$ [$_{\text{COMP}}$ how] [$_{\text{S}}$ John will solve the problem]]
    (d) *It is unclear [$\bar{\text{s}}$ [$_{\text{COMP}}$ how] [$_{\text{S}}$ PRO will solve the problem]]

In (66) (a), PRO cannot be governed by *unclear*, since it is separated from it by the bracketed S-bar, and we know from the BARRIER CONDITION (39) that S-bar is an absolute barrier to government: since PRO here is ungoverned (in accordance with (65)), the resultant sentence is well-formed. In (66) (b), we have a lexical NP. *John* in the same position, which is again ungoverned and hence caseless: but since the CASE FILTER (38) requires all overt lexical NPs to have case, the resultant sentence (66) (b) is ill-formed. In (66) (c), *John* is governed and assigned nominative case by the TENSE auxiliary *will*, so there is no violation of the CASE FILTER here. In (66) (d), PRO is likewise governed and assigned nominative case by *will*; but this violates the PRO-CONDITION (65), which specifically stipulates that PRO must always be ungoverned – hence the sentence is marked as ill-formed.

Notice that the Case Theory analysis of PRO sketched out above also predicts that PRO can never occur as the object of a verb or preposition, e.g. in sentences such as:

(67) (a) *John solved PRO
    (b) *John walked to PRO

since in the first case PRO would be governed and assigned objective case by the verb *solved* (thereby violating (65)), and in the second sentence PRO would be governed and assigned objective case by the preposition *to* (again violating (65)). More generally still, the Case Theory analysis predicts that PRO can only occur in an ungoverned NP-position. And since the only ungoverned NP-position (in general) is that of the subject of a bare infinitive complement, the Case Theory analysis indirectly predicts that PRO can occur only as the subject of a bare infinitive.

But not, in fact, as the subject of *any* bare infinitive, since we find contrasts such as:

(68) (a)   John tried to leave
      (b)   *John considers to be successful

i.e. in Chomsky's terms, the infinitive can have a PRO subject in (68) (a), but not in (68) (b). How can we handle this contrast? Recall that Chomsky assumes that infinitival complements after *try* have the status of S-bar superficially, whereas those after verbs like *consider* (cf. our discussion of (59)) have the status of S only (e.g. because of application of S-BAR DELETION). Thus, given Chomsky's assumptions, (68) (a) and (b) will have the respective superficial structures:

(69) (a)   John tried [$_{\bar{S}}$ [$_{COMP}$ e] [$_S$ PRO to leave]]
      (b)   John considers [$_S$ PRO to be successful]

If this is so, then notice that *tried* in (69) (a) will not govern PRO, because of the intervening S-bar; by contrast, *considers* will govern PRO in (69) (b) because there is no intervening S-bar here. The result will be that PRO is ungoverned in (69) (a), but governed in (69) (b). But since the PRO-CONDITION (65) stipulates that PRO must be ungoverned, then (69) (b) is ill-formed because it contains a governed PRO.

Chomsky (*Pisa Lectures*, 1980, p. 22) suggests that it might be possible to handle the following contrast along similar lines:

(70) (a)   It is impossible to win
      (b)   *It is certain to win (* in the sense of 'it is certain that some unspecified person will win')

if we suppose that *impossible* has an S-bar complement, but *certain* (and other similar RAISING predicates like *seem*, *appear*, *likely*, *sure*, etc.) takes simply an S-complement superficially. Then, (70) (a) and (b) would have the respective superficial structures:

(71) (a)   It is impossible [$_{\bar{S}}$ [$_{COMP}$ e] [$_S$ PRO to win]]
      (b)   It is certain [$_S$ PRO to win]

Given the analysis in (71), PRO would not be governed by *impossible* in (71) (a) because of the intervening S-bar, but PRO would be governed by *certain* in (71) (b) because there is no intervening S-bar. But since by (65), PRO can never be governed, then only (71) (a) and not (71) (b) is well-formed.

Thus far, we have overlooked an important theoretical question concerned with case – namely, the question of the *level* at which the case-marking rules operate. Do they operate at D-structure, or at S-structure, or at Surface Structure? In fact, Chomsky presents a rather complex *two-level* theory of case assignment: he distinguishes between *structural case* which is assigned to NPs at S-structure; and *inherent case* which is assigned to NPs in the Base (i.e. at D-structure). In the case of English, nearly all case-marking is *structural* in Chomsky's terms, so we'll begin by looking at structural case-marking.

Consider case-marking of the italicised NP in RAISING constructions like:

(72)   *John* seems — to like Mary

where (as we have seen) there is evidence (from idiom chunks, etc.) that the italicised NP originates in the position marked — as the subject of the subordinate infinitive complement, and is subsequently moved into main clause subject position by application of NP MOVEMENT. If this is so, then (72) will derive from the D-structure:

(73)   np seems [John to like Mary]

Let's suppose, for the sake of argument, that all case-marking takes place in the base, at the level of D-structure. If this is so, then *John* in (73) will fail to be assigned any case at all by *seems*, because *seems* is not a transitive verb (indeed, if the bracketed complement in (73) is underlyingly an S-bar, not just S, then *seems* will not even govern *John*). The net result will be that our grammar will then wrongly predict that sentences like (72) are ungrammatical, since – if all case-marking takes place at D-structure – *John* in (72) will fail to be assigned any case at all, and the sentence will then be marked as ungrammatical by the CASE FILTER (38). This is clearly a wrong prediction: it therefore suggests that our initial assumption about the level at which case-marking applies is wrong.

So let's assume instead that case-marking applies not at D-structure, but rather at S-structure. Assuming application of NP MOVEMENT to (73), and assuming also that RAISING predicates like *seem* have an S-complement in S-structure (not S-bar; cf. our earlier discussion of (71) (b)), then our sentence (72) will have the S-structure:

(74)   John$_2$ seems [$_S$ [$_{NP_2}$ e] to like Mary]

If (structural) case-marking takes place at S-structure, then *John* in (74) will of course be assigned *nominative* case, by virtue of being the subject of a tensed clause in S-structure (i.e. subject of the *seems*-clause). Since *John* now has case, the sentence no longer violates the CASE FILTER (38), and is correctly predicted to be well-formed. So it seems that we have strong empirical evidence for claiming that in such cases, case-marking must take place at S-structure, *not* at D-structure.

Furthermore, a little thought will show that if we assume that case-marking takes place at S-structure, then Case Theory provides us with a principled account of why NP MOVEMENT in structures such as (73) is apparently obligatory – i.e. why we cannot simply choose not to apply NP MOVEMENT in such cases, and end up with a sentence like:

(75)   *It seems John to like Mary

The reason is, of course, that (75) would have an S-structure along the lines of:

(76)   It seems [$_S$ John to like Mary]

and although *seems* governs *John* here (provided we follow Chomsky in assuming that the infinitive complement is an S, not an S-bar in S-structure), it cannot assign objective case to *John* because it is not a transitive verb, and rule (52) (b) stipulates that only *transitive* verbs assign objective case to NPs they govern. Thus, *John* in (76) fails to be assigned any case at all, and the resultant structure falls foul of the CASE FILTER (38). Hence it seems that Case Theory provides us with a principled account of why it seems that NP MOVEMENT is obligatory with RAISING predicates like *seem, likely*, etc.

But Chomsky goes further, and claims that Case Theory also provides a principled account of why NP MOVEMENT also appears to be obligatory in passive sentences in English (i.e. in effect, why English has no 'impersonal passive' sentences). Consider a passive sentence such as:

(77)   John was criticised

Underlying (77) would be the D-structure:

(78)   np was criticised John

Application of NP MOVEMENT to (78) will transform this into the S-structure:

(79)   John$_2$ was criticiseds[$_{NP_2}$ e]

And if case-assignment takes place at S-structure, then *John* in (79) will be assigned nominative case by virtue of being the subject of a tensed clause. But suppose that NP MOVEMENT fails to apply in (78), so that we are left with (78) as our S-structure, corresponding to the ungrammatical impersonal passive sentence:

(80)   *It was criticised John

How can we avoid generating (78/80) as an output of our grammar? Notice that Case Theory provides a simple answer to this question, if we make the not unreasonable assumption that passive participles like *criticised* are essentially *adjectival* in character. Given that *criticised* and *John* are sister constituents of the same VP in (78), then clearly *criticised* governs *John*. But if *criticised* is an *adjective* (or at any rate, not a *transitive verb*), it will fail to assign any case to *John*, since only transitive verbs and prepositions assign case to their complements. Thus, *John* in (78/80) will fail to be assigned any case at all, and the resultant sentence (80) will fall foul of the CASE FILTER (38). In a quite unexpected fashion, then, Case Theory provides a principled account of why NP MOVEMENT appears to be obligatory in both 'Raising' and 'Passive' constructions in English (as noted by Chomsky in 'Markedness and Core Grammar', 1980, p. 16).

Thus far, we have considered the case-marking of lexical NPs and PRO. But an obvious question to ask is: 'Do *traces* left behind by the application of NP MOVEMENT receive case-marking or not?' In the RAISING and PASSIVE constructions we have discussed so far, which give rise to S-structures such as:

(81) (a)   John$_2$ seems [$_S$ [$_{NP_2}$ e] to like Mary]
     (b)   John$_2$ was criticised [$_{NP_2}$ e]

it is clear that they do not. Thus, in (81) (a), although *seems* governs the NP-trace subject of the infinitive, it cannot assign objective case (or any other) to the trace because *seem* is not a transitive verb. Likewise, *criticised* in (81) (b) cannot assign objective case to the trace that it governs, if we assume that passive participles are not transitive verbs (hence are e.g. adjectives). Perhaps we can generalise from these two cases to the conclusion that:

(82)   NP-TRACE CONDITION
        'The trace of an NP MOVEMENT cannot be case-marked'
        (Chomsky, *Pisa Lectures*, 1980, p. 17)

Now it turns out that if indeed we do accept condition (82), then we get an interesting account of why NPs in certain sentence-positions cannot undergo NP MOVEMENT. Consider, for example, the impossibility of raising a subject out of an infinitival complement introduced by *for*: cf.

(83) (a)   It is necessary for *John* to leave
     (b)   **John* is necessary for — to leave

Underlying (83) would be the D-structure:

(84)   np is necessary [$_{\bar{s}}$ [$_{COMP}$ for] [$_s$ John to leave]]

Application of NP MOVEMENT to *John* here would result in the S-structure:

(85)   John$_2$ is necessary [$_{\bar{s}}$ [$_{COMP}$ for] [$_s$ [$_{NP_2}$ e] to leave]]

Assuming that case-marking takes place at S-structure, *John* would be assigned nominative case in (85) by virtue of being the subject of the tensed *is*-clause. But more importantly, the trace of *John* [$_{NP_2}$ e] will also be assigned case, since it is governed by the prepositional complementiser *for*, and hence will be assigned objective case. But since we know from (82) that NP-traces cannot carry case-marking, the resultant structure (85) and the corresponding sentence (83) (b) are both marked as ill-formed.

In much the same way, Case Theory also provides a principled account of why NP MOVEMENT is possible in passive but not active sentences. Consider the contrast, for example, between a passive D-structure like (86) (a) below, and its active counterpart (86) (b):

(86) (a)   np was arrested John (passive)
     (b)   np arrested John (active)

Applying NP MOVEMENT to *John* in each case will result in the respective S-structures:

(87) (a)   John$_2$ was arrested [$_{NP_2}$ e]
     (b)   John$_2$ arrested [$_{NP_2}$ e]

In both cases in (87), *arrested* governs the NP-trace; but in (87) (a), *arrested* is an adjectival passive participle, and hence fails to assign case to the NP-trace, whereas in (87) (b) *arrested* is a verb and hence assigns objective case to the trace. Since the NP-TRACE CONDITION (82) stipulates that traces of NP MOVEMENT cannot carry case, and since the trace in (87) (a) does not carry case but the trace in (87) (b) does, then only (87) (a), not (87) (b) is a well-formed structure. In other words, NP MOVEMENT is possible in passive, but not active sentences. More generally still, we see that Case Theory can provide an interesting account of when NP MOVEMENT is and is not optional/obligatory/impossible.

So far, we have limited our discussion of case-marking and movement rules to NP MOVEMENT. But an obvious question to ask is how case-marking works for constituents which undergo WH-MOVEMENT, and the traces of WH-MOVEMENT (let's call these *wh-traces*, and distinguish them from *np-traces*, the latter being traces left behind by NP MOVEMENT). In the case of WH-MOVEMENT, the situation is perhaps a little more complicated than with NP MOVEMENT. Consider, for example, the problem of case-marking the italicised *wh*-phrase in a sentence such as:

(88)   *Who* did they arrest?

Underlying (88) would be the D-structure:

(89)   [$_\bar{S}$ COMP [$_S$ they did arrest who]]

Assuming application of WH-MOVEMENT to adjoin the *wh*-phrase to COMP, and assuming also application of NP–AUX INVERSION, the resultant S-structure would be (ignoring details):

(90)   [$_\bar{S}$ [$_{COMP}$ who$_2$] [$_S$ did they arrest [$_{NP_2}$ e]]]

If we continue to assume – as before – that case-marking takes place at S-structure (i.e. after the application of transformations like NP MOVEMENT and WH-MOVEMENT), we now face the

338

apparent problem that *who* in (90) will fail to be assigned any case by our existing case-marking rules, so that the resultant sentence (90) will fall foul of the CASE FILTER (38) (which requires that every overt lexical NP carry case). Thus, sentence (88) will wrongly be predicted to be ungrammatical. However, one way out of this difficulty might be the following (suggested by Chomsky, *Pisa Lectures*, 1980, p. 9). Notice that in (90) the *wh*-trace $[_{NP_2} e]$ is governed by the transitive verb *arrest*, and hence assigned OBJEC-TIVE case. Let us now assume a convention that:

(91)   WH-CASE CONVENTION
         A moved *wh*-phrase inherits the case of its trace

Since the trace of the moved *wh*-phrase in (90) is assigned objective case, the *wh*-phrase itself will inherit this objective case-marking by (91) – hence the possibility of *whom* in more formal English in sentences like (88).

From the above discussion, it emerges that we have to distinguish two different types of traces. The traces left behind by NP MOVEMENT (= np-traces) are never case-marked, but traces left behind by WH-MOVEMENT (= *wh*-traces) can indeed carry case-marking (indeed if no trace of a moved *wh*-phrase carried case, the *wh*-phrase itself would have no case to inherit, and, being caseless, would fall foul of the CASE FILTER (38)). One consequence of this situation is that we are led to expect that WH-MOVEMENT will not be possible in contexts where its trace cannot be assigned case. Consider as a case in point a passive D-structure like:

(92)   COMP it was arrested who?

Assuming adjunction of the *wh*-phrase *who* to COMP, and NP–AUX INVERSION, the resultant S-structure will be:

(93) $[_{COMP}$ who$_2]$ was it arrested $[_{NP_2} e]$

Notice here that the *wh*-trace $[_{NP_2} e]$ is governed by *arrested*; but since *arrested* is not a transitive verb (e.g. it is an adjectival passive participle), it does not assign case to the *wh*-trace. Hence, *who* cannot inherit case from its caseless trace, and therefore *who* itself will be caseless. The resultant structure therefore violates the CASE FILTER (38): in other words, the proposed Case Theory analysis correctly predicts that the resultant sentence:

(94)   *Who was it arrested?

is ungrammatical.

In much the same way, the proposed Case Theory analysis also
rules out sentences like:

(95)   *Who will Mary try to go? (in the sense of 'Mary will try to
          ensure that *who* go?')

Underlying (95) would be the D-structure:

(96) $[_{\bar{S}_1}$ COMP$_1$ $[_{S_1}$ Mary will try $[_{\bar{S}_2}$ COMP$_2$ $[_{S_2}$ who to go]]]]

Successive cyclic application of WH-MOVEMENT to adjoin *who*
first to COMP$_2$, and then to COMP$_1$ (together with application of
NP–AUX INVERSION) will result in the following S-structure:

(97) $[_{\bar{S}}$ $[_{COMP}$ who$_2]$ $[_S$ will Mary try $[_{\bar{S}}$ $[_{COMP}$ np$_2]$ $[_S$ np$_2$ to go]]]]

(where we use the convention that lower case *np* = empty NP, and
in this case = trace). Notice that in (97), neither trace of
WH-MOVEMENT will be assigned case, since neither is governed
by the verb *try* because of the intervening S-bar (which counts as a
barrier to government, given the BARRIER CONDITION (39)).
Since neither *wh*-trace is assigned case, the *wh*-phrase *who* cannot
inherit case from any of its traces, and hence remains caseless.
Accordingly, the corresponding sentence (95) falls foul of the
CASE FILTER (38), since it contains a caseless lexical NP, *who*.

Let's summarise the assumptions which we have been making
about traces:

(98) (a)   NP-traces (= the trace of NP MOVEMENT) must never
           carry case
     (b)   WH-traces (= the trace of WH-MOVEMENT) can carry case
           (and at least one such trace must do if a *wh*-phrase is to inherit
           its case)

If you think about it carefully, you'll see that it follows from the
above (if we make certain reasonable assumptions) that we'd expect
that:

(99) (a)   an NP can only be moved by NP MOVEMENT out of a
           non-case-marked NP-position
     (b)   an NP can only be moved by WH-MOVEMENT out of a
           case-marked NP-position

In other words, we'd expect complementarity between the contexts in which NP MOVEMENT is possible, and those in which WH-MOVEMENT is possible; or, in plainer terms, we'd expect that NP MOVEMENT is possible only where WH-MOVEMENT is not possible, and WH-MOVEMENT is possible only where NP MOVEMENT is not possible. Let's see whether this prediction is fulfilled, by looking at a number of different NP-positions in turn, and seeing whether they can undergo (i) NP MOVEMENT, and (ii) WH-MOVEMENT.

Let's start by taking the subject of a tensed clause: can tensed clause subjects undergo NP MOVEMENT? Consider a D-structure like:

(100)   np is certain [$_{\bar{S}}$ [$_{COMP}$ e] [$_S$ John will resign]]

Application of NP MOVEMENT to move *John* into the empty main clause subject position here will result in the S-structure:

(101)   John$_2$ is certain [$_{\bar{S}}$ [$_{COMP}$ e] [$_S$ np$_2$ will resign]]

But notice here that the NP-trace np$_2$ will receive nominative case by dint of the fact that it is governed by the TENSE auxiliary *will* (or, more informally, because it is the subject of a finite clause). However, assignment of case to NP-traces is prohibited by the NP-TRACE CONDITION (82), which specifies that any sentence containing a case-marked trace of NP-MOVEMENT is ill-formed. Hence the structure (101) is ill-formed, as is the corresponding sentence:

(102)   *John is certain will resign

So, a tensed clause subject cannot undergo NP MOVEMENT.

But can a tensed clause subject undergo WH-MOVEMENT? Let's see. Consider the following D-structure:

(103)   COMP$_1$ it is certain [$_{\bar{S}}$ COMP$_2$ [$_S$ who will resign]

Successive cyclic application of WH-MOVEMENT here will adjoin *who* first to COMP$_2$, and then to COMP$_1$, giving the S-structure:

(104)   [$_{COMP}$ who$_2$] is it certain [$_{\bar{S}}$ [$_{COMP}$ np$_2$] [$_S$ np$_2$ will resign]]

Notice here that the rightmost trace will be assigned nominative case by virtue of being governed by the TENSE auxiliary *will* (or, equivalently, by virtue of being the subject of a tensed clause);

given the WH-CASE CONVENTION (91), the *wh*-phrase *who* will then inherit this nominative case-marking. Since *who* is assigned case, there is no violation of the CASE FILTER (38), and we thus predict that the resultant sentence:

(105)   Who is it certain will resign?

is well-formed. And certainly it is far more acceptable than (102). In other words, Case Theory gives us a principled account of why the subject of a tensed clause can be *wh*-moved, but not *np*-moved (i.e. can undergo WH-MOVEMENT, but not NP-MOVEMENT). Hence we no longer need to invoke the TENSED S CONDITION to account for this fact.

But what about the subject of an *untensed* clause (i.e. the subject of an infinitive)? Well, we have already seen that there are various types of infinitive complement in English. For the sake of brevity, let's just look at one type: namely the bare infinitive complements found after RAISING predicates like *seem, certain, likely, appear, sure*, etc. And indeed, let's take two sentences parallel to (102) and (105), namely:

(106) (a) John is certain — to resign
         (b) *Who is it certain — to resign?

Notice that this time the grammaticality judgements are reversed. How can we explain this? Well, let's assume following Chomsky that *John* in (106) (a) originates in the position marked — as subordinate clause subject, and is moved into main clause subject position by NP MOVEMENT. Let's also assume (again following Chomsky, as we discussed earlier in relation to (71) (b)) that bare infinitive complements of RAISING predicates have the S-structure status of S, not S-bar. Given these assumptions, then (106) (a) will have the S-structure:

(107)   John$_2$ is certain [$_S$ np$_2$ to resign]

Now in (107) *certain* does indeed govern the trace-subject of the infinitive (there is no S-bar separating the two, so the BARRIER CONDITION (39) is not violated) but it does *not* assign case to it, because adjectives are not case-assigners in English (only verbs, and prepositions, etc. are). Thus, the NP-trace in (107) is caseless, and hence satisfies the NP-TRACE CONDITION (82). Furthermore, *John* in (107) is assigned nominative case by virtue of being the subject of a tensed *is*-clause, so there is no violation of the CASE FILTER (38) either. Since the structure (107) violates none of the proposed *case-conditions*, the resultant structure is well-formed, and the sentence (106) (a) correctly predicted to be well-formed.

But what about (106) (b)? Here, *who* has been adjoined to the main clause COMP by WH-MOVEMENT, so that – if we again assume that bare infinitive complements of RAISING predicates have the status of S, not S-bar, in S-structure – the resultant S-structure this time is:

(108) $[_{COMP}$ who$_2]$ is it certain $[_S$ np$_2$ to resign$]$

Although the *wh*-trace subject of the infinitive here is governed by *certain* (because there is no intervening S-bar, and hence no violation of the BARRIER CONDITION (39)), it cannot be assigned case by *certain* because *certain* is an adjective, and adjectives in English are not case-assigners (only transitive verbs and prepositions etc. are). Thus, the trace subject of the infinitive complement in (108) is caseless; as a result, it has no case to transmit to the *wh*-phrase *who*, so that *who* also remains caseless. But this in turn violates the CASE FILTER (38), since *who* is an overt lexical NP, and (38) requires that overt lexical NPs have case.

If we summarise our discussion, we can see that the version of Case Theory outlined here makes two apparently correct predictions: namely that (i) the subjects of tensed clauses can undergo WH-MOVEMENT but not NP MOVEMENT; and (ii) that the subjects of (certain types of) bare infinitive complements can undergo NP MOVEMENT, but not WH-MOVEMENT.

So much for subject NPs. But what about *object* NPs? Let's begin first by looking at how the object of an active verb behaves. Take a D-structure like:

(109)   np will destroy the enemy

If we apply NP MOVEMENT to move *the enemy* into the empty main clause subject NP-position, the resultant S-structure will be:

(110)   The enemy$_2$ will destroy np$_2$

But notice here that the NP-trace np$_2$ is governed (and hence assigned objective case) by the transitive verb *destroy*; the structure (110) therefore violates the NP-TRACE CONDITION (82), and the resultant sentence is ill-formed:

(111)   *The enemy will destroy (with the structure (110))

So we see from the above discussion (as we saw earlier as well) that the object of a transitive verb cannot undergo NP MOVEMENT in English. But what about WH-MOVEMENT? Take a D-structure like:

(112)   COMP they will destroy who?

Assuming adjunction of *who* to COMP by WH-MOVEMENT, plus application of NP–AUX INVERSION, the resulting S-structure will be:

(113)   [$_{COMP}$ who$_2$] will they destroy np$_2$

Here, once again, the trace-object of *destroy* is governed by *destroy* and hence assigned objective case, since *destroy* is a transitive verb. The objective case-marking of the trace is then inherited by the *wh*-phrase *who*, given the WH-CASE CONVENTION (91). Since *who* is case-marked, there is no violation of the CASE FILTER (38), and the resulting sentence:

(114)   Who(m) will they destroy?

is correctly predicted to be well-formed. More generally still, the Case Theory analysis discussed here correctly predicts that the object of an active verb can undergo WH-MOVEMENT, but not NP MOVEMENT.

But what about the object (or, if you prefer, *complement*) of a passive verb? The passive counterpart of (109) would be a D-structure along the lines of

(115)   np will be destroyed the enemy

Application of NP MOVEMENT to (115) will result in the S-structure:

(116) (a)   The enemy$_2$ will be destroyed np$_2$

Here, *the enemy* is assigned nominative case because it is governed by the TENSE auxiliary *will* (or, if you like, because it is the subject of a tensed clause). By contrast, the NP-trace np$_2$ is assigned no case, because although it is governed by *destroyed*, the latter is not a transitive verb: rather, it is a quasi-adjectival passive participle, and hence cannot assign case to the trace. Thus, *the enemy* is assigned case, but its trace is not. The structure (116) (a) therefore satisfies both the relevant case-marking conditions – the CASE FILTER (82), and the NP-TRACE CONDITION (82). Hence our grammar correctly predicts that the resulting sentence:

(116) (b)   The enemy will be destroyed

is perfectly grammatical. That is, we correctly predict that passive objects can undergo NP MOVEMENT.

But can they also undergo WH-MOVEMENT? Consider the passive counterpart of (112) – i.e. the D-structure:

(117)   COMP it will be destroyed who

Application of WH-MOVEMENT here will adjoin *who* to COMP, so that after NP–AUX INVERSION the resultant S-structure will be:

(118)   [$_{COMP}$ who$_2$] will it be destroyed np$_2$

Here, the *wh*-trace (np$_2$) will fail to be assigned any case, since although it is governed by *destroyed*, the latter is not a transitive verb, but rather an (adjectival?) passive participle which does not assign case to its complements. Hence the *wh*-trace in (118) is caseless; as such, it has no case to transmit to the *wh*-phrase *who*, with the result that *who* falls foul of the CASE FILTER (38), since it is an overt lexical NP which carries no case. In other words, our grammar correctly predicts that the corresponding sentence:

(119)   *Who will it be destroyed?

is ungrammatical. More generally still, our grammar predicts that the object of an active verb can undergo WH-MOVEMENT but not NP MOVEMENT, whereas the object of a passive verb can undergo NP MOVEMENT but not WH-MOVEMENT.

Having looked at the possibility of moving subjects and objects of verbs, let's now go on to ask whether or not we can move the object of a preposition in English. Consider first the possibility of an NP which is the complement of a preposition undergoing NP MOVE-MENT. Let's start with a D-structure along the lines of:

(120)   np will be given the book to Mary

Suppose we now apply NP MOVEMENT to *Mary*: the result will be the following S-structure:

(121)   Mary$_2$ will be given the book to np$_2$

in which *Mary* is assigned nominative case by virtue of being governed by (i.e. being the subject of) the TENSE auxiliary *will*. But notice in addition that the NP-trace np_2 will be assigned objective case by virtue of the fact that it is governed by the preposition *to*, and prepositions assign objective case to NPs that they govern. However, assignment of case to the trace of an NP-moved constituent is prohibited under the NP-TRACE CONDITION (82). Therefore, the structure (121) is ill-formed, as is the corresponding sentence:

(122)   *Mary will be given the book to

In other words, the Case Theory analysis predicts that the object of a preposition cannot passivise in English (i.e. cannot undergo NP MOVEMENT).

But can the object of a preposition undergo WH-MOVEMENT? Consider a D-structure of the form:

(123)   COMP they will give the book to who?

Assume that WH-MOVEMENT applies to adjoin *who* to COMP, and that NP–AUX INVERSION also applies: this will give us the following S-structure:

(124) Who_2 will they give the book to np_2?

Observe that in (124) the *wh*-trace np_2 is assigned objective case because it is governed by (i.e. the object of) the preposition *to*. Given the WH-CASE CONVENTION (91), the *wh*-phrase *who* will inherit this objective case-marking, and hence will be assigned objective case. In other words, the Case Theory account sketched here correctly predicts that the corresponding sentence:

(125)   Who(m) will they give the book to?

is well-formed. (Incidentally – but I think *irrelevantly* – sentences like (125) sound slightly odd with *whom* instead of *who*: this is probably due to stylistic factors: i.e. stranding prepositions in English is a colloquial construction, whereas *whom* is a literary form.) More generally, then, we can say that the Case Theory account predicts that the object of a preposition in English can undergo WH-MOVEMENT, though not NP MOVEMENT. Once again, this prediction is – in general – correct.

We add the qualification 'in general' here, because there are in fact a number of potential counterexamples to the claim that the object of a preposition cannot passivise in English. Take sentences such as:

(126) (a) *Mary* was spoken to — by her father
    (b) *The story* was talked about — in the press
    (c) *The contract* was entered into — without due consultation

In each case in (126) it might be argued that the italicised NP originates in the position marked —, and is subsequently moved into the italicised position by NP MOVEMENT, in apparent contradiction of our claim that the object of a preposition never undergoes NP MOVEMENT. One frequently suggested way of dealing with such apparent counterexamples to the claim that prepositional objects cannot passivise in English is in terms of what is known as the RESTRUCTURING analysis. Let us suppose that certain sequences of the schematic form:

(127) $V - [_{PP} P - NP]$

can undergo a rule of RESTRUCTURING in the Base (i.e. *before* any transformations like NP MOVEMENT or WH-MOVEMENT apply), whereby the structure in (127) is restructured as:

(128) $[_V V - P] - NP$

What is going on here is that a Preposition which originally forms part of a Prepositional Phrase following a verb is *restructured* so that instead it forms a kind of 'complex verb' with the verb itself. So, for example, we might say that a structure like (129) (a) is restructured by the relevant RESTRUCTURING rule as (129) (b):

(129) (a) $[_V \text{speak}] [_{PP} \text{to} [_{NP} \text{someone}]]$
    (b) $[_V \text{speak to}] [_{NP} \text{someone}]$

If so, then we might say that the S-structure of a sentence like (126) (a) *Mary was spoken to by her father* would be:

(130) Mary_2 was [spoken to] np_2 by her father

In (130), *Mary* would be assigned nominative case, by virtue of being the subject of a tensed clause. But what of the trace np_2? The trace is governed by the complex passive participle *spoken-to*, but cannot be assigned case by the passive participle, since passive participles are not transitive verbs (e.g. they are adjectives). Thus, the NP-trace receives no case – precisely as is required by the NP-TRACE CONVENTION (82). In other words, the Case Theory analysis predicts that an NP following a Preposition can only passivise if the Preposition is (restructured as) part of the predicate (i.e. verb). The exact conditions under which a sequence like (127) can be restructured as (128) are far from clear: cf. apparently puzzling contrasts like:

(131) (a) *The church was gone into by the thieves
     (b) The question was gone into by the thieves

It is often suggested that RESTRUCTURING is blocked where there is some overt lexical material intervening between the V and the P – hence the fact that *given* and *to* cannot be restructured in (120) because of the presence of the intervening NP *the book*. Chomsky has also suggested that RESTRUCTURING might provide the answer to 'double passive' pairs like:

(132) (a) Advantage was taken of John
     (b) John was taken advantage of

if we suppose that in (132) (b) the chunk *take advantage of* can be optionally reanalysed (as a whole) as a complex verb.

Our entire discussion of *case* so far has been devoted to *structural case-marking* – i.e. case-marking as it applies at the level of S-structure. Recall, however, that earlier we said that there is a second kind of case-marking proposed by Chomsky – *inherent* case-marking, assigned in the Base (or, if you like, at the level of D-structure). To say that an NP is assigned *inherent* case is to say that it is assigned case in the Base (or, at D-structure). Let us suppose, for example, that English has an *inherent* rule of case-marking that in 'double NP' constructions (= *give someone something*) the second NP is assigned objective case *inherently* (= at D-structure), but the first NP is assigned case *structurally* (= at S-structure). This would mean that in a structure like:

(133)   John gave [$_{NP_1}$ him] [$_{NP_2}$ them]

NP_2 is assigned objective case *inherently* (= at D-structure), whereas NP_1 is assigned case *structurally* (= at S-structure). For sentences like (133) it might seem pointless to propose such a complex two-level theory of case-marking.

But now consider a passive D-structure such as:

(134)   np was given [$_{NP_1}$ Mary] [$_{NP_2}$ the book]

Let's assume that NP$_2$ here is inherently assigned objective case in the base (whereas NP$_1$ is not assigned any case inherently). If so, then the D-structure of (134) will be:

(135)   np was given [$_{NP_1}$ Mary] $\left[\begin{array}{l} \text{the book} \\ _{NP_2} \text{+ OBJECTIVE} \end{array} \right]$

in which *the book* is assigned objective case, but *Mary* is caseless. Let's now see how and whether NP MOVEMENT could apply to the structure (135). Suppose first of all that the rule does not apply. If so, then the NP *Mary* fails to be assigned case, since although it is governed by *given*, *given* is not a transitive verb (it is a passive participle, e.g. adjectival) and hence cannot assign case to *Mary*. The resulting structure therefore violates the CASE FILTER (38), since it contains an overt lexical NP *Mary* which is caseless. Therefore our grammar correctly specifies that the corresponding sentence:

(136)   *It was given Mary the book

is ungrammatical.

Now let's suppose that NP MOVEMENT does apply to the D-structure (135), to prepose the NP *Mary*. The S-structure thereby derived will be:

(137)   Mary$_2$ was given np$_2$ $\left[\begin{array}{l} \text{the book} \\ \text{+OBJECTIVE} \end{array} \right]$

Mary will subsequently be assigned nominative case *structurally* in S-structure, by virtue of being the subject of a tensed clause (the *was*-clause); and the NP-trace of *Mary np$_2$* will not be assigned case, because although it is governed by *given*, *given* is not a transitive verb, but rather an adjectival passive participle. Thus, *Mary* is assigned nominative case *structurally*, *the book* is assigned objective case *inherently*, and the np-trace is caseless. Since both lexical NPs *Mary* and *the book* have been assigned case, there is no violation of the CASE FILTER (38); and since the np-trace has not been assigned case, there is no violation of the NP-TRACE CONDITION (82) either. Hence, we correctly predict that the corresponding sentence:

(138)   Mary was given the book

is well-formed.

But now consider a third possibility – namely that NP MOVE-MENT applies to the D-structure (135) to prepose the NP *the book*. Assuming that the moved NP carries along with it the inherent (objective) case-marking it was assigned in the base, and assuming also that its trace retains this case-marking as well, application of NP MOVEMENT to prepose *the book* in (135) will result in the following derived structure:

(139) $\begin{bmatrix} \text{The book} \\ _{NP^2} \text{+OBJECTIVE} \end{bmatrix}$ was given Mary $\begin{bmatrix} \text{e} \\ _{NP^2} \text{+OBJECTIVE} \end{bmatrix}$

If *structural* case-marking now applies at S-structure, *the book* will be assigned nominative case (in addition to its inherent objective case) by virtue of being the subject of a tensed clause. The resulting S-structure will therefore be:

(140) $\begin{bmatrix} \text{The book} \\ \text{+OBJECTIVE} \\ _{NP^2} \text{+NOMINATIVE} \end{bmatrix}$ was given Mary $\begin{bmatrix} \text{e} \\ \text{+OBJECTIVE} \\ _{NP_2} \end{bmatrix}$

But there are three things wrong with the S-structure (140). Firstly, the lexical NP *Mary* fails to be assigned any case (because although *Mary* is governed by *given*, *given* is a passive participle, and hence does not assign case), and therefore falls foul of the CASE FILTER (38). Secondly, the np-trace of *the book*, np_2, carries (inherent) objective case, in violation of the NP-TRACE CONDITION (82) which specifies that 'The trace of an NP MOVEMENT cannot be case-marked.' And thirdly, the NP *the book* carries two conflicting case-specifications, objective and nominative. And yet, as we mentioned earlier in relation to sentences like (22), *case conflict* leads to ill-formedness: i.e. no NP can be assigned more than one distinct case (so, for example, a pronoun cannot have both the objective inflection *-m* and the genitive inflection *-'s* in English: **him's*). Since the S-structure (140) is three ways ill-formed, our grammar correctly predicts that the corresponding sentence:

(141)   *The book was given Mary

will be ill-formed.

From the above discussion, it should be fairly obvious that

inherent case-marking can be used as a device to prevent constituents from undergoing NP MOVEMENT (while still in fact
allowing them to undergo WH-MOVEMENT). Of course, there is
an obvious danger of *circularity* in such 'explanations': Ask 'Why
can such-and such an NP not undergo NP-MOVEMENT?' and the
answer is 'Because it is inherently case-marked.' Ask 'How do you
know that it's inherently case-marked?' and the answer is 'Because it
can't undergo NP MOVEMENT.' Circular hypotheses simply have
zero explanatory value: i.e. they are just ad hoc ways of cataloguing
a given set of facts.

Before we end, let's clear up a couple of minor pseudo-issues
which may seem puzzling. The first is: How exactly is *inherent
case* assigned in the Base? What does that mean? Well, there are a
number of simple solutions to this problem that can be made to
work mechanically. Since the issue is of no great importance (just a
trivial question of *execution*, Chomsky would say) let's just mention one possibility. We might suppose that our Lexicon will
contain a Lexical Redundancy Rule along the lines of:

(142)   In any lexical entry where a verb is subcategorised as occurring
          in a VP of the schematic form $[\!-\!\text{NP}_1 - \text{NP}_2]$ assign NP_2 the
          inherent case-feature [+OBJECTIVE]

A second problem of *execution* is how we relate case-marking to
phonetic form – i.e. how mechanically we account for the fact that
the nominative form of the relative pronoun is *who*, the objective
who(m), and the genitive *whose*? Here, the obvious solution is to
envisage a set of *spelling rules* (in traditional terms, morphophonological rules) which 'spell out' the phonetic form that NPs take
under case-marking (these rules operating *after* the case-marking
rules). For example, the most general such rule will specify that
genitive NPs are marked (in general, with exceptions, etc.) by *-'s*;
another rule will specify that for certain pronouns, objective
case-marking is represented by *-m* (cf. hi*m*, the*m*, who*m*). For
particular pronouns, we may just have to stipulate that they have
irregular phonetic forms, not predictable from more general rules:
i.e. we will have to stipulate that the third person feminine singular
personal pronoun objective/genitive case-form is spelled out as *her*.
Again, the question of the exact form of such rules is one of
execution: i.e. various alternatives might be envisaged, and when
we have developed an adequate universal theory of Morphology, we

may find that there are theory-internal (morphological) reasons to prefer one solution to another; but whatever solution is adopted to these morphophonological problems will be unlikely to have any bearing on the *syntactic theory of case* developed by Chomsky.

Before we leave *case*, let's just return to the question we raised earlier of the level at which structural case-marking takes place. Earlier we argued that this must be after movement transformations like NP MOVEMENT have applied, and we assumed that in consequence case-marking must take place at S-structure. But there was a further possibility which we did not discuss in detail – namely that case-marking might instead take place at Surface Structure, i.e. *after* rather than *before* the application of deletion rules. Are there any arguments as to why case-marking should take place before rather than after deletion, as we have implicitly assumed? Perhaps some slight evidence in favour of this assumption can be gleaned from the ill-formedness of phrases such as the following (parallel to our earlier example (71) (a)):

(143)   *something it is possible to happen

Underlying (143) would be a D-structure along the lines of:

(144)   something $[_{\bar{S}_1}$ comp it is possible $[_{\bar{S}_2}$ comp which to happen]]

Successive cyclic application of WH-MOVEMENT would adjoin *which* first to the empty COMP of S_2, then to the empty COMP of S_1, giving the S-structure:

(145)   something $[_{\bar{S}_1}$ $[_{COMP}$ which$_2]$ it is possible $[_{\bar{S}_2}$ $[_{COMP}$ np$_2]$ np$_2$ to happen]]

Subsequent application of WH-DELETION will then delete *which*, giving the Surface Structure:

(146)   something $[_{\bar{S}_1}$ it is possible $[_{\bar{S}_2}$ $[_{COMP}$ np$_2]$ np$_2$ to happen]]

How can we account for the ill-formedness of the resultant phrase (143) under such an analysis? If case-marking takes place at Surface Structure, it is not obvious how we could do this; neither of the traces of the moved *wh*-pronoun *which* is governed or assigned case by *possible*, because of the intervening S-bar barrier, $\bar{S}_2$, and because adjectives do not assign case in English anyway. Hence, there is no apparent violation of any case filter.

But now, let us suppose – by contrast – that case-marking takes place at S-structure rather than Surface Structure. In this case, since neither *wh*-trace in the S-structure (145) is assigned case, the *wh*-pronoun *which* cannot inherit case from either of its traces, and so remains caseless. But if we assume that the CASE FILTER (38) (which specifies that no overt NP can be caseless) operates at S-structure, not at Surface Structure, then we can handle the ill-formedness of (143) in terms of a violation of this filter. But this analysis commits us to the assumption that case-marking applies at S-structure (as indeed do case filters), not at Surface Structure. We shall thus assume as a working hypothesis that case-marking applies after movement, but before deletion (though admittedly our grounds for assuming this are heavily theory-internal, and perhaps rather tenuous).

Summary

In addition to Base Rules, Transformations, Constraints, Deletion Rules, Filters and so forth, our grammar also contains a set of case-marking rules which assign case to some NP-positions (e.g. an NP is assigned objective case if governed by a transitive V or P, and nominative case if governed by TENSE), though not to others (e.g. the subject of an infinitival S-bar is not assigned case); an associated set of case filters prevent overgeneration by the Case Component. There are two types of case-marking: *inherent* case-marking which applies in the Base, and *structural* case-marking which applies at S-structure. Our revised overall model of grammar thus looks something like this:

(147) (i) *Base*
      (a) Phrase Structure Rules
      (b) Lexicon (lexical entries, Lexical Redundancy Rules, Word-Formation Rules, Restructuring Rules, Inherent Case-marking Rules, etc.)
      (c) Lexical Insertion Rule
      Output of Base = D-structures
  (ii) *Transformational Component*
      (a) Transformations
      (b) Conditions (= Constraints) on Transformations
      Output of Transformational Component = S-structures
  (iii) *Case Component*
      (a) Case-marking Rules

        (b) Case Filters
        Output of Case Component = case-marked S-structures
    (iv) *Deletion Component*
        (a) Deletion Rules
        (b) Conditions on Deletion
        Output of Deletion Component = Surface Structures
    (v) *Surface Structure Filters*
        Output of Filters = filtered Surface Structures

The *case-marking rules* that we have been assuming here can be summarised as:

(148) (a)   NP is marked *nominative* if governed by TENSE
     (b)   NP is marked *objective* if governed by a transitive V or P
     (c)   NP is marked *genitive* if governed by POSS
     (d)   A moved *wh*-phrase inherits its case from its trace
     (e)   X governs Y iff X is the minimal governing node c-commanding Y and there is no S-bar or NP intervening between X and Y (= and there is no S-bar or NP containing (= dominating) Y but not X); governing nodes are lexical categories (V, P, N, A), TENSE, and POSS; X c-commands Y iff the first branching node dominating X dominates Y, and neither X nor Y dominates the other.

Among the *case filters* we posited are the following:

(149) (a)   CASE FILTER (38)
        No overt NP can be caseless
     (b)   CASE CONFLICT FILTER
        No NP can carry more than one case-marking
     (c)   PRO FILTER (65)
        PRO cannot be governed
     (d)   NP TRACE FILTER (82)
        The trace of an NP MOVEMENT cannot be case-marked

EXERCISES

Exercise I

Draw a P-marker representing the structure of the sentence:

(1)   John may want Mary to lend Paul her car

and discuss the case-marking of all the NPs in the sentence.

Exercise II

On the analogy of

(1)   While walking along the street, John fell down a hole

we might propose to analyse the sentence:

(2)   While walking along, John fell down

as (informally):

(3)   While walking along PRO, John fell down PRO

(where PRO is an empty pronominal NP): i.e. we might say that *along* and *down* in such cases are transitive prepositions which take an empty pronominal object. Why would such an analysis be inconsistent with the framework of Case Theory expounded here? What alternative analysis can you think of for sentences such as (2) which is consistent with our present framework?

Exercise III

In earlier work on TG, it was suggested that sentences like

(1)   The ball rolled down the hill

should be analysed as syntactically related to sentences like

(2)   John rolled the ball down the hill

In particular, it was suggested that we might analyse *the ball* as the underlying object of *roll* in both cases, and say that in (1) *the ball* moves out of underlying object position into the (empty) subject position by NP MOVEMENT. Under the NP MOVEMENT analysis, (1) would have the D-structure:

(3)   comp np rolled the ball down the hill

Movement of *the ball* into the empty subject NP position would give the S-structure:

(4)   comp the ball$_2$ rolled np$_2$ down the hill

In what way would such an analysis be incompatible with the version of Case Theory outlined here? What alternative analysis of sentences like (1) might be proposed, consistent with our present framework?

Exercise IV

Discuss the possibility that S-BAR DELETION may have to be lexically governed (i.e. the Lexicon will have to specify whether Verbs etc. optionally, obligatorily, or never trigger the rule) in relation to examples such as the following (assuming the grammaticality judgements given); pay particular attention to the case-marking of the subject of the bracketed infinitive complement:

(1) (a)   I believe [John to be the best candidate]
    (b)   *I believe [PRO to be the best candidate]

(2) (a)   *He claimed [Mary to be innocent]
   (b)   He claimed [PRO to be innocent]
(3) (a)   I expected [Mary to win]
   (b)   I expected [PRO to win]

What explanatory value do lexically governed rules have? Why?

*Exercise V

Show that S-BAR DELETION cannot be assimilated to other deletion rules like WH-DELETION. In this respect, consider which of the following possibilities would give the right results:

(1)   S-BAR DELETION operates:
         (i) after the Base Rules in (147), but before the Transformations
         (ii) after Transformations, but before Case-marking
         (iii) after Case-marking, like other Deletion Rules in (147)

Consider first of all which (more than one?) of the above hypotheses would correctly predict that sentences like:

(2)   I consider John to be incompetent

are grammatical (assuming that *John* is the subject of an infinitive complement which undergoes S-BAR DELETION). Now go on to consider which of the possibilities in (1) would also be compatible with the *successive cyclic* analysis of WH-MOVEMENT in sentences like:

(3)   *What* do you consider John to be —?

on which *what* would move out of the position marked — to be adjoined first to the empty COMP introducing the infinitive clause, and then to the empty COMP introducing the main clause.

Exercise VI

How might we account for the following contrasts in terms of Case Theory?

(1) (a)   For me to stay here overnight would be a mistake
   (b)   *For PRO to stay here overnight would be a mistake
(2) (a)   *Me to stay here overnight would be a mistake
   (b)   PRO to stay here overnight would be a mistake

Exercise VII

In relation to the examples below ((1) involving NP MOVEMENT and (2) involving WH-MOVEMENT) show how Case Theory obviates the need for positing either the TENSED S-CONDITION, or the SPECIFIED SUBJECT CONDITION in order to account for the ungrammaticality of the relevant sentences (and for the need to guarantee that NP MOVEMENT does, but WH-MOVEMENT does not obey the TSC and SSC):

(1) (a)   *John* seems — to be happy
    (b)   **John* seems — is happy
    (c)   **John* seems Mary to like —
(2) (a)   **Who* does it seem — to be happy?
    (b)   *Who* does it seem — is happy?
    (c)   *Who* does John seem to like —?

Are any of the ungrammatical sentences not accounted for by TSC and SSC, but accounted for by Case Theory? If so, what does that tell us about TSC and SSC?

*Exercise VIII

We have seen three different ways of blocking overgeneration: (i) Constraints, (ii) Surface Structure Filters, and (iii) Case Filters. Immediately below are three different devices (A, B and C) for blocking certain types of overgeneration by our Grammar:

A.   FIXED SUBJECT CONSTRAINT (Bresnan)
      No NP immediately following an overt COMP can be moved out of its containing clause
B.   FOR–TO FILTER (Chomsky and Lasnik)
      Any clause containing the complementiser *for* followed by *to* with no overt constituent separating them is ill-formed
C.   CASE FILTERS (Chomsky)
      (i) PRO must be ungoverned
      (ii) Lexical NP must have one and only one case-marking

Assume that without some device such as A, B, or C, our Grammar would generate all of the following as well-formed:

(1)   Who would you prefer for — to leave?
(2)   Who did you wonder whether — to come to the party?
(3)   Who don't you know where — to go?
(4)   Who would you like very much for — not to turn up?
(5)   I would prefer for PRO to leave
(6)   I'm not sure about whether PRO to come
(7)   You are preferred for — to keep quiet

Decide for yourself which of these sentences are ungrammatical; and then on the basis of your judgements, determine which of the devices (A, B, or C) can best handle the resultant overgeneration.

*Exercise IX

In discussing NP MOVEMENT in the text, we made three key assumptions:

A.   An NP moved by NP MOVEMENT does *not* inherit the case of its trace

B.   The trace of NP MOVEMENT cannot carry case

C.   No NP can be assigned more than one case

Show how these three principles can be used to account for why the italicised NP in the examples below cannot be moved out of the position marked —:

(1) (a)   **John* is thought — is innocent (OK . . . to be innocent)

    (b)   **Mary* is impossible for — to leave (OK it's impossible for M to leave)

    (c)   **Mary* was written a book about — (OK A book was written about Mary)

    (d)   **Mary* seems Bill to like — (cf. It seems Bill likes Mary)

Suppose now that we abandon the above account (to be more precise, we abandon A and B, and tighten up C), and replace all three principles, A, B and C, by the following *two* principles:

D.   Any moved constituent inherits the case of its trace (whether moved by NP MOVEMENT, or by WH-MOVEMENT); it may also have its own case

E.   No NP can carry more than one case-specification (e.g. an NP can't be marked for different cases, and can't be marked twice for the same case)

Show how the alternative account in terms of principles D and E can account for the same range of sentences in (1).

****Exercise X**

Below are a set of sentences containing embedded infinitive complements with and without overt complementisers introducing them. In each case, the infinitive in (a) has a lexical NP-subject, in (b) a PRO subject, in (c) a *wh*-trace subject and in (d) an *np*-trace subject. Decide for yourself which of the sentences are grammatical, and which ungrammatical. On the basis of your judgements, determine which of the sentences are – and which are not – accounted for adequately by the case rules and case filters we have presented in this chapter

(1)(a)   I would prefer (for) him to leave

   (b)   I would prefer (for) PRO to leave

   (c)   Who would you prefer (for) to leave?

   (d)   John is preferred (for) to leave

(2)(a)   We expect (for) him to win

   (b)   We expect (for) PRO to win

   (c)   Who do you expect (for) to win?

   (d)   John is expected (for) to win

(3)(a)   I arranged (for) him to be there

   (b)   I arranged (for) PRO to be there

(c)   Who did you arrange (for) to be there?
(d)   He was arranged (for) to be there
(4) (a)   John tried (for) Mary to come home early
(b)   John tried (for) PRO to come home early
(c)   Who did John try (for) to come home early?
(d)   John was tried (for) to come home early
(5) (a)   John claimed (for) Mary to be innocent
(b)   John claimed (for) PRO to be innocent
(c)   Who did John claim (for) to be innocent?
(d)   John was claimed (for) to be innocent
(6) (a)   John said (for) Mary to have escaped
(b)   John said (for) PRO to have escaped
(c)   Who did John say (for) to have escaped?
(d)   Mary was said (for) to have escaped.

**Exercise XI*

Kayne in two recent papers (1980) has argued that Chomsky's analysis of case-marking in English fails to account for the use of the objective form *whom* in some dialects of English in sentences such as:

(1)   a man *whom* I believe is right

Both Chomsky and Kayne would argue that sentence (1) is derived as follows. Its D-structure is:

(2)   a man $[_{\bar{S}_1}$ COMP $[_{S_1}$ I believe $[_{\bar{S}_2}$ COMP $[_{S_2}$ who is right]]]]

Application of WH-MOVEMENT on the $\bar{S}_2$ cycle will adjoin *who* to COMP$_2$ giving the derived structure:

(3)   a man $[_{\bar{S}_1}$ COMP $[_{S_1}$ I believe $[_{\bar{S}_2}$ $[_{COMP}$ who$_2$] $[_S$ np$_2$ is right]]]]

Reapplication of WH-MOVEMENT on the $\bar{S}_1$ cycle will then move *who* out of the subordinate COMP to be adjoined to the main clause COMP, giving the S-structure:

(4)   a man $[_{\bar{S}_1}$ $[_{COMP}$ who$_2$] $[_S$ I believe $[_{\bar{S}}$ $[_{COMP}$ np$_2$] $[_S$ np$_2$ is right]]]]

The essential assumption Chomsky makes is:

(5)   No Verb can govern an NP 'across' an intervening S-bar

In the light of this (and other familiar) assumption(s), what case would Chomsky's rules assign to *who* in the S-structure (4), and why?

Kayne rejects assumption (5), and replaces it by:

(6)   No Verb can govern an NP across *more than one* intervening S or S-bar constituent

What predictions will Kayne's analysis make about the case-marking of each of the traces in (4)? If both traces carry case-marking under his analysis, what modifications are going to be needed to the principle that a moved *wh*-phrase inherits case from any of its traces that are case-marked, in order to avoid case-conflict?

What predictions will Kayne's analysis make about the grammaticality of the objective form *whom* in the following:

(7) (a)   someone whom I am sure is right
   (b)   someone whom it appears is right
   (c)   someone whom it is obvious is right
   (d)   someone whom it is thought is right

Are these predictions correct?

What difficulties will Kayne's analysis face in respect of sentences like the following:

(8) (a)   *I don't know *whom* is right (OK = who)
   (b)   *He asked me about *whom* was coming (OK = who)

**Exercise XII

A basic assumption of the discussion in the text is that the subject of an infinitive introduced by *for* is assigned objective case by virtue of being governed by *for* (the latter being analysed as prepositional in nature). On the basis of the following example:

(1)   Who are you anxious for me to meet?

show that the above assumption is *incompatible* with the assumptions listed in (2) below:

(2) (a)   Case-marking of prepositional objects takes place at S-structure, hence after the application of WH-MOVEMENT
   (b)   WH-MOVEMENT applies successive cyclically
   (c)   *Wh*-phrases are Chomsky-adjoined to COMP

Assume that (1) derives from the D-structure:

(3) $[_{\bar{S}_1}$ COMP$_1$ $[_{S_1}$ you are anxious $[_{\bar{S}_2}$ $[_{COMP_2}$ for$]$ $[_{S_2}$ me to meet who$]]]]$

and that *who* is adjoined first to COMP$_2$, and then to COMP$_1$. Concentrate particularly on the structure of COMP$_2$ after *who* has been adjoined to it. Does *for* really govern *me*? Why not? Which of our assumptions might be revised to account for cases like (1)?

**Exercise XIII

In chapter 6, we argued that Trace Theory provides a natural account of contrasts like:

(1) (a)   Who do you wanna beat?
   (b)   *Who do you wanna win?

if we assume that the presence of a trace of *who* between *want* and *to* blocks TO-CONTRACTION from applying, and that *who* originates after *beat* in (1) (a), but between *want* and *to* in (1) (b). For the purposes of this exercise, assume that (1) (a) and (b) derive from the respective D-structures:

(2) (a)   COMP$_1$ you do want COMP$_2$ PRO to beat *who*
    (b)   COMP$_2$ you do want COMP$_2$ *who* to win

Also make the following assumptions:

(3) (i)   traces and lexical (= overt) constituents between *want* and *to* block contraction, but not PRO or an empty COMP
    (ii)   WH-MOVEMENT applies successive cyclically to adjoin *who* first to COMP$_2$, then to COMP$_1$

Show that given these assumptions, our grammar wrongly predicts that contraction is blocked in both (1) (a) and (1) (b).

Now make the same assumptions (2) and (3) as before, but in addition make the further assumption:

(4)   Non-case-marked (= caseless) traces undergo deletion at S-structure

Assuming that TO-CONTRACTION applies *after* S-structure, show that our revised analysis incorporating (2), (3) and (4) now makes correct predictions about the contrast in (1). For the purposes of TO-CONTRACTION (i.e. ignoring other complicating factors) would it matter whether we said that rule (4) was optional or obligatory?

FURTHER READING

The articles below are all primary literature, and extremely difficult to follow:

Chomsky (1980) 'On Binding', 'Markedness and Core Grammar', and *Pisa Lectures*
Kayne (1980) 'Extensions of Binding and Case-marking', 'On certain differences between French and English', and 'ECP extensions'
Rouveret and Vergnaud (1980) 'Specifying reference to subject'

11

Binding

Thus far, we have envisaged a grammar containing (at least) the following components:

(1) (i)   Base (Lexicon, Lexical Insertion, Categorial Rules, etc.)
   (ii)   Transformation(s) (& Conditions on Transformations)
  (iii)   Case-Marking Rules (and Case Filters)
  (iv)   Deletion Rules (and Conditions on Deletion)
   (v)   (Surface Structure) Filters

At this point, we turn away from *Syntax* for a moment to consider briefly the role of *Semantics* in the model proposed by Chomsky. Unfortunately, since our book is concerned with *Syntax*, we cannot here do justice to the question of how the semantic component of an EST grammar works: this is in itself the subject matter for another, yet-to-be-written book. Hence, in the ensuing discussion we confine ourselves to those aspects of semantic interpretation which turn out to have direct relevance to our discussion of Syntax.

First, some rather general remarks about semantic interpretation. Recall that within Chomsky's framework of *Autonomous Syntax*, the syntactic component of a grammar has the task of specifying which combinations of words in a language do and do not form grammatical sentences and what their syntactic structure is; whereas the semantic component of the grammar is concerned with specifying what those sentence-structures generated by the syntax actually mean. To take a simple example, consider the syntax and semantics of a pronoun like *it*. It is the task of the syntactic component to specify what sentence-positions the pro-NP *it* can occupy – i.e. that it can occupy typical NP-positions, as in:

(2) (a)   Lend me your dictionary, if you've got *it* handy
   (b)   My car isn't working, and I don't know what's wrong with *it*
   (c)   What will we do about oil when *it* runs out?

Syntax will specify that *it* can occur in a subject NP-position as in (2) (c), a direct object NP-position as in (2) (a), or a prepositional object position as in (2) (b). Semantics will specify what *it* can or cannot have as its antecedent – i.e. that *it* can be construed with *your dictionary* in (2) (a), with *my car* in (2) (b), and with *oil* in (2) (c).

Syntax, then, generates a set of syntactic structures; and Semantics specifies what those structures mean – i.e. in the case of proforms, Semantics specifies the possible or impossible antecedents for the proform. But the question of the interaction between Syntax and Semantics is made more complex by the fact that our schematic model (1) of a Grammar contains a variety of different subcomponents: thus, the *Base* generates a class of D-structures which are mapped onto S-structures by *transformations*, and case-marked by *case rules*; the resultant structures then undergo *deletion*, and are finally filtered through a set of *filters* to produce the corresponding Surface Structure. An obvious question to ask therefore is: 'What types of syntactic structures undergo semantic interpretation: D-structures, S-structures, Surface Structures, or what?'

Chomsky's proposal in his more recent work is that *case-marked S-structures* undergo semantic interpretation; that is, they are subject to a set of rules which map them onto an initial representation of their meaning which he refers to as *Logical Form* (= LF). Thus, in schematic terms, what he envisages is the following schema for a grammar:

(3) 1. Base Rules
     2. Transformations
     3. Case rules
     CASE-MARKED S-STRUCTURE

4. Deletion 5. Filters SURFACE STRUCTURE	6. Semantic Interpretation Rules LOGICAL FORM

Within the model (3), S-structure has a dual function: it serves both as the input to the Deletion Rules and Filters, and as the input to the Semantic Interpretation Rules. Unfortunately, it would take us too far astray here to present the highly complex empirical arguments justifying the assumption that Semantic Interpretation Rules operate on case-marked S-structures.

Rather than attempt to justify the organisation of a Grammar presented in (3), let us instead turn to look at one area of semantic interpretation crucial to our discussion of Syntax – that of *anaphora*. An essential task for any theory of semantic interpretation is to determine whether, in sentences containing more than one NP, a given NP can be interpreted as being *coreferential to* (i.e. referring to the same entity as) another. Before going any further, it is useful – following Chomsky – to distinguish between three distinct types of NP: viz. (i) *anaphors*, (ii) *pronominals*, (iii) *lexical NPs*. An *anaphor* is an NP which can have no independent reference, but rather which takes its reference from some other expression in the sentence, its *antecedent*. For example, *each other* is a *reciprocal anaphor* in English sentences like:

(4)   John and Mary like each other

since it takes its reference from its antecedent *John and Mary*. Since anaphors cannot have independent reference, but must take their reference from some antecedent, if an anaphor is used in a sentence where it has no antecedent, the sentence is *uninterpretable* (= *unsemantic* = semantically ill-formed) – as with:

(5)   *Each other have left

A second class of *anaphors* in English are *reflexive anaphors*: these are *self*-forms (*myself, ourselves*; *yourself, yourselves*; *himself, herself, itself, themselves*). Once again, they must take their reference from some antecedent, hence the contrast between:

(6) (a)   John cut himself
    (b)   *Himself resigned

In (6) (a) *himself* can be interpreted as having *John* as its antecedent and hence takes the reference of *John*; whereas in (6) (b), *himself* cannot be assigned any antecedent, and hence has no reference, and thus is uninterpretable.

A second class of NPs are *pronominals*. For the time being (to avoid unnecessary complexity) let's assume that this class comprises simply what are traditionally called 'personal pronouns' – i.e. the forms *I, me*; *you*; *he, him*; *she, her*; *it*; *we, us*; *they, them*. Semantically speaking, pronominals can fulfil either of two functions in English; they can either take their reference from some other NP (this is called their *anaphoric*, or *proximate* use), or they can refer independently (this is their *deictic* or *obviative* use). For instance, in a sentence like:

(7)   John thinks *he* is clever

the pronominal *he* could either be interpreted as referring back to *John* (an anaphoric or proximate use), or as referring to someone other than *John*, perhaps being pointed to by the speaker (its deictic or obviative use).

The third class of NPs distinguished by Chomsky are *lexical NPs*. This class comprises any overt NPs which are not either anaphors or pronominals – i.e. 'ordinary' NPs like *Nim Chimpsky*, *Snotty Snodgrass*, *the man next door*, *Debbie Harry*, etc.

As we noted earlier, one important task for any theory of semantic interpretation is to determine whether or not any given pair of NPs in a sentence can be interpreted as *coreferential*, and to find some way of representing this (non)coreferentiality. Consider first the problem of *representing* coreference. How can we represent the fact that in a sentence such as:

(8)   They shot the arrows at each other

the reciprocal anaphor *each other* can be anaphoric to (= can have as its antecedent) either the NP *they* or the NP *the arrows*? A traditional way of representing this type of relation is by using what are called *referential indices*: these are (usually numerical) subscripts appended to nodes. NPs with the same subscript are interpreted as coreferential, whereas NPs with different subscripts are interpreted as noncoreferential. Using referential indices, we could represent the ambiguity of (8) by saying that (8) can have either the interpretation (9) (i) below, or the interpretation (9) (ii):

(9) (i)   They$_2$ shot the arrows$_3$ at each other$_2$
    (ii)   They$_2$ shot the arrows$_3$ at each other$_3$

Likewise, again using subscripts, the ambiguity of (7) could be represented in terms of the two alternative interpretations (10) (i) and (ii) below:

(10) (i)   John$_2$ thinks he$_2$ is clever (= proximate interpretation for *he*)
     (ii)   John$_2$ thinks he$_3$ is clever (= obviative interpretation for *he*)

If we decide to represent coreference relations by using indices, then the question of determining whether any given pair of NPs in a sentence can or cannot be interpreted as coreferential can be reformulated as that of determining whether a given pair of NPs can or cannot be assigned the same referential index. Hence, we might say that we want to devise some INDEXING RULE which will assign appropriate indices to all the NPs in a sentence, thereby representing all the relevant coreference relations. For the time being, let's consider the possibility of a very general indexing rule along the lines of:

(11)   INDEXING RULE
            Assign every NP in a sentence an index (where the index is a random integer)

A rule like (11) would allow for the twin possibilities that any random pair of NPs might either share the same index, or be assigned different indices: thus in a sentence like (7) *John thinks that he is clever*, either *he* and *John* are assigned the same index – as in (10) (i) – and hence interpreted as coreferential, or *he* and *John* are assigned different indices – as in (10) (ii) – and hence interpreted as noncoreferential. In effect, then, the overgeneral rule (11) specifies:

(12)   Any random pair of NPs in a sentence can either be interpreted as coreferential, or as noncoreferential

Clearly the rule (11) – which makes the prediction (12) – is overgeneral, and will *overgenerate* in the sense of assigning to sentences interpretations which they cannot have. For example, rule (11) would give rise to interpretations like:

(13)   I$_2$ like yourself$_2$

in which *I* and *yourself* are *coindexed* (i.e. assigned the same index), and therefore wrongly predicted to be interpretable as coreferential. Of course, we could rule out 'impossible' interpretations like (13) by some condition like:

(14)   MATCHING CONDITION
            If two NPs are assigned the same index, they must 'match' in features (e.g. number, gender, person, etc.)

(14) would be a kind of 'semantic filter' – i.e. a filter which rules out some interpretations (indexed structures) as ill-formed. This is the same strategy that we used in the case of overgeneration by syntactic rules – namely to use *filters* (or: well-formedness conditions) to rule out the relevant overgenerated structures.

Even if supplemented by a condition like (14), however, our INDEXING RULE (11) will massively overgenerate in all sorts of ways. For example, it will generate 'impossible' interpretations such as the following:

(15) (a) John$_2$ hurt himself$_3$
 (b) John$_2$ hurt him$_2$
 (c) John$_2$ hurt Fred$_2$

Thus, in (15) (a) the rule would wrongly predict that *himself* can refer to someone other than *John*; in (15) (b) it would wrongly predict that *him* can·refer back to *John*; and in (15) (c), it would wrongly predict that *Fred* can be interpreted as referring to the same person as *John*. How are we to block this kind of overgeneration of unwanted (ill-formed) interpretations?

Chomsky's solution is to propose a number of indexing conditions, or – as he prefers to call them – *Binding Conditions*. The three conditions which he proposes to rule out overgenerated interpretations like those in (15) (a), (b) and (c) are respectively:

(16) (A) An anaphor must be bound in its governing category, if it has one
 (B) A pronominal NP must be free in its governing category if it has one
 (C) A lexical NP must be free everywhere

(Cf. Chomsky, 'Markedness and Core Grammar' (1980), p. 12.) To understand (16), we need the following definitions:

(17) (a) X is *bound* if X is an argument coindexed with a c-commanding argument; if not bound it is *free*
 (b) An *argument* is an NP-position within S or NP (subject, direct object, indirect object, etc.)
 (c) X *c-commands* Y if the first branching node dominating X dominates Y, and X does not dominate Y, nor Y, X.
 (d) X is the *governing category* for Y if X is the minimal NP or S which contains the constituent which governs Y
 (e) X *governs* Y if X is the minimal potential governor (= V, A, N, P, or TENSE) c-commanding Y, and there is no intervening S-bar or NP barrier between X and Y

Let's assume that the sentences in (15) have the structure:

(18)

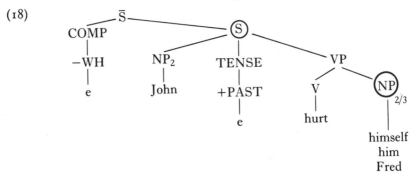

The encircled NP in (18) is *governed* by the verb *hurt* (more specifically, it is the direct object of the verb *hurt*). The minimal S or NP-node containing the verb *hurt* is the encircled S-node; hence the encircled S-node is the *governing category* for the encircled NP. If the encircled NP-position is filled by the reflexive anaphor *himself*, then condition (16) (A) specifies that *himself* must have a c-commanding coindexed antecedent NP within the encircled S. Now clearly, the NP *John* c-commands the encircled NP, since the first branching node above *John* is the S-node, and the S-node dominates the encircled NP. Thus, if *himself* is coindexed with John, as in:

(19)   John$_2$ hurt himself$_2$

then the resultant structure satisfies the Binding Condition (16) (A); but if *himself* has a different index from *John*, as in:

(20)   John$_2$ hurt himself$_3$

then the resultant structure (20) does not satisfy (16) (A), and hence the anaphor *himself* is *improperly bound* (i.e. uninterpretable).

Now suppose that the encircled NP is filled by the pronoun *him* instead. The governing category for *him* is the encircled S, as we established earlier. The Binding Condition (16) (B) stipulates that *him* must not be coindexed with a c-commanding NP within the encircled S; but the NP *John* c-commands the encircled NP *him*. Hence, *John* cannot be coindexed with *him*. Thus, of the two potential interpretations:

(21) (a)   John$_2$ hurt him$_2$
     (b)   John$_2$ hurt him$_3$

only the second one (in which *him* is marked as noncoreferential to *John*) satisfies the Binding Condition (16) (B). Or, more simplistically, the Binding Condition (16) (B) predicts (correctly) that *him* can only be interpreted as referring to someone other than *John*.

And what of the case where the encircled NP is filled by a lexical NP like *Fred*? Here, Condition (16) (C) in effect says that a lexical NP must not be coindexed with any c-commanding argument anywhere in the sentence containing it. If *Fred* is coindexed with *John* in (18), then this condition will be violated, since *John* c-commands *Fred*, as we have already seen. Thus, of the two possible interpretations:

(22) (a)   John$_2$ hurt Fred$_2$
     (b)   John$_2$ hurt Fred$_3$

only the second one (in which *John* and *Fred* are marked as noncoreferential) satisfies (16) (C). Or, more informally, Condition (16) (C) predicts that *John* cannot refer to the same person as *Fred* in such sentences.

So it seems that Chomsky's three Binding Conditions will deal quite adequately with overgeneration in all three of the cases we mentioned in (15). But will they also deal with other cases of overgeneration? Let's see. Consider now the following set of sentences:

(23) (a)   *Himself might hurt John
     (b)   He might hurt John

Let's assume that (23) have the following structure after IN-DEXING has applied:

(24)

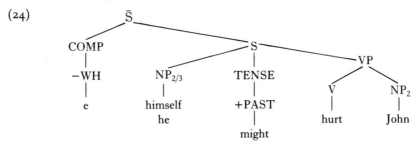

(24) is intended to represent the dual possibility that either

he/himself and *John* might be assigned the same index, or different indices. *He/himself* in (24) are governed by TENSE, and the minimal S or NP-node containing TENSE is the S-node, so that the S-node is the *governing category* for *himself/he*. *Himself* is a reflexive anaphor, and Binding Condition (16) (A) requires that an anaphor be coindexed with a c-commanding NP in its governing category: the governing category for *himself* is S, so for sentence (23) (a) to be well-formed, it would have to be the case that *himself* is coindexed with some NP which c-commands it within S in (24). But there is no NP c-commanding *himself* in (24): hence sentence (23) (a) is ill-formed irrespective of whether *himself* is assigned the same index as *John*, or a different one. *Himself* is therefore improperly bound, and uninterpretable.

But what about (23) (b), where we have *he* as the subject of the clause, not *himself*? Binding Condition (16) (B) says that a pronominal NP must not be coindexed with any NP which c-commands it within its governing category: the governing category for *he* is S. Hence, (16) (B) says that *he* must not be coindexed with any NP which c-commands it within S. But there is no NP which c-commands *he* at all. Does this therefore mean that we wrongly predict that sentence (23) (b) could have either of the interpretations:

(25) (a) He_2 might hurt $John_2$
     (b) He_2 might hurt $John_3$?

No, not at all. For while the pronoun *he* satisfies the relevant Binding Conditions in both (25) (a) and (25) (b), this is not true of the lexical NP *John*. Since *John* is a lexical NP, it is subject to the third Binding Condition (16) (C), which specifies that a lexical NP must not be coindexed with any other NP which c-commands it. But *John* in (24) is c-commanded by *he/himself*: hence any interpretation on which *he* and *John* are coindexed is ruled out by (16) (C). This means that only (25) (b) is a possible interpretation, not (25) (a): or in simpler terms, it means that *he* and *John* must be noncoreferential (or *disjoint in reference*, to use another favourite expression of Chomsky's). In short, Chomsky's three binding conditions make exactly correct predictions about possible and impossible coreference links in sentences like (23).

So let's move on to consider the following contrast:

(26) (a)   The soldiers disgraced themselves/them
    (b)   The soldiers' behaviour disgraced them/*themselves

Sentence (26) (a) is of course exactly parallel to our earlier sentences (15) *John hurt himself/him*: hence, no need to repeat that discussion here. Suffice it to say that the Binding Conditions (16) determine that *themselves* must be coreferential to *the soldiers*, but *them* must be disjoint in reference with *the soldiers*. But now consider the more interesting case (26) (b): let's assume that this would have the following structure, after INDEXING:

(27)

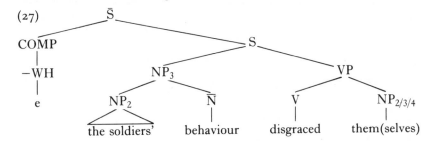

The NP *them(selves)* here is governed by the verb *disgraced*: the minimal S or NP containing the V *disgraced* is the S-node; hence the S-node is the *governing category* for the NP *them(selves)*. Take the case of *themselves*: this is a reflexive anaphor, and so subject to Binding Condition (16) (A), which says that an anaphor must have a coindexed c-commanding antecedent within its governing category. S is the governing category for *themselves* here, so (16) (A) amounts to claiming that *themselves* must be coindexed with some suitable antecedent which c-commands it within S. Apart from *themselves*, there are two other NPs within S, namely NP_2 *the soldiers'*, and NP_3 *the soldiers' behaviour*. Does either of these c-command *themselves*? Take NP_2 *the soldiers'*: the first branching node above this NP is NP_3, and quite clearly NP_3 does not dominate *themselves*; hence *the soldiers'* does not c-command *themselves*, and is therefore not a possible antecedent for *themselves*, since the relevant interpretation violates condition (16) (A). But does NP_3 (*the soldiers' behaviour*) c-command *themselves*? Yes it does, since the first branching node above NP_3 is S, and S dominates *themselves*. Does our grammar therefore (wrongly) predict that *themselves* can be coindexed with (and hence interpreted as referring back to) NP_3 *the soldiers' behaviour*? No, not at all, because this is ruled out by the MATCHING CONDITION (14), which specifies that an anaphor must match its antecedent in number, gender, person etc.: in this case, *themselves* is plural, and *the soldiers' behaviour* is singular: there is thus a mismatch of features which rules out any possibility of *themselves* referring back to *the soldiers' behaviour*. Had the features matched here, as in the case of:

(28)   *The soldiers' behaviour₂ condemns itself₂*

then the relevant interpretation would have satisfied all the proposed conditions, including the MATCHING CONDITION.

Now let's turn to sentences like:

(29)   *Mary* thinks that [s *she/*herself* will win]

Here, the subordinate clause subject *she/herself* is governed by the TENSE auxiliary *will*: the minimal S or NP containing *will* is the bracketed S, so that the bracketed S is the governing category for *she/herself*. *Herself* is a reflexive anaphor, and Binding Condition (16) (A) requires that an anaphor have a coindexed antecedent NP which c-commands it within its governing category (= S in this case). But there is no other NP within the bracketed S, so clearly this condition cannot be met. In other words, a sentence like:

(30)   *Mary thinks that herself will win

is ill-formed irrespective of whatever index is assigned to *herself*. But now consider *she* in place of *herself*: *she* is a pronominal, and hence subject to condition (16) (B) which says that a pronominal must not be coindexed with any c-commanding NP within its governing category (= S, here). But since *she* is the only NP within the bracketed S, clearly this condition will be met, irrespective of whether *she* is coindexed with *Mary* or not: i.e. both the interpretations (31) below will satisfy condition (16) (B):

(31) (a)   Mary₂ thinks that she₂ will win
     (b)   Mary₂ thinks that she₃ will win

Or, more informally, condition (16) (B) correctly predicts that *she* may refer either to *Mary*, or to someone else in a sentence like (29). Notice, interestingly, that previously we had assumed that we would require the TENSED S CONDITION (TSC) to block sentences like (30); now, by contrast, we see that we do not need to invoke the TSC to explain the ill-formedness of (30), since it follows automatically from our Binding Condition (16) (A). This opens up the interesting possibility that Binding Conditions like those in (16) might obviate the need for certain *constraints* like the TENSED S CONDITION.

Now let's contrast (29) with:

(32)   Mary considers [s *her(self)* to be the best candidate]

In (32), the italicised NP *her(self)* is governed by the verb *consider* (recall that *consider* is a verb which takes an S, not an S-bar infinitival complement in S-structure, and hence can govern the subject of that complement because there is no intervening S-bar): the minimal S or NP-node containing the governing verb *consider* is the main clause S – i.e. the bracketed S in (33):

(33)   [s Mary considers her(self) to be the best candidate]

Thus, the bracketed main S is the governing category for *her(self)* in (33) above. *Herself* is a reflexive anaphor, and hence subject to Binding Condition (16) (A) which requires that an anaphor have a coindexed c-commanding antecedent within its governing category (= the bracketed S in (33)). Now *Mary* is within the bracketed S, and also c-commands *herself* (since the first branching node above *Mary* is the bracketed S-node and this dominates *herself*): in other words *herself* is OK in (33), just in case it is coindexed with *Mary*, as in:

(34)   Mary$_2$ considers herself$_2$ to be the best candidate

If *herself* is not coindexed with *Mary*, then *herself* lacks any antecedent, and the resultant interpretation violates Condition (16) (A) – cf.

(35)   *Mary$_2$ considers herself$_3$ to be the best candidate

Thus, (16) (A) correctly predicts that a sentence like:

(36)   Mary considers herself to be the best candidate

is only well-formed if *herself* is construed with *Mary*.

But now suppose that we have *her* in place of *herself*. What happens then? Once again, *her* is governed by the verb *consider*, and hence the main S is the governing category for *her*. *Her* is pronominal, hence subject to condition (16) (B) which says that a pronominal must not be coindexed with any c-commanding NP within its governing category. Since *Mary* c-commands *her* and is contained within the main clause S which is the governing category for *her*, then this means that condition (16) (B) can only be met if *her* carries a different index from *Mary*: thus, of the two interpretations:

(37) (a)   Mary$_2$ considers her$_2$ to be the best candidate
     (b)   Mary$_2$ considers her$_3$ to be the best candidate

only the second one satisfies (16) (B). Or, in more concrete terms, Condition (16) (B) correctly predicts that in a sentence such as:

(38)   Mary considers her to be the best candidate

her must refer to someone other than *Mary*.

   Now let's move on to sentences like:

(39)   Mary wants John to help her(self)

Here, we see that *her(self)* is governed by (and the object of) the verb *help*; the minimal S or NP-node containing the verb *help* is the bracketed subordinate S-node in (40):

(40)   Mary wants [$_S$ John to help her(self)]

Hence the bracketed S-node is the governing category for *her(self)*. *Herself* is an anaphor, and hence subject to Condition (16) (A), which specifies that an anaphor must have a coindexed c-commanding antecedent within its governing category: but *John* is the only NP within the bracketed S in (40) that c-commands *herself*, so only *John* could be a possible antecedent for *herself*; however, even this reading would be ruled out perhaps by the MATCHING CONDITION (14), since there is an apparent gender conflict between *herself* and *John*. Nor could *Mary* be the antecedent of *herself*, since *Mary* is not contained within the bracketed S. In other words, sentence (39) is going to be odd, irrespective of whether *herself* is coindexed with *John*, *Mary*, or indeed assigned a unique index. Notice furthermore that we no longer need appeal to the SPECIFIED SUBJECT CONDITION to account for why *herself* cannot be coindexed with *Mary* in sentences like (39). So we have yet a further example where the proposed Binding Conditions obviate the need for some of the *constraints* that we looked at earlier (in this case, the SPECIFIED SUBJECT CONSTRAINT; and earlier the TENSED S CONDITION).

But what happens if we have *her* in place of *herself* in (40)? Once again, the governing category for *her* will be the bracketed S; and since *her* is pronominal, the Binding Condition (16) (B) requires that *her* not be coindexed with a c-commanding NP within the bracketed S; but this does not of course prevent *her* from being coindexed with an NP outside the bracketed S – e.g. with *Mary*, as in:

(41)   Mary$_2$ wants John$_3$ to help her$_2$

Alternatively, *her* might have a unique index, in which case it would be interpreted as *deictic* (or obviative): cf.

(42)   Mary$_2$ wants John$_3$ to help her$_4$

Either interpretation – (41) or (42) – would satisfy the Binding Condition (16) (B): the condition thus in effect predicts that in a sentence like

(43)   Mary wants John to help her

her can either refer back to *Mary*, or can refer to someone other than *Mary*.

So far, all the cases that we have considered are where the governing category is S, not NP. Do the Binding Conditions work also where the governing category is NP rather than S? Consider the sentence:

(44)   I like [$_{NP}$ the soldiers' pictures of them(selves)]

The governor of *them(selves)* here is the preposition *of*, and the minimal S or NP containing *of* is the bracketed NP; hence this bracketed NP is the governing category for *them(selves)*. Since *themselves* is a reflexive anaphor, by (16) (A) it must be coindexed with some c-commanding antecedent in the bracketed NP (its governing category); now if we assume that (44) has the structure:

(45)
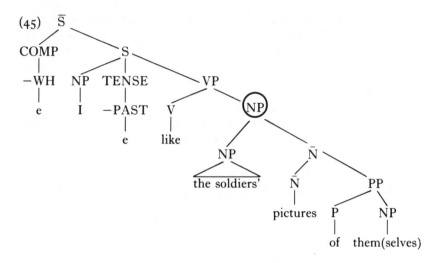

(where the encircled NP is the governing category for *them-(selves))*, then we see that the NP *the soldiers'* c-commands *them(selves)*, by virtue of the fact that the first branching node above *the soldiers'* is the encircled NP, and this dominates *themselves*; furthermore, *the soldiers'* is also contained within the encircled NP: hence if *themselves* is coindexed with *the soldiers'*, as in:

(46) I_2 like *the soldiers'*$_3$ pictures of *themselves*$_3$

the resultant interpretation satisfies the Binding Condition (16) (A).

But now suppose that we have *them* in place of *themselves*. Once again, it is the encircled NP in (45) which is the governing category for *them*; and since *them* is pronominal, condition (16) (B) requires that *them* have no coindexed c-commanding antecedent within the encircled NP; this condition will be met if *them* has a different index from *the soldiers'*, as in:

(47) I_2 like *the soldiers'*$_3$ pictures of *them*$_4$

but will obviously not be met if *them* is assigned the same index as *the soldiers'* – cf.

(48)   *I_2 like *the soldiers'*$_3$ pictures of *them*$_3$

In other words, Condition (16) (B) predicts that in a sentence like:

(49)   I like the soldiers' pictures of them

them must be disjoint in reference with (= must not overlap in reference with) *the soldiers'*.

But now contrast sentence (44) with:

(50)   The soldiers like [$_{NP}$ her picture of them(selves)]

Here, *them(selves)* is governed by *of*, and the minimal S or NP containing *of* is the bracketed NP, so that this bracketed NP is the governing category for *them(selves)*. Consider the interpretation:

(51)   The soldiers$_2$ like [$_{NP}$ her$_3$ picture of themselves$_2$]

This will be ruled out by condition (16) (A), because *themselves* has no coindexed antecedent within the bracketed NP which is its governing category. By contrast, if we replace *themselves* by *them*, then the interpretation:

(52)   The soldiers$_2$ like [$_{NP}$ her$_3$ picture of them$_2$]

is perfectly well-formed, since it satisfies the relevant Binding Condition (16) (B), because the pronominal *them* is not coindexed with any other NP within the bracketed NP which is its governing category. So, to answer our earlier question, it does indeed seem that the Binding Conditions work equally well for cases where the governing category is NP rather than S.

Hitherto, we have considered only cases where the antecedent of an anaphor is an overt NP. An obvious question to ask is whether *empty NPs* can also serve as antecedents. For example, can *traces* be antecedents for anaphors? Clearly this must be so, as we see from:

(53)   John$_2$ seems [$_S$ np$_2$ to have hurt himself$_2$]

(where np$_2$ is the trace of the NP-moved constituent *John*). *Himself* here is governed by the verb *hurt*, and the minimal S or NP containing *hurt* is the bracketed subordinate S, which is therefore the governing category for *himself*. Since *himself* is a reflexive anaphor, Condition (16) (A) requires that it have a coindexed c-commanding antecedent within the bracketed S. But does it have one? Only if we say that the trace np$_2$ serves as the antecedent for *himself*, since the trace np2 both c-commands *himself*, and occurs within the bracketed S. But this analysis of course commits us to the more general assumption that *traces* can serve as antecedents (or, more generally, can be coindexed with other NPs). The same would be true in a sentence like:

(54)   Who$_2$ [$_S$ np$_2$ might hurt himself$_2$]

(where np$_2$ this time is the trace of WH-MOVEMENT into COMP), where once again the structure (54) will only satisfy the relevant Binding Condition (16) (A) if we assume that traces can serve as antecedents, and more specifically that np$_2$ is the antecedent of *himself$_2$*.

In much the same way, PRO can also serve as the antecedent of an anaphor, as in:

(55)   John$_2$ wants [$_S$ PRO$_2$ to better himself$_2$]

Here, *himself* is governed by the verb *better*, and the minimal S or NP containing *better* is the bracketed subordinate S. Since *himself* is an anaphor, by (16) (A) it requires a coindexed c-commanding antecedent within the bracketed S. Clearly *John* does not qualify as such, since *John* is outside the bracketed S. By contrast, PRO does, since PRO c-commands *himself*, and also occurs within the bracketed S. Thus, our grammar will only make the correct prediction that the sentence:

(56)   John wants to better himself

is well-formed if we assume that PRO is the antecedent of *himself* in (55). It thus seems clear that not only lexical NPs, but also empty NPs (more specifically, trace or PRO) can serve as antecedents.

But a second, no less important question is whether empty NPs (PRO and trace) are subject to the Binding Conditions given in (16), and if so, to which one(s)? Let's begin by looking at PRO. PRO appears to have two rather different uses: compare:

(57) (a)   John is not clear what PRO to do
     (b)   It is not clear what PRO to do

In (57) (a), PRO refers back to *John*; or, to use Chomsky's terminology, *John* is the *controller* of PRO, and PRO is therefore *controlled by John*. But in (57) (b), PRO has no obvious controller (or antecedent): PRO in (57) (b) seems to have the nonspecific sense of 'anyone', 'people', 'one', etc. We might therefore say that PRO in (57) (b) is *uncontrolled* (i.e. has no antecedent, and therefore does not take its reference from some other NP).

This situation with PRO has an obvious parallel with the situation that we found with pronouns like *he, they,* etc.; for pronouns too have two uses: (i) a *proximate* use in which they take their reference from some other NP which they are coindexed with; and (ii) an *obviative* use in which they have independent reference. It seems that we can extend this to PRO as well, and say that PRO is *proximate* in cases like (57) (a) where it is controlled by another NP, and *obviative* in cases like (57) (b) where it is uncontrolled. Given this parallelism between *PRO* and *pronoun* (both having a proximate use and an obviative use), it seems clear that PRO should be treated as a *pronominal* (along with Pronoun). Hence we should expect that like other pronominals, PRO would be subject to the Binding Condition (16) (B), which specifies that pronominals should be free in their governing category. Let's see if this is true of PRO in cases like (57) (a) and (b). The answer is, of course, that condition (16) (B) can simply never apply to PRO, since PRO is always ungoverned (as we saw in our discussion of case), and therefore never has a governing category, and hence can never be subject to condition (16) (B) – or, if you like, (16) (B) applies *vacuously* to PRO. For example, in (57) (a) and (b), where we have the structure:

(58) (a)   John is not clear [$_{\bar{S}}$ what PRO to do]
     (b)   It is not clear [$_{\bar{S}}$ what PRO to do]

PRO cannot be governed by *clear* because of the intervening S-bar barrier (and S-bar counts as a barrier to government). Hence condition (16) (B) will apply only vacuously to PRO.

So it seems that the *Theory of Binding* in itself tells us little about the syntax or semantics of PRO, other than that PRO must occur in an ungoverned position – i.e. in effect, PRO can generally occur only as the subject of an infinitive. This leaves unanswered the vital question of how we know when PRO is proximate (i.e. controlled, hence referring back to some other NP), and when PRO is obviative (i.e. carries the sense of 'one/people/anyone'). These are questions which await the development of an adequate *Theory of Control* (independent perhaps of the Theory of Binding). The types of infinitive complement in which PRO occurs are essentially those in (59):

(59) (a)   It's difficult PRO to learn Welsh
(b)   It's not clear where PRO to go
(c)   John wants PRO to win the race
(d)   John persuaded Bill PRO to leave
(e)   John promised Bill PRO to leave

In (59) (a) and (b), PRO clearly has the obviative sense of 'anyone' – e.g. (59) (a) means 'it's difficult for people to learn Welsh'. In (59) (c), PRO cannot be obviative, but must be proximate, and furthermore can only be interpreted as controlled by (i.e. referring back to) *John*. In (59) (d) and (e), it seems clear that in each case *Bill* is the object of *persuaded/promised*, and that there is a missing subject for the following infinitive: cf. the parallel tensed clause construction:

(60) (a)   John persuaded Bill that he should leave
(b)   John promised Bill that he would leave

Thus, PRO in (59) (d) and (e) essentially corresponds to *he* in (60) (a) and (b). But notice that whereas in (59) (d) PRO is controlled by the main clause object *Bill* (i.e. PRO refers back to *Bill*), in (59) (e) by contrast, PRO is controlled by (i.e. refers back to) the main clause subject *John*. Generalising, we see that a PRO which is the subject of an infinitive complement after a verb like *want* or *promise* is controlled by the main S subject, whereas a PRO which is the subject of an infinitive complement embedded under a verb like *persuade* is controlled by the object of the verb *persuade*. This has led many linguists to propose a distinction between two types of verbs: those that take *subject control* (*want, promise*, etc. – i.e. verbs whose subject controls the PRO subject of a following infinitive); and those that take *nonsubject control* (*persuade*, etc. – i.e. verbs where the PRO subject of a following infinitive is governed by some complement of the higher verb which is not its subject, e.g. its object).

If we accept this classification, then we must distinguish three types of predicates which take infinitive complements with PRO subjects:

(61) (i)   those which have an *uncontrolled* PRO subject for the infinitive
(ii)   those which have a *subject-controlled* PRO
(iii)   those which have a *nonsubject-controlled* PRO

It will be for our yet-to-be-developed *Theory of Control* to provide a set of (hopefully universal) principles which will predict which of the three types in (61) any given predicate permitting an infinitive complement with a PRO subject will belong to. Pending the development of such a theory, it would seem to be necessary simply to specify in the lexical entry for verbs like *persuade* or *promise* whether they are subject-control or nonsubject-control verbs. This is unsatisfactory as a solution to the control problem, however, for a number of reasons. Firstly, arbitrary lists of properties associated with predicates have no predictive or explanatory value: ask the question 'How do you know this is a verb of subject control?', and you get the non-answer 'Because it's listed as a verb of subject-control in the Lexicon.' Secondly, treating *control* (of PRO) as a *lexically governed* phenomenon implies that control properties are entirely arbitrary, and hence will vary in random fashion from dialect to dialect, or language to language: this would lead us to expect that the counterpart of:

(62)   John persuaded Bill PRO to leave (cf. (59) (d))

in some other dialect or language would have subject control rather than nonsubject control (i.e. would have PRO interpreted as referring to *John* rather than to *Bill*). But as far as we know, this is not the case. And we would hope that an adequate Theory of Control should explain why this is not the case.

It seems likely that the question of whether a control predicate takes subject control or nonsubject control will ultimately turn out to follow directly from the meaning of the predicate concerned: indeed, it seems likely that classifying predicates strictly into a single control-class is a misguided enterprise. Consider the examples:

(63) (a)   John pleaded with Bill PRO to leave
     (b)   John pleaded with Bill PRO to be allowed to leave

(64) (a)   John appealed to Bill PRO to leave
     (b)   John appealed to Bill PRO to be allowed to leave

In (63) (a) and (64) (a), PRO has nonsubject control, and is interpreted as referring to *Bill*; but in (63) (b) and (64) (b), PRO has subject control and is interpreted as referring to *John* instead. Shall we then say that verbs like *plead* and *appeal* are dual control verbs (i.e. allow *either* subject *or* nonsubject control)? That's no good as a solution, because it wrongly predicts that PRO can refer to either *John* or *Bill* in all four of the sentences in (63) and (64). And to complicate matters still further, in sentences like:

(65)   John asked Bill PRO to leave

there are dialect disagreements over the preferred interpretation of PRO: for British speakers, PRO here must have nonsubject control and hence refer back to *Bill*; but for many American speakers, the preferred interpretation would be for PRO to have subject control, and hence refer back to *John*: to be more concrete, the difference of interpretation is over the question of whether (65) should be paraphrased as in (66) (a) or (b) below:

(66) (a)   John$_2$ asked Bill$_3$ if he$_3$ would leave
     (b)   John$_2$ asked Bill$_3$ if he$_2$ could leave

Does this control difference reflect a difference in the meaning of the verb *ask* in the two dialects? Answers to questions like these and many others are simply not forthcoming at the moment: a great deal more research needs to go into the whole question of *control*.

We remarked earlier that the *Theory of Control* is partly at least independent of the *Theory of Binding*. What we meant by that was that the Binding Conditions we have looked at so far do not predict in any way whether PRO in any given sentence is going to be uncontrolled, subject-controlled, or nonsubject-controlled. This does not of course mean that the Theory of Indexing developed for overt NPs does not apply to PRO. On the contrary, we assume that PRO is assigned a referential index by our INDEXING RULE (11) in the same way as other NPs. Random indexing will then generate interpretations like:

(67) (a)   John$_2$ persuaded Bill$_3$ PRO$_3$ to leave
     (b)   John$_2$ persuaded Bill$_3$ PRO$_2$ to leave
     (c)   John$_2$ persuaded Bill$_3$ PRO$_4$ to leave

It is for the *Theory of Control* to specify the principles that determine that only (67) (a), not (b) or (c), is a well-formed interpretation. The binding principles which do this will (apparently) have to be specific to PRO, and it is in this sense that the Theory of Control is independent of the Theory of Binding.

So far, we have only thought about NPs which get indexed as a result of the application of the INDEXING RULE (11). But recall that there is a second way in which an NP can be indexed. Under the Trace Theory of Movement Rules, a moved NP is automatically coindexed with its trace when it undergoes movement. Since *traces* carry indices, we might wonder whether they too are subject to the proposed *Binding Conditions*, and if so, to which one(s).

Let's start by considering traces of NP MOVEMENT (np-traces). Let's investigate the possibility that they might be treated as *nonlexical anaphors* ('empty' anaphors, if you like). If so, then we should expect that they would obey condition (16) (A) on anaphors – namely that they should be bound in their governing category. But is this the case with np-traces? Recall that there are two principal constructions which involve NP MOVEMENT, namely *Passive* and *Raising*. Let's consider first passive sentences like:

(68)   John was arrested

Underlying (68) would be the D-structure

(69)   np was arrested John

Application of NP MOVEMENT would yield the S-structure:

(70)   John$_2$ was arrested np$_2$

The trace *np$_2$* is governed (though not case-marked) by the passive participle *arrested*: the minimal S or NP containing this passive participle is the S containing the whole structure (70), and this S is therefore the governing category for the trace *np$_2$*. Does *np$_2$* have a coindexed c-commanding antecedent within this S? Of course it does – namely *John$_2$*. Hence, the structure (70) satisfies condition (16) (A), and is therefore well-formed. Notice that this time, however, we are using the Binding Condition in effect to monitor the output of a particular movement rule. So it seems as if Binding Conditions might obviate the need for certain *constraints on movement rules* of the type proposed in earlier research by Ross and Chomsky.

Now let's consider a rather different case of passivisation. Consider the sentence:

(71)   John is believed to be innocent

Underlying (71) would be the D-structure:

(72)   [$_S$ np is believed [$_S$ John to be innocent]]

Application of NP MOVEMENT to move *John* into the vacant main clause subject position would give:

(73)   [s John₂ is believed [s np₂ to be innocent]]

Let's see if the trace np_2 in (73) obeys the Binding Condition on anaphors (16) (A) which requires that an anaphor have a c-commanding coindexed antecedent within its governing category. The trace np_2 in (73) is governed by the passive participle *believed* (recall that *believe* is a verb which takes an S-complement, not an S-bar infinitival complement in S-structure); the minimal S or NP containing *believed* is the leftmost S; hence the leftmost S is the governing category for the trace. Does the trace have a c-commanding antecedent coindexed with it within the leftmost S? The answer is that it does – namely *John₂*. Hence, sentences like (71) are correctly predicted to be well-formed. Or, to put it another way, the Binding Condition (16) (A) permits NP MOVEMENT to apply in structures like (72).

But now compare (72) instead with:

(74)   np is believed [s̄ COMP [s John may be innocent]]

If we apply NP MOVEMENT in this case, we obtain:

(75)   John₂ is believed [s̄ COMP [s np₂ may be innocent]]

Is the trace-anaphor properly bound in respect of (16) (A) in (75)? No it is not: for the trace is the subject of the TENSE auxiliary *may*, and hence governed by *may*; the minimal S or NP containing *may* is the bracketed S; hence this bracketed S is the governing category for the trace np_2. But clearly the trace-anaphor has no coindexed c-commanding antecedent within the bracketed S, and therefore is *improperly bound* with respect to Binding Condition (16) (A). Hence, we correctly predict that the corresponding sentence:

(76)   *John is believed may be innocent

is ill-formed. But notice that here the Binding Conditions are in effect being used to 'block' the results of certain movement operations (NP MOVEMENT in this case). So it appears that the conditions which we originally proposed to deal with *anaphora* (more precisely, to deal with overgeneration by interpretive rules like the INDEXING RULE (11)), also deal with overgeneration by syntactic rules like NP MOVEMENT.

An obvious question to ask is whether the same is also true in Raising constructions involving NP MOVEMENT. Consider a D-structure along the lines of:

(77) $[_{S_i}$ np seems $[_{S_j}$ John to be unhappy]]

Application of NP MOVEMENT here would result in the S-structure:

(78) $[_{S_i}$ John$_2$ seems $[_{S_j}$ np$_2$ to be unhappy]]

in which *np*$_2$ is the trace of the NP-moved constituent *John*$_2$. Recall that Raising predicates take an S-complement (not an S-bar complement) in S-structure, and that a verb can govern the subject of an infinitive across an S, but not across an S-bar. This being so, then the trace-subject in (78) is governed by the verb *seems*; the minimal S or NP containing *seems* is S$_i$ (the main clause S), so that S$_i$ is the governing category for the trace-subject of the infinitive. Since traces of NP MOVEMENT are anaphors (we posit), let's ask whether the trace-anaphor in (78) is properly bound with respect to the Anaphor Binding Condition (16) (A). The answer is that it is, since S$_i$ is the governing category for the trace (as we just observed), and the trace does indeed have a coindexed c-commanding antecedent within S$_i$, namely *John*$_2$. Hence our Anaphor Binding Condition correctly predicts that the subject of an infinitive complement of a Raising predicate can undergo NP MOVEMENT, yielding grammatical sentences like:

(79) John seems to be unhappy

But can the object of an infinitive also undergo NP MOVEMENT in the same way? Let's see. Consider a D-structure such as:

(80) $[_{S_i}$ np seems $[_{S_j}$ John to like Mary]]

Application of NP MOVEMENT to *Mary* here would result in the S-structure:

(81) $[_{S_i}$ Mary$_2$ seems $[_{S_j}$ John to like np$_2$]]

Here, the trace is governed by the verb *like*, and the governing category for *like* is the embedded (subordinate) S-node S$_j$, since S$_j$ is the minimal S or NP-node containing *like*. Hence we now have to ask whether the trace is properly bound in S_j with respect to the Anaphor Binding Condition (16) (A). The answer is that it is not, since the trace lacks any coindexed c-commanding NP within S_j. Hence, the Anaphor Binding Condition correctly predicts that the resultant sentence:

(82)   *Mary seems John to like

is ill-formed. And, what's more, it does so without any need to invoke the SPECIFIED SUBJECT CONDITION, which we earlier used to account for the ungrammaticality of sentences like (82). So here again we have another case where Binding Conditions block not only overgeneration by semantic rules, but also overgeneration by syntactic rules.

Now let's consider a third possible case of NP MOVEMENT with a Raising predicate. Consider a D-structure such as:

(83)   np seems [$_{\bar{s}}$ COMP [$_s$ John may be unhappy]]

(cf. *It seems that John may be unhappy*). If we apply NP MOVEMENT to *John* here, we get the S-structure:

(84)   John$_2$ seems [$_{\bar{s}}$ COMP [$_s$ np$_2$ may be unhappy]]

Once again, the trace here is the subject of the TENSE auxiliary *may*, and hence is governed by *may*; furthermore, the bracketed subordinate S is the governing category for the trace, since it is the minimal S or NP containing its governor *may*. Is the trace properly bound in the bracketed S with respect to the Anaphor Binding Condition (16) (A)? Clearly it is not, since it lacks any coindexed c-commanding NP within the bracketed S. Thus, the ANAPHOR BINDING CONDITION (16) (A) correctly predicts that the subject of a tensed S cannot undergo 'Raising' (i.e. NP MOVE-MENT): i.e. it correctly predicts that sentences such as:

(85)   *John seems may be unhappy

are ill-formed. Recall that earlier we accounted for the ill-formedness of sentences such as (85) in terms of the TENSED S CONDITION. But now this condition – like the SPECIFIED SUBJECT CONDITION – is unnecessary, since both conditions can be subsumed under the ANAPHOR BINDING CONDITION (16) (A).

So far, we have only considered one type of trace – namely the trace of NP MOVEMENT. But what about the trace of WH-MOVEMENT (i.e. *wh*-traces)? These differ from np-traces (i.e. traces of NP MOVEMENT) in the crucial respect that np-traces are always caseless, whereas the (initial) trace of WH-MOVEMENT must have case in order for that case to be transmitted to the *wh*-phrase. In fact, *wh*-traces seem to have more in common with lexical NPs, since *wh*-traces and lexical NPs are both case-marked. Therefore, we might expect that *wh*-traces should be subject to the same Binding Condition as lexical NPs, namely condition (16) (C) that requires that they always be *free*. But what does *free* mean? *Free* means not coindexed with a c-commanding argument, where an argument is an NP-position *within S or NP*. Intuitively, to say that a *wh*-trace must be *free* is to say that WH-MOVEMENT cannot reorder constituents internally within an S or NP, or move them into another S or NP – but can in fact move them into COMP, into an S-bar. To see how this works, consider:

(86)   What will you do?

Underlying (86) would be the D-structure:

(87)   [$_{\bar{s}}$ COMP [$_s$ you will do what]]

Application of WH-MOVEMENT to adjoin *what* to COMP (plus NP–AUX INVERSION) would give the S-structure:

(88)   [$_{\bar{s}}$ What$_2$ [$_s$ will you do np$_2$]]

where *np$_2$* is a case-marked (assigned *objective* case) trace of WH-MOVEMENT. If *wh*-traces are subject to Binding Condition (16) (C), then the *wh*-trace in (88) must be *free* – that is, not coindexed with any c-commanding NP *contained within S or NP*. Now, although the trace is coindexed with *what*, *what* is not in an argument position, since *what* is contained within an S-bar – not within an S or NP (as an *argument* must be). Hence, in the technical sense of *free*, the *wh*-trace in (88) is *free*. As already noted, the effect of stipulating that *wh*-traces are subject to the same Binding Condition (16) (C) as lexical NPs is to specify that WH-MOVEMENT cannot move *wh*-phrases into any position within S or NP; but of course, if WH-MOVEMENT adjoins *wh*-phrases to COMP under S-bar, this condition will never be violated. Or, to put it another way, our Binding Condition (16) (C) predicts that *wh*-phrases cannot be moved by WH-MOVEMENT under S or NP, without the need to stipulate this as part of the rule of WH-MOVEMENT itself.

Now consider a more complex case, involving both NP MOVE-MENT, and WH-MOVEMENT. Let's start with a D-structure along the lines of:

(89) $[_{\bar{S}_i}$ COMP $[_{S_i}$ np is certain $[_{\bar{S}_j}$ COMP $[_{S_j}$ who to win]]]]

Assume that NP MOVEMENT applies, to give the derived structure:

(90) $[_{\bar{S}_i}$ COMP $[_{S_i}$ who$_2$ is certain $[_{\bar{S}_j}$ COMP $[_{S_j}$ np$_2$ to win]]]]

Assume that subsequently on the $\bar{S}_i$ cycle WH-MOVEMENT applies to adjoin the *wh*-phrase *who* to the main clause COMP, giving:

(91) $[_{\bar{S}_i}$ who$_2$ $[_{S_i}$ np$_2$ is certain $[_{\bar{S}_j}$ np$_2$ to win]]]]

Assume also, that at some stage of derivation the rule of S-BAR DELETION (triggered by Raising predicates like *certain*) applies. so that the S-structure associated with the corresponding sentence:

(92)   Who is certain to win?

is not (91), but rather (93) below:

(93) $[_{\bar{S}_i}$ who$_2$ $[_{S_i}$ np$_2$ is certain $[_{S_j}$ np$_2$ to win]]]]

Given all these assumptions (!), let's now ask whether the resultant S-structure (93) satisfies all the relevant Binding Conditions. Consider first the *rightmost* trace, the one which is the subject of *to win*. This trace is governed by *certain*, but receives no case, since adjectives do not assign case. The minimal S or NP containing *certain* is the main clause S_i, so that S_i is the governing category for the rightmost trace. Furthermore, the rightmost trace has no case, and hence is a trace of NP MOVEMENT; if we assume that caseless traces (i.e. np-traces) are treated as anaphors, then the rightmost trace will be subject to the Anaphor Binding Condition (16) (A): this means that it must be bound within its governing category, S_i. And sure enough, it is bound within S_i, since it is coindexed with the leftmost trace within S_i, and furthermore the leftmost trace c-commands it. Hence, the rightmost trace is proper-ly bound in (93).

But what of the leftmost trace? Is that properly bound as well? Well, the leftmost trace is assigned nominative case by virtue of being the subject of the tensed verb *is*. Since the leftmost trace is case-marked, it must be a *wh*-trace; hence it is subject to the Binding Condition (16) (C), which requires that a case-marked (*wh*-) trace be *free* – i.e. not coindexed with some NP which c-commands it within an S or NP. And indeed this is the case, since the leftmost trace is coindexed with *who*, and *who* is under S-bar, not under S. Hence, our two Binding Conditions correctly predict that the resultant sentence (92) *Who is certain to win?* is perfectly well-formed. Once again, then, we see that Binding Conditions serve not only to 'monitor' the output of semantic interpretation rules, but also the output of syntactic rules like NP MOVEMENT and WH-MOVEMENT. So, as we have already had occasion to remark, it seems as if our Binding Conditions obviate the need for many of the traditional constraints/conditions on transformations that we looked at earlier.

Summary

In addition to rules mapping S-structures onto Surface Structures, our Grammar also contains a set of Semantic Rules mapping S-structures onto associated Logical Forms (a preliminary representation of meaning), and perhaps further rules mapping Logical Forms onto Semantic Representations (a fuller representation of meaning). Among these rules is the INDEXING RULE which assigns every NP not already indexed by some movement rule a random integer as its index. The resulting indexed structures are then scanned by a set of 'semantic filters' called *Binding Conditions*, and these rule out certain indexed structures as ill-formed. The essential feature of the Binding Conditions is that they monitor not only the output of semantic rules like our INDEXING rule, but also the output of syntactic rules like NP MOVEMENT and WH-MOVEMENT; that is, the conditions rule out not only impossible coreference links between constituents, but also impossible movements. Subsequently, the properly indexed structures which satisfy the Binding Conditions undergo further semantic rules (which we have not been able to deal with here) mapping them onto a more adequate representation of meaning. Our revised overall model of grammar thus looks something like (94):

(94)   *Base*
      (a) PS rules
      (b) Lexicon (lexical entries,
           Redundancy, Restructuring,
           Inherent Case-marking Rules, etc.)
      (c) Lexical Insertion Rule
      Output of Base = D-structures
      Transformational Component
      (a) Transformations
      (b) Conditions on Transformations
      Output of Transformational Component = S-structures
      Case Component
      (a) Case-marking Rules
      (b) Case Filters
      Output of Case Component = case-marked S-structures

Deletion Component	*Semantic Component*
(a) Deletion Rules	(a) Semantic Rules (IN-
(b) Conditions on Deletion	DEXING, etc.)
Output of Deletion Component =	(b) Binding Conditions
Surface Structures	(c) etc.
Surface Structure Filters	Output of Semantic Component
Output of Filters = filtered Sur-	= representations of meaning
face Structures	(Semantic Representations)

The one semantic rule we discussed in the text was:

(95)   INDEXING RULE
      Assign every unindexed NP in any sentence an index (where the index is a random integer)

Among the Binding Conditions we discussed were the following:

(96)   MATCHING CONDITION
      If two NPs are assigned the same index, they must be compatible in terms of features (number, gender, person, etc.)

(97)   ANAPHOR BINDING CONDITION
      An anaphor (or *np*-trace) must be bound in its governing category, if it has one

(98)   PRONOMINAL BINDING CONDITION
      A pronominal NP must be free in its governing category, if it has one

(99)   LEXICAL BINDING CONDITION
      A lexical NP (or *wh*-trace) must be free everywhere

The relevant terminology can be defined as:

(100) (a) X is *bound* if X is an argument coindexed with a c-commanding argument; if not bound it is *free*

(b) An *argument* is an NP-position within S or NP (subject, direct object, indirect object, etc.)

(c) X *c-commands* Y if the first branching node dominating X dominates Y, and if neither X nor Y dominates the other

(d) X is the *governing category* for Y if X is the minimal NP or S which contains the constituent which governs Y

(e) X *governs* Y if X is the minimal governing node (V, A, N, P, or TENSE) c-commanding Y, and there is no intervening NP or S-bar barrier between X and Y

EXERCISES

Exercise I

Assuming that *each other* is a reciprocal anaphor, which of the sentences below do and do not satisfy the relevant Binding Conditions, and why? Do the predictions made by the binding analysis accord with your own intuitions about the well-formedness of the relevant examples?

(1)   They know that I mistrust each other

(2)   They think that each other will win

(3)   They want me to help each other

(4)   They want each other to be successful

(5)   They collect pictures of each other

(6)   They don't like my pictures of each other

(7)   Each other may annoy them

(8)   Rumours about each other annoy them

(9)   My pictures of each other didn't flatter them

(10)   I warned them about each other

(11)   I never talk to them about each other

(12)   Their incompatibility surprised each other

(13)   Their discussion of each other's ideas was frank

Exercise II

Discuss how Binding Theory would deal with possible and impossible interpretations of *he*, *him* and *his* in sentences such as the following. Do any of these sentences prove problematic for the theory?

(1)   John hates him

(2)   John lost his pen

(3)	John wants him to resign
(4)	He wants John to resign
(5)	John thinks that he is right
(6)	John expects me to help him
(7)	John's habits worry him
(8)	John's habits annoy his wife
(9)	John has no money on him
(10)	His mother worships John
(11)	Rumours about him annoy John
(12)	John blamed Paul for his failure
(13)	John blamed his failure on Paul

Exercise III

Discuss possible and impossible interpretations of PRO in the following sentences, and the extent to which Binding Theory correctly predicts these interpretations.

(1)	John wants PRO to try PRO to take the exam
(2)	John won't tell me how PRO to do it
(3)	It was silly of me PRO to misbehave
(4)	They put pressure on him PRO to resign
(5)	She begged me PRO not to say anything
(6)	She begged PRO to be allowed PRO to leave
(7)	Her decision PRO to leave was unexpected
(8)	The decision PRO to abort the mission was unfortunate
(9)	It is hard PRO to find the time PRO to relax
(10)	PRO to leave now would be a mistake

Exercise IV

Discuss the derivation and interpretation of the following sentences:

(1)	Who shot him?
(2)	John seems to despise him
(3)	How many arrows did they fire at each other?
(4)	Who do you think is likely to disgrace himself?
(5)	Which famous politician is alleged to have perjured himself?

Exercise V

Discuss the operation of NP MOVEMENT in examples such as the following, and the role of the Binding Conditions in filtering out the overgenerated sentences:

(1) (a)   *A book about Nixon* was destroyed —
   (b)   **Nixon* was destroyed a book about —
(2) (a)   *Mary* is alleged — to have stolen a ring
   (b)   **Mary* is alleged — has stolen a ring
(3) (a)   *John* seems — to be a nice guy
   (b)   **John* seems — is a nice guy
(4) (a)   *Andrew* seems — to fancy Debbie Harry
   (b)   **Debbie Harry* seems Andrew to fancy —

Assume in each case that the italicised NP originates in the position
marked — and is moved into the italicised position by NP MOVEMENT.

*Exercise VI

In (89)–(93) in the text, we proposed an analysis of the sentence (92) *Who
is certain to win?* and argued that this analysis was consistent with Binding
Theory. Now consider an alternative analysis: let's assume that the
D-structure is (as before):

(1) $[_{\bar{S}_i} \text{COMP}_i \; [_{S_i} \text{np is certain} \; [_{\bar{S}_j} \text{COMP}_j \; [_{S_j} \text{who to win}]]]]$

And assume also that the derivation of the sentence involves the
following steps:

(2) (i)   adjunction of *who* to COMP$_j$ by WH-MOVEMENT
   (ii)   movement of *who* out of COMP$_j$ into the empty subject *np* position
            preceding *is* by NP MOVEMENT
   (iii)   movement of *who* out of this NP-position to be adjoined to COMP$_i$ by
            WH-MOVEMENT
   (iv)   deletion of $\bar{S}_j$ by S-BAR DELETION

Show how this derivation would work, and why the resultant S-structure
would violate the Binding Conditions.

*Exercise VII

Given the indexed structure (1) below:

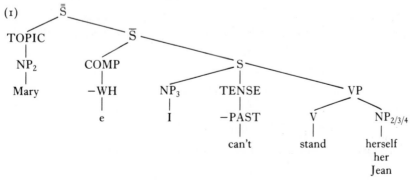

which interpretation(s) of the NP following *stand* would or would not be filtered out by the binding principles discussed in this chapter, and why? Do the binding principles make the correct predictions in each case?

**Exercise VIII*

Discuss the problems posed for Binding Theory by the interpretation of anaphors and pronominals contained inside a preposed *wh*-phrase in COMP, in relation to sentences such as the following:

(1)   Which picture of himself has John hidden?
(2)   Which picture of himself does John think I have hidden?
(3)   How many pictures of him did John take?
(4)   How many pictures of him did John's mother take?
(5)   Which of his paintings does John like best?

**Exercise IX*

English has a class of NPs which are sometimes referred to as *epithets* – expressions like *the idiot, the fool, the rotten bastard*, etc. On the basis of examples like those below, try and work out for yourself which of the Binding Conditions epithets are subject to (if any):

(1)   *John*, I can't stand the bastard ⎱ (Analyse italicised phrase
(2)   John has left, *the bastard* ⎰ as TOPIC – cf. Ex. VII above)
(3)   John can't stand the bastard
(4)   John thinks that the bastard likes me
(5)   John thinks that I like the bastard
(6)   John likes the bastard's pictures
(7)   John likes my pictures of the bastard
(8)   The bastard's mates betrayed John

**Exercise X*

Discuss the apparent problems posed for Binding Theory by the interpretation of the italicised constituents in sentences such as the following:

(1)   If I were you, I wouldn't marry *me*
(2)   Gary Glitter is *Gary Glitter's* greatest fan
(3)   John lost *his* temper with Harry
(4)   John told Harry PRO to pull *his* socks up
(5)   Only Nim Chimpsky understands *Nim Chimpsky*

To what extent are they real problems, or can you think of a solution to any of them?

****Exercise XI*

In the text, we assumed that sentences like (79) *John seems to be unhappy* are derived from a D-structure like (77) by application of NP MOVE-MENT and S-BAR DELETION, giving the resultant S-structure:

(1)   comp John$_2$ seems [$_S$ np$_2$ to be unhappy]

For the purposes of this exercise, assume that we entirely reject the use of transformations in syntactic analysis, in favour of an alternative model in which S-structures are directly generated by the Base Rules; and assume that our Base Rules will generate for us structures like:

(2)   comp John seems [$_S$ np to be unhappy]

Assume also that S-structures like (2) undergo the same INDEXING rule as other S-structures, whereby either *John* and *np* will be assigned the same index, as in:

(3)   comp John$_2$ seems [$_S$ np$_2$ to be unhappy]

or they will be assigned different indices, as in:

(4)   comp John$_2$ seems [$_S$ np$_3$ to be unhappy]

How could Binding Theory help us rule out structures like (4), while permitting those such as (3), and what assumptions would we need to make about the nature of the empty NP subject of the bracketed infinitival S for this to work?

See if you can devise a parallel base-generated (i.e. without NP MOVEMENT) analysis of passive sentences like:

(5)   John was arrested (cf. (68) in the text)

FURTHER READING

Note. The works cited below are all primary literature, and in most cases extremely difficult to follow:

Chomsky (1980) 'On Binding', 'Markedness and Core Grammar', *Pisa Lectures*, and 'On the representation of form and function'
Kayne (1980) 'Extensions of Binding and Case-marking', 'On certain differences between French and English', and 'ECP extensions'

SUGGESTED ESSAY
QUESTIONS

Note: You may find it helpful to consult both the Index and the relevant Exercises in the text when preparing your answers.

1. What problems arise in deciding whether sentences are *well-formed* or not?
2. What evidence is there that Language is *rule-governed*?
3. Why do we say that sentences have a *syntactic structure*?
4. What advantages does *X-bar Syntax* claim to offer over *Phrase Structure Syntax*? How real are they?
5. Discuss the role and organisation of the *Lexicon* in a grammar.
6. Discuss the arguments which might be put forward in support of positing any *one* transformation with which you are familiar.
7. Discuss the operation of *either* NP-MOVEMENT *or* WH-MOVEMENT in English.
8. Discuss the arguments for incorporating a level of *either* D-structure *or* S-structure into a grammar.
9. Analyse the arguments for incorporating *constraints* into a grammar of English.
10. What evidence is there in support of positing *deletion rules*, and what role do they play in a grammar?
11. 'The need for *filters* is simply an artefact of a badly formulated, excessively general set of sentence-formation rules.' Discuss.
12. What role is played by *case* in a grammar of English?
13. What are *Binding Conditions*, and what do they do?
14. What problems are posed by *overgeneration*? How do they come about, and how can they be solved?
15. Discuss the analysis of any *one* of the following in English:
    (i) reflexives; (ii) *wh*-questions; (iii) relative clauses; (iv) passives; (v) Raising; (vi) infinitives.
16. Discuss the role of *at least two* of the following in an EST grammar:
    (i) COMP; (ii) PRO; (iii) empty nodes; (iv) traces; (v) redundancy rules; (vi) subcategorisation.

BIBLIOGRAPHY

Where a work is cited in the text under an abbreviated title, the abbreviated title is given in brackets after the full title.

Akmajian, A. & Heny, F. (1975) *Introduction to the Principles of Transformational Syntax (Principles)*. MIT Press

Akmajian, A., Steele, S. M. & Wasow, T. (1979) 'The category AUX in Universal Grammar' ('Aux'), *Linguistic Inquiry* 10, pp. 1–64

Aronoff, M. (1976) *Word-Formation in Generative Grammar (Word-Formation)*, Linguistic Inquiry Monograph no. 1

Bach, E. (1974) *Syntactic Theory*. Holt Rinehart & Winston

Bach, E. & Harms, R. T. (eds.) (1968) *Universals in Linguistic Theory (Universals)*. Holt Rinehart & Winston

Baker, C. L. (1978) *Introduction to Generative-Transformational Syntax (Introduction)*. Prentice-Hall

Berko, J. (1958) 'The child's learning of English morphology', *Word* 14, pp. 150–77

Bresnan, J. (1976) 'The form and function of transformations', *Linguistic Inquiry* 7, pp. 3–40

Bresnan, J. (1978) 'A realistic transformational grammar' ('Realistic TG'), in Halle, M., Bresnan, J. & Miller, G. A. (eds.) *Linguistic Theory and Psychological Reality*. MIT Press

Chomsky, N. (1957) *Syntactic Structures*. Mouton

Chomsky, N. (1962) Paper presented to the session 'The logical basis of linguistic theory', Ninth International Congress of Linguists, Cambridge, Mass. Published in Lunt, H. (ed.) *The Proceedings of the Ninth International Congress of Linguists*. Mouton

Chomsky, N. (1965) *Aspects of the Theory of Syntax (Aspects)*. MIT Press

Chomsky, N. (1966) *Topics in the Theory of Generative Grammar (Topics)*. Mouton

Chomsky, N. (1968) Interview with S. Hamshire in *The Listener*, May 1968

Chomsky, N. (1972) *Language and Mind* (enlarged edition). Harcourt Brace Jovanovich

Chomsky, N. (1972) *Studies on Semantics in Generative Grammar (Studies)*. Mouton

Chomsky, N. (1975) *The Logical Structure of Linguistic Theory (Logical Structure)*. Plenum Press

Chomsky, N. (1976) *Reflections on Language (Reflections)*. Fontana

Chomsky, N. (1977) *Essays on Form and Interpretation (Essays)*. North-Holland

Chomsky, N. (1977) 'On Wh-Movement', in Culicover, P. W., et al. (eds.) *Formal Syntax*, pp. 71–132

Chomsky, N. (1980) 'On Binding', *Linguistic Inquiry* 11, pp. 1–46

Chomsky, N. (1980) 'Markedness and Core Grammar'. Unpublished paper, MIT

Chomsky, N. (1980) *Pisa Lectures on Binding and Governance (Pisa Lectures)*. Unedited transcript of a set of lectures given at the Scuola Normale, Pisa

Chomsky, N. (1980) 'On the representation of form and function'. Unpublished paper, MIT

Chomsky, N. (1980) *Rules and Representations*. Blackwell

Chomsky, N. & Lasnik, H. (1977) 'Filters and Control', *Linguistic Inquiry* 8, pp. 425–504

Culicover, P. W. (1977) *Syntax*. Academic Press

Culicover, P. W., Wasow, T. & Akmajian, A. (eds.) (1977) *Formal Syntax*. Academic Press

Dougherty, R. C. (1968) 'A transformational grammar of coordinate conjoined structures'. PhD thesis, MIT

Emonds, J. E. (1976) *A Transformational Approach to English Syntax (English Syntax)*. Academic Press

Fillmore, C. J. (1968) 'The case for case', in Bach & Harms *Universals*, pp. 1–68

Freidin, R. (1975) 'The analysis of passives' ('Passives'), *Language* 51, pp. 384–405

Fromkin, V. & Rodman, R. (1978) *An Introduction to Language (Introduction)*, second ed. Holt, Rinehart & Winston

Grinder, J. T. & Elgin, S. H. (1973) *Guide to Transformational Grammar (Guide)*. Holt, Rinehart & Winston

Gruber, J. S. (1976) *Lexical Structures in Syntax and Semantics (Lexical Structures)*. North-Holland

Harman, G. (ed.) (1974) *On Noam Chomsky: critical essays*. Anchor

Hoekstra, T. et al. (eds.) (1980) *Lexical Grammar*. Foris

Hornstein, N. & Lightfoot, D. (1981) *Explanation in Linguistics*. Longman

Huddleston, R. (1976) *An Introduction to English Transformational Syntax (Introduction)*. Longman

Jackendoff, R. S. (1969) 'Speculations on presentences and determiners'. Mimeo, Indiana University Linguistics Club

Jackendoff, R. S. (1972) *Semantic Interpretation in Generative Grammar (Semantic Interpretation)*. MIT Press

Jackendoff, R. S. (1974) *Introduction to the $\bar{X}$ Convention*. Mimeo, Indiana University Linguistics Club

Jackendoff, R. S. (1975) 'Morphological and semantic regularities in the Lexicon' ('Lexicon'), *Language* 51, pp. 639–71

Jackendoff, R. S. (1977) 'Constraints on Phrase Structure Rules' ('Constraints'), in Culicover et al. (eds.) *Formal Syntax*, pp. 249–83

Jackendoff, R. S. (1977) *$\bar{X}$ Syntax: A Study of Phrase Structure (Syntax)*. Linguistic Inquiry Monograph no. 2

Jacobsen, B. (1978) *Transformational-Generative Grammar (TG Grammar)*, second ed. North-Holland

Katz, J. J. & Postal, P. M. (1964) *An Integrated Theory of Linguistic Descriptions (Integrated Theory)*. MIT Press

Kayne, R. S. (1980) 'Extensions of Binding and Case-marking', *Linguistic Inquiry* 11, pp. 75–96

Kayne, R. S. (1980) 'On certain differences between French and English'. Unpublished paper, University of Paris VIII

Kayne, R. S. (1980) 'ECP extensions'. Unpublished paper, University of Paris VIII

Keyser, S. J. & Postal, P. M. (1976) *Beginning English Grammar (Grammar)*. Harper & Row

Kuno, S. (1973) 'Constraints on internal clauses and sentential subjects', *Linguistic Inquiry* 4, pp. 363–86

Lakoff, G. (1971) 'Presupposition and relative well-formedness', in L. A. Jakobovits & D. D. Steinberg (eds.) *Semantics*, pp. 329–40. Cambridge University Press

Lyons, J. (1968) *Introduction to Theoretical Linguistics (Introduction)*. Cambridge University Press

Palmer, F. (1971) *Grammar*. Penguin

Perlmutter, D. M. (1971) *Deep and Surface Structure Constraints in Syntax (Constraints)*. Holt, Rinehart & Winston

Perlmutter, D. M. & Soames, S. (1979) *Syntactic Argumentation and the Structure of English (Argumentation)*. University of California Press

Postal, P. M. (1974) *On Raising*. MIT Press

Ross, J. R. (1968) *Constraints on Variables in Syntax*. Mimeo, Indiana University Linguistics Club

Ross, J. R. (1969) 'Auxiliaries as main verbs' ('Auxiliaries'), *Studies in Philosophical Linguistics* 1, pp. 77–102

Ross, J. R. (1974) 'Excerpts from *Constraints on Variables in Syntax*' ('Excerpts'), in Harman (ed.) *On Noam Chomsky*, pp. 165–200

Rouveret, A. & Vergnaud, J–R. (1980) 'Specifying reference to subject: French causatives and conditions on representations', *Linguistic Inquiry* 11, pp. 97–202

Schwartz, A. (1972) 'Constraints on Movement Transformations', *Journal of Linguistics* 8, pp. 35–85

Selkirk, E. (1977) 'Some remarks on noun phrase structure' ('Structure') in Culicover et al. (eds.) *Formal Syntax*, pp. 285–316

Siegel, D. (1974) *Topics in English Morphology*. PhD dissertation, MIT

Smith, N. & Wilson, D. (1979) *Modern Linguistics*. Penguin

Vergnaud, J.–R. (1974) *French Relative Clauses*. PhD dissertation, MIT

Wasow, T. (1977) 'Transformations and the Lexicon' ('Lexicon'), in Culicover et al. (eds.) *Formal Syntax*, pp. 327–60

INDEX

Index